WORLD ON FIRE

How Exporting Free Market Democracy
Breeds Ethnic Hatred and Global Instability

AMY CHUA

WILLIAM HEINEMANN : LONDON

Published in the United Kingdom in 2003 by William Heinemann

3 5 7 9 10 8 6 4

Grateful acknowledgement is made to Penguin Books for permission to reprint material
from *Another Day of Life* by Ryszard Kapuściński

First published by The Doubleday Broadway Publishing Group,
a division of Random House, Inc.

William Heinemann
The Random House Group Limited
20 Vauxhall Bridge Road, London, SW1V 2SA

Random House Australia (Pty) Limited
20 Alfred Street, Milsons Point, Sydney
New South Wales 2061, Australia

Random House New Zealand Limited
18 Poland Road, Glenfield
Auckland 10, New Zealand

Random House (Pty) Limited
Endulini, 5A Jubilee Road, Parktown 2193, South Africa

The Random House Group Limited Reg. No. 954009

www.randomhouse.co.uk

A CIP catalogue record for this book is available from
the British Library

Papers used by Random House are natural, recyclable products made from wood grown
in sustainable forests. The manufacturing processes conform to the environmental
regulations of the country of origin

ISBN 0 434 01220 3

Printed and bound in Great Britain by
Clays Ltd, St Ives Plc, Bungay, Suffolk

To my mother and father

Acknowledgments

I am grateful to many people for their contributions to this book, but my greatest debt by far is to my husband Jed Rubenfeld, who for a decade has read every word I've written. I am the fortunate beneficiary of his kindness and genius.

I am also deeply grateful to a number of friends and professional colleagues. Strobe Talbott and Russell Pittman both read earlier drafts of the manuscript in its entirety and gave me tremendously helpful criticisms and suggestions. Others who provided invaluable comments on particular chapters include Bruce Ackerman, Yochai Benkler, Owen Fiss, Or Gozani, Jonathan Hecht, Donald Horowitz, Martin Michael, Elchi Nowrojee, Jeff Powell, George Priest, Susan Rose-Ackerman, Jennifer Roth-Gordon, David Steinberg, Alan Tan, and especially Amalia Anaya, Gonzalo Mendieta, and Jorge Patiño, who tried valiantly to correct my North American misconceptions. Errors, of course, are mine alone.

Many research assistants devoted dozens, in some cases hundreds, of hours to this book. In particular, I would like to thank Ivana Cingel, Alana Hoffman, David Penna, Rory Phimester, Lara Slachta, Brent Wible, and especially Jason Choy, who amazed me with his dedication and willingness to help at all hours. The following former students also provided extremely helpful assistance and often local expertise: Migai Akech, Homayoon Arfazadah, Hubert Baylon, Jennifer Becker, Jennifer Behr, Ikenna Emehelu, Jeff Federman, Ben Hance, Lidia Kidane, Nimrod Kozlovski, Bianca Locsin, Toni Moore, Gonzalo Zegarra

Mulanovich, Christina Owens, Caio Mario da Silva Pereira Neto, Tom Perriello, Emily Pierce, Uzi Rosha, Damian Schaible, Bill Scheffer, Daniel Sheridan, Saema Somalya, Suchon Tuly, Anders Walker, Kanchana Wang, and Tammy Zavaliyenko.

Many individuals were interviewed for this book, and I am thankful to them for their time and frankness. In most cases I have changed their names and other identifying factors to protect their anonymity.

This book is based on three earlier academic articles of mine: "The Paradox of Free Market Democracy: Rethinking Development Policy," *Harvard International Law Journal* 41 (2000): 287–379, "Markets, Democracy, and Ethnicity: Toward a New Paradigm for Law and Development," *Yale Law Journal* 108 (1998): 1–107, and "The Privatization-Nationalization Cycle: The Link Between Markets and Ethnicity in Developing Countries," *Columbia Law Review* 95 (1995): 223–303. I could not have written those articles without the friendship, support, and generosity of Dean Pamela Gann and Dean Katharine Bartlett of the Duke Law School and Dean Anthony Kronman of the Yale Law School.

Gene Coakley of the Yale Law School Library awed me with his energy and resourcefulness and has my great admiration and gratitude. I would also like to thank Miriam Abramowitz, Nicole Dewey, Frances Hamacher, and Patricia Spiegelhalter for their assistance and encouragement.

My love and thanks to Sophia and Louisa Chua-Rubenfeld for their patience and insights and for being my antidotes to despair.

Finally, I am deeply indebted to my agents Glen Hartley and Lynn Chu for believing in this project and to my brilliant editor, Adam Bellow.

Contents

PART THREE

Ethnonationalism and the West

WORLD ON FIRE

Globalization
and Ethnic Hatred

One beautiful blue morning in September 1994, I received a call from my mother in California. In a hushed voice, she told me that my Aunt Leona, my father's twin sister, had been murdered in her home in the Philippines, her throat slit by her chauffeur. My mother broke the news to me in our native Hokkien Chinese dialect. But "murder" she said in English, as if to wall off the act from the family, through language.

The murder of a relative is horrible for anyone, anywhere. My father's grief was impenetrable; to this day, he has not broken his silence on the subject. For the rest of the family, though, there was an added element of disgrace. For the Chinese, luck is a moral attribute, and a lucky person would never be murdered. Like having a birth defect, or marrying a Filipino, being murdered is shameful.

My three younger sisters and I were very fond of my Aunt Leona, who was petite and quirky and had never married. Like many wealthy Filipino Chinese, she had all kinds of bank accounts in Honolulu, San Francisco, and Chicago. She visited us in the United States regularly. She and my father—Leona and Leon—were close, as only twins can be. Having no children of her own, she doted on her nieces and showered us with trinkets. As we grew older the trinkets became treasures. On my tenth birthday she gave me ten small diamonds, wrapped up in toilet paper. My aunt loved diamonds and bought them up by the dozen, concealing them in empty Elizabeth Arden face moisturizer jars, some right on her bathroom shelf. She liked accumulating things. When we ate at McDonald's, she stuffed her Gucci purse with free ketchups.

According to the police report, my Aunt Leona, "a 58 year old single woman," was killed in her living room with "a butcher's knife" at approximately 8:00 P.M. on September 12, 1994. Two of her maids were questioned and confessed that Nilo Abique, my aunt's chauffeur, had planned and executed the murder with their knowledge and assistance. "A few hours before the actual killing, respondent was seen sharpening the knife allegedly used in the crime." After the killing, "respondent joined the two witnesses and told them that their employer was dead. At that time, he was wearing a pair of bloodied white gloves and was still holding a knife, also with traces of blood." But Abique, the report went on to say, had "disappeared," with the warrant for his arrest outstanding. The two maids were released.

Meanwhile, my relatives arranged a private funeral for my aunt, in the prestigious Chinese cemetery in Manila where many of my ancestors are buried in a great, white marble family tomb. According to the feng shui monks who were consulted, because of the violent nature of her death, my aunt could not be buried with the rest of the family, else more bad luck would strike her surviving kin. So she was placed in her own smaller vault, next to—but not touching—the main family tomb.

After the funeral, I asked one of my uncles whether there had been any further developments in the murder investigation. He replied tersely that the killer had not been found. His wife explained that the Manila police had essentially closed the case.

I could not understand my relatives' matter-of-fact, almost indifferent attitude. Why were they not more shocked that my aunt had been killed in cold blood, by people who worked for her, lived with her, saw her every day? Why were they not outraged that the maids had been released? When I pressed my uncle, he was short with me. "That's the way things are here," he said. "This is the Philippines—not America."

My uncle was not simply being callous. As it turns out, my aunt's death is part of a common pattern. Hundreds of Chinese in the Philippines are kidnapped every year, almost invariably by ethnic Filipinos. Many victims, often children, are brutally murdered, even after ransom is paid. Other Chinese, like my aunt, are killed without a kidnapping, usually in connection with a robbery. Nor is it unusual that my aunt's killer was never apprehended. The policemen in the Philippines, all poor ethnic Filipinos themselves, are notoriously unmotivated in these cases. When asked by a Western journalist why it is so frequently the Chinese who are targeted, one grinning Filipino policeman explained that it was because "they have more money."[1]

My family is part of the Philippines' tiny but entrepreneurial, economically powerful Chinese minority. Just 1 percent of the population, Chinese Filipinos control as much as 60 percent of the private economy, including the country's four major airlines and almost all of the country's banks, hotels, shopping malls, and major conglomerates.[2] My own family in Manila runs a plastics conglomerate. Unlike taipans Lucio Tan, Henry Sy, or John Gokongwei, my relatives are only "third-tier" Chinese tycoons. Still, they own swaths of prime real estate and several vacation homes. They also have safe deposit boxes full of gold bars, each one roughly the size of a Snickers bar, but strangely heavy. I myself have such a bar: My Aunt Leona Federal Expressed it to me as a law school graduation present a few years before she died.

Since my aunt's murder, one childhood memory keeps haunting me. I was eight, staying at my family's splendid hacienda-style house in Manila. It was before dawn, still dark. Wide awake, I decided to get a drink from the kitchen. I must have gone down an extra flight of stairs, because I literally stumbled onto six male bodies.

I had found the male servants' quarters. My family's houseboys, gardeners, and chauffeurs—I sometimes imagine that Nilo Abique was among those men—were sleeping on mats on a dirt floor. The place stank of sweat and urine. I was horrified.

Later that day I mentioned the incident to my Aunt Leona, who laughed affectionately and explained that the servants—there were perhaps twenty living on the premises, all ethnic Filipinos—were fortunate to be working for our family. If not for their positions, they would be living among rats and open sewers without even a roof over their heads.

A Filipino maid then walked in; I remember that she had a bowl of food for my aunt's Pekingese. My aunt took the bowl but kept talking as if the maid were not there. The Filipinos, she continued—in Chinese, but plainly not caring whether the maid understood or not—were lazy and unintelligent and didn't really want to do much else. If they didn't like working for us, they were free to leave any time. After all, my aunt said, they were employees, not slaves.

Nearly two-thirds of the roughly 80 million ethnic Filipinos in the

Philippines live on less than two dollars a day. Forty percent spend their entire lives in temporary shelters. Seventy percent of all rural Filipinos own no land. Almost a third have no access to sanitation.[3]

But that's not the worst of it. Poverty alone never is. Poverty by itself does not make people kill. To poverty must be added indignity, hopelessness, and grievance.

In the Philippines, millions of Filipinos work for Chinese; almost no Chinese work for Filipinos. The Chinese dominate industry and commerce at every level of society. Global markets intensify this dominance: When foreign investors do business in the Philippines, they deal almost exclusively with Chinese. Apart from a handful of politicians and a few aristocratic Spanish mestizo families, all of the Philippines' billionaires are of Chinese descent. By contrast, all menial jobs in the Philippines are filled by Filipinos. All peasants are Filipinos. All domestic servants and squatters are Filipinos. In Manila, thousands of ethnic Filipinos used to live on or around the Payatas garbage dump: a twelve-block-wide mountain of fermenting refuse known as the Promised Land. By scavenging through rotting food and dead animal carcasses, the squatters were able to eke out a living. In July 2000, as a result of accumulating methane gas, the garbage mountain imploded and collapsed, smothering over a hundred people, including many young children.

When I asked an uncle about the Payatas explosion, he responded with annoyance. "Why does everyone want to talk about that? It's the worst thing for foreign investment." I wasn't surprised. My relatives live literally walled off from the Filipino masses, in a posh, all-Chinese residential enclave, on streets named Harvard, Yale, Stanford, and Princeton. The entry points are guarded by armed, private security forces.

Each time I think of Nilo Abique—he was close to six feet and my aunt was four-feet-eleven-inches tall—I find myself welling up with a hatred and revulsion so intense it is actually consoling. But over time I have also had glimpses of how the Chinese must look to the vast majority of Filipinos, to someone like Abique: as exploiters, as foreign intruders, their wealth inexplicable, their superiority intolerable. I will never forget the entry in the police report for Abique's "motive for murder." The motive given was not robbery, despite the jewels and money the chauffeur was said to have taken. Instead, for motive, there was just one word—"Revenge."

My aunt's killing was just a pinprick in a world more violent than most of us ever imagined. In America we read about acts of mass slaughter and savagery; at first in faraway places, now coming closer and closer to home. We do not understand what connects these acts. Nor do we understand the role we have played in bringing them about.

In the Serbian concentration camps of the early 1990s, the women prisoners were raped over and over, many times a day, often with broken bottles, often together with their daughters. The men, if they were lucky, were beaten to death as their Serbian guards sang national anthems; if they were not so fortunate, they were castrated or, at gunpoint, forced to castrate their fellow prisoners, sometimes with their own teeth. In all, thousands were tortured and executed.[4]

In Rwanda in 1994, ordinary Hutus killed eight hundred thousand Tutsis over a period of three months, typically hacking them to death with machetes. Young children would come home to find their mothers, fathers, sisters, and brothers on the living room floor, in piles of severed heads and limbs.[5]

In Jakarta in 1998, screaming Indonesian mobs torched, smashed, and looted hundreds of Chinese shops and homes, leaving over two thousand dead. One who survived—a fourteen-year-old Chinese girl—later committed suicide by taking rat poison. She had been gang-raped and genitally mutilated in front of her parents.[6]

In Israel in 1998, a suicide bomber driving a car packed with explosives rammed into a school bus filled with thirty-four Jewish children between the ages of six and eight. Over the next few years such incidents intensified, becoming daily occurrences and a powerful collective expression of Palestinian hatred. "We hate you," a senior Arafat official elaborated in April 2002. "The air hates you, the land hates you, the trees hate you, there is no purpose in your staying on this land."[7]

On September 11, 2001, Middle Eastern terrorists hijacked four American airplanes. They destroyed the World Trade Center and the southwest side of the Pentagon, crushing or incinerating approximately three thousand people. "Americans, think! Why you are hated all over the world," proclaimed a banner held by Arab demonstrators.[8]

Apart from their violence, what is the connection between these episodes? The answer lies in the relationship—increasingly, the explosive collision—between the three most powerful forces operating in the world today: markets, democracy, and ethnic hatred.

This book is about a phenomenon—pervasive outside the West yet rarely acknowledged, indeed often viewed as taboo—that turns free market democracy into an engine of ethnic conflagration. The phenomenon I refer to is that of *market-dominant minorities:* ethnic minorities who, for widely varying reasons, tend under market conditions to dominate economically, often to a startling extent, the "indigenous" majorities around them.

Market-dominant minorities can be found in every corner of the world. The Chinese are a market-dominant minority not just in the Philippines but throughout Southeast Asia. In 1998, Chinese Indonesians, only 3 percent of the population, controlled roughly 70 percent of Indonesia's private economy, including all of the country's largest conglomerates. More recently, in Burma, entrepreneurial Chinese have literally taken over the economies of Mandalay and Rangoon. Whites are a market-dominant minority in South Africa—and, in a more complicated sense, in Brazil, Ecuador, Guatemala, and much of Latin America. Lebanese are a market-dominant minority in West Africa. Ibo are a market-dominant minority in Nigeria. Croats were a market-dominant minority in the former Yugoslavia. And Jews are almost certainly a market-dominant minority in post-Communist Russia.

Market-dominant minorities are the Achilles' heel of free market democracy. In societies with a market-dominant ethnic minority, markets and democracy favor not just different people, or different classes, but different ethnic groups. Markets concentrate wealth, often spectacular wealth, in the hands of the market-dominant minority, while democracy increases the political power of the impoverished majority. In these circumstances the pursuit of free market democracy becomes an engine of potentially catastrophic ethnonationalism, pitting a frustrated "indigenous" majority, easily aroused by opportunistic vote-seeking politicians, against a resented, wealthy ethnic minority. This confrontation is playing out in country after country today, from Indonesia to Sierra Leone, from Zimbabwe to Venezuela, from Russia to the Middle East.

Since September 11, 2001, this confrontation has also been playing out in the United States. Americans are not an ethnic minority (although we are a national-origin minority, a close cousin). Nor is there democracy at the global level. Nevertheless, Americans today are everywhere perceived as the world's market-dominant minority, wielding outrageously disproportionate economic power relative to our size and numbers. As a result, we have become the object of mass, popular resentment and hatred of the same kind that is directed at so many other market-dominant minorities around the world.

Global anti-Americanism has many causes. One of them, ironically, is the global spread of free markets and democracy. Throughout the world, global markets are bitterly perceived as reinforcing American wealth and dominance. At the same time, global populist and democratic movements give strength, legitimacy, and voice to the impoverished, frustrated, excluded masses of the world—precisely the people, in other words, most susceptible to anti-American demagoguery. In more non-Western countries than Americans would care to admit, free and fair elections would bring to power anti-market, anti-American leaders. For the last twenty years Americans have been grandly promoting both marketization and democratization throughout the world. In the process we have directed at ourselves the anger of the damned.[9]

The relationship between free market democracy and ethnic violence around the world is inextricably bound up with globalization. But the phenomenon of market-dominant minorities introduces complications that have escaped the view of both globalization's enthusiasts and its critics.

To a great extent, globalization consists of, and is fueled by, the unprecedented worldwide spread of markets and democracy. For over two decades now, the American government, along with American consultants, business interests, and foundations, has been vigorously promoting free market democracy throughout the developing and post-socialist worlds. At times our efforts have bordered on the absurd. There is, for example, the sad tale of a delegation of American free market advisers in Mongolia. Just before they leave the country, the Americans are thrilled when a Mongolian official asks them to send more copies of the voluminous U.S. securities laws, photocopied on one side of the page. Alas, it turned out that the Mongolian was interested in the documents not for their content, but for the blank side of each page, which would help alleviate the government's chronic paper shortage.[10]

There was also the time that the U.S. government hired New York–based Burson-Marsteller, the world's largest public relations firm, to help sell free market capitalism to the people of Kazakhstan. Among other ideas, Burson-Marsteller developed a television soap opera miniseries glorifying privatization. In one episode, two hapless families desperately want a new house but don't know how to build it. Suddenly a hot-air balloon descends from the sky, bearing the name "Soros Foundation" in huge letters. Americans spring out, erect the house, and soar away, leaving the awe-struck Kazakhstanis cheering wildly.[11]

In the end, however, stories about American naïveté and incompetence are just a sideshow. The fact is that in the last two decades, the American-led global spread of markets and democracy has radically transformed the world. Both directly and through powerful international institutions like the World Bank, International Monetary Fund, and World Trade Organization (WTO), the United States government has helped bring capitalism and democratic elections to literally billions of people. At the same time, American multinationals, foundations, and nongovernmental organizations (NGOs) have swept the world, bringing with them ballot boxes and Burger Kings, hip-hop and Hollywood, banking codes and American-drafted constitutions.

The prevailing view among globalization's supporters is that markets and democracy are a kind of universal prescription for the multiple ills of underdevelopment. Market capitalism is the most efficient economic system the world has ever known. Democracy is the fairest political system the world has ever known and the one most respectful of individual liberty. Working hand in hand, markets and democracy will gradually transform the world into a community of prosperous, war-shunning nations, and individuals into liberal, civic-minded citizens and consumers. In the process, ethnic hatred, religious zealotry, and other "backward" aspects of underdevelopment will be swept away.

Thomas Friedman has been a brilliant proponent of this dominant view. In his best-selling book *The Lexus and the Olive Tree,* he reproduced a Merrill Lynch ad that said "The spread of free markets and democracy around the world is permitting more people everywhere to turn their aspirations into achievements," erasing "not just geographical borders but also human ones." Globalization, Friedman elaborated, "tends to turn all friends and enemies into 'competitors.' " Friedman also proposed his "Golden Arches Theory of Conflict Prevention" which claims that "no two countries that both have McDonald's have ever fought a war against each other. . . ."[12] (Unfortunately, notes Yale history professor John Gaddis, "the United States and its NATO allies chose just that inauspicious moment to begin bombing Belgrade, where there was an embarrassing number of golden arches.")[13]

For globalization's enthusiasts, the cure for group hatred and ethnic violence around the world is straightforward: more markets and more democracy. Thus after the September 11 attacks, Friedman published an op-ed piece pointing to India and Bangladesh as good "role models" for the Middle East and arguing that the solution to terrorism and militant Islam is: "Hello? Hello? There's a message here. It's democracy, stupid!"—"[m]ulti-ethnic, pluralistic, free-market democracy."[14]

By contrast, the sobering thesis of this book is that the global spread of markets and democracy is a principal, aggravating cause of group hatred and ethnic violence throughout the non-Western world. In the numerous societies around the world that have a market-dominant minority, markets and democracy are not mutually reinforcing. Because markets and democracy benefit different ethnic groups in such societies, the pursuit of free market democracy produces highly unstable and combustible conditions. Markets concentrate enormous wealth in the hands of an "outsider" minority, fomenting ethnic envy and hatred among often chronically poor majorities. In absolute terms the majority may or may not be better off—a dispute that much of the globalization debate fixates on—but any sense of improvement is overwhelmed by their continuing poverty and the hated minority's extraordinary economic success. More humiliating still, market-dominant minorities, along with their foreign-investor partners, invariably come to control the crown jewels of the economy, often symbolic of the nation's patrimony and identity—oil in Russia and Venezuela, diamonds in South Africa, silver and tin in Bolivia, jade, teak, and rubies in Burma.

Introducing democracy in these circumstances does not transform voters into open-minded cocitizens in a national community. Rather, the competition for votes fosters the emergence of demagogues who scapegoat the resented minority and foment active ethnonationalist movements demanding that the country's wealth and identity be reclaimed by the "true owners of the nation." As America celebrated the global spread of democracy in the 1990s, ethnicized political slogans proliferated: "Georgia for the Georgians," "Eritreans Out of Ethiopia," "Kenya for Kenyans," "Whites should leave Bolivia," "Kazakhstan for Kazakhs," "Serbia for Serbs," "Croatia for Croats," "Hutu Power," "Assam for Assamese," "Jews Out of Russia." Romania's 2001 presidential candidate Vadim Tudor was not quite so pithy. "I'm Vlad the Impaler," he campaigned; referring to the historically economically dominant Hungarian minority, he promised: "We will hang them directly by their Hungarian tongue!"[15]

When free market democracy is pursued in the presence of a market-dominant minority, the almost invariable result is backlash. This backlash typically takes one of three forms. The first is a backlash against markets, targeting the market-dominant minority's wealth. The second is a backlash against democracy by forces favorable to the market-dominant minority. The third is violence, sometimes genocidal, directed against the market-dominant minority itself.

Zimbabwe today is a vivid illustration of the first kind of backlash—an ethnically targeted anti-market backlash. For several years now President Robert Mugabe has encouraged the violent seizure of 10 million acres of white-owned commercial farmland. As one Zimbabwean explained, "The land belongs to us. The foreigners should not own land here. There is no black Zimbabwean who owns land in England. Why should any European own land here?"[16] Mugabe himself was more explicit: "Strike fear in the heart of the white man, our real enemy!"[17] Most of the country's white "foreigners" are third-generation Zimbab-

weans. Just 1 percent of the population, they have for generations controlled 70 percent of the country's best land, largely in the form of
highly productive three-thousand-acre tobacco and sugar farms.

Watching Zimbabwe's economy take a free fall as a result of the mass
landgrab, the United States and United Kingdom together with dozens
of human rights groups urged President Mugabe to step down, calling
resoundingly for "free and fair elections." But the idea that *democracy* is
the answer to Zimbabwe's problems is breathtakingly naive. Perhaps
Mugabe would have lost the 2002 elections in the absence of foul play.
Even if so, it is important to remember that Mugabe himself is a product of democracy. The hero of Zimbabwe's black liberation movement
and a master manipulator of masses, he swept to victory in the closely
monitored elections of 1980, promising to expropriate "stolen" white
land. Repeating that promise has helped him win every election since.
Moreover, Mugabe's land-seizure campaign was another product of the
democratic process. It was deftly timed in anticipation of the 2000 and
2002 elections, and deliberately calculated to mobilize popular support
for Mugabe's teetering regime.[18]

In the contest between an economically powerful ethnic minority and
a numerically powerful impoverished majority, the majority does not always prevail. Instead of a backlash against the market, another likely outcome is a backlash against democracy, favoring the market-dominant
minority at the expense of majority will. Examples of this dynamic are
extremely common. Indeed, this book will show that the world's most
notorious cases of "crony capitalism" all involve a market-dominant ethnic minority—from Ferdinand Marcos's Chinese-protective dictatorship
in the Philippines to President Siaka Stevens's shadow alliance with five
Lebanese diamond dealers in Sierra Leone to President Daniel Arap
Moi's "business arrangements" with a handful of Indian tycoons in Kenya
today.

The third and most ferocious kind of backlash is majority-supported
violence aimed at eliminating a market-dominant minority. Two recent
examples are the ethnic cleansing of Croats in the former Yugoslavia and
the mass slaughter of Tutsi in Rwanda. In both cases a resented and disproportionately prosperous ethnic minority was attacked by members
of a relatively impoverished majority, incited by an ethnonationalist gov-

ernment. In other words, markets and democracy were among the causes of both the Rwandan and Yugoslavian genocides. This is a large claim, but one that this book will try to defend.

To their credit, critics of globalization have called attention to the grotesque imbalances that free markets produce. In the 1990s, writes Thomas Frank in *One Market under God,* global markets made "the corporation the most powerful institution on earth," transformed "CEOs as a class into one of the wealthiest elites of all time," and, from America to Indonesia, "forgot about the poor with a decisiveness we hadn't seen since the 1920s."[19] Joining Frank in his criticism of "the almighty market" is a host of strange bedfellows: American farmers and factory workers opposed to NAFTA, environmentalists, the AFL-CIO, human rights activists, Third World advocates, and sundry other groups that made up the protesters at Seattle, Davos, Genoa, and New York City. Defenders of globalization respond, with some justification, that the world's poor would be even worse off without global marketization. With some important exceptions, including most of Africa, recent World Bank studies show that globalization's "trickle down" has produced benefits for the poor as well as the rich in developing countries.[20]

More fundamentally, however, like their pro-globalization counterparts, Western critics of globalization have overlooked the ethnic dimension of market disparities. They tend to see wealth and poverty in terms of class conflict, not ethnic conflict. This perspective might make sense in the advanced Western societies, but the ethnic realities of the developing world are completely different from those of the West. As a result, the solutions that globalization's critics propose are often shortsighted and even dangerous when applied to non-Western societies.

Essentially, the anti-globalization movement asks for one thing: more democracy. Thus Noam Chomsky, one of the movement's high priests, has clarified that there is no struggle against "globalization" in the general sense, only a struggle against the global "neoliberalism" perpetuated by a few "masters of the universe" at the expense of a truly democratic community. Similarly, at the 2002 World Social Forum in Brazil, Lori

Wallach of Public Citizen rejected the label "anti-globalization," explaining that "our movement, really, is globally for democracy, equality, diversity, justice and quality of life." Wallach has also warned that the WTO must "either bend to the will of the people worldwide or it will break." Echoing these voices are literally dozens of NGOs who call for "democratically empowering the poor majorities of the world."[21]

Given the ethnic dynamics of the developing world, and in particular the phenomenon of market-dominant minorities, merely "empowering the poor majorities of the world" is not enough. Empowering the Hutu majority in Rwanda did not produce desirable consequences. Nor did empowering the Serbian majority in Serbia.

Critics of globalization are right to demand that more attention be paid to the enormous wealth disparities created by global markets. But just as it is dangerous to view markets as the panacea for the world's poverty and strife, so too it is dangerous to see democracy as a panacea. Markets and democracy may well offer the best long-run economic and political hope for developing and post-Communist societies. In the short run, however, they are part of the problem.

"Markets," "democracy," and "ethnicity" are notoriously difficult concepts to define. In part this is because there is no single correct interpretation of any of these terms. Indeed, I hope precisely to show in this book that the "market systems" currently being urged on developing and post-Communist countries are very different from the ones now in place in contemporary Western nations; that the process of "democratization" currently being promoted in the non-Western world is not the same as the one that the Western countries themselves went through; and that "ethnicity" is a fluid, artificial, and dangerously manipulable concept.

Nevertheless, some clarification of my usage of these terms is in order. In the West, terms like "market economy" or "market system" refer to a broad spectrum of economic systems based primarily on private property and competition, with government regulation and redistribution ranging from substantial (as in the United States) to extensive (as in the Scandinavian countries). Ironically, however, for the last twenty years the United States has been promoting throughout the non-Western world raw, laissez-faire capitalism—a form of markets that the West abandoned long ago. In this book, unless otherwise indicated, terms like "marketization," "markets," and "market reforms" will refer to the kinds of pro-capitalism measures *actually being implemented today* outside the West. These measures characteristically include privatization, elimination of state subsidies and controls, and free trade and pro-foreign investment initiatives. As a practical matter, they rarely, if ever, include any substantial redistribution measures.

Similarly, while "democracy" can take many forms,[22] I will use the term "democratization" to refer to the political reforms actually being promoted and implemented in the non-Western world today. Thus, "democratization" will refer principally to the concerted efforts, heavily U.S.-driven, to implement immediate elections with universal suffrage. Needless to say, an ideal democratic society would surely include more substantive principles, such as equality under law or minority protections, but to build such principles into the definition of democracy would be to confuse aspiration with reality. It is striking to note that at no point in history did any Western nation ever implement laissez-faire capitalism and overnight universal suffrage at the same time—the precise formula of free market democracy currently being pressed on developing countries around the world.

Ethnicity is another controversial concept that has generated much debate. For purposes of this book, I will assume that "ethnicity" is not a scientifically determinable status. Rather, "ethnicity" will refer to a kind of group identification, a sense of belonging to a people, that is experienced "as a greatly extended form of kinship."[23] This definition of ethnicity is intended to be very broad, acknowledging the importance of subjective perceptions. It encompasses differences along racial lines (for example, blacks and whites in the United States), lines of geographic origin (for example, Malays, Chinese, and Indians in Malaysia), as well as linguistic, religious, tribal, or other cultural lines (for example, Kikuyu and Kalenjin tribes in Kenya or Jews and Muslims in the Middle East).

Ethnic identity is not static but shifting and highly malleable. In Rwanda, for example, the 14 percent Tutsi minority dominated the

Hutu majority economically and politically for four centuries, as a kind of cattle-owning aristocracy. But for most of this period the lines between Hutus and Tutsi were permeable. The two groups spoke the same language, intermarriage occurred, and successful Hutus could "become Tutsi." This was no longer true after the Belgians arrived and, steeped in specious theories of racial superiority, issued ethnic identity cards on the basis of nose length and cranial circumference. The resulting much sharper ethnic divisions were later exploited by the leaders of Hutu Power.[24] Along similar lines, all over Latin America today—where it is often said that there are no "ethnic divisions" because everyone is "mixed-blooded"—large numbers of impoverished Bolivians, Chileans, and Peruvians are suddenly being told that they are Aymaras, Incas, or just *indios,* whatever identity best resonates and mobilizes. These indigenization movements are not necessarily good or bad, but they are contagiously potent.

At the same time, ethnic identity is rarely constructed out of thin air. Subjective perceptions of identity often depend on more "objective" traits assigned to individuals based on, for example, perceived morphological characteristics, language differences, or ancestry. Try telling black and white Zimbabweans that they are only imagining their ethnic differences—that "ethnicity is a social construct"—and they'll at least agree on one thing: that you're not being helpful. Much more concretely relevant is the reality that there is roughly zero intermarriage between blacks and whites in Zimbabwe, just as there is virtually no intermarriage between Chinese and Malays in Malaysia or between Arabs and Israelis in the Middle East. That ethnicity can be at once an artifact of human imagination and rooted in the darkest recesses of history—fluid and manipulable yet important enough to kill for—is what makes ethnic conflict so terrifyingly difficult to understand and contain.

There are a number of misunderstandings about my thesis that I frequently encounter. I will do my best to dispel some of them here by making clear what I am *not* arguing. First, this book is not proposing a universal theory applicable to every developing country. There are certainly developing countries without market-dominant minorities: China and Argentina are two major examples. Second, I am not arguing that ethnic conflict arises only in the presence of a market-dominant minority. There are countless instances of ethnic hatred directed at economically oppressed groups. Last, I am emphatically not attempting to pin the blame for any particular case of ethnic violence—whether the mass killings perpetuated by all sides in the former Yugoslavia or the attack on America—on economic resentment, on markets, on democracy, on globalization, or on any other single cause. Numerous overlapping factors and complex dynamics, such as religion, historical enmities, territorial disputes, or a particular nation's foreign policy, are always in play.

The point, rather, is this. In the numerous countries around the world that have pervasive poverty and a market-dominant minority, democracy and markets—at least in the form in which they are currently being promoted—can proceed only in deep tension with each other. In such conditions, the combined pursuit of free markets and democratization has repeatedly catalyzed ethnic conflict in highly predictable ways, with catastrophic consequences, including genocidal violence and the subversion of markets and democracy themselves. This has been the sobering lesson of globalization over the last twenty years.

———

Part One of this book discusses the economic impact of globalization. Contrary to what its proponents assume, free markets outside the West do not spread wealth evenly and enrich entire developing societies. Instead, they tend to concentrate glaring wealth in the hands of an "outsider" minority, generating ethnic envy and hatred among frustrated, impoverished majorities.

What happens when democracy is added to this volatile mixture? Part Two addresses the political consequences of globalization. In countries with a market-dominant minority, democratization, rather than reinforcing the market's efficiency and wealth-producing effects, leads to powerful ethnonationalist, anti-market pressures and routinely results in confiscation, instability, authoritarian backlash, and violence.

Part Three discusses the phenomena of market-dominant minorities and ethnonationalism in the West, past and present. It also addresses the future: What should be done about the explosive instability that market-dominant minorities inject into the pursuit of free market democracy? I suggest that the United States should not be exporting markets in the unrestrained, laissez-faire form that the West itself has repudiated, just as it should not be promoting unrestrained, overnight majority rule—a form of democracy that the West has repudiated. Ultimately, however, I argue that the best hope for democratic capitalism in the non-Western world lies with market-dominant minorities themselves.

PART ONE

THE ECONOMIC IMPACT
OF GLOBALIZATION

Since the creation of Microsoft, the software industry has produced the largest crop of billionaires and multibillionaires in
American history. Now imagine that all these billionaires were
ethnic Chinese, and that Chinese-Americans, although just 2 percent of the population, also controlled Time Warner, General
Electric, Chase Manhattan, United Airlines, Exxon Mobil, and
the rest of America's largest corporations and banks, plus Rocke-
feller Center and two-thirds of the country's prime real estate.
Then imagine that the roughly 75 percent of the U.S. population
who consider themselves "white" were dirt poor, owned no land,
and, as a group, had experienced no upward mobility as far back
as anyone can remember.

If you can picture this, you will have approximated the core
social dynamic that characterizes much of the non-Western
world. Throughout South and Southeast Asia, Africa, the Caribbean and the West Indies, much of Latin America, and parts of
Eastern Europe and the former Soviet Union, free markets have
led to the rapid accumulation of massive, often shocking wealth
by members of an "outsider" or "nonindigenous" ethnic minority.

Americans don't hate Bill Gates, even though he has owned as
much as 40 percent of the American population put together.[1]
They don't feel cheated or exploited by him, or that he has humiliated Americans by making billions "on their soil." Not so in
societies with a market-dominant minority. In these societies,

class and ethnicity overlap in a particularly dangerous way. The extremely wealthy stick out—whether because of their origins, skin color, religion, language, or "blood ties"—from the impoverished masses around them, and they are seen by these majorities as belonging to a different ethnicity or people—as "outsiders" who look different, speak differently, or as Fiji's nationalist leader George Speight recently said of his country's market-dominant Indian minority, "smell different."[2]

When the U.S. Department of Justice sued Microsoft, accusing it of engaging in monopolistic practices to try to destroy its competitors, Americans did not want to lynch Bill Gates or strip him of his assets or even take him down a few notches. On the contrary, polls found that most Americans wanted the government to leave Gates alone, so that he could "get back to making bucks."[3] But in the numerous non-Western countries with a market-dominant minority, the plutocrats are ethnic outsiders. And while Bill Gates does not generate mass ethnic resentment in the United States, Indian tycoons in Uganda, Eritrean businessmen in Ethiopia, and Jewish oligarchs in Russia do.

Most Americans—whether ordinary citizens, commentators on globalization, or policymakers—are unaware of this problem. As a result, we have been confidently exporting free market capitalism to the rest of the world, oblivious to the ethnic hatred and instability we are systematically helping to breed.

Today's global economy did not appear overnight, but to a large extent represents the triumph of five decades of American foreign policy. After the Second World War, and consciously to promote capitalism and contain Communism, America drove the creation of the World Bank, the International Monetary Fund (IMF), the Organization for Economic Cooperation and Development, and the free trade organization, GATT. In the 1960s the U.S. Agency for International Development and private organizations like the Ford Foundation poured millions into "modernization" projects aimed at bringing economic and legal progress to the developing world through the export of capitalist institutions. With the collapse of the former Soviet Union in 1989, capitalism was seen around the world as triumphant and inexorable. In the developing countries of Africa, Asia, and Latin America, the IMF and World Bank pushed through privatization programs and foreign investment and trade liberalization by conditioning desperately needed loans on these market reforms.

As of the late nineties, more than eighty developing and post-socialist countries were privatizing. Pro-market tax codes, investment codes, and securities laws, often drafted by American lawyers and academics, proliferated from Peru to Bulgaria to Vietnam. By 1996, Kazakhstan alone had adopted over 130 market-friendly laws. In Argentina, President Carlos Menem passed a flurry of pro-capitalism laws on an "emergency" basis. Stock exchanges—some hand-operated—appeared everywhere, including in Mozambique and Swaziland.[4]

In the new millennium, globalization and the worldwide spread of free markets continue to accelerate, with America at the helm. At the same time it is now possible to look back and begin to assess what the economic impact of globalization has been, not just in the United States, but around the world. As the next four chapters will show, the disturbing reality is that global markets, even if marginally "lifting all boats," have consistently intensified the extraordinary economic dominance of certain "outsider" minorities, fueling virulent ethnic envy and hatred among the impoverished majorities around them.

CHAPTER 1

Rubies and Rice Paddies

Chinese Minority Dominance
in Southeast Asia

I n Burma,* tattoos are traditionally used to protect against snakebite. In 1930 and again in 1938, enraged Burmans applied these tattoos to achieve invulnerability against bullets and then proceeded to slaughter Indians in an orgy of violence. Even monks were said to have participated. At the time, Indians, along with British colonialists, were a starkly economically dominant ethnic minority in Burma and the object of mass antipathy. Killing Indians was an act simultaneously of revenge and nationalist pride among a long-downtrodden people. As a contemporary observer put it, "The average Burman on the street felt that at least once he had proved his superiority over the Indian."[1]

Today there is only a small community of Indians left in Burma. Hundreds of thousands fled in the sixties, in response to another wave of ethnic violence. But a new market-dominant minority has taken their place, far wealthier than the Indians ever were.

---

*Members of the majority ethnic group in Burma are called *Bamahs* (in the spoken language) or *Myanmahs* (in the written language). The newly independent state that emerged from the end of British colonial rule in 1948 was called the Union of Burma. In 1989, SLORC changed the country's name to Myanmar. (It also changed the names of various cities: Rangoon, for example, is now called Yangon.) In deference to the democratic opposition party, which has refused to acquiesce in the name change, the United States government currently refers to the country as Burma, and I do the same. Unless otherwise indicated, "Burman" refers to the majority ethnic group, who comprise about two-thirds of the population, while "Burmese" refers to any citizen of the country.

Markets, Junta Style, and the Chinese Takeover

Burma has one of the most repugnant military governments in the world—the State Law and Order Restoration Council, or SLORC,** which seized power in September 1988 after gunning down thousands of unarmed demonstrators. SLORC held multiparty elections in 1990, but then refused to honor the landslide victory of 1991 Nobel Peace laureate Aung San Suu Kyi, placing her instead under house arrest and earning the widespread hatred of the Burmese people.[2]

From its inception, SLORC has been aggressively pro-market. Reversing three decades of disastrous, socialist central planning, SLORC in 1989 launched "the Burmese way to capitalism." Apart from enriching corrupt SLORC generals, who are all ethnic Burmans, the ensuing decade of marketization brought virtually no benefits to the indigenous population, the vast majority of whom still engage in traditional agriculture. One group, however, has benefited tremendously.

Since Burma's shift to a market-oriented, open-door economy, both Rangoon, the modern capital, and Mandalay, the ancient City of Gems and royal seat of the last two Burmese kings, have been taken over by ethnic Chinese. Some of these Chinese are from families that have lived in Burma for generations. Like the Indians but to a lesser extent, the Chinese were disproportionately wealthy during the colonial period (1886–1948), which was characterized by essentially laissez-faire policies superimposed on Burma's traditional rural economy. Although much of their wealth was confiscated during the socialist era (1962–88), the Chinese remained active in Burma's black markets and, in a few cases, opium trafficking.

In Burma's new market economy, the Sino-Burmese minority have been transformed almost overnight into a garishly prosperous business community. In addition, tens of thousands of poor but entrepreneurial immigrants from China, sweeping down from nearby Yunnan, have bought up the identity papers of dead Burmans for as little as three hundred dollars, becoming Burmese nationals overnight. Today, ethnic

---

**In 1997, SLORC was purged of many members, reorganized, and renamed the State Peace and Development Council. But most Burmese continue to call the government SLORC.

Chinese Burmese—looking uncomfortable in *longyis,* the traditional Burmese unisex sarongs—own nearly all of Mandalay's shops, hotels, restaurants, and prime commercial and residential real estate. The same is more or less true in Rangoon. Only a tiny, dying handful of Burman-owned establishments (mainly printing houses and cheroot factories) are left, dwarfed by the Chinese-built and Chinese-owned high-rise buildings around them.

Typical of Southeast Asia, the Chinese dominate Burmese commerce at every level of society. Massive joint ventures—such as the Shangri-La Hotel deal between Lo Hsing-han, the Sino-Burmese chairman of the Asia World conglomerate, and Sino-Malaysian tycoon Robert Kuok—have turned Mandalay and Rangoon into booming hubs for mainland Chinese and Southeast Asian Chinese business networks. (Non-Burmese Chinese investors are easy to spot. They're the ones not in *longyis* but in cowboy boots and sunglasses, walking around with bottles of Johnny Walker Red.) At the humbler end of the spectrum, Chinese hawkers make an excellent living selling cheap bicycle tires from China—often more than thirty thousand tires a month—for rickshaws in Burma. Nor is Chinese dominance only an urban phenomenon. After two years of severe flooding in southern China, large numbers of Chinese farmers—over a million, some estimate—poured into northern Burma. These new Burmese "citizens" now grow rice on the cleared hill country they have taken over. Entire Chinese villages have sprung up in this way.[3]

With the United States boycotting Burma on human rights grounds, globalization for Burma has had a disproportionately Chinese face, although the presence of French and German foreign investors can be felt as well. "Name a large infrastructure project anywhere in Myanmar these days and there is a strong possibility it will be in the hands of Chinese contractors," observed *The Economist* a few years ago. "Chinese engineers are working on improvements to the highway from Mandalay to Yangon. Chinese companies are developing the railway line from Mandalay to Myitkyina, near the Chinese border, and the line from Mandalay to the capital. With the help of chain gangs from Myanmar's prisons, they are also building a line from Ye to Tavoy in Myanmar's far south-east. . . . Against international competition, Chinese contractors have won the contract to build a big bridge across the Chindwin river.

Other Chinese ventures range from a new international airport for Mandalay to housing for the armed forces and 30 irrigation dams. It was the Chinese, in association with Siemens, who last year installed a ground satellite station serving the capital."[4]

The Chinese in Burma dominate not only legitimate trade and business but also more sordid black market activities. Indeed, the line between licit and illicit commercial activity in Burma, as in many developing countries, is often vague. Some of the country's most influential businessmen are former—possibly current—drug kingpins. "Drug traffickers who once spent their days leading mule trains down jungle paths are now leading lights in Burma's new market economy," lamented former U.S. secretary of state Madeline Albright a few years ago.[5]

Burma-born, ethnic Chinese tycoon Lo Hsing-han, for example, was an infamous opium warlord in the 1960s, thought to be responsible for much of the heroin that wound up in American veins. According to Burma scholar Bertil Lintner, Lo started off in his native Kokang Province as a lieutenant to the pistol-toting lesbian opium queen, Olive Yang. In 1989, Lo cut a deal with SLORC, persuading fellow ethnic warlords to accept a cease-fire with the junta in exchange for valuable timber and mineral concessions. Today, Lo's "Asia World" commercial empire includes a container shipping business, Rangoon port buildings, and tollbooths on the resurfaced Burma Road. Lo insists that he is now a legitimate businessman. "Since the market economy appeared in Myanmar," he explains, "it is easier to earn money trading vehicles on the Chinese border."[6] Whether or not Lo is clean, Burma's "Chinese underworld" remains as dominant in drug traffic and money laundering as Chinese merchants are in Mandalay's booming, lawful markets.

Chinese Plutocrats, Burman Misery

Ever since SLORC embraced markets, Burma has been hemorrhaging natural resources, especially teak, jade, and rubies. Apart from SLORC generals, the beneficiaries have been almost exclusively ethnic Chinese and a handful of hill tribe smugglers.

Burma's forests hold more than 70 percent of the world's teak. The Burmese teak is a magnificent tree, sometimes reaching 150 feet, with opposing egg-shaped leaves and clusters of white flowers. Its timber is dark, heavy, oily, of unusual strength and durability. Long the wood of Burmese royalty, immortalized by Rudyard Kipling ("Elephints a-pilin' teak / In the sludgy, squdgy creek, / Where the silence 'ung that 'eavy you was 'arf afraid to speak! / On the road to Mandalay . . . "), teak to-day is America's wood of choice for boat decking and salad bowls.

For over a decade now, Burma's hill tribes, particularly the Shan, have been selling enormous quantities of teak to Chinese buyers at fire-sale prices. Technically these sales are contraband, violating SLORC's of-ficial monopoly on timber exports. In reality, SLORC generals struck a deal with hill tribe insurgents a decade ago, granting them economic freedom in exchange for a cease-fire. As a result, since 1989, convoys of trucks loaded with teak logs—sometimes over ten feet in diameter, from trees hundreds of years old—travel daily, snaking along the moun-tainous old Burma Road across the border into China's Yunnan Province.

Meanwhile, SLORC's official timber policy has been aggressive globally-oriented marketization under government concessions. In-sisting that teak logging will facilitate Burma's economic development, SLORC has invited the full support of the private sector in promoting "forestry" (i.e., deforestation), even exempting forestry exports from commercial tax. Along with European and Chinese foreign investors, most of SLORC's business partners are Sino-Burmese tycoons who have close ties to Thai Chinese logging companies. Leading industrialist "May Flower" Kyaw Win, born to a poor Chinese family in the Northern Shan State, is a prominent example. Since moving into the timber business in 1990, Kyaw Win—also the managing director of Yangon Airlines and often spotted with top-ranking generals—has become one of the wealthiest men in Burma.[7]

By contrast, ethnic Burmans have profited almost not at all from the country's market-driven deforestation. Shan tribespeople continue to earn money smuggling teak to Yunnan, but adding insult to injury, the Shan, along with the paid-off Burmese border officials, spend their pro-ceeds almost entirely on coveted consumer goods imported from China and sold by Burmese Chinese. As a result the Chinese end up with both the teak and the money, while the Shan and the Burmans are left with cheap Chinese-made ghetto blasters, Michael Jackson T-shirts, sports shoes, condoms, and beer.[8]

In addition to teak, Burma is famous for her gems: pigeon-blood rubies, ultramarine sapphires, and imperial jade. Prior to 1989, under Burmese-style socialist rule, only the state was permitted to engage in gem mining and gem sales. Thus in the 1980s, when a private miner discovered, and then sold on the black market, a raw ruby weighing an incredible 469.5 carats, he was promptly arrested and imprisoned. SLORC recaptured the ruby in 1990 and proudly proclaimed it the property of the state. Christened Na Wa Ta, or the "SLORC ruby," its picture was displayed across the country in the state-owned *Working People's Daily*. (Around the same time, the government also announced the discovery of two raw sapphires, one weighing 979 carats, the other around 1,300 carats.) During the socialist period, when all industry was nationalized, the Burmese government sold gems to foreign companies by holding annual "gem emporiums." Private gem sales were conducted underground by hundreds of traders operating largely out of Mandalay's 34th and 35th Street black markets.[9]

In a watershed pro-market reversal, the Burmese government in the early nineties privatized much of its gem industry. Since 1995, private mining concessions have been sold on the basis of competitive bidding, costing as much as $83,000 per acre for virgin gem mines. Once again, virtually all the concessionaires have been Sino-Burmese businessmen. One Chinese-owned jewelry company reportedly controls 100 gem mines and produces over 2,000 kilograms of raw rubies a year. Lo Hsinghan's visible holdings, valued at an estimated $600 million, include valuable ruby concessions as well as "a mining stake in the northern 'jade rush' town of Phakent—said to harbor a 300-ton jade boulder, buried so deep in the jungle it can't be moved." Lo's Asia World conglomerate is now the most popular partner for foreigners investing in Burma. Along with private mining, SLORC also legalized private gem sales. Today, Burma's gem industry is dominated by thriving Burmese Chinese at every level, from the financiers to the concession operators to the owners of scores of new jewelry shops that sprang up all over Mandalay and Rangoon.[10] Needless to say, SLORC officials are also handsomely paid off at every level.

It is an understatement to say that, in terms of financial and human capital, the vast majority of indigenous Burmans, roughly 69 percent of the population, cannot compete with the country's 5 percent Chinese minority. Three-quarters of the Burmans live in extreme rural poverty, typically engaging in paddy production or subsistence farming. Despite land reforms during the socialist era, an estimated 40 percent of Burman peasants are landless. For rural Burmans, saving money is virtually impossible; anything earned is spent just to stay alive. As a result, most Burmans have little or no capital and have not profited from economic liberalization.[11]

Lack of financial capital is not the only problem. Since abandoning socialism in 1988, SLORC has slashed real spending on health and education. According to United Nations agencies, nearly 40 percent of Burmese children never enroll in school and up to 75 percent drop out before the fifth grade. Moreover, because of the ruling junta's paranoia about student-led civil unrest, Burma's universities were closed for three-and-a-half years, until July 2000. Human capital levels among indigenous Burmans are thus abysmal. All these factors, along with possible cultural obstacles—some have suggested that there is a native prejudice against "greedy" profit-seeking—make it extremely difficult for Burmans to compete in a market economy.[12]

In urban areas, Burmans may actually have suffered from marketization. Most of the native residents of Mandalay were historically artisans, who made their living weaving tapestry, carving gold leaf, crafting furniture, or polishing precious stones. In recent years, low wages in these traditional industries relative to the skyrocketing prices of consumer goods have pushed the standard of living of thousands below subsistence. Meanwhile, since 1989, the price of rice in Mandalay has been rising steadily—at one point, over 1,000 percent in seven years—with no end in sight. For many Burmans, whose average per capita income is only around $300 a year, this translates into something close to starvation.

Further, as ethnic Chinese developers in the nineties snapped up all the prime real estate in Mandalay—making fast fortunes as property values doubled and tripled in the chaotic new markets—indigenous Burmese Mandalayans were pushed farther and farther away from their

native homes. (In 1990, SLORC had already forcibly relocated dissidents and Mandalayan monks.) Today, thousands of poor, displaced
Burmans live in satellite shantytowns on the outskirts of Mandalay,
within eyeshot of the gaudy, fenced-off mansions of the SLORC generals, many of whom are openly parasitic on Chinese businessmen.[13]

Free markets are supposed to lift all boats, and indeed often do. But
this is distinctly not the perception of Burma's roughly 30 million ethnic
Burman majority. In their view, markets and economic liberalization
have led to the domination and looting of their country by a relative
handful of "outsiders," chiefly ethnic Chinese, in symbiotic alliance with
SLORC. Mandalay's central business district is now filled with Chinese
signs and Chinese music pouring out of Chinese shops. Burmese-made
products have been almost entirely displaced by cheaper Chinese imports. Chinese restaurants serving grilled meat and fish overflow with
loud Mandarin-speakers. "To go to Mandalay," snaps a character in a local cartoon strip, "you need to master Chinese conversation." When the
sun sets, Mandalay's new money heads to Chinese-owned karaoke bars,
where young Chinese hostesses sing along to the latest songs from laser
discs made in Hong Kong. On weekends, wealthy Chinese relax in the
mountaintop resort of Maymyo, where they have bought up as vacation
homes the grand Victorian houses left behind by British colonialists.[14]

Meanwhile, just below the surface, anti-Chinese hostility seethes
among the Burman majority. As hatred of SLORC intensifies, hatred for
the Chinese intensifies as well, not without justification: Crony capitalis-
tic relationships between SLORC generals and Chinese entrepreneurs,
not to mention arms sales from China, have been critical in propping up
Burma's reviled ruling junta. But in the current reign of fear, there is no
avenue for venting resentment, whether against SLORC, the rich
Chinese, or the market-oriented policies that have allowed both of these
groups to make hundreds of millions while indigenous Burmans become
an increasingly subjugated underclass in their own country. Alcoholism
is sharply on the rise among Burmans, all the more startling given that
liquor consumption is considered a sin according to one of the Five
Commandments of Burmese Buddhism. Fittingly, the alcohol chiefly
consumed is Chinese Tiger Beer, imported from China.[15]

Today, ordinary Burmans speak bitterly of "the Chinese invasion" or "recolonization by the Chinese." "The people who put up these new buildings say they are Burmese, but we know they are really from China," a Burman shopkeeper explained angrily. "They are taking over our business and pushing us out of our homes."[16] Notwithstanding massive government repression—the Internet and all forms of political organization and free expression are banned—indigenous hostility against the Burmese Chinese is palpable and growing.

Chinese Market-Dominance in Historical Context

No other country has Burma's lurid combination of Orwellian government, bulging rubies, and vast fields of opium poppies (which the current junta insists are being replaced with limes and soybeans). Nevertheless, the basic dynamic in Burma just described—Chinese market dominance and intense resentment among the indigenous majority—is characteristic of virtually every country in Southeast Asia.

Ethnic Chinese have played a disproportionate role in the commercial life of Southeast Asia since long before the colonial era. In the early 1400s, when the Grand Eunuch Admiral Cheng Ho led a fleet of three hundred vessels around Southeast Asia on behalf of the Ming dynasty, he discovered an enclave of fellow Chinese already prospering in Java, now in Indonesia. The admiral observed that the Chinese had fine food and clothing, in contrast to "the natives of the country, who were very dirty and were fond of eating snakes, insects, and worms, and who slept and ate together with the dogs."[17]

Around the same time, in another part of what is now Indonesia, the much more advanced Tabanan was the seat of one of Bali's most powerful and cultured royal courts. The Tabanan kingdom, recounts Clifford Geertz, was full of "rebellious conspiracies, strategic marriages, calculated affronts, and artful blandishments woven into a delicate pattern of Machiavellian statecraft." Tabanan was also the center of the now world-famous Balinese music and theater arts. Nevertheless, even six hundred years ago, all foreign trade in the kingdom was conducted by a single wealthy Chinese, with the remainder of the tiny Chinese community acting as his agents. Indigenous commerce was practically nonexistent. Half a millennium later, little in this respect had changed. As late as

1950, virtually all the stores and factories in Tabanan were Chinese owned.[18]

In the Philippines, when the Spanish in 1571 founded the city of Manila on the island of Luzon, they encountered Chinese settlements that had preceded them by more than a century as well as belligerent Chinese traders, who sailed up in their junks, firing rockets and cannons. Animosity between the Chinese and the Spanish is a constant theme in the Philippines' colonial history. The Spaniards subjected the Chinese to severe taxes and restrictions, and sequestered them in fenced-in quarters called the Parián. At the same time, the Spanish were utterly dependent on the Chinese, who, as traders, tailors, locksmiths, bakers, and so on, seemed to occupy every critical economic niche.

On May 23, 1603, three Chinese mandarins, wearing all their official insignia, and carrying a box of seals as if they were still in China, arrived in the Philippines. After receiving homage from Manila's Chinese residents, the mandarins

> presented a letter to the Spanish Governor explaining that they had come to investigate a hill of gold and silver, as yet unexploited they understood, of which the Chinese Emperor had heard tell. They bore themselves with the dignity befitting the emissaries of All Under Heaven, moving through Manila as though it were Chinese territory, and administering floggings as they saw fit. The Spaniards did not quite know what to make of it. Was it a curtain-raiser to a Chinese takeover of the Philippines? . . . Taking immediate precautions, the Governor issued orders for all Chinese on the island to be registered, and for the men to be divided and housed in groups of three hundred.[19]

The Chinese resisted, and hostilities broke out. After a Spanish envoy was killed in Parián, the Spanish took their vengeance, massacring twenty-three thousand Chinese and hungrily looting their property. Afterward, however, the Spanish regretted having killed so many Chinese, for, as one of them lamented, they had no food and "no shoes to wear, not even at excessive prices."[20]

The Chinese eventually returned and were massacred by the Spanish many more times. In the end, the Chinese outlasted the Spanish.

Chinese economic dominance in Vietnam dates back even further. Vietnam's recorded history begins in 208 B.C., when a renegade Chinese general conquered Au Lac, a domain in the northern mountains of Vietnam populated by the Viet people, and declared himself emperor of Nam Viet. A century later the powerful Han dynasty incorporated Nam Viet into the Chinese empire, and for the next thousand years Vietnam was ruled as a province of China. During this period of Chinese colonization, and for many centuries afterward, waves of Chinese immigrants—bureaucrats, scholars, and merchants as well as soldiers, fugitives, and prisoners of war—settled in Vietnam. By the end of the seventeenth century a distinct Chinese community, known in Vietnam as the Hoa, had formed within Vietnamese society.[21]

The Chinese in Vietnam were notoriously enterprising. Unlike the British, Dutch, and Japanese, the Chinese were not only traders but also manufacturers, of everything from black incense to fine silk. They acted as middlemen between the Europeans and the local Vietnamese. In Hoi An, Vietnam's busiest trading port from the sixteenth to eighteenth centuries, Chinese merchants monopolized Vietnam's gold export business and dominated the local trade in paper, tea, pepper, silver bars, arms, sulphur, lead, and lead oxide. Resentment against Chinese success coupled with repeated attempts by China to conquer Vietnam sparked recurrent anti-Hoa reprisals, including the 1782 massacre of Chinese in Cholon, Saigon's Chinatown. Nevertheless, by the time the French arrived in the mid-eighteenth century, Vietnam's tiny Chinese minority dominated the indigenous Vietnamese majority in virtually every urban market sector as well as in trade and mining.[22]

As throughout Southeast Asia, the Chinese prospered under colonial laissez-faire policies. Indeed, favorable economic conditions brought a rapid influx of Chinese immigrants, which continued until the middle of the twentieth century. Almost all of these Chinese settled in South Vietnam. By the 1930s the gaps between the large-scale manufacturing, commercial, and financial enterprises of the French were filled by the smaller businesses of the Chinese. The magnitude of the Chinese minority's economic power was astounding. Constituting just 1 percent of Vietnam's population, the Chinese controlled an estimated 90 percent of non-European private capital in the mid-1950s and dominated Vietnam's retail trade, its financial, manufacturing, and transportation sectors, and all aspects of the country's rice economy. Although there were also numerous wealthy Vietnamese in the commercial class, Chinese economic dominance produced a bitter outcry against "the Chinese stranglehold on Indochina," "the Chinese cyst," and "the Chinese excrescence."

During the Vietnam War (which the Vietnamese call the American War), the wealth of the Chinese in South Vietnam, particularly Saigon, intensified. Vietnamese Chinese pounced on the lucrative business opportunities that came with the arrival of American troops, who needed a trade and services network. At the same time the South Vietnamese government deregulated the economy, adopting relatively liberal market practices. Local Chinese businessmen aggressively seized these opportunities as well, extending their dominance to include light industry.

Following the country's reunification in 1976, the revolutionary Vietnamese government singled out the entrepreneurial Chinese of the south as "bourgeois" and perpetrators of "world capitalism," arresting and brutalizing thousands and confiscating their property along with that of their Vietnamese counterparts. "Employing the techniques Hitler used to inflame hatred against the Jews," reported *U.S. News & World Report*'s Ray Wallace in 1979, "Hanoi is blaming day-to-day problems in Vietnam on resented Chinese control of commerce and the Mekong Delta."[23] As Vietnam was transformed into a socialist economy, thousands of Chinese either died laboring in Vietnam's "new economic zones" or fled the country.

Today in Vietnam, both markets and the Chinese are back. The government's post-1988 shift to market liberalization, or *doi moi* ("renovation"), has led to an astounding resurgence of Chinese commercial dominance in the country's urban areas. Vietnam's 3 percent Chinese minority cluster in Ho Chi Minh City (still Saigon to most Vietnamese), where they control roughly 50 percent of that city's market activity and overwhelmingly dominate light industry, import-export, shopping malls, and private banking. Once again, resentment among the indigenous Vietnamese is building.[24]

Globalization and the Explosion of Chinese Wealth

Vietnam, however, is still technically a socialist country, with the state retaining control over major sectors of the economy. By contrast, in most of Southeast Asia, global markets have catapulted wealth creation—and wealth disparities—to an entirely different order of magnitude. In Thailand, Malaysia, the Philippines, and Indonesia, ethnic Chinese tycoons, richer than entire nations, oversee multibillion-dollar financial empires stretching from Shanghai to Kalimantan to Mexico City.

For several decades prior to the 1980s, most of the Southeast Asian governments pursued disastrous non-market economic policies. Starting in the 1980s and 1990s, in what the World Bank has called "the third wave of globalization," the countries of Southeast Asia embarked on aggressive market reforms, including free trade and pro-foreign investment policies, deregulation, and privatization of state-owned enterprises. These reforms generated rapid economic growth throughout the region, particularly in the labor-intensive, export-oriented manufacturing industries. At the same time, the turn to free markets unleashed the entrepreneurial energies of Southeast Asia's Chinese minorities, enormously enhancing their visibility and economic dominance.

Thailand, for example, was isolationist in the fifties and sixties, its economy mired in state-owned enterprises. Over the next several decades, internationalization and market-oriented policies led to the dramatic emergence of a massive export-oriented, large-scale manufacturing sector, which in turn jump-started the economy. Virtually all of the new manufacturing establishments, including the now behemoth Siam Motors, were Chinese controlled. Indeed, a recent survey of Thailand's roughly seventy most powerful business groups found that all but three were owned by Thai Chinese. (Of these non-Chinese groups, one was controlled by the Military Bank, another by the Crown Property Bureau, and the third by a Thai-Indian family.)[25]

In Malaysia, too, privatization and other market policies have starkly magnified the economic dominance of the country's Chinese minority. This is true despite extensive affirmative action policies for the indigenous Malay majority, which have been in place ever since bloody anti-

Chinese riots in 1969 left nearly a thousand dead in Kuala Lumpur. Today, the Malaysian Chinese—the largest Chinese minority in Southeast Asia, representing about a third of the population—account for 70 percent of the country's market capitalization.[26]

A good portion of this 70 percent figure is attributable to Robert Kuok, who started off selling palm oil but now commands a sprawling business empire that includes everything from manufacturing to real estate (including hotels in Burma) to media. Kuok is "the quintessential Asian tycoon," *The Economist* wrote recently, "amassing wealth, spreading it across countries and industries to reduce risk, and above all keeping quiet about it." "Gregarious and chatty, Mr. Kuok nevertheless ensures that virtually nothing of substance is known about him." When an international investigative agency probed into Kuok's empire a few years ago, this is the profile they came up with: "Name—Robert Kuok; political affiliation—unknown; adversaries—none identified; litigation—nothing known; ambitions—not known." According to *Forbes* in 2002, the Kuok group's net worth is around $4 billion.[27]

Chinese market dominance in the Philippines is equally striking, if slightly more complex. Filipino Chinese range widely in cultural identity: from highly assimilated, fourth-generation Chinese mestizo families, like the Cojuangcos; to relatively recent immigrants like my own family, who retain more of their Chinese culture and insularity; to the latest arrivals from mainland China, who are widely disliked—even by other Chinese Filipinos—because they are "loud and pushy" and "spit everywhere." Further, unlike in other Southeast Asian countries, the Chinese in the Philippines share their economic dominance with a powerful and glamorous "Spanish-blooded" gentry class. Today these *hacienderos* still live like feudal lords and control almost all of the land in the countryside.

Although the *hacienderos* also have extensive businesses, it was the country's tiny Chinese minority whose economic power exploded with the pro-market reforms of the late-1980s and 1990s. Today, Filipino Chinese, just 1 to 2 percent of the population, control all of the Philippines' largest and most lucrative department store chains, major supermarkets, and fast-food restaurants, including the McDonald's franchise and the Jollibee chain, which makes "Filipino-style" burgers with soy sauce. With one exception, all of the Philippines' principal banks are now Chinese-controlled, including George Ty's Metrobank Group, the country's largest and most aggressive financial conglomerate.

The Manila Stock Exchange, located near Chinatown, is dominated by Filipino Chinese stockbrokerage firms. Ethnic Chinese also dominate the shipping, textiles, construction, real estate, pharmaceutical, manufacturing, and personal computer industries as well as the country's wholesale distribution networks. Outside of commerce and finance, Chinese Filipinos control six out of the ten English-language newspapers in Manila, including the one with the largest daily circulation. Apart from the aristocratic Zobel de Ayala family and possibly the Marcos family (Ferdinand and Imelda's son Bong Bong and daughter Imee are currently both elected officials in the Philippines), all of "the top billionaires in the Philippines" are Filipino Chinese or Chinese-descended, at least according to a recent report in the (Chinese-owned) *Philippine Star*.[28]

Even the relatively unmarketized economies of Cambodia and Laos are showing signs of Chinese market dominance. Cambodia's capital city Phnom Penh is now teeming with thousands of prospering Chinese businesses. In Laos, which has almost no indigenous commercial culture, the 1 percent Chinese minority more or less constitute the country's entire business community, profiting eagerly from every grudging inch of globalization-induced market opening.[29]

Globalization has unquestionably had some positive effects even for Southeast Asia's poor indigenous majorities. According to a recent World Bank report, global integration and market policies since 1980 have reduced absolute poverty in a number of Southeast Asian countries, including Thailand, Malaysia, and the Philippines, raising average incomes in these countries at all levels.[30] Unfortunately, this kind of statistic hides a number of troubling facts.

First, even with these income improvements, the indigenous majorities in these countries remain unmistakably, often shockingly poor. Impoverished Filipinos do not rejoice in World Bank empirical studies showing that their per capita income has increased by a few cents per day. Second, more fundamentally, globalization and free markets since 1980 have aggravated, in appearance and almost certainly in reality, the grotesque ethnic wealth disparities in the region. In the eyes of Southeast Asia's indigenous majorities, global markets have produced multimillionaires, billionaires, and multibillionaires—but only among members of another ethnic group. As a result, despite marginal increases in their income, indigenous Southeast Asians often feel that free markets benefit only "outsiders"—ethnic Chinese and foreign investors—along with a handful of corrupt indigenous politicians in their pockets.

In all the countries of Southeast Asia, free markets have produced countless rags-to-riches success stories among the ethnic Chinese, but remarkably few among the region's indigenous majorities. As an informal illustration of globalization's disproportionate ethnic effects, consider two roughly contemporaneous vignettes of Southeast Asian economic history.

Bean Curd or Chicken Feed?

Between bean curd and chicken feed, which would have been the better business bet in 1920s Southeast Asia? It's hard to imagine two humbler products. As it happens, a bean curd industry in Java and a chicken feed industry in Bangkok emerged around the same time. The first, operated by indigenous Javanese, has remained virtually unchanged for eighty years and today is suffering badly from globalization and market competition. The second, founded by two Chinese brothers, is now a $9 billion global agro-industrial conglomerate.

In 1920, in the east Javanese town of Mojokerto, a local Javanese woman started manufacturing bean curd in a bamboo shack. Soon afterward, four similar bean curd factories appeared. This part of town became known as the "Bean Curd Neighborhood," because almost all of its inhabitants over the age of ten were involved in producing bean curd in one way or another. In his 1963 book *Peddlers and Princes: Social Change and Economic Modernization in Two Indonesian Towns,* anthropologist Clifford Geertz describes the production process:

Bean-curd, a small piece of which most Javanese eat with every meal, and which is probably their major source of protetin, is made from soya bean. . . . The beans are soaked in water for about six hours until they become mushy. They are then ground between one fixed stone and one movable one, the movable one being rotated by hand through an ingenious spindle-and-pulley arrangement suspended from the ceiling. The result of this operation, which may take a half-hour or so, is a semiliquid pulp which is then screened for major impurities and cooked in a large vat for several hours. This cooking is an attention-demanding job because the pulp must be added gradually, can by can, and must be stirred continually. While still boiling, the cooked product is now screened again, this time through a piece of cheesecloth stretched over a vat, and vinegar is added to cause the by now milk-like substance to curdle. The separated liquid is siphoned off, and the curds are placed in a bamboo tray to dry in the sun, this whole straining, siphoning, and curdling process taking perhaps ten or fifteen minutes. When, in about an hour, the curds are dry, or reasonably so, they are carefully molded into squares through a process of enclosing them in a small piece of cloth and dextrously folding the cloth into a flattened cube. Next, the little patties thus formed are pressed even dryer with a flat board, and then they are fried in deep fat for about a half-hour. Finally, they are wrapped separately in paper for sale; and this, as bean curd does not keep, must take place within a day or two of manufacture.[31]

These details of bean curd making are worth noting not just for the craft, but because they have remained essentially unchanged for eighty years. Today, tofu manufacturing in Indonesia is still a cottage industry, in the hands of small indigenous producers, many of whom cater to street vendors. In Jakarta's smog-filled streets, hundreds of these vendors peddle their *ta-fu* and *tempeh* (fermented tofu cakes) in pushcarts known as *kaki lima,* or "five-legs," for the two legs of the peddler, the two wheels of the cart, and the post it rests on. According to a 2001 Javanese bean curd industry website, the equipment used to make tofu still consists of the "rolling machine, wok, boiler, soaking basin, and boiling basin." Of the thousands of Javanese families that have engaged in this business since it began, none has introduced major technological innovations or become dominant through greater efficiencies. Nor has there been any product diversification or vertical integration to speak of.

Globalization and economic liberalization, moreover, thus far have brought only pain for Indonesia's tofu producers. Whereas soybeans were locally grown when Geertz described Mojokerto's tofu industry, Indonesia today imports most of its soybeans from the United States. When the rupiah crashed in 1998, the price of soybeans soared—a disaster for Indonesia's tofu producers, whose monthly income is only around twenty-seven dollars and who are unable to pass higher costs along to their even poorer vendors and customers. Some eighty-four hundred tofu producers in East Java went out of business in 1998. Meanwhile, to control a ballooning budget deficit, the IMF and the World Bank are urging Indonesia to do away with government subsidies for fuel oil, which currently sells for only about a quarter of its world market price. Fuel prices have already increased significantly. For family-based tofu businesses, which typically buy one hundred liters of fuel a day to fire the ancient pressure cookers that turn their soybeans into slurry, free market policies have made Indonesians choose between starvation and removing their children from school—both to put them to work and to eliminate the cost of tuition.[32]

Also around 1920, two young immigrant brothers—who had left China virtually penniless just a few years earlier—scraped together enough capital to open their tiny Chia Tai seed shop in Bangkok. Over the next few decades the brothers, Chia Ek Chor and Chia Siew Whooy, struggled, importing seeds and vegetables from China, exporting pigs and eggs to Hong Kong, experimenting incessantly while living on next to nothing. In the 1950s the brothers began specializing in animal feed, especially for chickens, establishing the Charoen Pokphand Feedmill in 1953. Through the 1950s and 1960s the Chia family—now surnamed Chiaravanont—vertically integrated, combining their feedmilling operations with chicken breeding. By 1969 the Charoen Pokphand (CP) Group had an annual turnover of between $1 and $2 million.

As Thailand opened up its economy in the 1970s, embracing globally-oriented market policies, the CP Group took off, entering into various business arrangements with major Thai banks, the Thai government, and foreign companies. The core of the CP Group's agribusiness was contract farming: The company supplied Thai farmers with chicks and feed and taught them how to raise chickens. In turn, the farmers sold the grown chickens back to the CP Group, which processed the chickens and then marketed them to high-volume buyers such as grocery stores, restaurants, and fast-food franchises. At the same time, the CP Group expanded internationally, exporting their contract farming formula first to neighboring Indonesia and Malaysia, then to the rest of Asia, and eventually all over the world, from Mexico to Turkey to Alabama.

In the 1980s, with Thailand now aggressively privatizing and in full free market mode, the CP Group moved into aquaculture, applying their contract farming formula to raising and marketing shrimp. In 1987 the group acquired the 7-Eleven and Kentucky Fried Chicken franchises for Thailand. It also moved into Shanghai, manufacturing motorcycles with a license from Honda and brewing beer with a license from Heineken. In 1989 the CP Group entered the petrochemical business through a joint venture with Solvay, one of Belgium's largest firms. In 1992 the group signed a contract to rebuild Thailand's telecommunications system, a $3 billion project. In 1994 it signed a joint venture agreement with Wal-Mart to establish super-retail stores throughout Asia. Today the CP Group claims $9 billion in assets and is among the most powerful business conglomerates anywhere in the world.[33]

Needless to say, these two stories do not amount to a scientific sample; they are intended only to be suggestive. And they do suggest a number of points. For one thing, the key to success doesn't turn on what product you start with, whether bean curd or chicken feed. My own family in the Philippines started off manufacturing fish paste, another humble product best thought of as mashed anchovies. To save on costs, my family members decided to produce their own containers. They eventually dropped the fish paste to focus exclusively on plastics.

Nor does the existence of "social networks" explain economic success. Both the Javanese bean curd industry and the CP Group operate substantially through kinship networks. In Mojokerto, tofu production was essentially communal, involving about fifty close-knit families. The

CP Group is now headed by Dhanin Chiaravanont, the youngest son of the elder Chia brother, and the founders' other twelve sons are all on the board of directors.

What distinguishes the CP Group from the Javanese tofu industry is not social networks or the nature of its products, but rather its breathtaking dynamism. Moreover, while the Chiaravanont family's economic success is extreme in magnitude, it is representative of Chinese success stories at all levels of Southeast Asian society.

It seems safe to say that this entrepreneurial dynamism—together with frugality, hard work, willingness to delay gratification, and intense desire to accumulate wealth almost as an end in itself—cannot be traced to any single cultural, much less genetic source. (There are plenty of individual Chinese in Southeast Asia who do not exemplify these qualities. My own maternal grandfather was a poor schoolteacher who had an aversion to commerce.) A given ethnic group can be entrepreneurial and market-dominant in one setting, but not in another. The Chinese in China were market-dormant, so to speak, for centuries.

Why some groups prosper disproportionately over others has been the subject of a long and fascinating debate ever since Max Weber described the Protestant work ethic and desire to accumulate wealth as "the spirit of capitalism" itself.[34] Explaining the market dominance of various ethnic groups is not the focus of this book. I leave this debate to others more qualified to resolve it.[35]

The critical point, however, is that today the "spirit of capitalism" may no longer be enough. What economists call "path-dependence" now plays a tremendous, unavoidable role in group economic success. Access to capital is so important to economic success in a modernized global economy that already-prosperous ethnic groups have an enormous market advantage. The Chinese minorities have a worldwide head start advantage of roughly $2 trillion in assets, not to mention their famous "social networks" of business connections, which are not merely intra-ethnic but include Western and Japanese foreign investors as well. In much of the world, history may have moved beyond the point where a poor ethnic group could, fortuitously or otherwise, develop the "spirit of capitalism" and thereby attain market dominance.

Jakarta Burning

Although Americans prefer to forget this, Indonesia's General Suharto was a longtime darling of the United States government and business community because of his rejection of populist redistribution in favor of liberal markets and foreign investment. Starting as early as the 1970s, and in exchange for the support of the United States, the World Bank, and the IMF, Suharto pursued raw, globally-oriented free market policies.[36]

As in all the Southeast Asian countries, the result was an influx of foreign capital, unprecedented levels of growth, and spectacular Chinese economic success. By 1998, Sino-Indonesians occupied a position of economic dominance wildly disproportionate to their numbers. Just 3 percent of the population, the Chinese controlled approximately 70 percent of the private economy. All of Indonesia's billionaires were ethnically Chinese, and almost all of the country's largest conglomerates were owned by Sino-Indonesian families. The major exceptions to this rule were companies owned by the children of Suharto, which themselves depended on state favors and Chinese entrepreneurialism. More generally, although Chinese Indonesians were certainly not all well-off, they were economically dominant at every level of society. Ethnic Chinese dominated petty trading occupations in rural areas. They also dominated both retail and wholesale trade in urban areas as well as the country's informal credit sector. Indeed, almost every tiny town had a Chinese-run general store that was the center of local economic life.[37]

The extraordinary market-generated economic growth of the 1980s and 1990s almost certainly left Indonesia's roughly 200-million-strong indigenous (or *pribumi*, "of the soil") majority better off, at least in terms of average income. But that was not their perception. On the contrary, there was a pervasive belief among the *pribumi* that Suharto's market liberalization favored the "already rich" Sino-Indonesians at the expense of indigenous Indonesians. Even though most Chinese Indonesians are struggling and hardworking members of the middle class, with no political connections whatsoever, all the *pribumi* majority seemed to see in the years leading up to 1998 was a handful of brazen Chinese plutocrats accumulating immense wealth by exploiting their corrupt ties with the increasingly hated Suharto.

One of Suharto's most prominent Chinese cronies was Liem Sioe Liong, who emigrated to Indonesia from Fujian Province, China in 1938 at the age of twenty-one. Liem started off in his uncle's peanut oil shop in a backwater Javanese town, eventually scraping together enough savings to start his own business. Along the way he adopted the Indonesian-sounding name Sudono Salim and won the favor of an ambitious army officer named Suharto. After Suharto became president in 1966, he granted Salim lucrative franchises in banking, flour milling, and telecommunications. In return, Salim financed Suharto's pet projects, both private and public—developing Indonesia's steel sector, for example—while adding enormously to the personal wealth of the Suharto family. Meanwhile, by forming alliances with foreign industrial and commercial enterprises, Salim aggressively acquired technology, information, and market expertise. By 1997 the Salim Group was reportedly the world's largest Chinese-owned conglomerate, with $20 billion in assets and some five hundred companies.[38]

Ethnic Chinese timber tycoon Bob Hasan was another of Suharto's close business associates. In the 1980s, Hasan wielded so much influence over the president that he could essentially write legislation favoring his own group of rattan and plywood companies.[39] Hasan's logging companies further maximized profits by using environmentally disastrous burning methods to clear land. During the last few months of 1997, vast areas of Southeast Asia were smothered by thick smoke from massive forest fires in Indonesia. At the height of the fires, provinces in Sumatra and Kalimantan (the island formerly known as Borneo) were recording air pollution levels hazardous to human life. Eighty percent of the fires—burning 1.4 million hectares in Kalimantan alone—were caused by the behavior of Chinese-owned commercial entities. According to a recent, unpublished World Bank report, all of Sumatra's lowland forests will be extinct by 2005, and Kalimantan's by 2010.[40]

By the end of the 1990s the spectacle of Suharto and a handful of Chinese cronies engorging themselves at the nation's expense had provoked massive, widespread, long suppressed hostility among the *pribumi* majority. Suharto's resignation in May 1998 was accompanied by an eruption of vicious anti-Chinese violence. Even as globalization's enthusiasts celebrated the fall of Indonesia's dictatorship and the good judgment of global markets—"Who ousted Suharto?" Thomas Friedman would later write. "It wasn't another state, it was the Supermarkets, by withdrawing their support for, and confidence in, the Indonesian economy"[41]—thousands of torch-carrying Indonesians headed for Jakarta's Chinese neighborhoods.

For three long days, terrified Chinese shop owners huddled behind locked doors while screaming Muslim mobs smashed windows, looted shops, and gang-raped over 150 women, almost all of them ethnic Chinese. Salim's Jakarta home was burned to the ground as were nearly five thousand other homes and stores owned by ethnic Chinese. In the end, over two thousand people died, including many *pribumi* rioters trapped in flaming shopping malls. The resulting $40 billion to $100 billion of capital flight, almost all Chinese-controlled, plunged the economy into a crisis from which the country has not recovered. At the time, however, the prevailing view among the *pribumi* majority was that it was "worthwhile to lose ten years of growth to get rid of the Chinese problem once and for all."[42] Meanwhile, the U.S. State Department called resoundingly for free markets and democratic elections.

After the May 1998 riots, anti-Chinese violence, often preceded by spray-painted symbols marking Chinese shops and homes as targets, continued to break out, not just in Jakarta but throughout Indonesia's cities. Unlike Salim or other tycoons, most Chinese Indonesians did not have the wherewithal to leave the country. They remained in the only home they had ever known, stockpiling weapons to defend themselves. Hundreds of Chinese Indonesians purchased "anti-rape corsets": a stainless steel chastity belt, complete with tiny key, developed by a Chinese entrepreneur.[43]

Much of the capital that fled Indonesia in 1998 ended up in Singapore. (Australia was another favorite destination.) Often disappointingly sterile to Western visitors, Singapore has for years been a multipurpose haven for Sino-Indonesians. Today, violence in Indonesia has subsided, and even as the great majority of *pribumi* Indonesians struggle to survive, the Friday afternoon Garuda Airlines flight to Singapore is packed with gaily jabbering *ibu*—the wives of Chinese Indonesian businessmen going to Singapore for the weekend to shop and dine. The latest rage in Singapore is "medical tourism." Given Indonesia's frightening hospital and health statistics, a constant stream of Indonesian Chinese fly to Singapore for cutting-edge medical care, from chemotherapy to liposuction and, especially popular among young Chinese women, operations on the epicanthic fold to produce Caucasian "double eyelids."

Indonesia's population is 210 million; Singapore's population is just over 3 million. Whereas the Chinese are a market-dominant minority in Indonesia (and the rest of Southeast Asia), in Singapore they are an 80 percent market-dominant *majority*. Indonesia's per capita income is around $2,000—and it's that high only because of the country's many wealthy Chinese. Singapore's per capita income is around $27,000, higher than that of France, Germany, and the United Kingdom.[44] Ethnic violence in Singapore is virtually unheard-of. For Indonesian Chinese, explains one Singaporean law professor, "Singapore is seen as Valhalla: a place where things work, where things are what they should be and would be if Chinese were in charge."

The Wrath of the Many

The Chinese are not the only market-dominant minority in Asia. Throughout the region, resentment and vindictive terror have been directed at other disproportionately successful minorities with the same ferocity. India, for example, has no market-dominant minority at the national level, but plenty of market-dominant minorities at the state level. Thus, in the oil-rich northern state of Assam, Bengali immigrants, now roughly 40 percent of the population, have for years dominated commerce and the professions. Between 1979 and 1983, enraged members of the Assamese majority repeatedly attacked Bengalis in widespread, vicious ethnic riots.[45] In Sri Lanka, the Ceylon Tamils, historically more educated, prosperous, and "advanced" than the Sinhalese majority, dominated the economy until a wave of anti-Tamil reprisals in the 1970s; ethnic strife continues to this day. Recently, writes Thomas Sowell, "a Tamil woman picked at random was dragged off a bus in Sri Lanka, doused with gasoline, and set ablaze by a Sinhalese mob in which people danced and clapped their hands while she died in agony."[46]

Nevertheless, no minority in Asia is, or has ever been, as stunningly wealthy or glaringly market-dominant as the ethnic Chinese communities of Southeast Asia, who collectively control virtually all of the region's most advanced and lucrative industries as well as its economic crown jewels. As the U.S. government and international financial institutions continue to call for faster and tougher market reforms, there festers among the region's indigenous majorities deep anti-Chinese resentment, rooted not just in poverty but in feelings of envy, insecurity, and exploitation. Such resentment is ready at any moment to be catalyzed, whether by another economic downturn, a charismatic hate-monger, or simply a dispute between a Chinese employer and an indigenous laborer. Even during relatively stable periods the Chinese throughout Southeast Asia are repeatedly subjected to kidnapping, vandalism, and violence. Just recently a Muslim Filipino kidnapping gang known as "The Pentagon" executed two Chinese hostages, both employees of a multimillion-dollar irrigation project in Mindanao, and vowed to behead a third if a $10 million ransom was not paid. Reacting to another series of kidnappings last year, one Filipino official shrugged and said, reflecting widespread sentiment, "The Chinese can afford the ransom."

Thus globalization and free markets in Southeast Asia have generated not only tremendous growth but also tremendous ethnic hatred and instability. During the 1998 Indonesian crisis I did a brief stint at the World Bank. At one point it was suggested that I join a delegation to Jakarta. A few days later, however, I was told not to go, as I was of Chinese descent and thus at risk. This surprised me; I thought my American passport and the auspices of the World Bank would surely be sufficient to protect me. One of my colleagues at the bank explained that Indonesian officials were apparently marking the passports of anyone "with Chinese blood" with a red stamp, Hitler-style. I don't know if the rumor was true, but the sad truth is that it easily could have been, given the intensity of anti-Chinese fury in Indonesia at the time.

The situation developing in Burma today is dangerously similar to the one that eventually sent much of Jakarta up in flames. Indeed, in its pro-market, pro-Chinese military dictatorship, the Burmese government is openly modeling itself on Suharto's Indonesia, despite the latter's disastrous collapse. If anything, SLORC is even more universally hated than was the Suharto regime, and the Burmese Chinese—SLORC's financiers—are seen as even more flagrantly plundering. Symbolically, near the border town of Ruili, a Chinese-owned factory houses three hundred Burmese brown bears. The wretched beasts are packed into cages one cubic meter in size and further restrained by metal harnesses used to collect the bile from their gall bladders.[47] The bile is a highly prized Chinese medicine, exported at great profit to Hong Kong and South Korea. As well-intentioned Americans and international human rights organizations properly celebrate the release of Aung San Suu Kyi, and earnestly demand democratization, they are completely oblivious that global markets, SLORC-style, have turned Burma into a powder keg.

CHAPTER 2

Llama Fetuses, Latifundia, and La Blue Chip Numero Uno

"White" Wealth in Latin America

I n the fall of 1999 a graduate student from Bolivia named Augusto Delgado raised his hand in my Law and Development seminar. Always frank and incisive, and one of the best students I have ever had, Augusto said: "I believe, Professor Chua, that my country is a perfect counterexample to your thesis. In Bolivia, we have all the conditions you mention. A very small light-skinned minority dominates the economy, while 65 percent of the population are impoverished Aymara and Quechua Indians. But in Bolivia today there would never be an *ethnic* movement against the market-dominant minority. The reason for this is because ethnicity has no appeal in Bolivia. No Indian would ever want to identify himself as an Indian. They are willing to think of themselves as campesinos, or peasants, but as *indios*—no."*

Augusto's comments are typical of a sentiment that has prevailed in Latin America for many decades: that "there is no ethnic conflict" in Latin America, certainly by comparison to Africa or Southeast Asia. There may be class conflict, or political conflict, but little distinctively

---

*Unlike in Argentina, Chile, and parts of the United States, no mass slaughter of the indigenous population ever took place in Bolivia. On the contrary, powerful Amerindian uprisings in the 1780s and 1890s have helped shape the country's history. The revolution of 1952 led to universal suffrage as well as large-scale expropriation of land from the Spanish elite and redistribution to Amerindians. After the 1952 revolution, however, as part of an effort to unify the country, explicitly "ethnic" identity was downplayed, and instead the idea that "everyone is a mestizo" emphasized.

ethnic conflict. The reason most commonly given is that almost every-one in Latin America, high and low, is "mixed-blooded."

Less than two years later, when Augusto was back in La Paz working as a corporate lawyer, he contacted me by e-mail. He explained that he was writing to take back his earlier words. At that very moment, angry indigenous coca peasants were marching on La Paz, protesting the gov-ernment's decision to eradicate coca—for Bolivians, a "sacred plant," widely used in legal, nonaddictive forms; for the U.S.-sponsored anti-drug campaign, the source of cocaine. Calling for a constitutional as-sembly to organize a new "majority-based" government, the peasants had set up road blockades, paralyzing the country's major cities. Meanwhile, seemingly from nowhere, a powerful Amerindian move-ment—led by Felipe Quispe, an Aymaran Indian known as Mallku, or the Great Condor in Aymaran—was threatening to take over parts of Bolivia. The worst thing about Mallku's movement, wrote Augusto, was that it was explicitly antiwhite. "For the first time in our history, an or-ganized Aymara leader is asking those who are not 'indigenous' to leave the country. . . . Boredom is easily swept away by the passion I feel for my country and by the intense historical movement we are living in."

Bolivia's elites, of which Augusto is one, were stunned by the bitter-ness and venom of Quispe's rhetoric. Bolivia's land "belongs to the Aymara and Quechua Indians and not the whites," Mallku declared at several points.[1] After negotiations between protesting Amerindian farm-ers and the cabinet broke down, Quispe shouted at the (white) minis-ters: "The whites should leave the country. We cannot negotiate the blood of my brothers. Kill me if you are men!"[2] Years before, when asked by a journalist why he was engaging in terrorist activity, Quispe lashed back, "So that my daughter will not have to be your maid."

Despite a tendency for Westerners to romanticize indigenous lead-ers—the *Financial Times* recently described Quispe as a "natural-born rebel with a cause"—Quispe is not an altogether savory character. He was jailed in the 1990s for guerrilla warfare, has been accused of cor-ruption, and may have participated in blowing up electrical infrastruc-ture a few years ago.[3] The Bolivian establishment was thus appalled by the level of Amerindian support, at least in certain rural provinces, for Mallku, who, as one government minister said incredulously, "is encouraging acts of violence" and "operating under a mentality of 400 years ago."[4] Another view common in Latin America (although not in Bolivia, whose history includes many indigenous insurrections)[5] is that Amerindians, perhaps because of years of exclusion, are apathetic and "fatalistic." As a Chilean professor put it a few years ago, "They don't seem to care about politics—they are totally out of the system."

What Latin American elites are learning is that poor, "apathetic and fatalistic" masses are prime targets for charismatic demagogues. Increasingly, indigenous leaders like Mallku are offering the region's demoralized majorities a package that is hard to beat: a natural scapegoat (rich, corrupt "whites") and a sense of pride, ownership, and identity. Sometimes that identity is "Aymara"—the Aymara are a fiercely independent people whose ancestors created architectural marvels many centuries before the Incan conquest; other times, it is "Quechua," "Mayan," "Inca," or just *indio*.

But however charismatic, indigenous leaders like the Great Condor face formidable obstacles, including the entire weight and momentum of Latin American history since the European conquest. The last lines of Augusto's e-mail to me are revealing. "The political conflict will surely be over by June," he concluded, "and that would be a wonderful time for you to finally visit Bolivia. Lake Titicaca is especially beautiful then, and we can visit my friend's vacation house overlooking the water." Even in the midst of immense turmoil, Augusto was confident that within a few months, things in Bolivia would be "back to normal." And so they were.

Bolivia and Other Countries
with Amerindian Majorities

At Augusto's urging, I visited La Paz in June 2001 along with my husband and two daughters, and gave a lecture at the Catholic University of Bolivia. La Paz is breathtaking, literally and metaphorically. The city rises up out of a gigantic crater, surrounded by the Andes, with the magnificent Mount Illimani towering over the other snow-capped peaks. Despite its stark beauty, La Paz attracts relatively few tourists, in part because its eleven-thousand-foot altitude leaves the unaccustomed with headaches and even the locals with low energy. My family and I were no exception. Arriving in early June 2001, we spent most of the first day resting, as Augusto had advised, downing aspirin and *mate de coca* (tea from coca leaves), venturing out only late in the day to do some exploring. As it happens, the first souvenir I bought was a dried llama fetus.

Revolting as it may sound, my poor stillborn llama is actually rather cute. Frozen in the fetal position and dried stiff like beef jerky, it has the gentle, smiling face of a camel and plenty of soft, if slightly formaldehyde-scented, fur. I bought the llama fetus partly because it horrified me, but also for educational purposes, so that my eight-year-old daughter Sophia could show it to her class. (She refused to bring it in.)

Bolivians buy llama fetuses to ward off evil in its many guises. Bolivian miners—who, with a life expectancy of forty-five years, basically live their entire adult lives dying—look to llama fetuses for protection against dynamite explosions and the lung-destroying silicon particulates they inhale all day. Downing high-proof alcohol also helps. "The purer the alcohol, the purer the minerals I find," one miner told me wryly.

Llama fetuses can be found everywhere in Bolivia if you just know where to look. (So can live llamas and, at least in La Paz, llama steaks.) I bought my llama fetus at the Mercado de las Brujas, or Witches' Market, on Calle Sagárnaga. Like virtually all the market vendors in Bolivia, the person who sold me my llama fetus was an Amerindian woman: in this case an Aymara wearing the distinctive bowler hat and ruffled skirts seen all around La Paz. (Along with most tourists, I assumed that these wonderful hats and skirts were traditional, indigenous costumes; in fact, they reflect early indigenous efforts to look more "Spanish.") Our vendor was friendly and inquisitive. Her skin was typically sun-leathered—La Paz is the highest, most radiated capital in the world—and to my untrained eye she could have been anywhere between thirty and sixty years of age. She spoke almost no English and a nonstandard Spanish, infused with numerous Aymara words.

Nevertheless, it was obvious that this vendor of fetuses—pig and lamb as well as llama—and other traditional amulets was an adroit entrepreneur. After five minutes of her marketing, cajoling, bargaining, and lifetime guarantees, I eagerly paid the woman twenty dollars (about 8,000 percent the going market price, I later learned) for a souvenir that, it turns out, scares the living daylights out of everyone I know.

Legend has it that Amerindians are famous traders, long used to money and markets. The vendors in La Paz's open markets work hard, wheedling and charming locals and tourists alike from dawn to dusk. They are frugal and aggressive; one Mexican anthropologist said fifty years ago that they have a distinctly "commercial libido."[6] Yet, along with the rest of Bolivia's 65 percent indigenous majority, these Aymaran booth vendors are part of the country's entrenched, appallingly poor, Amerindian economic underclass. Compared to the West, this ethnic "underclass" is, relatively speaking, huge, encompassing the great majority of the Bolivian people, most of whom have no access to heat—not even in the high plateau areas, where it is freezing cold at night—clean water, or medical care. "Only the rich can afford real doctors," a Quechuan driver said to me. "For most of us Bolivians, if you get sick, you pray to *pachamama* (Mother Earth). But you probably die."

———

The same day that I bought the llama fetus, I met some of Augusto's friends at a dinner party at his apartment. They were an urbane and witty group. Two were descended from former presidents of Bolivia. Several held notable political positions. A cabinet-level minister was there; she was a beautiful woman whose parents had been schoolteachers. Her husband, also present, had been head of a different department in a previous administration; his family once owned what is now an entire neighborhood in La Paz (although at the time, he explained, the land was not valuable). Another guest, a jovial, self-made cement magnate, was a vice presidential candidate in the coming election, who had a few years earlier survived a harrowing kidnap. Not all of Augusto's friends were well-off. One was a quirky, erudite polyglot, who had co-taught with the philosopher Adorno in Frankfurt for many years. "Augusto and I come from one of the oldest families in Bolivia," he whispered to me at one point, "but we were not businesspeople, and today we are the poor cousins here." "I can't bear this horrible Indian folk music," he announced loudly at another point, requesting that Augusto put on a different CD. Another guest was a newspaper columnist who made ends meet by acting as a guide for European and North American tourists.

We dined on quail eggs, homemade pâté, and fresh trout from Lake

Titicaca, all prepared by Augusto's Aymaran housekeeper. The conversation was principally in English. Although Bolivians typically stress that everyone in the country has some indigenous blood ("no one is pure white," as one of Augusto's friends put it), and although one guest at Augusto's dinner looked distinctly *indio,* most were what North Americans would consider "white"—light-skinned, blond and blue-eyed, auburn-haired and green-eyed, and so on. They were also disproportionately good-looking and on average about a foot taller than the indigenous maid and manservant serving us. Most had European ancestors, and not just from Spain. Augusto's mother, for example, was of Scottish descent.

Characterizing Bolivia's ethnic makeup is tricky, given the high historical rates of "racial mixing" and phenomena such as *"encholamiento,"* in which a white man and an Amerindian or mestiza woman (a *chola*) have a son, who, if successful, marks his success by marrying a white woman. Today, Bolivian society is loosely divisible into three layers. To use the terminology of Bolivia's census as late as 1976, "whites" make up 5 to 15 percent of the population, "mestizos" make up 20 to 30 percent, and "Indians" 60 to 65 percent. These classifications are of course highly artificial; wealth can turn a "mestizo" or even an "Indian" into a white. As the Bolivian intellectual Tristán Marof wrote decades ago, " 'Whites' are all that have fortune in Bolivia, those that exercise influence and occupy high positions. A rich mestizo or Indian, although he has dark skin, considers himself white."[7]

Nevertheless, the bottom line in Bolivia is this. The country's Amerindian majority, many of whom lived as serfs until 1952, are largely excluded from the modern economy. Most live in poverty, with no secondary education, no access to sanitation, and terrible teeth. According to the government's own statistics, 90 percent of rural Bolivians—overwhelmingly Amerindians—cannot satisfy basic necessities.[8] Among the "mestizo" group, economic success is more mixed. But Bolivia's whites* enjoy wildly disproportionate wealth and status.

---

*For the remainder of this chapter I will use the term "whites" without quotation marks, but it should be understood that this term is not only highly artificial, but may have a somewhat different meaning in Latin American usage than it has in the United States.

Together with foreign investors, Bolivia's white elite, defining itself through European or North American cultural habits, controls the vast part of Bolivia's wealth, including the country's most valuable natural resources and its most modern and advanced economic sectors. Private schools, foreign degrees, international business contacts, and fluency in English (as well as French and German, in many cases) reinforce the market dominance of this minority over Bolivia's Aymara and Quechua Indian majority, many of whom speak only indigenous languages.

The market dominance of the white minority in Bolivia does not necessarily imply superior entrepreneurialism on their part. Most of the people I met through Augusto—even those in business—did not pride themselves on being particularly good entrepreneurs (although some clearly were). "Corporate law in Bolivia is not like in New York," explained Augusto, who is also an essayist and political commentator. "I could, I guess I probably should, work harder—go out and find new business perhaps. But I prefer to spend my time reading books and writing." Observers have long noted a disdain for commerce and industry among Hispanic elites. Some have attributed this disdain to Spain's and Portugal's eight-hundred-year conflict with the Moors, in which soldiers and priests were glorified while merchants and bankers—roles often occupied by Jews or Muslims—were denigrated. Whatever the reason, the Spanish and Portuguese colonizers of Latin America were famous for proclaiming their contempt for business and manual labor.[9]

Something of this "gentleman's complex" may persist today. On the other hand, many families in the Bolivian elite have strong entrepreneurial roots as well. In the late nineteenth and early twentieth centuries, small but enterprising waves of immigrants from Germany, France, Italy, England, and Spain developed Bolivia's—indeed much of the Andean region's—import-export, finance, mining, transportation, and manufacturing sectors.

In the 1980s and 1990s, Bolivia, following the dictates of the World Bank and IMF, and advised by U.S. economists like Harvard's Jeffrey Sachs, pursued aggressive privatization and free market policies. These policies were spectacularly successful in many respects. Under President Gonzalo Sanchez de Lozada—a mining tycoon educated at the University of Chicago—annual growth rose from negative rates to 4 to 5 percent, and foreign investment more than doubled between 1996 and 1999.[10] Globalization, moreover, has definitely created opportunities for "mestizo" Bolivians; among the upper crust today there are those with darker skin and unmistakably Amerindian features. Globalization has even produced some benefits for the indigenous majority. Growing tourism means that Amerindian entrepreneurs can sell more animal fetuses, peddle more Coca-Colas, even act as tour guides if they learn a little English. On a less wholesome note, there are an increasing number of Aymaran merchants prospering from illegal contraband businesses.

Yet global markets have, if anything, intensified the economic dominance of Bolivia's white elite—the natural business partners of Western investors—over the country's growth-stunted, impoverished indigenous majority. Certainly globalization has intensified the visibility of Bolivia's wealth disparities, as condominiums and tony art galleries boom in the major cities of La Paz, Cochabamba, and Santa Cruz while the rural parts of the country continue to be mired in abject poverty. Indeed, for many indigenous Bolivians, market reforms have meant infuriating increases in utility rates, layoffs—to reduce hyperinflation a few years ago, the government slashed social spending and closed state-owned tin mines, sending the unemployment rate soaring—and hollow promises of trickle-down.[11] "Free trade?" scoffed a Quechuan tour guide named Osvaldo, who accompanied us to the surreally beautiful Uyuni salt flats after we left La Paz. "That just means that we now sell our gas to Brazil, while there is no heat here in Bolivia." Osvaldo added with a shrug, "The same families make all the money in Bolivia, whatever policies we have."

Bolivia is one of only four countries—the others are Peru, Guatemala, and Ecuador—in which Amerindians still constitute a majority or near majority of the population. In all these countries, the same basic ethnic reality holds. Centuries of racial intermixing and immigration have produced the ethnic complexity distinctive to Latin America. In Cuzco, for example, the former Inca capital of Peru, many among the elite have Amerindian features and speak Quechua. Similarly, the most recently elected Miss Peru publicly celebrated her mixed heritage, including a dark-skinned mother, a Chinese grandfather, and a great-grandmother who was a Spanish vice countess. Nevertheless, the fact remains that in all these countries, Amerindians represent a distinct, recognizable, mass underclass, often the object of condescension, controlling only a tiny portion of the nation's wealth. Meanwhile, whites—however artificial the term and however permeable the category may sometimes be—are a starkly market-dominant minority.

"Pigmentocracy" in Latin America

But the phenomenon of white market dominance in Latin America is not confined to these four countries. It is equally visible even in countries where indigenous communities are much smaller and the vast majority of the population is "mestizo." With the exception of Argentina, Chile, and Uruguay (where from early on indigenous peoples were largely extinguished), Latin American society is fundamentally *pigmentocratic:* characterized by a social spectrum with taller, lighter-skinned, European-blooded elites at one end; shorter, darker, Indian-blooded masses at the other end; and a great deal of "passing" in between. The roots of pigmentocracy are traceable to the colonial era.

Unlike their (evidently more repressed) British counterparts in, say, India or Malaysia, the Spanish colonialists freely and prolifically procreated with indigenous women. From the outset, Spanish and Portuguese chroniclers waxed enthusiastic about the charms of Amerindian women, who were "beautiful, and not a little lascivious, and fond of the Spaniards" by one account and "very handsome and great lovers, affectionate and with ardent bodies" by another.[12] In an important sense, the Spanish Conquest of the Americas was a conquest of women. The Spanish obtained Amerindian girls both by force and by peaceful means—sometimes, for example, as tokens of friendship from the Indian caciques. Intermarriage, concubinage, and polygamy were common.

Although this "racial mixing" might suggest a readiness among Latin America's colonizers to transcend ethnic boundaries, in reality it was nothing of the sort. On the contrary, what emerged was an invidious social system known as the Society of Castes *(sociedad de castas),* in which individuals were classified in accordance with the lightness of their skin, with whites occupying the highest stratum.

The names of the specific *castas* that emerged in Spanish America varied across different regions and changed over the years. The following list is illustrative of eighteenth-century New Spain:

1. Spaniard and Indian beget mestizo
2. Mestizo and Spanish woman beget castizo
3. Castizo woman and Spaniard beget Spaniard
4. Spanish woman and Negro beget mulatto
5. Spaniard and mulatto woman beget morisco
6. Morisco woman and Spaniard beget albino
7. Spaniard and albino woman beget torna atrás
8. Indian and torna atrás beget lobo
9. Lobo and Indian woman beget zambaigo
10. Zambaigo and Indian woman beget cambujo
11. Cambujo and mulatto woman beget albarazado
12. Albarazado and mulatto woman beget barcino
13. Barcino and mulatto woman beget coyote
14. Coyote woman and Indian beget chamiso
15. Chamiso woman and mestizo beget coyote mestizo
16. Coyote mestizo and mulatto woman beget ahí te estás[13]

That the Spaniards were supposed to be "pure-blooded" is, to say the least, ironic. Among the numerous groups that, by the Middle Ages, had inhabited and commingled with each other on Iberian soil were Celts, Phoenicians, Greeks, Carthaginians, Romans, Visigoths, Jews, Arabs, Berbers, and Gypsies.[14]

Nevertheless, the disdain of a "pure white" Spanish elite for the "colored" masses is a deeply ingrained feature of the history of every modern Latin American nation. In Mexico, mixed-blooded mestizos were for years prohibited from owning land or joining the army or clergy. In Peru, even intellectuals believed that "the Indian is not now, nor can he ever be, anything but a machine." In Chile, victory in the War of the Pacific (1879–83) was often attributed to the "whiteness" of the Chileans, as compared with the "Indians" of Bolivia and Peru, the defeated nations. In Argentina, a popular writer wrote in 1903 that mestizos and mulattos were both "impure, atavistically anti-Christian; they are like the two heads of a fabulous hydra that surrounds, constricts and strangles with its giant spiral a beautiful, pale virgin, Spanish America." And throughout Latin America, landowners preferred their daughters to marry penniless *peninsulares* (arrivals from Spain) rather than wealthy criollos (American-born Spaniards). The fact of being born in the Old World was supposedly good proof of being "pure white"—something that could not be assumed of even the wealthiest members of the colonial aristocracy, "whose ancestors had been living for years alongside not just the Indians but also the blacks."[15]

Today, while ethnic lines in Latin America are much more muted than elsewhere in the developing world, the phenomenon of a market-dominant, ethnically distinguishable minority—here, the light-skinned, landowning (and increasingly, stockowning), Western-educated elite—remains an important feature of all but a few Latin American countries.

Mexico: Dark-Skinned Poverty, Light-Skinned Plutocrats

Pigmentocracy certainly thrives in Mexico, where I spent a good deal of time between 1989 and 1991. During that period I was an associate with a Wall Street law firm, working around the clock representing the Mexican government in the landmark privatization of Teléfonos de México (Telmex), Mexico's national telephone company. Almost without exception the Mexican officials, lawyers, and business executives we dealt with were light-skinned and foreign educated, with elegant European names. Meanwhile, the people doing the photocopying and cleaning the floors were all shorter, darker, and plainly more "Indian-blooded."

While considerable social fluidity exists in Mexico, it is also true that lightness of skin correlates directly and glaringly with increasing wealth and social status. Mexico's roughly 9 to 10 million indigenous peoples, about one-tenth of the population, have the highest rates of illiteracy and disease in the country. In the state of Chiapas, just thirty-five years ago, Amerindians were forbidden to walk on sidewalks or look lighter-skinned Mexicans in the eye. Not surprisingly, according to Mexican writer Enrique Krauze, Indian women desire to have children with mestizos—"not to betray their race but out of a desire to spare their progeny a bleak future."[16]

At the other end of the spectrum, all of Mexico's most lucrative corporate sectors—oil, finance, media and telecommunications, heavy industry, luxury hotels, transportation—are controlled by a small, clubby, light-skinned market-dominant minority who play golf with each other on weekends (and often weekdays). While working on Telmex, I remember being a little surprised when our local counsel, an elegant, baritone-voiced, European-looking man by the name of Alejandro Duclaud Gonzalez de Castilla, married the daughter of one of Telmex's (equally elegant) senior officers. I was even more surprised when, in the spring of 2001, I learned that Alejandro—whom I liked enormously and had spoken with regularly for two years—was being sued by the U.S. Securities and Exchange Commission, along with his wife, his brother, and other family members, for allegedly making nearly $4 million from insider trading. He settled with the SEC without admitting or denying the charge after judgment was entered against him.[17]

My surprise, however, was probably naïve. Although insider trading is of course illegal, insider profiteering from developing-world privatization is the rule rather than the exception. Back in the early nineties, I believed that the proceeds of privatization, as a World Bank official put it, would go to roads, "potable water, sewerage, hospitals, and education to the poor." Like many in the 1990s, however, I was viewing emerging-market privatization through a rose-colored lens. Just a few years after the Telmex privatization was completed, Mexico City's La Jornada reported, "The booty of privatization has made multimillionaires of 13 families, while the rest of the population—some 80 million Mexicans—has been subjected to the same gradual impoverishment as though they had suffered through a war."[18]

In retrospect, I still believe that privatizing Telmex, and bringing in Southwestern Bell to modernize the company, was on balance a good thing for the Mexican people. Since Telmex was privatized in 1990, more than $13 billion has been invested to upgrade and extend phone service, including in remote rural areas. A fiber optics network stretching more than twenty thousand miles has been built, and callers no longer have to wait two minutes for a dial tone. At the same time, many believe that the principal domestic beneficiaries of Mexico's privatization process were former President Carlos Salinas de Gortari, his family, his cronies, and multibillionaire Carlos Slim.

Slim, who has been outplaying his blue-blooded counterparts at the game of globalization, merits a brief digression. Before the Telmex privatization, Slim was unknown in the United States. I knew only that he was around fifty and the son of a Christian Lebanese immigrant, that his name was incongruous in light of his rather substantial figure, and that his investment bank Grupo Carso, along with foreign partners Southwestern Bell and France Telecom, were planning to bid as a consortium for a controlling stake in Telmex.

Slim's successful acquisition of Telmex catapulted him to international prominence, at least in financial circles. With Slim at the company's helm, Telmex stock—once worth only pennies a share—soared after the privatization, and unlike many non-U.S. stocks, kept on soaring. Telmex's market capitalization today hovers around $37 billion, making the company, as the *Financial Times* put it, "*la blue chip numero uno*" in Latin America. After Salinas's presidency ended in 1994, there was a flurry of reports exposing pandemic corruption within Mexico's ruling PRI. Because of his close identification with Salinas, Slim was often mentioned in the U.S. press, but always vaguely, hintingly, never with any concrete allegations.

In any case, whereas Salinas is now in disgrace and exile, Carlos Slim has never been wealthier. *Forbes* magazine recently listed him as Latin America's richest man—every two minutes Slim reportedly makes $5,000, more than the average Mexican earns in a year—and he is popularly compared to the legendary American investor Warren Buffett. In the last few years, Carlos Slim has become an increasingly prominent figure in the United States as he continues to buy up large blocks of CompUSA, Barnes & Noble, OfficeMax, Office Depot, Circuit City, Borders, and other major U.S. retailers.

The bulk of Slim's holdings, of course, are still in Mexico, where he controls most of Mexico's local phone service, long distance, and Internet access, not to mention half of the nation's stock market. Slim also owns Sanborns (Mexico's most popular restaurant chain), a major ATM network, a mining company, numerous factories engaged in tire, metal, and other forms of industrial production, massive resort developments in Cancún, and Grupo Financiero Inbursa, a financial services company that sells insurance to, and invests the savings of, millions of ordinary Mexicans. The running joke about Slim is that he began investing abroad because there was nothing left to acquire inside Mexico.[19]

Slim's focus these days is on the Internet and global markets. To attract Spanish-speaking web surfers, Slim began offering bilingual service through Prodigy, the U.S.'s third-largest Internet service provider, which Slim bought outright in 1997 for $100 million in cash and $150 million in debt assumption. After Slim took over, Prodigy's subscriber base in the United States increased by 1,000 percent. Meanwhile, a month after acquiring CompUSA, Slim launched what he predicts will be the largest Spanish-language portal in all of North and South America, a joint venture between Telmex and Microsoft called Tlmsn. Most recently, Telmex spun off its fast-growing cellular phone and international division in a $15 billion listing of America Movil SA on the New York Stock Exchange; the Slim family still indirectly controls both companies. In addition to its U.S. holdings, America Movil has telecom, wireless, and broadband interests in nine Latin American countries. Slim's goal is reportedly for America Movil to dominate both the U.S. Hispanic and Latin American cellular and Internet markets.

Needless to say, Slim has no Amerindian ancestors. As elsewhere in the world, the Lebanese community in Mexico is very tight: Slim's late wife was also Christian Lebanese, and, reportedly, most members of Slim's extended family have married other Christian Lebanese; virtually all are extremely wealthy.[20]

As Carlos Slim illustrates, the line separating rich and poor in Latin America is not as simple as "old Spanish" landowning families on the one hand and Amerindian and mestizo masses on the other. Instead, white wealth takes two very different forms: old Spanish (or in Brazil's case, Portuguese) wealth, typically rooted in the plantation, or *latifundia,* system; and more recent immigrant wealth, often reflecting enormous entrepreneurialism. Although both result in white market dominance, the history and economics behind them are totally different.

Latifundia and Global Markets: Nonentrepreneurial White Dominance

The market dominance of Latin America's European-descended landowners owes as much to colonial oppression as to commercial dynamism. By all accounts the Spaniards easily conquered the vastly more numerous Amerindians they encountered in the New World. They managed this through a combination of superior technology, European germs that decimated an estimated 95 percent of the pre-Columbian indigenous population—and sheer trickery. In *Guns, Germs, and Steel,* Jared Diamond describes, in the words of a contemporary observer, the trap set by conquistador Francisco Pizarro for the Incan emperor Atahuallpa:

> On the next morning a messenger from Atahuallpa arrived, and [Governor Pizarro] said to him, "Tell your lord to come when and how he pleases, and that, in what way soever he may come I will receive him as a friend and brother. I pray that he may come quickly, for I desire to see him. No harm or insult will befall him."

Later that day, when Atahuallpa arrived with his squadrons of "Indians dressed in clothes of different colors, like a chessboard," some dancing and singing, others bearing great quantities of gold and silver furniture—Pizarro's troops ambushed them. "Cavalry and infantry, sallied forth out of their hiding places straight into the mass of unarmed Indians crowding the square, giving the Spanish battle cry, 'Santiago!' " Once Atahuallpa was captured,

> Pizarro proceeded to hold his prisoner for eight months, while extracting history's largest ransom in return for a promise to free him. After the ransom—enough gold to fill a room 22 feet long by 17 feet wide to a height of over 8 feet—was delivered, Pizarro reneged on his promise and executed Atahuallpa.[21]

Similarly, in 1572, another Inca ruler, Tupac Amaru, a nephew of Atahuallpa, was seized by the Spanish and converted. At the Plaza of

Cuzco he eloquently asked his subjects to abandon paganism. "After he finished his address," as a Spanish chronicler put it, "his head was cut off; this caused the Indians incredible pain."[22]

Through the colonial period, small numbers of Spanish administered and exploited vast indigenous populations through the *encomienda,* a notorious institution by which Amerindians were distributed among and forced to pay heavy tributes to conquistadores, or *encomenderos.* The theory was that the *encomendero* would "protect and civilize" (i.e., Christianize) his Amerindians. In reality, the Amerindians served as pools of forced labor for the *encomenderos,* who quickly amassed huge amounts of wealth. The *encomiendas* were often very large; in Peru, for example, some conquistadores had as many as ten thousand Indian heads of household under their control.

The psychological effects of the Spanish Conquest were crushing and lasting. "The death of the sun—the strangulation of the Inca," writes sociologist Magnus Mörner, was a "profound shock, reinforced later on by the beheading of Tupac Amaru." Contemporary indigenous dances still reflect the profound "Trauma of Conquest." Meanwhile, the missionaries, backed up by Spanish military force, did their best to destroy indigenous rituals, traditions, and kinship systems, all viewed as incompatible with the Christian faith, again with devastating effects. For example, before the conquest, consumption of intoxicating drinks among the Andean Indians was confined to ceremonial occasions. After the conquest, alcoholism became an outlet for indigenous frustration and has remained so ever since.[23]

At the same time, the Spanish confiscated indigenous land wholesale. Conversion of communal properties into private holdings occurred in Mexico, Guatemala, Ecuador, Peru, Bolivia, and elsewhere in Latin America. Bit by bit the communal landholdings of Amerindians were turned over to the expanding plantation economy. By 1910 over 80 percent of all rural families in Mexico were landless while Amerindians in Guatemala had such minuscule holdings *(minifundia)* that most of them came under the vagrancy laws requiring them to work for subsistence wages on coffee plantations. In virtually all of the Latin American countries, *latifundios*—large agricultural estates owned by a handful of

Spanish-blooded families—grew more and more immense at the expense of an increasingly demoralized, expropriated rural proletariat.[24]

Today, Bolivia, Mexico, and Peru are the major exceptions in Latin America. Because of extensive agrarian reforms, these countries (along with Cuba) have largely dismantled their *latifundia* systems, at least to a much greater extent than elsewhere in Latin America. Virtually everywhere else in Latin America, the *latifundia* system is not only intact but poised to boom with each new round of pro-market, pro-globalization reforms.

Export-oriented plantations of over one thousand hectares represent just 1.5 percent of all farms in Latin America yet account for 65 percent of the region's total farm acreage. The exclusive social clubs of Latin America's major cities—where multimillion-dollar business deals are casually arranged and foreign investors are often wined and dined—are typically still controlled by men whose families derived their original wealth from plantation farming.[25] Not surprisingly, the market-oriented reforms of the 1990s disproportionately benefited Latin America's Spanish-blooded *latifundistas,* who because of their capital, education, foreign connections, and conservative social policies historically have tended to be the soul mates, if not the relatives, of political leaders championing economic liberalization.[26]

Throughout Latin America's countrysides, from Guatemala to Costa Rica, from Venezuela to Paraguay, the same stark pigmentocratic reality holds. Tall, light-skinned, Voltaire-steeped owners of *latifundios* dominate—and in many cases browbeat and brutalize through private militias—the vastly more numerous, shorter, darker, Indian-featured peasants who labor for them, usually barefoot, alongside children whose bellies are bloated with parasites.

In Brazil, which I'll say more about in a moment, 50,000 (less than .01 percent) of the country's 165 million population still own most of the country's land. Again, the *latifundio* owners are unmistakably white; the peasants, however, are typically descendants of African slaves. The bodily differentiation between higher-class and lower-class Brazilians in the countryside is not marked solely by skin color and facial features. In the sugar-producing Zona da Mata, many of the dark-skinned plantation workers have lost a limb or several fingers due to the gruesome dangers of caning. Moreover, according to the late Brazilian nutritionist Nelson Chaves, even slaves were better fed than the contemporary sugar workers of the Zona da Mata. "[T]he rural worker of today," Chaves wrote in 1982, "is primarily a carrier of worms, and his stature is diminishing considerably over time, so that it is actually approaching that of the African pygmy."[27]

Latin America's Immigrant Entrepreneurs

The other form of white market dominance in Latin America stems not from plantation wealth but from the entrepreneurial energies of relatively recent immigrant groups, who are dramatically overrepresented among the region's business elite. Thus, a study from the 1960s found that of Mexico's thirty-odd outstanding business leaders, almost half reported a foreign paternal grandfather. Similarly, a 1965 survey of Bogotá executives revealed that although Colombia has had relatively little immigration, 41 percent of the country's leading entrepreneurs were foreign born.[28]

Some of Latin America's most stunningly successful immigrant entrepreneurs have been Lebanese or Jewish. In terms of numbers, both groups are tiny, representing almost negligible minorities in their countries of residence. In terms of economic dynamism, however, both groups have been extraordinary. In addition to Slim, a surprising number of Latin America's wealthiest businessmen are Lebanese. Moreover, Lebanese Latin Americans have held high-profile political positions. Both Ecuador's recently ousted former president Jamil Mahuad, for example, and Argentina's recently ousted former president Carlos Menem, were Lebanese—and avid proponents of privatization and market reform.

From the 1890s on, most Jews entered the countries of Latin America as poor peddlers. In Judith Elkin's words, with "packs on their backs and account books in their pockets," they trudged the streets of major cities and towns, selling small items of mass consumption such as matches, razor blades, scissors, sandals, cloth, tableware, and jewelry. Even the mountainous Andean countries were tackled by the indomitable Jewish peddler. As one foreign visitor observed in 1940:

In Bolivia you see the Eastern Jew who does not attend courses to learn Spanish, but who speaks the dialect of the Indios. They appear in the most outlying villages, where hardly any Europeans have ever been, and manage to eke out an existence, sleeping in their wagons under the stars. Hardly a German immigrant has dared or would dare to do this. . . . Without wishing to be critical, but to complete the picture, I must say that the first care of each German is to get an apartment. As far as the German is concerned, an apartment must have a bath.[29]

Jews are no longer peddlers in Latin America today. In a matter of a few generations the Jewish communities of Latin America have transformed themselves from struggling immigrants into financially powerful businessmen and professionals. In 1994 nearly 53 percent of employed Jews in Mexico identified themselves as directors, managers, or administrators while another 26 percent identified themselves as professionals. Throughout Latin America the rate of upward social mobility among Jewish communities has been astounding over the last century. In Brazil, the Jewish Klabin and Lafer families, linked by marriage ties, are among the wealthiest in the country; their jointly owned, diversified industrial firm is the largest newsprint producer in Latin America. More generally, approximately two-thirds of Brazilian Jews belong to the "elite." In Panama, the minuscule Jewish minority—only .25 percent of the population—disproportionately dominates the country's wholesale, retail, real estate, and services sectors and represents 40 percent of the traders in the Colon Free Trade Zone (after Hong Kong, the world's second largest free trade zone), through which in 1997 alone over $5 billion worth of goods was imported and re-exported.[30]

In Argentina, the largest landowners and producers of beef in the country are now two Jewish brothers, rather startling in light of Argentina's long, proud tradition of cattle raising. In fact, Eduardo and Alejandro Elsztain—who in 1997 doubled their rural landholdings to 1.1 million acres—are revolutionizing Argentine ranching with biotechnology. Their farm company Cresud recently entered into a joint venture with the Texas-based Cactus Feeders to begin fattening one hundred thousand head of cattle a year with corn rather than traditional pampas grass. Argentina's gauchos were incredulous: Corn-fed cattle produce marbled beef, and as anyone who has tried (and been disappointed by) *bife de lomo* knows, Argentinians like their beef very lean. The Elsztains, however, have their eye on global markets. Cresud's cows are being corn-fed both to increase yields and to appeal to the multibillion-dollar, fat-loving markets of North America and Asia.[31] (Think porterhouse and Kobe beef.)

———

The presence of commercially dynamic immigrant populations—not just Jews and Lebanese, but also Germans, Italians, Palestinians (in Belize and Honduras), and other groups—is observable in virtually every country in Latin America. These relatively recent arrivals are important in that they have broken up the traditional economic stranglehold of the old, "Spanish-blooded" landowning oligarchies. But they have not altered the basic pigmentocratic reality of Latin American society. These immigrant groups have become part of the tiny white minority that, in almost every Latin American country, controls nearly all of the nation's wealth, including the most advanced, lucrative sectors of the economy.

Countries without Market-Dominant Minorities

The major exceptions to the rule of pigmentocracy in Latin America are Argentina, Uruguay, and arguably Chile. These countries have only small or negligible Amerindian populations. In Uruguay, for example, the indigenous and famously fierce Charrúa and Guaraní Indians largely perished in seventeenth-century battles with Spanish and Portuguese forces. The last Charrúa Indian died in 1948, and supposedly only 8 percent of present-day Uruguayans are mestizos.[32] Furthermore, all three countries saw enormous waves of European immigrants around the turn of the twentieth century.[33] Unlike in the rest of Latin America, the descendants of these immigrants eventually came to represent a majority of the population. Consequently, the wealthy in Argentina, Chile, and Uruguay are not ethnically distinguishable from the less-well-off majorities around them. Indeed, by Western standards, most people in Argentina and Uruguay, wealthy or not, are "white."

Chile is a slightly more complicated case. Chile's indigenous peoples, including the increasingly activist Mapuche Indians in the south, currently number roughly 1 million out of a total population of 15 million. Compared to Argentina and Uruguay, a much greater percentage of Chileans are mestizos, but still this percentage is nowhere near a majority. Precise figures are difficult to obtain, in part because of the deeply subjective dimension of ethnic identity: Many Chileans who have some Amerindian ancestry would be the last to admit it. Throughout Chile, many among not just the upper, but also the middle classes, pride themselves on their "whiteness" and, according to historian Frederick Pike, "by and large believe[] in the inferiority of Indians and mixed bloods."[34]

Unspoken White Dominance in Brazil

Brazil, famous for being a "racial democracy," offers perhaps the most fascinating example of a deeply internalized but suppressed color hierarchy. For generations, Brazilians of all classes have been told, and to some extent have apparently believed, that centuries of racial mixing had erased the color line, making racism impossible. For many Brazilians, the contrast between the racial harmony in their country and the racial conflict in the United States has long been a source of pride.

But in fact, as throughout Latin America, the stark reality in Brazil is that a tiny, light-skinned, market-dominant minority has always had a stranglehold on economic and political power. Throughout Brazil the most prestigious and highest-paying jobs in business, politics, and universities are held by those with light skin.[35] Brazil's exclusive private schools are glaringly white. In a country where a vast majority of the population is (by U.S. standards) black, writes Eugene Robinson in his recent book *Coal to Cream,* the leading tycoons, wealthiest landowners, fanciest neighborhoods, and toniest social clubs, not to mention the virtual entirety of Brasilia's limo-riding bureaucratic elite, are wildly disproportionately white.

In the opening scene of *Coal to Cream,* Robinson describes a remarkable exchange he had with acquaintances on Ipanema Beach. Robinson, who is African-American and an editor at the *Washington Post,* asked his colleague's Brazilian girlfriend Velma—a small woman with "flaring nostrils, high cheekbones, and brown skin at least a couple of shades darker than mine"—what it was like being black in Brazil. Velma responded with a look of genuine surprise. "But I'm not," she said. "I'm not black."

To Robinson, however, "it was obvious at first glance" that Velma was primarily a descendant of African slaves, and he blurted out, "But you must be, Velma. I'm black, and you're as dark as I am." Velma, however, maintained that she most definitely was not black and, moreover, that as far as she was concerned, Robinson wasn't really "black" either. Later, after Velma had left, another Brazilian explained to Robinson "that Velma had long, straight hair, and that she also enjoyed the considerable status and income that came from her job as a lawyer. So naturally—and this was said as if it were the most natural thing in the world, though it made no sense at all to me—she called herself white."

At first Velma's reaction causes Robinson to question his own American inclination to identify as "black" anyone who has a visible African heritage. Gradually, however, Robinson sheds his initial infatuation with Brazil, which, on first encounter, seemed "a great black nation—unadvertised as such," a wonderful "mélange of blacks and browns and tans and taupes, of coppers and cinnamons." As Robinson looks deeper into Brazil, he begins to see a startling degree of racial inequity combined with pervasive racial denial.[36]

The millions of African slaves brought over to work Brazil's plantations far exceeded the number brought into the United States. Slavery in Brazil outlasted that in the United States by a generation. Today, Brazil's tens of millions of grotesquely impoverished, slum-dwelling or cane-cutting *pobres* are, again by U.S. standards, overwhelmingly black. Dark-skinned Afro-Brazilians occupy Brazil's lowest-rung jobs and fill Brazil's disease-ridden prisons. As late as 1988, poor blacks in Brazil were disenfranchised on illiteracy grounds. Meanwhile, "mulattoes" or persons of "mixed race," although said to enjoy slightly greater mobility than their darker-skinned counterparts, are starkly underprivileged as compared to the "white" minority.[37]

For years the myth of racial democracy has covered over these stark ethnic disparities in wealth. It may be wondered whether the poorest, dark-skinned Afro-Brazilians ever believed in this myth. Nevertheless, many Brazilians high and low often insist that "race" is not an important factor in Brazil, because "people are always passing" and because "people can essentially become 'white' by becoming wealthy." They argue that the distinctly African influences on Brazil's music, food, religion, even standards of beauty have gone a long way in eliminating the harshest aspects of racism.

In emphasizing that poor African-blooded Brazilians can achieve upward mobility by "lightening themselves"—for example, by making a fortune (which almost never happens) or by marrying someone with lighter skin (which more often does)—Brazilians don't seem to see the extent of racism and ethnic self-hatred that pervades Brazilian society. As Eugene Robinson eventually realized, "In Brazil, most people with some measure of African blood"—again a large majority of the country's population—"demanded to be *not* thought of as black." As a result, concludes Robinson, there was no black consciousness or indignation: "[N]obody saw these neighborhoods that were running with blood as *black* neighborhoods. Nobody saw that blood that was flowing as *black* blood."[38]

Brazil, moreover, is not exceptional in this regard. Throughout Latin America, centuries of ethnic degradation and discrimination, not to mention disenfranchisement and violence, have left deep, lasting psychological scars. A dashing blond, water-skiing Bolivian recently assured me that "in my country everyone is mestizo, everyone has some Indian blood," then later in the same conversation asserted, with equal equanimity, that "no member of the upper class would even think of marrying a Quechua."

Treated as "subhuman," even "bestial," Latin America's indigenous populations have internalized a profound and debilitating sense of inferiority. It is no wonder that throughout Latin America—right up to the cusp of the twenty-first century—ethnicity had little appeal. During most of the second half of the twentieth century, Latin America's poor have not wanted to think of themselves as "Indian" or "indigenous." Political, even populist movements have been organized around class, almost never ethnic, lines. And because in election after election, despite coup after coup, political and economic power always remained in the same light-skinned, "illustrious-blooded" hands, "apathy and fatalism" among the indigenous populations spread and deepened.

Globalization and the Kindling of Ethnic Resentment

All this, however, is changing. To the extent that ethnicity has been downplayed in the last several decades in Latin America, globalization, together with the demise of Marxism, is revitalizing it. Capitalism, it is often said, "transcends national boundaries," but so too can ethnic consciousness, ethnic demagoguery, and ethnic anger—with just as much speed and even greater intensity and passion.

Along with global markets and global media, "Indian-ness" is spreading across Latin America with technologically unprecedented zeal. Particularly in those countries where Amerindians constitute a majority of the population—and even in countries like Mexico, Chile, or Venezuela, where they do not—Latin America's poor masses are being ethnicized, increasingly through radio, television, and most recently the Web. They are being reminded—by cellphone-wielding leaders like Bolivia's El Mallku, Venezuela's Hugo Chavez, or Mexico's Zapatista leader Subcomandante Marcos—that they are Aymaras, *pardos,* Indians, *cholos,* whatever identity best mobilizes great numbers of frustrated, long degraded, dark-skinned masses.

Peru's Amerindian Alejandro Toledo, who swept to landslide victory in the 2001 presidential elections, offers the best of examples. "You're one of us—win for us!" shouted thousands of wrinkled Amerindian women in bowler hats, weeping as Toledo campaigned through the streets in a truck emblazoned with the ancient Inca symbol of the sun. Reversing five hundred years of ethnic degradation, Toledo—who many insist resembles Pachacutic, the Incas' greatest ruler—highlighted his indigenous origins, wearing Indian garb, calling himself *el cholo,* and appealing explicitly to Peru's dark-skinned majority "who look like I do." Indeed, reclaiming ethnic pride was Toledo's central campaign message. "After so many years of bowing our heads, it's time we all held them up in pride," declared Toledo, who rose out of poverty in Peru's coastal slums to study at Stanford University. "For as long as I can remember, we have been taught to hate the Indian inside us," explained a Quechuan supporter of Toledo's. "But now I see that self-hate fading. After so many servile years, we are finally asking important questions like 'How dare they look down on me because I am proud of my culture?' "[39]

But there are dangers, too—dangers that the region's white elites have always been aware of. ("Bolivia's rulers have always harbored a deep fear that the country's Indian majority might one day rise up and kill them in their beds—or more realistically, trap them in their cities," William Finnegan recently wrote in *The New Yorker*.)[40] Alejandro Toledo's approval ratings have plummeted to 32 percent, as it has become increasingly clear that his pro-market policies will not immediately improve the lives of Peru's impoverished majority. Meanwhile, elsewhere in Latin America, distinctively ethnic resentment against market-dominant light-skinned elites is on the rise.

In Ecuador, for example, the vigorously pro-market government led by President Jamil Mahuad was toppled in January 2000 by an Amerindian uprising that turned into a military coup. At the time of the uprising President Mahuad's approval ratings had dropped to just 6 percent, and the coup appears to have been supported by a majority of Ecuador's impoverished population, 40 percent of whom say they are "pure Indians" and 90 percent of whom are increasingly identifying themselves as "indigenous-blooded." One triggering event for the coup was the decision by Mahuad—who is ethnic Lebanese, Harvard-educated, and part of the country's white business elite—to replace Ecuador's currency with the U.S. dollar as part of a larger plan to open up the country's battered economy to international investors. The "dollarization" program was bitterly opposed by Ecuador's largely Amerindian peasant majority, who saw "the measure as just another scheme by bankers and businessmen to further impoverish them." "The dollar may be fine for mestizos and the big folks, but we are peasants and do not know how to manage dollars," seethed Apolinario Quishpe, one of thousands of Amerindian farmers who marched on Quito.[41]

Ecuador's recent upheaval was intensely anti-market and anti-globalization. It was also an explicitly Amerindian-based movement, led by the National Confederation of Indigenous Nationalities of Ecuador (Conaie), and deeply, angrily ethnic in its mobilizing rhetoric. "The shamans say change is coming," thundered Fernando Villavicencio, one of Conaie's leaders. "They say we are entering the age of the condor; they say that the Red Warrior has returned!"[42] In a country where not long ago newspaper advertisements offered haciendas for sale with Indians and cattle included in the price, Villavicencio's championing of Amerindian blood has galvanized large, formerly "apathetic" segments of the population, unifying urban and rural poor alike, and pitting them against an "arrogant," often corrupt white elite that represents only 7 percent of the population.

Even in Brazil, globalization is increasing racial and ethnic consciousness. Black identity and black power have begun to hit Brazil's marginalized youth, in part through the ripple effect of American popular culture. Throughout the country's garbage-filled favelas, or shantytowns, the angry lyrics of a U.S.-influenced but distinctly Brazilian rap and hip-hop movement can be heard. This movement is openly "unBrazilian" in its relentless attacks on the country's racial inequality. In songs like "The Periphery Continues Bleeding," "Just Another Wake," and "Surviving in Hell," rappers aggressively expose social injustice against blacks, emphasizing that only 2 percent of Brazil's university students are black, that three out of four people killed by the police are black, and that every four hours a black man dies violently in São Paulo.

In place of a "racial democracy," Brazil's urban favelados increasingly see an impoverished, humiliated black majority and a privileged, powerful white minority. Almost overnight, the hot group Racionais—which recently won a number of prestigious Brazilian MTV awards—has popularized expressions like "4P" *"poder para o povo preto"* ("power for the black people") and *"preto tipo a"*—literally "class A black" but referring to blacks who are proud and fight for their rights. Similarly, in "Stop Sucking Up," hip-hop star MV Bill scathingly attacks Brazilian blacks who deny their African heritage. A recent poll revealed that a startling 93 percent of those surveyed in Rio de Janeiro now believe that racism exists in Brazil.[43]

Nonetheless, the reality so far is that racial consciousness remains surprisingly muted in Brazil, with the myth of Brazilian racial democracy still broadly defended by many Brazilians spanning different social classes. As a Brazilian graduate student recently said to me, "For better or worse, there is no serious sign of ethnic conflict or ethnic mobilization in Brazil. Poor favelados are totally marginalized and Brazilian rap is certainly not changing that or posing any real threat to whites. In fact, Brazilian hip-hop is extremely popular among white university students." Most Brazil watchers agree that the economic and political dominance of a white elite in Brazil is probably guaranteed for a long time to come.

––––––––

Obviously, Latin America differs from Southeast Asia in countless respects. Because of extensive miscegenation, ethnic and racial lines in this region are not nearly as starkly drawn, and Latin America has been able to avoid the extreme ethnic animus and violence seen in Southeast Asia. Moreover, throughout Southeast Asia economic and political power have historically been divorced, with entrepreneurial Chinese minorities always at the political mercy of the indigenous majorities around them. By contrast, in Latin America a small landowning and to a certain extent hereditary elite has historically held both economic and political power.

Nevertheless, despite these and other differences, the same striking phenomenon holds. Like the indigenous populations of Southeast Asia, the uneducated, disease-ridden, desperately poor but numerically vast Indian- or African-blooded majorities of Latin America experience little or no economic benefit from privatization and global markets while finding themselves suddenly filled with contradictory new materialistic and consumerist desires. Meanwhile, along with their foreign investor partners, a tiny, well-connected, ethnically distinguishable minority dominates virtually every aspect of the modern economy, from export agriculture to wireless telecom, and uses liberalization, privatization, and globalization to increase its advantages. Moreover, despite the vast incidence of ethnic intermixing in Latin America, Latin America's white elite tend, like the Chinese in Southeast Asia, to be surprisingly endogamous, intermarrying only amongst themselves. As in Southeast Asia, so too in Latin America these by-now hypercapitalized market-dominant minorities are, as a practical matter, economically untouchable.

They may not, however, be politically untouchable. In 1998, to the shock of Venezuela's business elite, former paratrooper Hugo Chavez swept to landslide presidential victory, attacking free markets and "oligarchs" and championing the rights of the country's brown-skinned *pardo* majority. A silver-haired tycoon I met in Bolivia predicted worse for his country. "Bolivia," he said, "is a country where 3 percent of us control everything, and 65 percent of the population have no future. This place is definitely going to blow. It's only a matter of time." Most of my former student Augusto's other friends were not nearly so pessimistic. But this is the subject of Part Two.

CHAPTER 3

The Seventh Oligarch

The Jewish Billionaires
of Post-Communist Russia

I n the spring of 2000, a professor whom I'll call Jerry White was furiously trying to finish up an article on the debacle of Russian privatization. Jerry and his coauthors had served as legal advisers to the Russian government during the country's mass privatization process in the late 1990s. The article described, from an insider's hindsight perspective, how Russia's pro-market reforms (which he and other Western advisers had helped devise) had gone horribly awry. Instead of dispersing ownership and creating functioning markets, these reforms had allowed a small group of industrialists and bankers to plunder Russia, turning themselves almost overnight into the billionaire-owners of Russia's crown jewels while the country spiraled into chaos and lawlessness. Although not yet published, the article had already created a stir. It was to be a major mea culpa, a candid exposé of the naïveté of Western advisers, in hopelessly over their heads.

I stopped by Jerry's office one day after reading a near-final version of the article. Something about the oligarchs described in his article had struck me, and I wanted to run it by him.

It seemed to me, I said to Jerry, that most of the key players in the privatization and eventual economic takeover of Russia were Jewish. Was it possible?

"Oh, no," Jerry replied instantly, with a frown. "I don't think so."

"Are you sure?" I pressed him. "If you look at their names—"

"You can't tell anything from names," Jerry snapped impatiently, clearly not wanting to discuss the topic any further.

As it turns out, six out of seven of Russia's wealthiest and (at least until recently) most powerful oligarchs are Jewish. This fact became public knowledge in the United States just a few months after my conversation with Jerry, when Chrystia Freeland in *Sale of the Century* offered a journalist's firsthand account of how, without actually breaking the law, a handful of extraordinarily savvy businessmen—all but one of them Jewish—used the privatization process to become the owners of vast amounts of Russia's mineral wealth and the overwhelming victors in Russia's "gladiator capitalism."[1] Around the same time, John Lloyd wrote in a cover story for the *New York Times* magazine that "in a country where Jewishness is best kept quiet, nearly all [of Russia's] oligarchs are Jewish."[2] Yet Jerry, who was there in Russia, himself Jewish, and moreover writing an article meant to be provocative, wasn't willing to touch the Jewish question.

Not all Jews, of course, react like Jerry. When I first mentioned to my husband, who is Jewish, that six out of seven of Russia's wealthiest tycoons are Jewish, he raised an eyebrow. "Just six?" he asked calmly. "So who's the seventh guy?"

The seventh oligarch—the only "full-blooded ethnic Russian" among them—is Vladimir Potanin. ("While the other oligarchs were still decorating their offices with leopard skins and mirrors, Potanin was buying graciously battered English antiques," writes Freeland.)[3] The six Jewish businessmen most frequently called oligarchs are: Roman Abramovich, Pyotr Aven, Boris Berezovsky, Mikhail Friedman, Vladimir Gusinsky, and Mikhail Khodorkovsky. Together, these men came over the course of the 1990s to wield mind-boggling political and economic influence.

The height of their oligarchic influence was reached in 1996, when the Yeltsin government hung on the verge of political and financial collapse. Among other problems, Yeltsin had suffered a heart attack; his approval ratings hovered between 5 and 8 percent; the Russian treasury was strapped for cash; and in the parliamentary elections the Communists and Vladimir Zhirinovsky's extreme nationalists had captured two-thirds of the seats of the lower house, paralyzing the government.[4]

Already wealthy by that time, the oligarchs collectively put forth the so-called "loans-for-shares" deal—now notorious, but at the time grudgingly endorsed by Western advisers and Russian economists as well as England's *The Economist*. Essentially, the oligarchs offered loans and political support to the government in exchange for majority shares—at a fraction of their potential market value—in the behemoths of the Russian economy, a half dozen massive enterprises breathtakingly rich in nickel, gold, and oil deposits. When in 1996 it appeared that Boris Yeltsin might lose his reelection to the Communists, the oligarchs poured millions into Yeltsin's campaign and began flooding the television airwaves (which they owned) with pro-Yeltsin "news" items while conspicuously failing to give any airtime to the opposition.[5]

With Yeltsin's victory, the loans-for-shares deal was finalized, catapulting the oligarchs from a small group of millionaires to a small group of billionaires. A few years later the oligarchs "guaranteed"[6] that Vladimir Putin, like Yeltsin before him, would get elected in Russia's 2000 presidential elections.

Russia has roughly 147 million inhabitants. The National Conference on Soviet Jewry estimates that Jews make up less than 1 percent of the population.[7] Given these demographics, how is it that six Jewish businessmen came to wield such astounding economic and political power?

Russian Jews in Historical Perspective

In general, it is much harder to talk about Jewish economic dominance than that of any other group. This is because of the numerous episodes in which exaggerated or even patently false claims of Jewish economic dominance led to vicious discrimination, ghettoization, and some of the worst atrocities in human history. As a result, whereas one can relatively freely explore and talk about the phenomenon of, say, a 3 percent Chinese minority controlling 70 percent of a country's wealth, it is far more difficult to ascertain or even discuss the extent of Jewish economic influence in any given context.

Nevertheless, Jews have been in many ways the quintessential market-dominant minority. Jews do not appear to have been particularly economically successful during antiquity—but that's about the last time in history that they weren't, at least when left alone to pursue their livelihoods. During the Middle Ages, despite recurrent anti-Jewish restrictions and persecutions, Jews prospered visibly and disproportionately as merchants and middlemen and eventually as international traders, particularly between Christian Europe and the Muslim lands. Indeed, Jewish entrepreneurialism during this period played a crucial role in the economic development of Europe. The enormous wealth that Jews were forced to leave behind when expelled from Spain in 1492 helped finance the voyage of Columbus that led to the discovery of the Americas.[8]

Fast forwarding five hundred years, Jews occupied a commanding economic position in many Eastern European countries during the early twentieth century. Jews in interwar Romania, although just 4 percent of the population, controlled most of the private capital in the export, transportation, insurance, textile, chemical, housing, and publishing industries. Although their access to universities was restricted, they were also strongly represented in law, medicine, journalism, and banking. In Poland, as of 1921 over 60 percent of all commerce was conducted by Jews, who comprised just 11 percent of the population. Around the same time, Lithuania's Jewish minority accounted for more than three-quarters of the country's commercial activity. Meanwhile, in Hungary, Jews in 1910 represented nearly one-quarter of the population of Budapest—earning the capital the epithet "Judapest." As of 1920, Jews constituted 23 percent of Hungary's actors and musicians, 34 percent of the country's authors, 51 percent of the attorneys, 60 percent of the doctors in private practice, and the overwhelming majority of those "self-employed" in business and finance.[9]

Discussing Jewish economic success in present-day Russia is especially fraught because of the virulent history of Russian anti-Semitism. For centuries, anti-Jewish policies in Russia—expulsions (dating to as early as 1727), harsh economic restrictions, coerced twenty-five-year terms of military service, persecutions, pogroms, and so on—were to a large extent successful in preventing Jews from prospering, let alone being economically dominant.

In the late eighteenth century, Russia annexed much of eastern Poland and, along with the territory, acquired large numbers of Jews. Not wanting them to "spread throughout the country," the tsarist government confined the Jews to certain relatively undeveloped regions, collectively known as the Pale of Settlement. Moscow, St. Petersburg, and, for a while, Kiev and Warsaw, for example, were all "beyond the Pale" and thus off-limits to Jews.[10]

The 1800s saw periods of relatively benign neglect toward the Jews, campaigns to assimilate them, and campaigns to annihilate them. The Russian statesman Konstantin Pobedonostsev, adviser to the tsars, supposedly predicted that Russia's "Jewish problem" would be solved "by having one-third of them killed, one-third of them converted to Christianity, and one-third driven out of the country forever."[11] Some Jews prospered. Around the thriving port of Odessa—on the Black Sea coast and within the Pale—Jewish bankers, traders, and businessmen were commercially prominent (and frequent targets of anti-Jewish mob violence). Jews also played a central role in Russia's lucrative vodka industry, operating many of the large commercial distilleries on Great Russian estates as well as smaller-scale enterprises in the Pale. Trade in vodka—one of the largest sources of imperial income—made millionaires out of Jewish financiers, such as the Ginzburg and Poliakov families, both of which played major roles in the building of Russia's railroads. The Ginzburgs were eventually ennobled. Meanwhile, at the other end of the social spectrum, the Jewish tavern-keeper cut a familiar figure throughout Eastern Europe.[12]

Nevertheless, restricted to the Pale, subjected to economic discrimination, and victimized by recurrent anti-Jewish plundering and violence, most Russian Jews at the turn of the twentieth century lived in cruel poverty. (Of course, most other Russians also lived in poverty; the Russian population, was, after all, one of the world's poorest at the time.) From Warsaw to Lodz in the Polish territories, in Vilna (Vilnius) in the north and Odessa in the south, the Jewish proletariat, along with the Russian, eked out a hungry, miserable existence. At the turn of the century it was not uncommon for Jewish factory employees to work seventeen, even twenty hours a day, usually with only primitive sanitation. In many Jewish communities within the Pale it was typical for up to 40 percent of the population to be unemployed at any given time; begging was commonplace. Around 1900 an estimated 35 percent of Russia's Jewish population depended on relief provided by Jewish welfare institutions. Between 1881 and 1914 over a million and a half Jews left Russia for the United States.[13]

Although Jews were disproportionately represented among the leaders of the Bolshevik Revolution of 1917, Russia's deep ambivalence toward Jews persisted throughout the Communist era. Jews paid an especially terrible price during Stalin's purges; virtually all the cultural leaders of Soviet Jewry were executed, and many Jewish academics and students were purged from institutions of higher learning. On the other hand, Jews tended to be overrepresented among the bureaucratic elite (although never at the top level), among doctors and lawyers, and in the Soviet Academy of Sciences.[14] In addition, along with other "outsider" ethnic groups such as Chechens and Azerbaijanis, Jews played a disproportionate role in the Soviet Union's black market system—a vast array of underground enterprises which, in the dysfunctional, shortage-stricken Communist economy, were a crucial source of necessities and consumer goods. Nevertheless, no one (outside the Politburo) got billionaire-rich in the former Soviet Union, and Jews were no exception.

Not so in the post-Soviet era. During the 1990s, seven entrepreneurs, six of them Jewish, came to control the overwhelming part of Russia's newly privatized economy, including most of its vast natural resource wealth. Despite the inevitable rumors, these men did not become billionaires through violence or *mafiya* tactics. Rather, they became billionaires by playing the game more effectively and ruthlessly than anybody else during Russia's free-for-all transition to capitalism. Russia's incipient corporate economy operated in practically a legal vacuum at the time, with no laws prohibiting insider trading or other forms of self-dealing. "Russia has been looted all right," says Freeland, "but the biggest crimes haven't been clandestine or violent or even, in the strict legal sense, crimes at all. Russia was robbed in broad daylight, by businessmen who broke no laws, assisted by the West's best friends in the Kremlin."[15]

The Rise of the Oligarchs

When I first began to research the oligarchs, I arranged a series of informal interviews with recent Jewish émigrés from the former Soviet Union. One of the people we spoke with was a financial analyst named Sonia living in New York's Brighton Beach, who still has many relatives in Russia and speaks Russian at home.

At one point we asked Sonia if she had any thoughts as to why so many of the oligarchs were Jewish.

Sonia shook her head. "You don't understand," she said dismissively. "These oligarchs—they are 95 percent Russian and only 5 percent Jewish. They are fully assimilated, products of the Russian environment. The Jews in Russia, it is not like the Jews in the U.S. In the U.S., there is an active Jewish community, synagogues, organizations. In Russia there is nothing. For most people, it is just something they have stamped on their passport."

But wasn't it strange, we persisted, that so many of the oligarchs should be Jewish?

"You know Jews!" Sonia laughed. "They gravitate towards business! So, many became involved in the black market. In the Soviet era it was difficult to get goods, so the black market prospered. Everyone, from regular people to Communist officials, used the black market. Of course, it was against 'official policy,' but it was an open secret and mostly tolerated by the government. These [entrepreneurs] had a head start when private business began to be allowed."

Sonia's impression that Jews were significant in the former Soviet Union's black markets was repeated by another interviewee named Tanya, who is also Jewish and whose family moved to New York from the Ukraine six years ago.

" 'Black market' sounds terrible," she said. "But what are considered black markets in a Communist economy would be perfectly legitimate businesses in a capitalist system. My uncle, for example, had one of these underground firms. He manufactured shoes on his own. Later he sold the shoes either at the weekend flea market or through an 'off-the books' arrangement with a state-owned shoe store. What my uncle did was considered illegal. Yet everyone liked him and depended on him. There would have been no shoes on the shelves without people like my uncle."

In 1987 and 1988, as part of Gorbachev's initial tentative embrace of markets, small private businesses were legalized (with certain restrictions). By January 1990 roughly two hundred thousand businesses—misleadingly named *kooperativs*—were in operation.[16] The underground shoe business run by Tanya's uncle was, after 1988, one of the early, authorized private enterprises operating in Russia's incipient capitalist economy. "It made sense," Tanya explains. "The people who ran the illegal businesses in the Soviet era were the people who understood at least the basics of how the free market functioned. That gave them an advantage over the rest of the Russian public when the country transitioned to capitalism."

Despite the (generally accurate) stereotype of former directors of Soviet enterprises as inept, fist-thumping Communist Party officials representing everything markets do not, some Soviet directors were more entrepreneurial than others. The father of Tanya's boyfriend (who is also Jewish), for example, transformed himself from a middling manager of a state-owned enterprise into one of Russia's wealthy "new businessmen." "In the former Soviet Union," recalls Tanya, "he was one of the more business-minded directors of a state-owned railroad line. As soon as individuals were permitted to set up private enterprises, Mr. Yurkovsky organized a company for transporting raw materials—using not just railroads, but also ships and planes. He made a massive fortune—and very quickly. He eventually moved to San Francisco, where he bought a huge house and a BMW for each member of his family."

Like Tanya's uncle, all the Jewish oligarchs were dabbling in quasi-clandestine private enterprise before *glasnost*. Mikhail Friedman—who was rejected by the "MIT of the Soviet Union" because of his Jewish origins and relegated instead to the less prestigious Institute of Steel and Alloys—started a ticket scalping agency while a student in the economically stagnant early eighties. Friedman paid Moscow university students to wait in line to buy theater tickets, which could then be bartered on the black market. Although ticket scalping existed long before Friedman came on the scene, he was the first to organize it into a well-disciplined business, employing 150 scholars—on full salary if they waited overnight, or half salary if they queued up in the early morning—and "managers" from every university department. Friedman, as a kind of controlling shareholder, would meet once a week with his managers to review their business plans.[17]

When private enterprises were legalized in 1987, Friedman and some college friends jumped at the opportunity. Friedman's *koopera-tiv*—the predecessor of Russia's now incredibly powerful Alpha Group—tried everything, from selling Siberian wool shawls to breeding white mice for laboratories. Friedman hit pay dirt with a window washing business. Within half a year his income was over ten thousand rubles a month, a pittance in dollar terms but forty times the combined salaries of his parents. After that, Friedman branched out to importing Western cigarettes and photocopy machines, then to exporting oil. By 1991 he was a dollar millionaire. A few years later, drawing on government connections formed during the *glasnost* era, Friedman set his sights on Russia's mass privatization process. He quickly mastered the art of buying up large stakes in firms that would interest Western multinationals when shares in those firms were still selling at steep discounts. Western banks, including Credit Suisse First Boston, were astonished by how astutely Friedman's Alpha Group anticipated where the profits lay in this first stage of privatization.[18]

Next, Friedman recruited Pyotr Aven, Yeltsin's first trade minister, who later became an oligarch in his own right. Suddenly, Alpha had access to "the golden trough" of government contracts and oil export licenses. In 1996, Friedman and Aven were at the core of the clubby group that underwrote Yeltsin's presidential campaign. Today the Alpha Group controls Russia's largest private bank, 50 percent of Tyumen Oil Company (TNK), Russia's fourth-largest oil company, as well as Crown Resources, an international commodities trading company with an annual turnover of some $5 billion.[19]

According to John Lloyd, there are allegations in Russian security agency dossiers that Friedman ("born in 1964 in the city of Lyov, former Ukrainian Republic, a Jew") engaged in illegal activities to further Alpha's businesses. When Lloyd asked Friedman about these accusations during an interview, Friedman shrugged and said, "That stuff's always around."[20]

———

The other Jewish oligarchs followed roughly similar paths. Vladimir Gusinsky's boyhood dream was to be a physicist, but, like Friedman, he was rejected from his university of choice because of his Jewish background. In 1987 he abandoned his career as a provincial theater director for the turbulent new world of Russian business. From driving a gypsy cab to hawking blue jeans on the black market, the hustling, volatile Gusinsky finally broke through with copper bracelets, a kind of New Age fad that was supposed to prevent high blood pressure. Gusinsky then put his money in real estate and construction before realizing that the real money was to be made in banking. Shamelessly cultivating his relationship with Yuri Luzhkov, Moscow's powerful mayor, Gusinsky was soon making millions managing the city's operating capital. Snapping up newspaper, magazine, and television interests right and left—in some cases letting the business run into the ground while pocketing the assets—Gusinsky became in the nineties the most powerful man in Russian media. By turning his television station NTV into a massive propaganda machine for Yeltsin, Gusinsky—along with his sometimes-ally, sometimes-nemesis fellow oligarch Boris Berezovsky—played a crucial role in Yeltsin's 1996 victory over the Communists.[21]

"I cannot say I am an absolutely honest man, an example for everyone," Gusinsky admitted in an interview with Chrystia Freeland. "Nor can any person who survived in this country before 1985, or who built great things after 1985. We all have things that we would not like to tell our children."[22]

Like Friedman and Gusinsky, Mikhail Khodorkovsky was unable to realize his childhood dream, which in this case was to work in a leading Soviet defense plant, because of his Jewish ancestry. But Khodorkovsky had an important advantage over his fellow Jewish oligarchs: He had served in the Communist Youth League and from the outset enjoyed the patronage of senior Soviet-era government officials. Thus in the late 1980s, when Khodorkovsky ventured into private business with the establishment of Menatep Bank, he had the support and protection of the Communist regime. After 1990, Khodorkovsky served as economic adviser to the prime minister of the Russian Federation—a role he apparently had no trouble playing while continuing to run Menatep.

Just as Gusinsky made his initial fortune managing Moscow's money, Khodorkovsky made untold millions while managing the federal government's finances. In the early nineties, Khodorkovsky's Menatep went on a "mass privatization shopping spree" in which it bought, at bargain basement prices, everything from a titanium-magnesium plant to glass and textile factories to food-processing companies.[23] In 1996, Khodorkovsky emerged from the loans-for-shares deal as the powerful chairman of Yukos, Russia's second-largest oil company, with an estimated $170 billion in oil reserves. In addition to Yukos, Khodorkovsky today controls massive mineral and timber interests as well as the *Moscow Times, St. Petersburg Times,* and other newspaper interests. In 2002, *Forbes* named him the richest man in Russia.[24]

Many, to put it mildly, have a low opinion of Khodorkovsky. He is famous for his ruthlessness. In one company he took over, he installed surveillance cameras in every office to monitor his new employees. He decided that over a third of them weren't working hard enough, so he fired them.[25] After his Menatep Bank collapsed in 1998, Khodorkovsky transferred its good assets to a different entity, leaving its creditors empty-handed. A court-appointed manager was unable to trace the transactions, as a truck carrying most of Menatep Bank's records mysteriously drove off a bridge into the Dybna River.[26]

Probably the most notorious of Russia's oligarchs is Boris Berezovsky. "Slight and balding, with lovingly manicured hands and a fondness for larding his conversation with Latin phrases," Berezovsky, who is older than most of the other oligarchs, holds a Ph.D. in applied mathematics and spent twenty-five years at the Russian Academy of Sciences.[27]

With the introduction of markets, Berezovsky abandoned science for car sales. Starting in 1989, Berezovsky parlayed his Logovaz car dealership into an immensely lucrative and sophisticated international financial structure, complete with reputable Swiss partners, shell companies in Panama and Dublin, and tax havens in Cyprus and the Cayman Islands.[28]

At the same time, without violating the law, Berezovsky played to a naïve Russian public, which almost overnight had become an easy target for get rich quick schemes. In the convulsive first stages of Russian capitalism, when wealth was suddenly permissible and a few of their compatriots became very visible millionaires, ordinary Russians were in a panic not to miss out on the rags-to-riches moment. Riches seemed to be there for the taking, if one only had the courage to make investments. In this atmosphere, schemes of all sorts reached dizzying heights.

In 1993 the Russian public poured $50 million into Berezovsky's Avva Fund, which, according to a massive advertising campaign, would be used to develop a fabulous new Russian "people's car" through a joint venture with General Motors (GM). Unfortunately for Avva's investors, GM, alarmed by Russia's rampant gangsterism and corruption, backed out, rendering Avva securities almost instantly worthless.[29]

Berezovsky quickly became Russia's iconic nouveau-riche capitalist. Ostentatiously roaring around Moscow in a dark blue bulletproof Mercedes, flanked by bodyguards in Mitsubishi jeeps on either side, Berezovsky sent his two eldest daughters to Cambridge University and married a glamorous young second wife. In 1993, Berezovsky went for the real kill. Brazenly setting out to penetrate Yeltsin's inner circle, he befriended the ghostwriter of the president's memoirs, who in turn recommended to Yeltsin that Berezovsky publish the book. Berezovsky did—and (with the help of some Finnish companies) "did the Kremlin proud. The book was rolling off the presses within a few weeks and the color was brighter and the pages were thicker than the washed-out onionskin text that Russian publishers produced." Moreover, Berezovsky published the book not as a business transaction, but as a "free" favor to the president. In return, Yeltsin gave Berezovsky a membership to the President's Club, whose only members were close friends and family of Yeltsin. Berezovsky, an accomplished networker, used his membership to full advantage and within a matter of months had key connections throughout the Kremlin.[30]

In 1994, using Gusinsky's NTV network (which often criticized Yeltsin) as a foil, Berezovsky convinced the Kremlin to privatize ORT, the state-owned television network, and to give Berezovsky control of it. Shortly afterward, he acquired control of the state oil company Sibneft and Russia's national airline Aeroflot. In 1997, *Forbes* named Berezovsky Russia's wealthiest tycoon.[31]

But that was during the Yeltsin era. Under President Vladimir Putin, it was Berezovsky's (also Jewish) protégé and former partner Roman Abramovich who, as the *Washington Post* put it in 2001, became "the man to see in Russia." An orphan before the age of four, Abramovich has in the last several years orchestrated a takeover of the world's richest aluminum industry and bought out Berezovsky's share of the ORT television network. Moreover, on Christmas Eve 2000 the thirty-four-year-old Abramovich was, surreally, elected the new governor of Chukotka, a miserable, poverty-entrenched, below-freezing region in the remotest corner of Russia's Far East, just across the Bering Strait from Alaska. Abramovich's campaign strategy? Spending tens of millions from his own pocket airlifting food, boots, and parkas for the locals and flying thousands of them to sunny beach vacations. When asked about his motives, Abramovich says that he has grown tired of simply making money. "I do it for pleasure," he explains.[32]

———

Why were so many of the oligarchs Jewish? How did it happen that, even as Russia sank from Soviet superpower to post-perestroika immiseration, members of a minuscule "outsider" ethnic minority came to wield almost unimaginable economic and political power?

Certainly the answer is not that Boris Yeltsin had a special fondness for Jewish interests. Yeltsin agreed to loans-for-shares because he desperately needed capital, both to salvage a collapsing economy and to finance his reelection. And the soon-to-be oligarchs had capital. By the early nineties they had already accumulated far more wealth than anyone else in the country.

For one reason or another, for better or worse, in Russia's nearly anarchic transition to a market economy, Jews rose to the top. Long before most Russians—including the country's leaders—had any real understanding of how markets work, the six Jewish oligarchs mastered the game. These men started with next to nothing; most were actually disadvantaged by their Jewish ancestry. They were not particularly sophisticated. They may have been ruthless, but they were plainly smart, unsurpassed entrepreneurs who built their empires from scratch.

The Seventh Oligarch

The contrasting story of Vladimir Potanin, the non-Jewish oligarch, provides a stark counterpoint. Unlike the others, Potanin essentially inherited his wealth from the former Soviet Union. The well-connected son of a senior Soviet foreign trade official, Potanin was privileged all his life. During the Communist era he traveled widely with his father, to places like New Zealand and Turkey. He never had to barter theater tickets or hawk blue jeans. Instead, he attended Moscow's Institute of International Relations, the prestigious training ground for Soviet diplomats, then began his climb up the bureaucratic power structure. In 1992, Potanin started a bank. It was not especially successful. Yet when Russia's state-owned International Bank of Economic Cooperation collapsed, and the panicking Kremlin needed someone to take over its accounts, it was perfectly natural that they chose the golden boy Potanin. "He went straight from a promising Soviet career to a $300-million bank," writes Freeland. "Even in a country where most fortunes were built on the back of government connections, Potanin earned an enduring reputation as the *nomenklatura's* favorite capitalist, the tycoon who had been appointed by the old elites, rather than making his own way."[33]

In 1994 it was Potanin who conceived of loans-for-shares and, after getting the other oligarchs on board, it was Potanin who sold the scheme to the Kremlin. He was, after all, one of them: an archetypical Russian with a pug nose, pink skin, and sandy hair, and just the kind of "home-bred tycoon" Yeltsin's pro-market reformers had hoped the market revolution would create. With the cash-hungry state behind them, Potanin and the other oligarchs wrested control of Russia's crown-jewel natural resource companies away from their highly corrupt "red" directors. Potanin grabbed Norilsk Nickel, Russia's metals colossus, Khodorkovsky took Yukos, Berezovsky and Abramovich got Sibneft, and so on.[34]

All the oligarchs were ruthless. In this respect, however, the oligarchs essentially personified Russia's agonizing, lawless transition to a market economy. The capitalism that emerged in Russia beginning in the 1990s was not the Pareto-optimal paradise of efficient, voluntary market exchange that Western economists envisioned. Instead, in the words of John Lloyd, Russian capitalism was "a deformed and ugly beast."[35] Nevertheless, the fact remains that Russian capitalism was made and is still dominated by a tiny handful of immensely successful entrepreneurs, most of them Jewish.

Retaliation, Reform, and Mass Resentment

For at least two of the oligarchs, life has gone downhill since former KGB official Vladimir Putin came to power. A week before being elected president on March 26, 2000, Putin warned Russia's billionaires that their days of running the country were over: "[T]hose people who fuse . . . power and capital—there will be no oligarchs of this kind as a class."[36] So far, Putin's main targets have been Vladimir Gusinsky and Boris Berezovsky, both media moguls who dared to cover the president unfavorably. Indeed, many Russia watchers are concerned that free speech in Russia is under serious threat. According to *The Economist,* for example, "Gusinsky, owner of NTV, the only independent national television station, was jailed on June 13th on a spurious-sounding allegation of fraud. Before that, the press minister had called him a 'bacterium,' anti-Semitic remarks were broadcast about him on state-controlled television and masked police had raided his headquarters."[37] Gusinsky is now in exile.

Also in exile is Gusinsky's former rival Boris Berezovsky, who is lashing back at Putin from his new home in London. According to one source, Berezovsky is planning to release a documentary "proving" that Russian security forces were behind a series of bombings that in 1999 killed over three hundred people in Moscow and other major Russian cities. Berezovsky claims that the bombings were conducted to incite hatred against Chechens in a calculated effort to rally public support for Putin.[38]

The consensus in Moscow, however, is that the popular Putin has nothing to worry about. "The rating of [Russia's security police] is way higher than Berezovsky's own rating, not to mention the president," explains one Moscow journalist. Stanislav Kucher, another Moscow journalist, is even less sympathetic. In his view Berezovsky is simply rankled "that he no longer can influence the development of this country." "He was absolutely sure that had he not been Jewish he would make president. And of course, he would say that with bitter regret."[39]

Meanwhile, the oligarchs remaining in Russia have, at least in appearance, shaped up under the Putin presidency. In a recent interview with Matthew Brzezinski, Vladimir Potanin waxes eloquent: "We are coming to the end of the first phase of Russia's capitalist transition: the accumulation of capital." Now, in the "second stage," we must make our holdings "profitable, restructure them into viable concerns, change the system." "What was okay two years ago is no longer acceptable."[40] Similarly, Mikhail Friedman "applauds" the government's recent economic and rule-of-law reforms, "but wishes they could be pushed through more quickly." And Mikhail Khodorkovsky in a recent interview with the *Los Angeles Times:* "We used to think that all that mattered was to have good production figures. We considered other matters less important: the environment, investor relations, public affairs, corporate governance as a whole. And suddenly it hit us over the head, hard, and we realized we were wrong."[41]

The Jewish oligarchs in particular are keenly aware that they are increasingly at President Putin's mercy. According to the Union of Councils for Soviet Jews, Putin "is gaining popularity by what is seen as a crackdown on widely hated, mostly Jewish, tycoons."[42] The most recent shakeup occurred in January 2002, when Roman Abramovich, an oligarch formerly favored by Putin, was replaced by Viktor Geraschenko as Russia's "top business leader." According to journalist Andrei Grigoriev, Putin's move "did not make Abramovich any poorer but his weight did go down." As recently reported by the National Conference on Soviet Jewry, political anti-Semitism appears to be on the rise in Russia, with prominent politicians, particularly those associated with the Communist Party, employing anti-Semitic rhetoric in parliamentary sessions, on television, in newspapers, and at mass rallies in order to further their own political ambitions.[43]

As is sadly so often the case with market-dominant minorities, struggling ordinary Russian Jews, with no political connections or billion-dollar fortunes, bear the brunt of Russian anti-Semitism. According to the chairman of the Glasnost Public Foundation in Moscow, a majority of Russians today believe that "they have been impoverished at the expense of rich Jews."[44] (Along with the oligarchs, many of the Yeltsin government's key market reformers—including former prime minister Sergei Kiriyenko, shock therapy advocate Yegor Gaidar, and the now-despised "privatization tsar" Anatoly Chubais—are also well known to be part Jewish.)[45] Russian websites today are filled with references to the "zioncrats" and "bloodsucking Yids" who "hijacked the privatization process," "control the economy," and are "stealing the wealth of the Russian people."

The financial collapse in 1998 brought a burst of popular anti-Semitism, including the bombing of synagogues, the beatings of two rabbis, a number of neo-Nazi marches in Moscow, and the desecration of Jewish cemeteries around the country. Russian National Unity, a paramilitary and virulently anti-Semitic extremist group, is thought to have at least 6,000 active members and up to 50,000 nonactive members, spread across twenty-five Russian regions. One of the group's leaders was recently sentenced to two years in prison for inciting ethnic hatred. At the trial a Russian Orthodox priest testified that according to the Jewish Talmud, Jews "kill children, gather blood" and "use it to make matzah."[46] Around the same time, hundreds of posters appeared in the Siberian city of Novosibirsk with the slogan, "Jews are Rubbish!" In the Kuban region of Krasnodar, mailboxes were filled with leaflets saying: "Help save your dear, flourishing Kuban from the damned Jews—Yids! Smash their apartments, set their homes on fire! They have no place on Kuban territory. . . . Anyone hiding the damned Yids will be marked for destruction the same way. The Yids will be destroyed. Victory will be ours!"[47]

Obviously, Russian anti-Semitism is not caused by economic liberalization or capitalism. As discussed earlier, there was plenty of anti-Semitic sentiment and violence long before 1989, both during the tsarist era and in the former Soviet Union. Nevertheless, the fact remains that the chaotic, post-perestroika transition to markets has generated starkly concentrated and visible Jewish wealth, bringing to the surface tremendous ethnic resentment and hostility among the "indigenous" Russian majority. According to recent polls, most Russians are deeply "ambivalent" about Jews and thus susceptible to manipulation by politicians, particularly during periods of economic downturn and distress. In one independent survey of 1,509 Muscovites, 52 percent opposed Jewish social-political organizations operating in Russia, while 34 percent favored quotas limiting the number of Jews holding leading positions in Russia. "The basic problem is the economic situation," Adolf Shayevich, Russia's chief rabbi, said a few years ago. "People have no work and no prospects. Historically, that's when Russians look for scapegoats."[48]

Even today, with Putin popular and the economy on the upswing, anti-Semitism shows no sign of waning. On February 28, 2002, the *Moscow Times* reported that a new political party was formed, calling for a better deal for ethnic Russians and explicitly blaming Jews for stealing the country's wealth. "Look on the list of Russia's richest people," urged Vladimir Miloserdov, head of the party's executive committee, "and you will see no ethnic Russians among them." The head of the new party is Gen. Igor Rodionov, who served as defense minister under Yeltsin. His policy platform: The oligarchs "must return what they have looted in Russia and publicly repent to the Russian people for the crimes that Jewish terrorists and extremists have committed." The new party expects to be registered with the Justice Ministry in May 2002.[49]

CHAPTER 4

The "Ibo of Cameroon"

Market-Dominant Minorities in Africa

O f all the world's regions, scarcity-stricken Africa has the greatest abundance and variety of market-dominant minorities. Some of these minorities are indigenous Africans. Others are "entrepreneurial" immigrant groups like the Indians or Lebanese. Still others are former European colonizers. All are deeply resented and, at times, the objects of homicidal fury.

The problem is starkest in southern Africa. In country after country, a handful of whites engorged themselves on natural resources and human labor, creating enclaves of spectacular wealth and modernization, surrounded by mounting, justifiable hatred among the indigenous black majority. The typical result has been horrific violence.

A tragic example is Angola, now largely forgotten in the West. For many the country, with its shocking death tolls and endless atrocities, is simply too depressing to think about. But Angola's problems can be traced to a familiar colonial history.

Under the Portuguese, Angola suffered from one of the most oppressive forms of colonial rule: Until the nineteenth century, Portugal used the area as a "slave pool" for its more lucrative colony in Brazil while plundering Angola's precious gemstones and metals. Even just thirty years ago, 335,000 Portuguese colonialists ruthlessly ran and controlled the virtual entirety of Angola's economy. In *Another Day of Life*, Ryszard Kapuściński describes their almost overnight departure in 1975, when Angola was granted independence in the midst of rising chaos and violence:

At the airport in Lubango a group of terrified, sweaty, apathetic Portuguese sat on kit bags and suitcases beside their even more terrified wives, and their children asleep in the women's arms. They rushed for the plane before it had even shut off its motors. . . .

Everybody was in a hurry, everybody was clearing out. Everyone was trying to catch the next plane to Europe, to America, to anywhere. Portuguese from all over Angola converged on Luanda. . . . People lived in the open, perpetually soaked because it was always raining. They were living worse now than the blacks in the African quarter that abutted the airport, but they took it apathetically, with dismal resignation, not knowing whom to curse for their fate. . . .

At about this time, someone brought news to the hotel that all the police had left!

Now Luanda, of all the cities in the world, had no police. When you find yourself in such a situation, you feel strange. On the one hand everything seems light, loose, but on the other hand there is a certain uneasiness. The few whites who still wandered the city accepted the development with foreboding. Rumors circulated that the black quarters would descend upon the stone city. Everyone knew that the blacks lived in the most awful conditions, in the worst slums to be seen anywhere in Africa, in clay hovels like heaps of smashed cheap pottery covering the desert around Luanda. And here stood the luxurious stone city of glass and concrete—empty, no one's. . . . But according to the terrified Portuguese who passed themselves off as experts on the native mentality, the blacks would burst in, swept up in a madness of destruction and hatred, drunk, drugged with secret herbs, demanding blood and revenge. Nothing could hold back that invasion. . . . Everyone is lost and it will be the most hideous death—stabbed to death in the streets, hacked with machetes on their own doorsteps.[1]

Most of the Portuguese got out safely, leaving the country to disintegrate into a civil war of unspeakable brutality. According to the World

Bank, the Portuguese took "with them the skills needed to run the economy; this lack of capacity has exacerbated Angola's political and economic woes."[2] Although the United States was involved in Angola's strife in the 1970s and 1980s, it lost interest when the Cold War ended.

The question for the other countries of southern Africa—all of which still have starkly market-dominant white minorities—is whether they can avoid Angola's fate. In Zimbabwe, millions of dollars worth of sugar, tobacco, and maize has gone up in flames as gangs of landless "war veterans" continue to invade, loot, and burn white-owned commercial farms. In Namibia, widely praised for its racial harmony, President Nujoma recently condemned his country's white farmers for their imperialist exploitation. "We have the capacity to fight you," he declared at another point. "We will get you. I warn those whites it is the first and last time I hear you insulting us."

Meanwhile, all hopes are on South Africa. Perhaps, inspired by Nelson Mandela's inclusive vision, the country can beat the region's bloody record. This was not the view expressed by the African National Congress (ANC) official who, stopped in November 1997 for driving while intoxicated, told the policeman: "When Mandela dies, we will kill you whites like flies."[3]

Market-Dominant Whites in Southern Africa

In September 1997, I was invited by a young Afrikaner professor whom I'll call Lucien to give some lectures at the University of South Africa, better known as UNISA, in Johannesburg. When I walked into UNISA's lecture room I was taken aback. I had of course expected racial imbalance. Everyone knew that seventy years of white-minority rule would have lasting, nefarious effects. Still, I was not prepared to see an entire room filled with only white faces (and perhaps one person of South Asian descent). South Africa's demographics are roughly the opposite of America's: 77 percent of the population is black and 11 percent is white. In 1997, Mandela and his ANC party had been in power three years. Yet in one of the country's major universities—at a lecture on democracy and race, no less—there was not a single black professor or student in the room.

After the lecture I asked to see Soweto, one of the unimaginably squalid, teeming black "townships" that surround South Africa's urban centers. (Soweto, whose name originated as an abbreviation for South Western Township, was the site of the famous 1976 police massacre.) My hosts looked stricken. This could probably, possibly, perhaps be arranged, they equivocated, mumbling something about the difficulty of finding cars and drivers. But for the moment something else had already been planned. Along with a few other professors, I was going to Lucien's house near Pretoria, the country's genteel capital, for lunch. Lucien's wife and family were waiting.

I'm not sure exactly what I expected Lucien's home to be like, but I wasn't close. Lucien's "home" turned out to include a private safari park, covering not tens or hundreds, but thousands of acres of breathtakingly serene grassy slopes filled with waterfalls, streams, zebras, giraffes, hippo pools, ostriches, kingfishers, impala, kudu, gemsbok—seemingly every species of bird and antelope. Lucien's wife Marina, a beautiful woman with some Italian ancestry, greeted us at the lodge with a rifle and three adorable daughters and gave us a private tour in a jeep she drove herself. We picnicked outside an 1800-era stone and timber-beamed farmhouse, which Marina's brother operated as an inn. Lunch was grilled cheese sandwiches and warthog pie—I thought they were kidding, but it was a specialty of the house—served to us by a black manservant in a white jacket.

The really amazing thing was that, among whites in South Africa, Lucien and Marina didn't count as wealthy. Lucien described himself to me as a struggling, middle-class descendant of Boer farmers. Land, yes, they had—he and his family never ceased being grateful for, and humbled by, the beauty of their surroundings. But truth be told, his professor's salary was barely enough to cover his daughters' tuition and music lessons. Like many Afrikaners, Lucien was not at all interested in business. That was the province of the so-called "English-speaking" whites, including most prominently the Oppenheimer family (of De Beers fame), who historically controlled the country's most lucrative industries: gold, platinum, and diamond mining, finance, insurance, technology.

South African whites fall into two general categories: Afrikaners, descendants of seventeenth-century Dutch and French Huguenot settlers, and "English speakers," most of whom have British origins. The English speakers have more of a claim to being "entrepreneurial." Indeed, throughout much of the twentieth century the Afrikaners were a rural, economically backward underclass compared to the commercially dominant British.[4] (This changed with the aggressive pro-Afrikaner affirmative action policies pursued by the Nationalist Party between 1948 and 1976). But the main reason that South Africa's present-day whites are so overwhelmingly market-dominant, vis-à-vis the black majority, is not because of any superior "entrepreneurialism." It is because they have a gargantuan economic head start.

They have this head start because generations ago, their forebears turned the black majority around them into a mass pool of uneducated, disenfranchised, dehumanized labor held in check by a police state. For seventy years, while whites advanced and luxuriated—South Africa has fabulously engineered roads, first-class hospitals where some of the world's first heart transplants were performed, and resplendent vineyards—the apartheid regime deliberately and systematically destroyed the human capital of the black majority. So-called Coloureds (people of mixed African and European descent) and Asians, together about 11 percent of the population, occupied an intermediate niche, above blacks. They too, however, were disenfranchised and barred from living and mingling with whites.

Catching up will not be easy. Any way you look at them, the statistics are awful. Sixty-five percent of South African blacks today live in abject poverty. Eighty-eight percent have less than a high school education. A quarter over the age of twenty have had no formal schooling at all. In townships like Soweto, it is common for four thousand residents to share five toilets; electricity, where it exists, is generated with car batteries. There is almost no intermarriage between blacks and whites. AIDS is pandemic—in recent years, 40 percent of all adult deaths in South Africa have been AIDS-related—and strikes blacks extremely disproportionately. Seven years after the end of apartheid, whites still own 80 percent of South Africa's land and account for 90 percent of the country's commercial agricultural production.

Economic liberalization has produced some success stories. The case everyone knows is that of Cyril Ramaphosa, who went from trade union leader to chief negotiator for the ANC to media tycoon. A few former township dwellers have made it to Harvard. But while the hope is that in the long run free market policies will create thousands more such success stories, at the moment the unemployment rate among blacks is a frightening 48 percent. The townships are not shrinking but *growing,* at a rate of a million black Africans a year. As of August 2000, blacks controlled only 1.7 percent of the Johannesburg Stock Exchange's total capitalization. According to a recent report released by South Africa's Black Economic Empowerment Commission, almost all of South Africa's mines, banks, and major corporations remain in white hands.[5]

———

Like South Africa, both the neighboring countries of Namibia and Zimbabwe have a market-dominant white minority who, because of their huge and hugely-undeserved head starts, would under laissez-faire market conditions overwhelmingly economically dominate the black majorities around them.

Unknown to most Americans, Namibia is one of the most mysteriously beautiful places in the world, from the wild Skeleton Coast in the north (vast stretches of foggy beach punctuated by eerie, rusting shipwrecks) to the brilliant red dunes of the Namib Desert to the immense Fish River Canyon in the south. Namibia was colonized by the Germans, who starting in the late 1890s turned the dozen or so major ethnic groups constituting black Namibia into forced labor—almost annihilating the particularly rebellious Herero tribe. Following the Second World War, Namibia was annexed by a belligerent South Africa. The country's arable land was parceled into some six thousand lavish farms for white settlers. Members of the black majority were relegated to newly demarcated "tribal homelands," where they received an offensively inferior education. Until the 1990s, 75 percent of Namibian children completed less than five years of schooling.

Today Namibia's population of about 1.6 million has one of the African continent's highest GDPs—but also, according to a recent World Bank report, one of the highest levels of income inequality in the world. While the great majority of black Namibians engage in communal subsistence farming, a tiny minority of roughly eighty thousand whites own the most productive land and control all the most lucrative and globally-oriented sectors of the economy. A decade after the end of apartheid, Namibia's business community is still almost entirely white.[6]

Meanwhile, South Africa's Oppenheimer family has controlled Namibia's diamond mines—the richest in the world—since 1908. (De Beers entered into a joint venture with Namibia's current government in 1994). The Oppenheimers have been called "pioneers of globalization"; De Beers has offices all over the world and currently controls 60 percent of the global trade in rough diamonds. The conglomerate's latest technological gambit is deep-sea diamond mining. "Special drill bits," marvels *Fortune*'s Nicholas Stein, "23 feet in diameter, burrow into the ocean floor, releasing a mix of diamond and ore that is sucked through 300 feet of tubing to the surface, where machines separate the diamonds from the surrounding material and pack them, like chunky soup, into aluminum cans."[7]

In 2000, De Beers recovered roughly 570,000 carats of high quality diamonds off the Namibian coast. That same year, roughly 60 percent of Namibia's black majority had no access to sanitary toilets. Namibia also has what may be the world's largest uranium mine. It, however, is owned by a British company.[8]

Zimbabwe, too, previously known as Rhodesia, is a country of glorious natural beauty. But you would never know it from our newspapers, which for decades have had nothing to report but human ugliness in Zimbabwe: from Ian Smith's grotesquely oppressive white rule; to the guerrilla downing of two civilian airplanes in the late seventies, followed by the rape and hacking to death of crash survivors; to the recent confiscations and violence instigated by President Robert Mugabe.[9]

The British initially colonized Zimbabwe in the late nineteenth century, and whites continued to control the country's economy and politics until 1980. Unlike South Africa, where Afrikaners own most of the land, the majority of Zimbabwe's forty-five hundred white farmers are of British and Irish ancestry. Only fifty or so are of Dutch heritage.

For a variety of reasons, outside observers tend to regard the Anglo elite throughout southern Africa with greater sympathy than the descendants of the Boers. In South Africa the Afrikaners are viewed as the chief architects and perpetuators of apartheid, with many Anglo whites belonging to the opposition. In the case of Zimbabwe there is no doubt that Anglo whites were responsible for the worst oppressions. Yet the general impression, it seems, is that Zimbabwe's white farmers, with their sun-leathered skin and khaki shorts, do not—despite their multiple servants and ownership of the country's best land—live in the aloof luxury of their Afrikaner counterparts in South Africa. "With Zimbabwe's whites," mused a U.S. Justice Department official, "there seems to be more of a feel of a hard-working, dirt-under-the-fingernails, landowner class rather than a true idle upper or gentry class." Along slightly different lines, London's *Guardian* recently observed, only partly tongue-in-cheek, that "Zimbabwe's white landowners, being of British and Irish ancestry, get a much better press than do Afrikaners. Those sandy-faced Boers, with faces out of rural scenes by obscure Flemish painters, never sat well with British liberals. But the white elite of Zimbabwe, 0.6% of the population owning 70% of the land, seem to be a jolly good bunch: nice foreheads, English names, English accents even."[10]

However affable, Zimbabwe's whites did not come by their wealth legitimately. The original British settlers duped, killed, and expropriated their way to control of the country's best land, leaving the indigenous majority to scrubby, marginal areas infested with the dreaded tsetse fly. In the 1930s white supremacy was legislated in the form of laws excluding black Africans from ownership of arable farmland, from skilled trades and professions, and from settling in "white areas," including all towns and cities. The result was that Zimbabwe's blacks were forced to work on white-owned farms, in white-owned mines, and in white-owned factories.

Although political power finally changed hands in 1980, the hard fact of white market dominance remains. With their vastly superior education, land, technological skills, foreign investment connections, and corporate and horticultural experience, members of Zimbabwe's tiny white minority have a century-old edge that makes them as market-dominant as the Chinese in Southeast Asia. Throughout the eighties and nineties, forty-five hundred white commercial farmers produced more food than a million black farmers. In Hippo Valley, for example, two large-scale sugar estates, both white-owned, together produced about five hundred thousand tons of sugar annually, half of it for export. As late as 2000, Zimbabwe's whites, not even 1 percent of the population, essentially owned and ran the country's modern, immensely productive, commercial-agriculture-based economy, thriving on global markets, employing over two million people, and fueling the country's high growth rates.[11] Predictably, this enormous racial concentration of wealth and market expertise has produced combustible political conditions, not just in Zimbabwe but in Namibia and South Africa as well.

Kenyan Cowboys and "Capitalistic" Kikuyus

Ever since Hugh Cholmondeley, England's third baron of Delamere, arrived in 1897 after a two-thousand-mile camel ride from Somalia, Kenya also has had an inordinately prosperous, disproportionately skilled white minority. Today numbering only about five thousand, they live, completely segregated, in the beautiful Nairobi suburbs of Langata and Karen, named after the Danish settler Karen Blixen. They live in large houses with small windows (to keep out the sun) and magnificent, sprawling gardens filled with fuchsias and English roses and avenues of jacaranda and eucalyptus trees.

Back in the days of Happy Valley—Nairobi's legendary enclave of witty, winsome, morphine-and-orgy-addicted expatriate aristocrats—Kenya's whites included luminaries like Evelyn Waugh, Edward, Prince of Wales, and the American millionaire Northrop MacMillan. After the dashing Josslyn Hay, earl of Erroll, was found murdered on the floor of his Buick with a bullet in his head—sixty years later the mystery remains unsolved—Happy Valley was never the same again.[12]

Today these aristocrats are mostly gone. Nowadays the most prominent white Kenyans are probably the Leakeys: a family of paleontologists and conservationists who first arrived in Kenya from Great Britain three generations ago. In the 1990s, Richard Leakey transformed the Kenya Wildlife Service, crucial for the country's tourist trade, from a shabby, demoralized department into the pride of Kenya's public sector, with its own efficient paramilitary force. Leakey's recent foray into electoral politics, however—off-limits to whites since independence—

prompted angry charges of "recolonization" from President Daniel Arap Moi and led to Leakey being whipped and beaten by Moi supporters. The two men have since made up. Astounding everybody, Moi appointed Leakey head of Kenya's civil service in 1999, to help root out the "twin evils" of "corruption and inefficiency." Most observers interpret Moi's move as an attempt to court Western foreign aid donors, who have grown increasingly disgusted with Kenya's kleptocratic politics.

Meanwhile, the so-called "Kenyan Cowboys," or "KCs," try to maintain the legacy of Happy Valley. Fun-loving, decadent, bafflingly immature, these young men and women are stuck in a time warp, somewhere in the heyday of British colonialism. While the great majority of Kenya's roughly 31 million blacks struggle to survive on less than two dollars a day—45 percent are unemployed—the KCs spend their days sipping tea and playing bridge, polo, or cricket. Weekends, they go on safari. In the summer they jet set to Europe. The rest of the time they frequent anachronistic private clubs like Nairobi's Muthaiga Country Club, where their predecessors amused themselves in the 1930s by swapping wives, throwing gramophones out the window, or shooting bullets into the stuffed lion still displayed in the hallway. The KCs strive to carry on this tradition, mainly through drinking and such activities as putting "butter pats on the carnations on the dinner table and throw[ing] them up at the ceiling to see if they will stick." Although discrimination against Africans and Asians officially ended in the 1960s, the Muthaiga Club's membership remains predominantly white. All the staff are black.[13]

In addition to wealthy white former colonialists, Africa is also full of successful and in some cases market-dominant African minorities. This often comes as a surprise to Americans, who, because of the reality of our own inner cities, tend to associate "African" and "minority" with "poverty" and "economic backwardness." But throughout Africa, for usually hotly disputed reasons, some indigenous ethnic groups have consistently prospered more than others.

Kenya's Kikuyus, who are concentrated in the fertile Central Province and the capital city Nairobi, provide a typically complicated example. The Kikuyus are a minority in the sense that they represent roughly 22 percent of the population. On the other hand, out of Kenya's approximately forty African ethnic groups, the Kikuyu are numerically the largest. (Kenyans do not use the term "ethnic group," preferring instead the English word "tribe" or its Swahili equivalent *kabila*.) Next in size are the Luhya, with around 14 percent of the population, the Luo (13 percent), and the Kalenjin (12 percent).

As is often the case with ethnic statistics, however, these figures are somewhat misleading because there are cross-cutting cleavages within ethnic groups as well as complex, opportunistic relations between members of different ethnic groups. The Kalenjin, for example, comprise several smaller groups; President Moi belongs to one such group, the Tugen. Similarly, the Kikuyu, the powerful group of Kenya's first president, Jomo Kenyatta, embraces two highly competitive factions: the Kiambu Kikuyu and the Nyeri Kikuyu.[14]

Despite these important qualifications, it remains the case that the Kikuyu view themselves, and are perceived by other Kenyans, as a distinct and distinctly successful group. Before colonization, Kikuyu territory stretched from Nairobi to the slopes of Mount Kenya. The British expropriated their land in order to produce cash crops (especially tea and arabica coffee), at the same time displacing nomadic groups like the Kalenjin, the Turkana, and the Maasai. Forcefully evicted from their homes, the Kikuyu became laborers and domestic servants on European farms or found employment in the cities. Many Kikuyu believe that as a group they suffered disproportionately under British colonization. Many non-Kikuyu disagree. In any event, as early as the 1920s, while the country was still under British rule, the Kikuyu emerged as a disproportionately urban, "capitalist" elite among Kenya's indigenous tribes. The Kikuyu were also the driving force behind the country's independence movement. In the fifties, the Mau Mau uprising was led principally by Kikuyu (although it was also a civil war among the Kikuyu), and as already noted, Kenya's first president, Jomo Kenyatta, was a Kikuyu.

Under Kenyatta's rule, which lasted between 1963 and 1978, the economic prominence of the Kikuyu intensified. In part this is because Kenyatta adopted ethnically biased economic policies blatantly favoring the Kikuyu, especially his own family members. One component of Kenyatta's "Africanization" campaign, for example, was to transfer to the Kikuyu large tracts of the fertile, cash-crop-producing land formerly controlled by whites to the exclusion of other groups. By 1978, Kenya had developed an indigenous "capitalist bourgeoisie" that was predominantly Kikuyu.[15] But the reasons behind Kikuyu economic success remain bitterly disputed.

I recently posted on the web the following question: "Why have the Kikuyu been more economically successful than other Kenyans?" (In Kenya, the term "Kenyans" is still understood to mean black Kenyans.) Many Kenyans, including self-identified Kikuyus, Luos, and Kalenjin, responded. Here is a sampling of their comments.

> W: The Kikuyu, of which I'm one, have become successful economically due to various reasons. One, civilization came early to our community when the colonial settlers settled in our land and introduced the start of the Kenyan economy. Second, the Kikuyus have a different attitude. They like to invest and try ventures, however small they are. They believe that being a small business owner is better than being a manager here or there. . . . In my family, there is no one who is an employee. We believe that the worst offense you can do to yourself is to remain an employee. Rightly so, wealth is created by those who engage in business.
>
> K: IT IS OUT OF HARD WORK. HARD HARD WORK AND CONFIDENCE. THE SAME REASONS ALL OTHER PEOPLE BECOME STRONG ECONOMICALLY.
>
> S [responding to K]: You are a sick puppy. If I remind you of Kamaliza [a Swahili name for "exterminator" and a nickname used by some Kenyans to refer to President Kenyatta], you will realize that your fathers and mothers had an unfair advantage vis-à-vis other Kenyans. During Kenyatta's reign, he transferred all the "white settlers" land to Kikuyus. Please don't give me that BS of I work hard and own my own business. If you don't care to learn history then stop spouting ignorance. . . . You should at the very least stop corrupting this media with misinformation. Please acknowledge the sins of your ancestors, then propose solutions. Non-Kikuyus sat on the sidelines while Kamaliza and his Kikuyu henchmen raped the country, denying other Kenyans jobs

and land. We are all hard working folks and don't think for a moment that your likes have cornered the market on success, by virtue of being Kikuyu.

J: This is what you say to a stranger, with no idea about Kenya and how Kikuyus got wealthy! You say that Kikuyus were outright thieves?! Next time check your words!!! I insist, Kikuyus are not thieves. They were aided to their wealth, but nobody makes it to financial success without help. That is why banks offer loans. The difference is that Kikuyus appreciate the little they have and have a drive towards enterprising like no other tribe in Kenya. I was brought up by my aunt, she fed us by selling the local brew, and now she owns a restaurant!! Am I not allowed to be proud of that??? She was never a relation of a certain minister and neither did she finish her formal education!! . . . You being a Kenyan should have some sensitivity on what you write!!! The Kikuyu bashing has to stop!! I am tired of everyone picking on Kikuyus because we happen to be the first at the top!!!!!!

S: What I am trying to tell your kinsmen is that hard work is not a genetic trait of Kikuyus only. . . . You have to accept facts such as outright stealing favoring Kikuyus that was perpetrated by Kamaliza henchmen—like the series of Kikuyu Governors and department heads that were in charge of the Central Bank. Moi and his henchmen [who are Kalenjin] may be stealing now, but is he doing anything different from what Kamaliza did? You don't have to defend Kamiliza because you are a Kikuyu.

P: Guys, calling each other names IS NOT going to resolve anything. I suggest you respect each others opinions or positions, and stick with ONLY THE FACTS.

M: It is as simple as having self-determination and being afraid of poverty. To be poor means being hopeless to a Kikuyu. You are not accorded respect by other men. They can even swindle your wife, they regard you like garbage. These are some of the reasons that make Kikuyus economically strong. It is like part of a culture of the people. But not anymore, not under Moi.

However contested the reasons, at least one basic fact is not: Among black Kenyans, deservedly or not, the Kikuyu have for generations been disproportionately wealthy. Even today under President Moi, who has openly pursued pro-Kalenjin policies, the Kikuyu continue to have an unusually solid business and middle class. Kikuyu elite remain the owners of large tracts of valuable land, much of it handed to them under Kenyatta. Of the few black members of the Muthaiga Club, almost all are Kikuyu, who are fighting tooth and nail to keep out the emerging new Kalenjin elite.

The Market-Dominant Ibo of Nigeria

The Kikuyu are by no means an exceptional case. Disproportionately successful African minorities can be found in virtually every corner of the African continent. The Ibo, known as the "Jews of Nigeria," for example, are famous the world over for being an unusually driven and enterprising "trader" minority. Within Nigeria, Ibo subcommunities dominate key economic sectors. Ibo in Nnewi overwhelmingly control Nigeria's auto parts industry. Ibo operating out of Aba specialize in shoes and textiles. Ibo in Onitsha have long operated the country's long distance transportation sector. (The Onitsha Market is the largest open market in Africa, perhaps in the world. Dominated by Ibo, it has even inspired its own literature, the so-called Onitsha Market Literature: folk comedies, romances, poems, and plays, written by dozens of Nigerian writers living and working in Onitsha and published by printing houses in the marketplace.)[16] Despite explicitly anti-Ibo economic policies in recent years, there is virtually no commercial sector in Nigeria without a strong Ibo contingent. "The Ibo are merchants," a Nigerian lawyer explained to me. "They sell practically anything—electronics, clothing, tires, mattresses, you name it."

As with the Kikuyu, there are different theories about the reasons for Ibo economic success. Non-Ibo groups in Nigeria will sometimes attribute Ibo success to corruption or crime. It is a fact that Ibos are disproportionately represented not only in legitimate trade but also in fraud and drug trafficking in Nigeria—although in part this might be because the Ibo have in recent years been shut out from legitimate economic sectors. (Ibos are thought to be at the center of the international advance-fee-fraud scams, more popularly known as 419, which bilk

Americans out of about $100 million a year.) On the other hand, many Nigerians, especially Ibo, believe the explanation is genetic. Some have suggested that the Ibo are a lost tribe of Israel; this theory appears to have been discredited.

Other theories emphasize the unusually open and "achievement-oriented" character of Ibo society; similar arguments have been made for the Kikuyu.[17] In addition, like the Chinese or Koreans, the Ibo have sophisticated social networks that are almost impenetrable by outsiders. Moreover, the Ibo are in a sense immigrants even in Nigeria, and according to some this experience has contributed to a stronger "work ethic." Because of overpopulation and infertile soil in Iboland, which is located in the southeast, many Ibo migrated to the urban centers of northern and western Nigeria. Like the Chinese in Southeast Asia then, the Ibo effectively became landless migrants, arguably with a survivalist work ethic and higher "tolerance" levels for suffering.[18] In any event, there is no denying the bottom line. The Ibo are a disproportionately dynamic, urban, and prosperous minority—not just in Nigeria, but everywhere they go. In West Africa it is often said that the banks in countries like Benin or Côte d'Ivoire would collapse if the Ibo withdrew their deposits. In the United States there are strikingly successful Ibo communities in Atlanta, Houston, Los Angeles, and other major cities.

———

Indeed, not only the Ibo but other Nigerian ethnic groups like the Hausa and the Yoruba have become the preeminent petty traders of West Africa. While the far more lucrative import-export business is dominated by Lebanese with ties to the global marketplace (to be discussed below), a stroll through the alleyways of any West African market makes clear that most goods bought and sold by the "mama benzes" and "marché mamas" aren't exactly part of the technologized global marketplace. Rather they're the products of West African, and particularly Nigerian, industry.

Nigeria is the economic powerhouse among the West African states, with a towering industrial leg up on the other countries in the region. In part because of this industrial head start, Nigerians dominate petty trading throughout the cities and villages of West Africa. It's not unusual to find Ibo selling auto parts in the most remote village markets of Benin, Togo, or Burkina Faso. Ibo merchants travel with their goods, ferrying the products of the Nigerian auto parts industry across the West African bush because they have the contacts, know the terrain, and can do it most cheaply.

In the stalls of Marché Dantokpa in Cotonou, Benin, one is more likely to hear the merchants speaking Pidgin English, Ibo, or Yoruba (another Nigerian language) than French, the national language of Benin, or Fon, the language of the ethnic majority. The spillover from Nigerian industry ultimately ends up in markets like Dantokpa, not quite global but regional in reach, where the local equivalent of the Western-educated MBA is the Nigerian with family contacts on both sides of the border who uses her familiarity with the corrupt and often dangerous Nigerian highway to her advantage. At Dantokpa's taxi station, cars leave regularly for Nigerian border towns, Lagos, and beyond. The Nigerians return burdened with cheap goods that eventually make their way, usually through Nigerian hands, to the smallest market towns in West Africa. Indeed, while West Africa has not yet undergone the homogenization (with an American face) caused elsewhere by global markets, it has seen a regional homogenization (with a Nigerian face): There may not be a McDonald's on every corner, but in every West African market Nigerians sell the same goods from the same factories at the same prices. Hence, the ubiquitous plastic African sandals and housewares decorated with the faces of former Nigerian strongmen.

The global marketplace has so far had minimal effects in West Africa, benefiting principally European and Lebanese expatriates and local political elites. But indigenous West Africans are connected in a vibrant regional marketplace, dominated by the Ibo and other ethnic groups from Nigeria. These groups have created ethnic enclaves in the region's major cities that tend to be more ostentatious than the other neighborhoods, earning Nigerians a reputation as fierce hagglers and crafty traders. While wealth inequality is already stark in many cases, as globalization finally reaches African shores the disparities are likely to grow, enriching these groups that already know how to manipulate the markets.

The "Ibo of Cameroon" and
Other Successful Indigenous African Minorities

In the same half-admiring, half-insulting way that the Ibo are called
the "Jews of Nigeria," the "aggressive and commercially vigorous"
Bamiléké are known as the "Ibo of Cameroon." Even before independence in 1960 the Bamiléké had come to dominate petty trading, retail,
and transportation in Douala, Cameroon's largest city and principal port. Today, the Bamiléké—the so-called "merchant tribe of
Cameroon"—control most of the country's commerce (except possibly
in East Cameroon, where, historically, Ibo immigrants from Nigeria
dominated). In addition to owning luxury hotels, breweries, clothing
stores, and other large businesses in the major cities, small Bamiléké
communities operate the local grocery stores and mom-and-pop businesses in almost every town. The Bamiléké are also the country's financiers. Through a robust nationwide network of interest-bearing *tontines,*
or local lending associations, the Bamiléké operate an informal capital
market so efficient it constantly threatens to put government-owned
banks out of business.[19]

There are many other disproportionately wealthy black minorities
throughout Africa, each with a different, complex story—some with
horrible endings. In tiny Rwanda, the Tutsi minority were historically
not particularly "entrepreneurial," but they were a cattle-raising elite
who for four centuries (the last one under Belgian colonial rule) dominated economically and politically over the country's 80 percent Hutu
majority. Meanwhile, in neighboring Burundi, where they comprise
roughly 14 percent of the population, the Tutsi still control approximately 70 percent of the country's wealth. Burundi's capital Bujum-
bura—the only city and the only pocket of wealth in the country—is
known as Tutsi Tinsel Town.[20]

In Ethiopia, Eritreans long constituted a starkly successful merchant
class, concentrated mainly in Addis Ababa. The examples get more obscure, but the pattern is the same. In Togo, the Ewe—fortuitous beneficiaries of a missionary education—were an economically advanced
minority favored first by German and later by French colonialists. In
Guinea, the 20 percent Susu are a disproportionately educated, eco-

nomically (and at present politically) powerful tribe. In Uganda, the Baganda minority dominated economically over the rest of the country even before the British employed them to help rule the country. In Tanzania, the brown-toothed Chagga minority—the brown water they drink is staining—live on the fertile slopes of Mount Kilimanjaro and are not only wealthy coffee farmers but flourishing businessmen and bureaucrats.[21]

With varying degrees of intensity, all of these African groups have been the objects of widespread resentment. In Uganda, for example, the politically dominant groups of the north have repeatedly subjected the economically powerful Baganda of the south to bloody purges. In Nigeria in 1966, tens of thousands of Ibo were slaughtered indiscriminately by furious mobs. In Ethiopia, the relatively prosperous Eritreans were recently expelled en masse. In Cameroon, "la Probleme Bamiléké" has been called "the most critical source of inter-ethnic tension" in the country today, with hostility seething among Cameroon's two hundred other tribes and even priests lashing out against Bamiléké "exploitation" of "the weak and the poor."[22] Finally, in Rwanda, the genocidal massacre of the Tutsi minority is inextricably connected with their historic economic dominance.

The Indians of East Africa and the Lebanese of West Africa

Most of the disproportionately wealthy African minorities discussed above do not dominate their respective economies to anywhere near the extent that, say, the Chinese do in Southeast Asia or whites do in southern Africa. (The Bamiléké in Cameroon and the Tutsi in Burundi may be exceptions.) Indeed, their relative advantage vis-à-vis other indigenous groups often pales by comparison to the much starker market dominance of nonindigenous ethnic minorities—not only descendants of former European colonizers but also so-called entrepreneurial "pariah" minorities such as Indians and Lebanese.

In Kenya, for example, notwithstanding the disproportionate success of the Kikuyu, an overwhelming percentage of the country's businesses—from car dealerships to the fish processing industry to the country's largest corporations, hotels, and banks—are operated by Indians. (A notable exception is the small-scale manufacturing sector, which is dominated by black Kenyans.) "A tiny handful of Asians control the entire economy," is the common, bitter view among black Kenyans. They "behave like colonizers," and own "most of the companies, the big companies." "The whole area is dominated by them. There is not one African. . . . They collude and make sure you go down."[23]

These statements reverberate with prejudice, and most Americans would probably be tempted to dismiss them as groundless stereotyping. Unfortunately, they hold more than a grain of truth. Kenya's roughly seventy thousand Indians, less than 2 percent of the population, are in fact dramatically more affluent as a group than the vastly more numerous black Kenyans around them. While Kikuyu run Kenya's tea and coffee plantations, "Asians" (as they are known) comprise most of the country's merchant class and, partly because of their international connections, benefit extremely disproportionately from globalization and market liberalization. They live, clustered and endogamous, in relatively upscale Nairobi neighborhoods like Westlands, where sari-clad women devouring the latest issue of *India Today* are driven around in Peugeots by black Kenyan chauffeurs. The Indian community has been a major source of funding for both the Kenyatta and Moi regimes. Most recently an unfortunate number of Indians have been willing to act as frontmen for Moi and his cronies. Moi currently co-owns extensive businesses with several Indian tycoons.[24]

It is often suggested—not only by Kenyans but also by Westerners—that Indian economic dominance in Kenya is due to their manipulation of the political process as opposed to any superior entrepreneurialism.[25] There is no doubt that some Indian businessmen are thickly mired in the corrupt cronyism of the Moi regime. The infamous "Goldenberg case," involving allegations that Indian tycoon Kamlesh Pattni siphoned off $400 million from Kenya's Central Bank with the connivance of government officials, has been in litigation since 1994. Nevertheless, the suggestion that political cronyism is the sole or even principal explanation of Indian economic dominance in Kenya overstates the case.

Unlike Africa's white settlers, who came over with guns and the might of Europe behind them, most of Kenya's Indians descend from "coolie" laborers imported by the British in the late 1800s to build the Uganda-Kenya railway. The descendants of these laborers worked as struggling artisans, clerks, or traders. They rose from destitution not through political favoritism, but rather despite discriminatory restrictions by colonial whites on one side and intense animosity from native Africans on the other. As early as 1924 there were a surprising number of Indian doctors and lawyers, almost all self-made. Indeed, in the same year Indians already controlled a stunning 80 to 90 percent of Kenya's commercial trade. Few of these early Indian businessmen had anything to do with politics.

Today in Kenya, not only Moi's Indian cronies are successful. Indian merchants, famous for their extreme thriftiness and tiny profit margins, dominate commerce at every level of society. The same is true in Dar es Salaam and Zanzibar in Tanzania, Uganda's capital Kampala, and Rwanda's capital Kigali.[26]

Throughout East Africa over the last two decades, the market reforms and globally oriented policies called for by the World Bank and IMF have starkly magnified the economic dominance of the region's insular and entrepreneurial Indian minorities. In Tanzania, for example, the turn from socialism to markets in the 1980s led to the reemergence of the Indian minority as a powerful economic force. Majority fears that these "outsiders" would "overwhelm and take over everything" led to bitter anti-Indian brutality. Similarly, Zambia's "very greedy" Indians, who were once accused of purchasing the body parts of mutilated African children, were targeted in bloody mass riots in the mid-1990s. In one furious participant's words, "Indians are the ones getting the chances. They've got millions and millions."[27]

In Kenya, after a failed military coup in 1982, the market-dominant Indian minority was confronted with the unleashed hatred of some of Kenya's 16 million African majority. Looters and rioters targeted Indian shops and businesses, smashed what could not be taken, and raped at least twenty Indian women. Today, with Kenya's Indian community prospering visibly from global markets—and several Indian billionaires in open cahoots with President Moi—anti-Indian hostility continues to grow, occasionally exploding in ethnic riots and mass violence. As African opposition leaders intensify their ethnic hatemongering—

Kenneth Matiba has promised to expel the Asians from Kenya if he becomes president[28]—Kenya's Indian minority finds itself uncomfortably
dependent on the corrupt and increasingly authoritarian President Moi.
Meanwhile, the U.S. government has for years been calling reflexively
for more markets and more democracy, not just in Kenya but in all of
Africa.

———————

Whereas Indians are known as the "Jews of East Africa," the Lebanese
are the preeminent market-dominant minority in West Africa, a term
that refers loosely to eleven countries along Africa's Atlantic coast
(Senegal, The Gambia, Guinea-Bissau, Guinea, Sierra Leone, Liberia,
Côte d'Ivoire, Ghana, Togo, Benin, and Nigeria) and three inland countries (Burkina Faso, Mali, and Niger).

Sierra Leone offers an example that is surprisingly parallel to the
Angolan tragedy. Most Americans have some knowledge of the brutal
rebel war in Sierra Leone, which has been called "the worst place on
earth" and "the darkest corner in Africa."[29] A few may know that the
rebels were chopping off children's limbs principally to gain control of
the country's lucrative diamond fields. But who ran Sierra Leone's diamond industry for years before the rebels took it over? A tiny handful of
principally Lebanese dealers.

The extent of Lebanese market dominance in Sierra Leone—historically and at present—is astounding. The first Lebanese (then called
"Syrians") arrived in Sierra Leone around 1895, probably at the port
city of Freetown, today the nation's capital. Unlike the Europeans, who
were unable or unwilling to penetrate the bush, the Lebanese headed
straight for the interior of the country. Before long Lebanese traders
could be found on every street corner peddling mirrors, beads, poma-
tum, iron pocketknives, jewelry, and cheap imported textiles to their
African customers.

The Lebanese did not just sell. They also bought produce (particularly rice and palm products) from African farmers, which they held until prices rose and then transported and sold to European firms. With
their profits from street trading, the Lebanese opened shops. Displacing
rival indigenous traders (mostly so-called Creoles, from the coast) was

easy. The Lebanese worked from dawn to dusk and had much lower overheads. They spent practically nothing on lodging, often sleeping on the same counter where meals were prepared and eaten. Moreover, because of their reputation for industriousness and commercial acumen, European firms were disposed to grant Lebanese long-term credit, an advantage they exploited to the hilt.[30]

By the 1920s, the Lebanese had established themselves as indispensable middlemen, linking European firms located in Freetown with African consumers and producers in the interior. By the 1930s, the Lebanese controlled the country's road transport industry. By the late 1950s, when Sierra Leone was still an English protectorate (independence would come in 1961), Lebanese middlemen dominated the two most lucrative sectors of the economy: agriculture and diamond dealing.[31]

The perception of Lebanese economic dominance at this time was vividly captured in Graham Greene's novel *The Heart of the Matter,* set in a "West African coastal town" that is almost certainly Freetown. (Greene worked for the British secret service in Sierra Leone during World War II.) The place is described by one English character to a newcomer as follows:

> "This is the original Tower of Babel," Harris said. "West Indians, Africans, real Indians, Syrians, Englishmen, Scotsmen in the Office of Works, Irish priests, French priests, Alsatian priests."
> "What do the Syrians do?"
> "Make money. They run all the stores up-country and most of the stores here. Run diamonds too."
> "I suppose there's a lot of that."
> "The Germans pay a high price."[32]

By the early 1990s, on the eve of civil war, the Lebanese—not even 1 percent of the population—dominated all the most productive sectors of the economy, including diamonds and gold, finance, retail, construction, and real estate. During the war, rebel forces—rumored to be funded by Liberia's president Charles Taylor, who in turn is said to be funded by a Lebanese Liberian businessman—took over the diamond mines for two years, with disastrous economic effects.[33] Although many Lebanese left during these years, the tiny, internationally connected Lebanese merchant community in Sierra Leone continues to be the country's most dynamic economic force.

As the country struggles to recover, black Sierra Leoneans' feelings toward the Lebanese are decidedly ambivalent. I had the good fortune recently of meeting with a group of five native Sierra Leoneans. The group's leader, whom I'll call Mr. Michaels, was a prominent Freetown lawyer and law professor. The other four were his adulating and exceptionally smart students. All were visiting New Haven as part of an exchange program sponsored by Yale Law School's human rights clinic. We met in a student coffee bar.

Filled with ghastly visions of amputees, child armies, and villagers burned alive, I was struck by the optimism of the Sierra Leoneans I met in New Haven. Putting on a good face for the outside world was clearly a priority.

After discussing at length the latest cease-fire with the Revolutionary United Front (RUF) and the ongoing U.N.-supervised truth and reconciliation process, I turned to the question of economics. "So, who's rich in your country?" I asked.

"Anyone who works hard," one student immediately answered. (English is the official language in Sierra Leone.)

"Not just corrupt people?"

"No, this is not Nigeria." They all laughed—except for Mr. Michaels, who had a lot of gravitas for a thirty-six-year-old.

"How is Sierra Leone's educational system?" I asked. According to the United Nations, nearly 70 percent of Sierra Leone's population is illiterate.

"We used to be the Athens of West Africa," they replied, almost collectively. "The best students from Kenya, Nigeria, everywhere in Africa came to study." Fourah Bay College, they reminded me several times, was established in 1827. "Of course, education has taken a nosedive since the war. But we are on the way back up again."

There was more optimism, on almost every issue. When I asked whether some groups in Sierra Leone prospered more than others, Mr.

Michaels shook his head, almost as if he disapproved of my question. "Tribalism is not a serious problem in Sierra Leone," he replied. "We are not like Kenya. We are all first Sierra Leoneans." Also from Mr. Michaels: "Sierra Leoneans are a very open-minded, hospitable people. We treat foreign investors better than our own kinsmen." He even said, although 75,000 Sierra Leoneans have been killed and 30,000 maimed in the civil war, "Our country is a land of opportunity. Our constitution bars any form of discrimination."

When I specifically mentioned the Lebanese, however, a more complex picture emerged. "What is the status of the Lebanese today?" I asked.

"Oh, they dominate business. They are very rich," was the uniform reply.

But the Lebanese no longer dominated the diamond industry?

No, the students explained. The diamond fields were now under the control of the United Nations. "Of course," they added, "the Lebanese are still smuggling."

Was there much resentment or discrimination against the Lebanese minority? I asked.

The students found this question exasperating. "You have it backwards," they replied. (Mr. Michaels kept quiet.) "It is the Lebanese who are not equitable toward Sierra Leoneans. They feel they are better. Their community is closed. They attend private Lebanese schools. These schools are very expensive, and almost no Sierra Leoneans can afford them."

But didn't Sierra Leone still have laws discriminating against Lebanese? I asked them about section 27(4) of their constitution, which essentially authorizes discrimination against "non-native" citizens of Sierra Leone, including ethnic Lebanese who were born in Sierra Leone and whose families have lived there for four generations.

"It is the Lebanese who discriminate against Sierra Leoneans," one of the students repeated while the others nodded. "For example, no Lebanese woman would ever marry a (black) Sierra Leonean man. I have never heard of a single case. Some Lebanese men do marry Sierra Leonean women, but those women are then treated as second-class citizens. Sometimes their children are even taken away from them!"

The same student then added: "But I like the Lebanese. I have many Lebanese friends, and I discuss these issues honestly with them."

Compared to the reviled soldiers of the RUF, the Lebanese today are in most Sierra Leoneans' relatively good graces; the psychotic brutality of the rebels in many ways unified the country. Nevertheless, in postwar Sierra Leone the Lebanese remain the country's principal commercial group, controlling access to most international capital. Although not all Lebanese are prosperous, there are several highly visible Lebanese tycoons, and as a group they are starkly disproportionately wealthy. Meanwhile, despite the optimism of the Sierra Leoneans I met in New Haven, 80 percent of Sierra Leoneans continue to live in desperate, disease-ridden poverty. In 2001, the United Nations listed Sierra Leone as the country with the lowest human development index ranking in the world, behind Bangladesh and Rwanda.[34]

A similar dynamic holds throughout West Africa, which includes some of the world's poorest countries. In The Gambia—which sits in the middle of Senegal—the tiny Lebanese community owns nearly all the stores and restaurants in the capital Banjul and controls the groundnut industry, the country's predominant cash crop. The Gambia's tourism industry is dominated by foreign investors, mainly from the United Kingdom (although Russians have recently come onto the scene). In relatively prosperous Côte d'Ivoire, the Lebanese (only 150,000 strong) and French multinationals jointly control the modern economy while 65 percent of the indigenous population of 14 million live in extreme rural poverty. Similarly, in Benin, Ghana, and Liberia, tiny numbers of Lebanese, along with a handful of European expatriates and foreign investors, dominate the most advanced, lucrative sectors of the private economy.

In many of these countries the Lebanese are often regarded as no different from the old colonialists. Living in isolated and heavily guarded villas, they zoom through the streets in fancy cars and glimmering motorcycles while most Africans drive second- and third-hand rusting mopeds. Outside of Sierra Leone many Lebanese businesses are of relatively recent vintage, owned by tycoons in Beirut who send their youngest children to cut their management teeth on the African investments. The youngsters play for a few years, indulging in various excesses, before returning to test their new skills in a business back home. Needless to say, none of this wins them much favor among the locals, even those who chauffeur and guard them.

Meanwhile, vast numbers of West Africans live so far outside the modern economy that privatization, trade liberalization, and foreign investment have virtually no effect on them whatsoever. Compared to the still largely traditional West African majorities around them, the Lebanese are far better educated (usually abroad or in private Lebanese schools) and have vastly superior access to capital and distribution networks. Sometimes collaborating with, sometimes competing against European investors, the market-dominant Lebanese are West Africa's link to, and principal beneficiaries of, global capitalism.

Colonialism and Market-Dominant Minorities

It is especially appropriate in the context of Africa to add a note about colonialism. From the British in India to the Portuguese in Angola to the Spaniards in upper Peru, all the Western colonizers were essentially market-dominant minorities: prosperous, more advanced outsider groups surrounded by generally impoverished and exploited indigenous masses. Indeed, the colonial period, with its enormous cross-border, cross-ocean capital flows, was in many ways the first modern wave of globalization. Like today's market-dominant minorities, the colonialists profited enormously and wildly disproportionately from international trade and what is sometimes misleadingly referred to as "colonial laissez-faire policies."

The evils of colonialism are well documented, particularly the shameless exploitation of natural resources and native labor. The arguable benefits of colonization are also well documented: the establishment of infrastructure and in some selective cases, education for the colonized populations.

The only point I wish to highlight here is that there are important links between colonialism and the phenomenon of market-dominant minorities. Not only were the colonialists themselves market-dominant minorities, but colonial divide-and-conquer policies favored certain groups over others, exacerbating ethnic wealth imbalances and fomenting group tensions. Indeed, in some cases these policies may have created "ethnic identities" and "ethnic differences" where they previously did not exist. Today, moreover, most starkly in southern Africa but also in Latin America and elsewhere, many market-dominant minorities are the descendants of former colonizers. Thus, the pervasive existence of market-dominant minorities throughout the developing world is one of colonialism's most overlooked and most destructive legacies.

Africa and Globalization

In the West, Africa is often seen as a vast continent of incomprehensible tribalism, endemic corruption, and almost intrinsic misery and violence. Cast in this way, Africa is irredeemable, its problems unique and uniquely insoluble.

But Africa fits solidly into a much larger global pattern; the same basic processes that are destabilizing Southeast Asia, Latin America, and Russia are operating in Africa, too. In Africa, as in virtually every other region of the non-Western world, market-dominant minorities control virtually all the most valuable and advanced sectors of the modern economy, monopolizing access to wealth and global markets, and producing seething, often unmobilized ethnic resentment and hatred among the indigenous African majorities around them.

To be sure, Africa also differs in important respects from other developing regions of the world. No other region is poorer or has Africa's complexity of tribal, linguistic, ethnic, and subethnic divisions. Africa was the last region to be decolonized. Corruption and looting have occurred in Africa on a scale unknown to the rest of the world. Ethnic violence and civil warfare—certainly not all involving market-dominant minorities—occur more frequently and with more intensity, or at any rate with more primitive weapons, than elsewhere.

Nevertheless, taking a global perspective, it becomes clear that Africa is no more exceptional or hopeless than other regions of the non-Western world. On the contrary, like Southeast Asia or Latin America—but probably to a greater extent—Africa is plagued with the problem of market-dominant minorities. As a result, economic liberalization, free markets, and globalization are aggravating Africa's extreme ethnic concentrations of wealth, provoking the same dangerous combination of frustration, envy, insecurity, and suppressed anger that can also be seen among the impoverished indigenous majorities of Indonesia, Russia, Guatemala, or Sri Lanka. What happens when democratization—or more accurately, immediate elections with universal suffrage—is added to this volatile mixture is the sobering subject of Part Two.

PART TWO

THE POLITICAL CONSEQUENCES OF GLOBALIZATION

Thus has the spread of global markets produced vast, inflammable ethnic wealth imbalances all over the world. But globalization has also had a crucial political dimension: namely, the American-led worldwide promotion of free elections and democratization.

That markets and democracy swept the world simultaneously is not a coincidence. After the fall of the Berlin Wall a common political and economic consensus emerged, not only in the West but to a considerable extent around the world. Markets and democracy, working hand in hand, would transform the world into a community of modernized, peace-loving nations. In the process, ethnic hatred, extremist fundamentalism, and other "backward" aspects of underdevelopment would be swept away.

The consensus could not have been more mistaken. Since 1989, the world has seen the proliferation of ethnic conflict, the rise of militant Islam, the intensification of group hatred and nationalism, expulsions, massacres, confiscations, calls for renationalization, and two genocides of magnitudes unprecedented since the Nazi Holocaust. The following four chapters will attempt to explain why.

In the last twenty years democratization has been a central, massively funded pillar of American foreign policy. In the 1990s the U.S. government spent approximately $1 billion on democracy initiatives for the post-socialist countries of Eastern Europe and the former Soviet Union. At the same time, America aggressively promoted democracy throughout Africa, Latin America, the Caribbean, and Southeast Asia. Haiti alone received more than $100 million in democracy aid after 1994. With the glaring exception of the Middle Eastern states, there is almost no developing or transitional country in the world where the United States has not actively championed political liberalization, majoritarian elections, and the empowerment of civil society. As of 2000, an estimated 63 percent of the world's population, in 120 countries, lived under democratic rule, a vast increase from even a decade ago.[1]

The global spread of democratization reflects the powerful assumption in Western policy and intellectual circles that markets and democracy go hand in hand. But in the numerous countries around the world with a market-dominant minority, just the opposite has proved true. Adding democracy to markets has been a recipe for instability, upheaval, and ethnic conflagration.

In countries with a market-dominant minority and a poor "indigenous" majority, the forces of democratization and marketization directly collide. As markets enrich the market-dominant minority, democratization increases the political voice and power of the frustrated majority. The competition for votes fosters the emergence of demagogues who scapegoat the resented minority, demanding an end to humiliation, and insisting that the nation's wealth be reclaimed by its "true owners." Thus as America toasted the spread of global elections through the 1990s, vengeful ethnic slogans proliferated: "Zimbabwe for Zimbabweans," "Indonesia for Indonesians," "Uzbekistan for Uzbeks," "Kenya for Kenyans," "Ethiopia for Ethiopians," "Yids out of Russia," "Hutu Power," "Serbia for Serbs," and so on. More moderate candidates, who disavow ethnic politics, are made to look like traitors. As popular hatred of the rich "outsiders" mounts, the result is an ethnically charged political pressure cooker in which some form of backlash is almost unavoidable.

This backlash typically takes one of three forms. The first is a backlash against markets, targeting the market-dominant minority's wealth. The second is a backlash against democracy by forces favorable to the market-dominant minority. The third and most ferocious kind of backlash is ethnic cleansing and other forms of majority-supported ethnic violence, as occurred most recently in the former Yugoslavia and Rwanda.

In other words, in the numerous countries around the world with a market-dominant minority, the simultaneous pursuit of free markets and democracy has led not to widespread peace and prosperity, but to confiscation, autocracy, and mass slaughter. Outside the industrialized West, these have been the wages of globalization.

CHAPTER 5

Backlash against Markets

*Ethnically Targeted Seizures
and Nationalizations*

In Zimbabwe, for three years now, furious mobs wielding sticks, axes, crossbows, iron bars, sharpened bicycle spokes, and AK-47 automatic rifles have invaded and ripped apart white-owned commercial farms. Usually by the hundreds, sometimes a thousand at a time, the invaders—with noms de guerre like "Hitler" and "Comrade Jesus"—ransack and destroy, hurling stones and gasoline bombs, singing revolutionary songs, drinking crates of looted beer, fighting over bread and tinned beef, beating, raping, abducting. "They were really like wild dogs," sobbed a terrified victim. After grabbing food, money, and clothing, they "grabbed four chickens, cut their throats and barbecued them as they watched the house they had set on fire burn down." Hospitals are flooded with victims of violence: resisters, black or white, faces smashed to a pulp, deep welts zigzagging down their backs, some shot at point-blank range.[1]

These assaults have not been spontaneous. Rather, they have been sponsored and encouraged by the Zanu-PF government of President Robert Mugabe, which has designated over three thousand farms, covering millions of acres and overwhelmingly white-owned, for confiscation. "We are taking our land," Mugabe has said. "We cannot be expected to buy back our land that was never bought from us, never bought from our ancestors!" To thousands of cheering supporters in December 2000, he declared, "Our party must continue to strike fear in the heart of the white man—our real enemy. The white man is not indigenous to Africa. Africa is for Africans. Zimbabwe is for Zimbabweans."When middle-aged Zimbabweans marched for peace, they were bludgeoned by police.[2]

Many have described the violence directed at Zimbabwe's white farmers and their black farmhands as "anarchy." But if this is anarchy, it is an anarchy born of democracy. Moreover, this "anarchy" follows a highly predictable, worldwide pattern. Democratization in Zimbabwe arrived with independence in 1980, in the face of a 1 percent former-colonizer minority owning 70 percent of the nation's best land.

Mugabe was a hero of Zimbabwe's revolutionary movement. In 1976 he declared, "in Zimbabwe, none of the white exploiters will be allowed to keep an acre of their land."That promise helped him sweep to over-whelming victory in the closely monitored 1980 elections, and repeat-ing that promise has helped him win every election since.[3] On taking power in 1980, Mugabe was as popular as Nelson Mandela was in newly postapartheid South Africa.

It is easy to demonize Mugabe. But in an ugly sense Mugabe has be-haved as a highly rational vote-seeking politician, and the recent vio-lence and seizures are direct products of the democratic process. In 1980, heavily pressured by Britain, Mugabe agreed to a ten-year mora-torium on major land reform: Zimbabwe's whites would be allowed to keep their vast estates in exchange for their tacit political support. After the deal expired in 1990, Mugabe stepped up his rhetoric about nation-alizing white-owned land, particularly whenever elections rolled around. Nevertheless, largely out of fear of losing foreign investment and World Bank and IMF loans, Mugabe redistributed almost no white farmland in the nineties.

Meanwhile, Mugabe's popularity waned. Complying with IMF free market austerity measures led to sharp price hikes, unemployment, and widespread disenchantment among Zimbabwe's poorest. These hard-ships were exacerbated by drought and massive crop failure. Crime rates increased. At the same time, Mugabe was plagued by one corrup-tion scandal after another. In the late 1990s, Zimbabwe's white farmers and corporations, anxious over Mugabe's intensifying calls for confisca-tion of their land and sensing weakness in his constituency, swung their support fully behind the free-market-oriented opposition Movement for Democratic Change (MDC). Along with the British government,

Zimbabwe's whites poured funding into the MDC.[4] Furious, Mugabe—called a "master manipulator" of the populace even by his detractors—responded as he always had: by playing the race card.

Starting in 1998, in anticipation of the 2000 parliamentary elections, Mugabe called for the immediate seizure of hundreds of commercial farms owned by the "sons of Britain" and "enemies of Zimbabwe." These calls were delivered at mass rallies and broadcast on national television. As the 2002 presidential elections approached, Mugabe intensified the hatemongering and expropriations. Subordinates were sent into white-owned tobacco fields to mobilize support: "Vote for Zanu PF and you will all be given land, farms, houses. Vote for Zanu PF and there will be peace, jobs, prosperity. Vote for MDC and there will be war. We will get our guns." Their slogans were: *"Down with the whites. Down with colonialism. Down with the MDC. Down with Britain."* The seizures began in earnest in 2000 and have accelerated since.[5]

The results have been catastrophic. Zimbabwe's currency, stock market, tourism sector, and foreign investment have all collapsed. Vast fields of tobacco, maize, sunflower, and sugar lay in charred ruins. Tens of millions of dollars in export earnings have literally gone up in flames. Aid agencies estimate that more than half a million people in Zimbabwe face starvation.

It is generally assumed in the Western media that the opposition MDC, which repudiated the violent land seizures, would have won the 2002 elections had they been free and fair. This might well be true: Mugabe set up far more polling stations in rural areas, where his support was strongest, than elsewhere, and there are plenty of reports of intimidation. On the other hand, African governments have uniformly praised the 2002 elections, which in fact were no more irregular than other elections in Africa that the West has deemed "free and fair."[6]

More important, the MDC was in fact, and was known to be, sponsored and funded by whites. "The problem with MDC," as one observer bluntly puts it, is that "[d]espite being led by trade unionist Morgan Tsvangirai, despite taking 57 seats in the election (most, but not all, of its candidates were black), despite appealing hugely to an urban black electorate, this is still a party designed for and by whites." At the MDC party headquarters in Harare last June, according to news reports, "the only black face visible was the security guard outside the front entrance. Within, it was a sea of pale political strategists, organizers, media spinners and volunteers."[7]

Even if MDC had won in 2002, pressures for the massive redistribution of white holdings would not have gone away. The land problem—specifically, the problem of a 1 percent market-dominant white minority controlling the country's best land in the form of three-thousand-acre commercial farms while most members of the black majority live in land-hungry poverty—would remain, ready for another firebrand politician to exploit, if not next year, then two or five or ten years down the road. Nor should it be forgotten that the harsh, free market, belt-tightening policies urged on Zimbabwe in the early 1990s by the United States, World Bank, and IMF created hardship among the nation's poorest, contributing to the mass popular frustrations that in turn made Mugabe's confiscatory campaigns all the more appealing. Zimbabwe's dilemma is that foreign investors and global capital flee whenever the country proposes to upset the white minority's landholdings—which is why, from 1980 to the late 1990s almost no land redistribution occurred. But placating the interests of the market-dominant minority and the international business community throws fat on Zimbabwe's democratic fire. Today's bloody confiscations and the resulting economic collapse are the direct product of the collision between free markets and democratic politics.

Meanwhile, in neighboring South Africa—which prides itself on its differences from Zimbabwe—five thousand people marched in July 2001 on Kempton Park near Pretoria. At the helm were leaders of the Pan Africanist Congress (PAC), a black opposition party that has campaigned with the slogan "One settler—one bullet!" since its inaugural meeting in 1989. ("Settlers" refers to whites.) The marchers, most of whom were homeless, demanded revolution and the right to occupy land. After years of black majority rule, they protested, they still had nothing to show for it. The PAC leaders egged them on, promising Mugabe-style invasions throughout the country. "This is just a small microcosm of what is potentially a time-bomb," declared the PAC secretary general. Furious, the Mbeki government evicted the squatters, condemning the PAC leaders as "dangerous demagogues" and "hypocrites and opportunists who will jump at the slightest opportunity to exploit the plight of our people."[8] But since the Kempton Park incident, President Mbeki has accelerated land redistribution efforts.

At the same time, the country's multibillion-dollar mining industry is facing what London's *The Times* recently called "[t]he biggest shake-up in South African ownership rights since the discovery of diamonds and gold in the [nineteenth] century." If signed into law, the new Minerals Development Bill, acrimoniously fought by the white-dominated mining industry, "will abolish private ownership of mineral rights, transfer title to the State, and grant it the sole power to award licenses for prospecting and mining." The Mbeki government denies charges that it is conducting "back-door nationalization." A number of influential whites agree that the scope of the bill is greatly exaggerated. Nevertheless, mining giants like De Beers and Anglo-American are deeply troubled about a clause in the bill that gives the minister for minerals and energy enormous discretionary power to "confiscate any property or any right for black empowerment purposes" without the right of appeal. The current minister, Phumzile Mlambo-Ngcuka, has publicly declared that "the twenty-first century is not going to allow a white-dominated mining industry to continue."[9]

————

The land seizures in Zimbabwe are part of a much larger global pattern. Throughout the non-Western world, wherever a small "outsider" market-dominant minority enjoys spectacular wealth in the midst of mass destitution, democratization has invariably produced tremendous popular pressures to "take back the nation's wealth" for its "true owners." This is true today from Indonesia to Russia to Venezuela, as I will address momentarily. But the same phenomenon—ethnically targeted confiscation—has been common ever since democratization came to the developing world in the early part of the twentieth century.

Understanding the History of Nationalization in the Developing World without Cold War Blinders

Throughout the twentieth century, bursts of nationalization repeatedly punctuated and damaged the economic growth of Asia, Africa, and Latin America. Most American economists and policymakers, steeped in

decades of Cold War dynamics, tend to assume that all these nationalizations were motivated by socialist or Communist thinking. In fact, however, nationalization in the Third World has always been far less an
expression of Communism than of popular frustration and vengeance
directed at a market-dominant minority.

With a few exceptions (China, Cuba, Vietnam), nationalization programs in Third World countries—unlike those in the former Soviet
bloc—never sought to eliminate private property or eradicate all economic classes. On the contrary, in the vast majority of countries in Asia,
Africa, and Latin America, nationalization programs have targeted explicitly and almost exclusively the assets and industries of hated market-
dominant minorities.

Pre-1989 examples of nationalizations targeting a market-dominant
minority are so numerous that I'll give only a few illustrations here. In
newly independent Indonesia, President Sukarno's sweeping nationalizations in the 1950s and 1960s targeted both the market-dominant Dutch
and, very explicitly, the market-dominant Chinese. Indeed, through nationalization and other anti-Chinese measures, Sukarno "indigenized"
key sectors of the economy—finance, mining, batik, rice, import-
export, industry—all formerly dominated by Europeans and Chinese.
Although Sukarno's "Guided Democracy" was in many ways undemo-
cratic, his anti-Chinese nationalizations were overwhelmingly and fever-
ishly supported by the *pribumi* majority. Indeed, most indigenous
Indonesians thought Sukarno was "too soft" on the Chinese.[10]

In Sri Lanka, which has maintained a troubled parliamentary democracy for nearly half a century, the disproportionate economic power of
the Tamil minority had produced bitter resentment among the (largely
Buddhist) Sinhalese majority by the 1950s. Solomon Bandaranaike—
Oxford-educated and a consummate politician—capitalized on this ethnic resentment. Converting from Roman Catholicism to Buddhism, he
swept to electoral victory in 1956 by scapegoating Tamils and championing the cause of "Sinhala Only." After Bandaranaike's assassination in
1959, his wife Sirimavo became prime minister, again through democratic elections. Once in office, Mrs. Bandaranaike began radically nationalizing land and industry. These nationalizations had nothing to do
with socialism; they did not affect Sinhalese business interests. Rather

their express purpose was to elevate the "true" Sri Lankans over Tamils, Christians, and other ethnic minorities.[11]

In postindependence Burma, U Nu, the country's first democratically elected prime minister, openly sought to "Burmanize" the economy through nationalization. "The wealth of Burma has been enjoyed firstly by big British capitalists, next the Indian capitalists, and next the Chinese capitalists," U Nu declared in a famous tract from 1949. "Burmans are at the bottom, in poverty, and have to be content with the leftover and the chewed-over bones and scraps from the table of foreign capitalists." In the sixties and seventies, Gen. Ne Win's expropriations of over fifteen thousand commercial enterprises again expressly targeted Westerners and the despised market-dominant Indian and Chinese minorities.[12]

In Pakistan, Zulfikar Ali Bhutto won the support of the impoverished masses (as well as members of his own, landowning zamindaar class) through rousing public speeches that accused "Twenty-Two Families"—almost all *Mohajir* immigrants from India—of stealing the nation's wealth. It was intolerable, he campaigned, that Pakistan's indigenous majority (comprising four major ethnic groups: the Punjabi, Sindhi, Baluchi, and Pashtuns) should remain at the mercy of a tiny minority of "outsider" *Mohajir* industrialists and bureaucrats.

After sweeping to power, Bhutto's "socialist" Pakistan People's Party showed itself to be not socialist at all, but deeply ethnonationalist. Bhutto left almost completely intact the massive estates of the wealthy Sindhi zamindaar families, including his own. As late as the 1970s the Bhutto family's own estate was measured in terms of miles rather than acres, extending across several successive train stops. Nor did Bhutto ever try to nationalize all private business. Instead, Bhutto aggressively targeted firms owned by the market-dominant ethnic *Mohajirs*. Thus, in January 1972, along with a few Punjabi businesses, Bhutto nationalized thirty-one heavy industrial firms, representing almost all of the hated Twenty-Two Families' industrial wealth. Bhutto's 1974 nationalizations of banking and insurance attacked any remaining *Mohajir* holdings. Through ethnically targeted nationalizations, Bhutto successfully undercut the *Mohajir* minority's stark dominance of Pakistan's industrial and commercial sectors.[13]

The nationalization movements that swept across Latin America in the first half of the twentieth century present a somewhat more complicated picture. Nationalizing politicians in Latin America undoubtedly mobilized mass support for their movements with class-based appeals and Marxist rhetoric. Nevertheless, the conventional wisdom that sees these nationalization movements as solely or even principally Marxist overlooks the core of ethnic nationalism that often gave them force.

Nationalization in Latin America was in a surprising number of cases fueled by the desire to reclaim the wealth of the nation for its true, ethnically defined owners. In country after country, revolutionary leaders sought to reverse the historical obsession with white superiority, either by glorifying Amerindian blood or by celebrating "mixed-bloodedness." Indeed, in the early twentieth century the resentment engendered by Latin American racism, always interwoven with the struggle between rich and poor, was a powerful engine of revolutionary change throughout the region.

In Bolivia in 1951, for example, Victor Paz Estenssoro, head of the revolutionary party Movimiento Nacionalista Revolucionario (MNR), won the presidential elections by mobilizing the largely mestizo middle class with slogans like, "The land to the Indians, the mines to the State." Properly terrified, the distinctly "non-Indian" mining elite supported a military takeover. After the MNR recaptured power in a bloody coup in 1952, one of Estenssoro's first acts was to extend universal suffrage and free education to the Indian majority, consciously seeking to reverse the ethnically based disdain that had imbued Bolivian society at every level since the colonial period. The government then nationalized all major mines and expropriated six thousand vast estates from the "illustrious-blooded" hacendados, redistributing them in family-size plots among the landless Amerindian majority.[14]

But revolutionary as they were, Bolivia's nationalizations were not really Communist: They did not seek to abolish private property in any thoroughgoing fashion. Rather, they were majority-supported confiscations directed at a market-dominant minority. The nationalization movements in Mexico, Peru, and elsewhere similarly targeted, along with "foreign imperialists," the wealthy "white" elite with their links to foreign capital and vast latifundia landholdings.[15]

There are many more examples, from all parts of the developing world. Not all nationalizing leaders were democratically elected (although many were). But virtually all were supported with wild enthusiasm by the indigenous majority when they expropriated the riches of the market-dominant minority.

———

After 1989, many proclaimed that nationalization was a thing of the past. The Soviet Union had fallen, Communism had been discredited, and developing countries would never again be moved to nationalize. Unfortunately, all this is true only if nationalization in the developing world genuinely rested on Communist ideology. But as I have tried to show, this is not the case. To a far greater extent than has been recognized, nationalization movements in the developing world have been fueled by popular resentment among abjectly poor majorities against market-dominant minorities. Thus it should be no surprise that nationalization and confiscation persist today, even after the collapse of the former Soviet Union. Indeed, almost everywhere market-dominant minorities exist, post-1989 democratization has generated a volatile combination of anti-market sentiment and ethnic scapegoating. As a result, in a striking number of countries, even as markets triumphantly swept the world in the 1990s, a backlash of nationalization and confiscation began.

These nationalizations and confiscations have been anti-market, but only in a limited sense. They target not the institution of private property itself, but rather the wealth of a hated ethnic minority. They are based not on an ideal of a Communist utopia, but rather on a deluded vision in which the indigenous masses somehow step into the capitalist shoes of the minority so that they, "the true owners of the nation," can be the market's prosperous beneficiaries. In Zimbabwe, the ongoing mass seizures of white-owned farmland are hardly motivated by socialist thinking. On the contrary, these confiscations are quintessential expressions of ethnic nationalism directed at a deeply resented "outsider" market-dominant minority. The recent anti-Chinese confiscations in newly democratic Indonesia provide another vivid illustration.

Post-Suharto Indonesia:
Markets Plus Democracy Equals Ethnic Confiscation

As discussed earlier, market-oriented policies in Indonesia during the 1980s and 1990s led to the astounding economic dominance of the country's 3 percent Chinese minority along with widespread, seething hostility among the *pribumi* majority against both General Suharto and the country's "greedy Chinese locusts."

After Suharto's fall, Indonesians were euphoric. After the words "free and fair elections" hit the U.S. headlines, Americans were euphoric. Democratic elections, it was thought, would finally bring to Indonesia the kind of peace and legitimacy perfect for sustaining free markets. Indeed, Thomas Friedman has suggested that this is "one of the real lessons of globalization's first decade"—that democratic processes give the public a sense of ownership in market reforms, thus making the majority more patient and tolerant of the inevitable "pain of globalization reforms."[16]

That's not what happened in Indonesia. The fall of Suharto's autocracy was accompanied by an eruption of ferocious anti-Chinese violence in which delirious, mass-supported Muslim mobs burned, looted, and killed anything Chinese, ultimately leaving two thousand people dead. (Many of the dead were non-Chinese Indonesians trapped in blazing shopping malls.) Overnight democratization in the midst of all this naturally gave rise to ethnic scapegoating and demagoguery by opportunistic, vote-seeking politicians. The Islamic right, recalls Clifford Geertz, attacked the frontrunner candidate Megawati Sukarnoputri "as not really a Muslim but some sort of Javanist Hindu, beholden to Christians and Chinese. . . ." Megawati, meanwhile, assured frenzied crowds that she was speaking daily with her dead father, Indonesia's nationalist hero and founding president, Sukarno.[17]

Tarred by having been Suharto's vice president, presidential candidate and interim president Bucharuddin Jusuf Habibie played brilliantly on both anti-market and anti-Chinese sentiment. To screaming crowds, Habibie and his right-hand man Adi Sasono preached their vision of a New Deal for Indonesia: a true "people's economy" to be achieved by breaking up Chinese conglomerates and redistributing them to "the long suffering masses" in the form of indigenous cooperatives. "It's a matter of economic justice," Sasono declared. "One race cannot control 90 percent of the economy!" yelled adulating supporters.[18]

While president, Habibie expropriated the Chinese-controlled rice industry by canceling rice distribution contracts with hundreds of ethnic Chinese businessmen and awarding them instead to members of the Indonesian majority—most of whom hadn't the foggiest idea what to do. The results were disastrous, part of a food crisis in which tens of millions of Indonesians were at one time reportedly eating only one meal a day. The new state-run rice cooperatives were immediately saturated with corruption, inefficiency, and scandal (one official was accused of trying to export illegally nineteen hundred tons of rice to Malaysia while his own constituents were starving). Predictably, indigenous officials and businessmen began to secretly subcontract work out to Chinese traders again. Still, the anti-Chinese and anti-market campaign rhetoric continued—and didn't stop until most of the wealthiest Chinese Indonesians had left the country, along with $40 to $100 billion of Chinese-controlled capital. It was only when the World Bank and IMF realized that this capital was gone that they started to be concerned about ethnic conflict in Southeast Asia and to urge the Indonesian government to come to an "accommodation" with the country's Chinese business community.[19]

Today—as a result of what one Jakarta-based consultant calls "Asia's largest nationalization since the Communist takeover of China in 1949"—the Indonesian government sits on roughly $58 billion in industrial assets consisting of equity stakes in over two hundred companies ranging from automobile production to cement. Most of these nationalized assets were formerly owned by Chinese tycoons. For several years now these nationalized companies—once immensely productive Chinese "money making machines" as one government official described them—have simply stagnated while the country descends further into frustrated poverty. (As of last year, a frightening 40 million *pribumi* Indonesians were unemployed or underemployed.)[20]

Although there may have been economic justifications for the state takeovers of Indonesia's failing, corruption-soaked banks, it is telling that most of the vast nationalized holdings have not been reprivatized despite the availability of buyers, the ongoing massive economic waste, and the government's repeated assurances that the assets will be sold. Apart from bureaucratic incompetence and infighting, the explanation is that the potential buyers are typically ethnic Chinese or foreign investors, and the government has been paralyzed by fear that sales to such groups will trigger another violent nationalist backlash. As a result, Indonesia is "now like a communist country," one observer recently lamented, "where the government owns, controls or manages almost 80 percent of productive assets." Four years after Suharto's fall, intense ethnic resentment and xenophobia continue to drive Indonesian economic policy. Among the *pribumi* majority there is a pervasive dread that ethnic Chinese and other "foreigners" will "swoop in like vultures" to carry off the nation's resources. These "vultures" include the hated ethnic Chinese Salim Group, which is rumored to be making a rebid for its former companies from Singapore.[21]

Anti-Semitism and Nationalization in Democratic Russia

In Russia, economic and political liberalization has unleashed widespread—and in parts of the country like Cossack-dominated Krasnodar, virulent—anti-Semitism. As chapter 3 discussed, many of the Yeltsin government's most reviled market reformers—including "shock therapy" champion Yegor Gaidar and "privatization tsar" Anatoly Chubais—are well known to be part Jewish. Moreover, the principal beneficiaries of Russia's chaotic transition to capitalism were also disproportionately Jewish.

To repeat, it would be preposterous to suggest that Russian anti-Semitism is caused by either markets or democracy. Anti-Semitism has poisoned Russia since long before 1989. Over a century ago, for example, Fyodor Dostoyevsky, in his self-published magazine *A Writer's Diary,* blamed the "Yids" for their exploitation of the noble Russian peasant:

And so the [tsar] liberator came and liberated the native People [the serfs]; and who do you think were the first to fall upon them as on a victim? Who was foremost in taking advantage of their weaknesses? Who, in their eternal pursuit of gold, set about swindling them? Who at once took the place, wherever they could manage it, of the former landowners—with the difference that though the landowners may have thoroughly exploited people, they still tried not to ruin their peasants, out of self-interest, perhaps, so as not to wear out the labor force, whereas the Jew doesn't care about wearing out Russian labor; he takes what he can and he's gone."[22]

The point, however, is that the combined effect of post-perestroika marketization and democratization has been to galvanize anti-Semitism in Russia (as well as in Ukraine, Belarus, and the Baltic republics) in highly predictable fashion. Markets have generated starkly visible Jewish wealth—*Forbes* in 2002 listed Jewish oligarchs Mikhail Khodorkovsky, Roman Abramovich, and Mikhail Friedman as Russia's three richest billionaires, with Vladimir Potanin in fourth place—while democracy has made anti-Semitism a political force with a strength not seen in Russia since Stalin.

Since perestroika, the new democratic rights of free speech and free association have given rise to eighty nationalist political parties and organizations, including three that have openly adopted neo-Nazi symbols and rhetoric. At the same time, politicians all over the country, including powerful elected officials, publicly engage in anti-Semitic baiting.

In October 1998, for example, Gen. Albert Makashov, a Communist Party representative in the Russian Parliament, accused Jews of ruining the country's economy. "Who is to blame?" railed Makashov in recorded testimony before the Duma. "The executive branch, the bankers, the mass media are to blame. Usury, deceit, corruption, and thievery are flourishing in the country. That is why I call the reformers Yids." A "Yid," he elaborated in an editorial in the newspaper *Zavtra,* is "a bloodsucker feeding on the misfortunes of other people. They drink the blood of the indigenous peoples of the state; they are destroying industry and agriculture." Makashov subsequently led two fiery rallies in which he shouted, "I will round up all the Jews and send them to the next world!" A few months later, Viktor Ilyukhkin, Communist chairman of the

Russian Parliament's security committee, blamed Jews in Yeltsin's government for effecting "a genocide against the Russian people."

When asked by Yeltsin to censure Makashov and Ilyukhkin, Gennadi Zyuganov, head of Russia's still powerful Communist Party, endorsed them instead. In a letter to the Ministry of Justice and the national security chief, Zyuganov declared that Zionism is among the "most aggressive imperialist circles striving for world domination." "Communists . . . rightly ask how it can be that key positions in a number of economic sectors were seized by representatives of one ethnic group. They see how control over most of the electronic media—which are waging a destructive campaign against our fatherland and its morality, language, culture and beliefs—is concentrated in the hands of those same individuals." Zyuganov has also said, "Too many people with strange sounding family names mingle in the internal affairs of Russia."

Anti-Semitism is moderate in Moscow compared to other parts of Russia. "At least in Moscow there's some regulation," explained the distressed leader of the local Jewish Association in the Siberian city of Novosibirsk, where a synagogue was recently vandalized and the name of the neofascist group, Russian National Unity, painted on the walls. Aleksandr Barkashov, the leader of the group, subsequently told a rally in Yekaterinburg (Sverdlovsk) that he was changing the name of his organization to "Movement Against the Jews." Anti-Semitism is probably most intense in Krasnodar, a city along Russia's southern border that is home to numerous Cossacks. Since his coalition's landslide election in 1996, Communist-Nationalist governor Nikolai Kondratenko has openly spewed anti-Semitic hatred. "What is the result of Zionism?" boomed Kondratenko's deputy governor in 1998. "The result is the collapse of Russia. Native Russians never would have allowed all these reforms to happen." And the governor himself recently proclaimed to cheering crowds: "Why haven't we revolted against that scum, a bunch of people for whom Russia, Russians, patriotism, the land of Russia is something alien? Their policy is the losing one, and those who will continue torturing Russia will burn more than just their tongues."[23]

During Russia's 1998 election campaign, calls for renationalization of the oligarchs' holdings—widely viewed as "stolen" from the Russian people—were everywhere.[24] Like Yeltsin before him, Vladimir Putin most likely would not have won the presidential election without the oligarchs' massive funding and media support. Not surprisingly, Putin did not campaign on a renationalization or anti-Semitic platform. Once in power, however, Putin made sweeping promises to "bring the house in order" and "move the oligarchs away from power," gaining popularity with every new attack on the oligarchs.

In particular, Putin recently turned on Jewish media moguls Vladimir Gusinsky and Boris Berezovsky. In a murky corporate coup in 2001, the Kremlin-controlled natural gas monopoly Gazprom took over Gusinsky's independent NTV station, which had made the mistake of poking fun at the First Lady. Then, in January 2002, Putin pulled the plug on Berezovsky's TV-6 station—cutting off a show in midsentence—leaving the Kremlin with a monopoly on television for the first time since the collapse of the Soviet Union. Berezovsky's unfavorable television coverage of the *Kursk* submarine disaster the previous year had infuriated the Kremlin.[25]

Officially, Putin's shutdown of Berezovsky's TV-6 station was supported by a court ruling that the station was bankrupt. Nevertheless, even Putin's supporters concede that his confiscation techniques in both cases—involving intimidation, dozens of armed secret service raids, and mysterious backroom deals—were highly suspect. In the West, Putin's actions provoked a firestorm of criticism that he was "destroying free speech," "silencing critics," and returning to "Soviet-style terror." In Russia, however, negative reaction has been much more muted while many have openly supported Putin's moves against the oligarchs. Although Putin himself has never engaged in anti-Semitic rhetoric, he is no doubt aware that significant sectors of the population believe that they "have been impoverished at the hands of rich Jews" and that, as a result, his confiscations of Gusinsky's and Berezovsky's media holdings would generate little popular opposition.[26]

It is important to stress that President Putin himself has not adopted anti-Semitic rhetoric and that he has also targeted non-Jewish businessmen in Russia. The fact remains that the three wealthiest people in Russia today are Jewish oligarchs Khodorkovsky, Abramovich, and Friedman. With Gusinsky and Berezovsky now in exile, hatemongering demagogues waiting in the wings, and draft nationalization bills constantly being debated in the Duma, these oligarchs are increasingly at Putin's mercy. Meanwhile, the new political party headed by Yeltsin's former defense minister, Gen. Igor Rodionov, if approved, will have as its explicit policy agenda reclaiming from Russia's "Zionists" the wealth they "looted" from "the Russian people."[27]

Anti-market Backlash in Venezuela

In Venezuela, a small minority of cosmopolitan "whites"—including descendants of the original Spanish colonizers as well as more recent European immigrants—historically dominated both the country's economy and its politics. As elsewhere in Latin America, this minority is very closely knit. As one Venezuelan jokingly put it, "In Venezuela there are more boards of directors than there are directors."

But in 1998, the Venezuelan people—respecting their democratic institutions and to the horror of the United States—elected as president the wildly anti-market former army paratrooper Hugo Chavez. Like President Alejandro Toledo in Peru, Chavez swept to his landslide victory on a wave of ethnically tinged populism. Demanding "a social revolution," Chavez aroused into impassioned political consciousness Venezuela's destitute majority, who make up 80 percent of the population, and who, like "the Indian from Barinas"—as Chavez refers to himself—have "thick mouths" and visibly darker skin than most of the nation's elite. "He is one of us," wept cheering, growth-stunted washerwomen, maids, and peasants. "We've never had another president like that before."[28]

According to Moisés Naím, former Venezuelan Minister of Trade and Industry and now editor of *Foreign Policy*, "What differentiates Hugo Chavez from his political rivals" is "his enthusiastic willingness to tap into collective anger and social resentments that other politicians failed to see, refused to stoke, or more likely, had a vested interest in not exacerbating." Whereas Peru's Toledo reached out to his country's elite, Chavez deliberately fomented class conflict, lacing it with ethnic resentment. Chavez, writes Naím, "broke with the tradition of multiclass political parties and the illusion of social harmony that prevailed in Venezuela for four decades."

Like Bolivia's Amerindian rebel leader Mallku and Ecuador's Villavicencio, Chavez generated mass support by attacking Venezuela's "rotten", largely white elites. "Oligarchs tremble," he campaigned to great, agitated crowds. "The plan of battle" was to "take every piece of space by assault." Chavez's platform could not have been more anti-market. He relentlessly attacked foreign investors and Venezuela's business elite, calling them "enemies of the people," "squealing pigs," and rich "degenerates." He lashed out at "savage capitalism," describing Cuba as "a sea of happiness." "I will bring about the end of the *latifundia* system," he repeatedly declared, "or stop calling myself Hugo Chavez." Over and over, Chavez has said that he is not proposing "anything like Communism." Rather, he intends "urgently" to expropriate the "idle" land of the agrarian elite and redistribute it to "the Venezuelan people."[29]

After taking power, Chavez changed the country's name to the Bolivarian Republic of Venezuela, in honor of the revolutionary hero Simón Bolívar. He passed a new constitution, hailing it as the most democratic in the world. The right to food, he proclaimed, was more important than corporate profit. Displaying distinctly autocratic tendencies, Chavez disbanded the "worm-eaten" Congress and Supreme Court. He stopped privatization of the oil sector, "outlawed" large landowners, and guaranteed free education and worker benefits for "housewives."[30] He "decreed" almost fifty anti-market laws. In 2001, Chavez threatened to nationalize all banks that refuse—in accordance with one of Chavez's new laws—to grant credit to small farmers and small businesses. "Not only can we nationalize any bank," declared Chavez, "any banker who does not abide by the law could go to jail."[31]

Chavez swept to electoral victory not by offering any affirmative economic policy. Rather, in Naím's words, he "catered to the emotional needs of a deeply demoralized nation," employing an "inchoate but very effective folksy mixture of Bolivarian sound-bites, Christianity, collectivist utopianism, baseball and indigenous cosmogony, peppered with diatribes against the oligarchy, neoliberalism, foreign conspiracies and globalization." That Chavez would even try to play the ethnic card—and proudly describe himself as "the Indian from Barinas"—is remarkable. Unlike Bolivia or Ecuador, Venezuela has only a tiny Amerindian population and, despite the glaring disproportionate whiteness of the wealthy minority, many middle- and upper-class Venezuelans will still insist that their country has "no ethnic divisions" and that to see otherwise is to impose a lens of North American racism. Ironically, given Chavez's constant railing against globalization, it was one of globalization's major components—democracy—that allowed Chavez to convert generations of bitterness and frustration into a powerful political engine. Stirred to political consciousness by the demagogic Chavez, Venezuela's 80 percent dark-skinned majority, most of whom live below the poverty line, voted for a leader whose nationalization and other anti-market policies seem to Westerners utterly irrational.

Unfortunately, democratization in Venezuela ran smack against free markets. Chavez's antibusiness policies have had a devastating effect on the economy. As soon as Chavez took office, Venezuela's wealthy whites, fearful of confiscation, whisked away more than $8 billion out of the country, mostly to the United States. As Chavez's incompetent state interventions accelerated, foreign investment fled. The real battle, however, occurred in the oil industry, which generates 80 percent of Venezuela's export revenues and represents the country's lifeblood. Although technically state-owned, Venezuela's oil company PDVSA has for years been professionally run by members of the business elite—"oligarchs," in Chavez's view. In spring 2002, Chavez fired PDVSA's president, Gen. Guaicaipuro Lameda, widely admired by foreign investors for his efficient steering of the company. In Lameda's place, Chavez installed a radical left-wing academic with little business experience. Chavez also appointed five new left-leaning directors to PDVSA's board. PDVSA's blue-blooded senior management fought back. Chavez retaliated.[32]

The coup that momentarily deposed Chavez in April 2002 was a classic effort led by a market-dominant minority to retaliate against a democratically elected government threatening their wealth and power. Although supported at first by trade union leaders and skilled labor, the regime that was briefly installed to replace Chavez "looked like it had come from the country club." Interim president Pedro Carmona, a wealthy white, was head of the country's largest business association. Union representatives were completely excluded from positions of authority. "All of them oligarchs," scoffed a dark-skinned street vendor, referring to the country's wealthy white minority. "Couldn't they have appointed one person like us?" The new leadership was "pure business"; its exclusion of anyone but "country club" elites as well as its attempt to dissolve the democratically elected national congress turned even supporters of the coup against it.[33]

To the dismay of the Bush administration, which hailed the coup as a "victory for democracy," the high-handed actions of the Carmona regime combined with Chavez's still-considerable support among Venezuela's poor majority returned Chavez to power with stunning speed. But in many cases, as the next chapter will show, market-dominant minorities have much more success in their collisions with poor, democratic majorities.

CHAPTER 6

Backlash against Democracy

Crony Capitalism and Minority Rule

W hen a poor democratic majority collides with a market-dominant minority, the majority does not always prevail. Instead of a backlash against the market, there is a backlash against democracy. Often, this antidemocracy backlash takes the form of "crony capitalism": corrupt, symbiotic alliances between indigenous leaders and a market-dominant minority. For the global marketplace, this is a cozy solution. The indigenous regime protects the market-dominant minority's wealth and businesses. In turn, the World Bank and IMF supply loans. In the short run the result is a boom in foreign investment, economic growth, and riches for the rulers and their cronies. At the same time, however, the country's inner furies begin to boil. Sooner or later—and it is usually sooner—the situation explodes.

In the late 1990s, members of Sierra Leone's rebel force, the Revolutionary United Front (RUF), often gave their victims a choice. Farmers could either rape their own daughters or have both hands cut off. Young girls could either have their fathers shot or their mothers and sisters burned alive. The mass butchery suffered by the people of Sierra Leone is most startling because children perpetrated much of it. High on cocaine, children as young as six wielded machetes, following orders to chop off fingers, hands, arms, legs, and ears. In the January 1999 invasion of Freetown—known as Operation No Living Thing among the RUF—the rebels first killed all the patients in the hospitals to make room for their own injured. They then slaughtered an estimated six thousand civilians, raped thousands of women, and hacked off the limbs of thousands more. The central villains behind the mass murders and mutilations include RUF leader Foday Sankoh and Liberian president Charles Taylor.[1]

In the West we tend to think of Sierra Leone as a country where modernization and globalization have not yet penetrated. But Sierra Leone reached this state of savagery in part as a result of modernization and globalization. Sierra Leone was a classic case of the collision between markets and democracy in the face of a market-dominant minority—here, the entrepreneurial Lebanese, who for decades controlled the country's diamond mines. There was a backlash against democracy, an extended period of crony capitalism, and then the inevitable explosion.

Sierra Leone attained independence in 1961. By that time the Lebanese already controlled most of the country's modern commerce, including the diamond trade, and were the objects of enormous popular resentment. In a familiar pattern, there followed a period of anti-Lebanese, anti-market policies in the name of the indigenous African majority. Restrictions were placed on Lebanese economic activity, and persons of "European or Asiatic origin," which included Lebanese, were denied citizenship. "Africanization" and nationalization were in the air, and both markets and the Lebanese, less than 1 percent of the population, were in trouble.[2]

The decisive backlash against democracy came in the 1970s, when the populist president Siaka Stevens, a mild socialist in his early years, did an about-face. He decided that capitalism—more specifically, piggybacking on Lebanese wealth and entrepreneurialism—was the best way to outmaneuver his political rivals and cash in on his country's enormous diamond resources. An alliance with the Lebanese, however, was not an option democratically available. In 1971, therefore, Stevens declared a "state of emergency," stamped out political competition, and formed a shadow alliance with five economically powerful but politically vulnerable Lebanese diamond dealers who had extensive access to international markets. Stevens also invited Guinean troops into the country to protect his government from political opposition. In 1978, Stevens officially turned Sierra Leone into a one-party state.[3]

The most powerful of Stevens's Lebanese cronies was Jamil Said Mohammed. Technically "Afro-Lebanese"—his father was Lebanese, his mother was African—the wily Mohammed has always been seen as "basically Lebanese," perhaps because he was educated in Lebanon, married to a Lebanese wife, and steeped in Lebanese contacts. Mohammed began his climb to multimillions by buying a truck for $500 and transporting rice, ginger, and groundnuts to the country's commercial centers. During Sierra Leone's 1955 diamond boom, Mohammed, along with a handful of other Lebanese, won the race for instant riches, eventually operating as a dealer in the "diamond towns" of Sefadu, Yengema, Nimikoro, and Njaiama. By the late 1970s, after a brief jail sentence for diamond smuggling, Mohammed was one of the five wealthiest men in the country. His business interests included not just diamonds but also gold, fishing, salt, soap, cement, banking and financing, construction, import-export, and, last but not least, explosives.[4]

The deal struck between President Stevens and Mohammed and four other Lebanese businessmen was classic. Stevens protected the Lebanese politically, and in exchange the Lebanese—who had business networks in Europe, the Soviet Union, and the United States—worked economic wonders, generating enormous profits and kicking back handsome portions to Stevens and other high-ranking indigenous officials. Stevens and key cabinet ministers also made sure that the most valuable government contracts were awarded to the Lebanese, who of course returned the favors. (Mohammed's London office was decorated with a life-size photograph of President Stevens.) By the early 1980s the influence wielded by the five Lebanese was so great that they were referred to as Sierra Leone's "invisible government." Indeed, according to a recent Canadian study, Mohammed was seen as the country's "co-President" during the seventies and eighties. Virtually nothing from the country's vast diamond wealth went to Sierra Leone's indigenous majority.

Needless to say, these policies did not endear President Stevens or the Lebanese to the Sierra Leoneans, who saw a handful of "outsiders" apparently siphoning off the wealth of the nation at the expense of the country's development. After Stevens, other autocrats followed, each one in turn complying with Western advisers, courting foreign investment, and allying themselves flagrantly with the Lebanese plutocrats. It was widely believed that these plutocrats paid no taxes and lived opulent lives while the majority of Sierra Leoneans lived in indescribable poverty. Hardship among Sierra Leonean citizens markedly increased in 1989 and 1990, as a result of what IMF negotiators called "bold and decisive" free market measures. To control inflation, the IMF required that subsidies to the general public be phased out. As a result, rice prices rose 180 percent and oil prices rose 300 percent, leaving ordinary Sierra Leoneans in desperate straits. Many frustrated Sierra Leoneans blamed their plight on the wealthy Lebanese. By the early 1990s, popular resentment and alienation were widespread, particularly in the provinces where most of the diamond mines were located. Conditions were ripe for the anarchy that followed.[5]

RUF leader Sankoh found no difficulty recruiting soldiers from the hungry, disaffected, and angry teenagers in provincial areas. He promised them jobs, free education, and a mission. "That was all the motivation they needed," as James Traub has put it.[6] The RUF movement was by no stretch socialist or populist; it had no ideology. It was a blatant grab for power and wealth, mobilizing foot soldiers from a destitute, demoralized, 70 percent illiterate provincial population that for years had seen the nearby diamond mines generating fantastic wealth for a handful of Lebanese cronies and corrupt politicians.

In the years of chaos and carnage that followed, an estimated 75,000 were killed and another 4.5 million displaced. The Lebanese plutocrats—their diamond mines taken over by rebels—were the first to leave. The rest of the tiny Lebanese community soon followed. Sierra Leone's Lebanese population dropped from 20,000 to 2,000 as of 1999.[7] Some have since returned.

Needless to say, these events cannot be blamed on markets, democracy, or globalization. The reign of terror that destroyed Sierra Leone between 1991 and 1999 was the deliberate handiwork of vicious, self-interested butchers and thieves. Nevertheless, it is a mistake not to see how markets, democracy, and a market-dominant minority interacted to make this scenario possible. Since at least 1973, Sierra Leone's indigenous leaders suppressed democracy to go into cahoots with a deeply resented market-dominant minority. Despite the conditions of enormous instability that resulted, global markets generally approved of these arrangements. At the same time, the pro-market austerity measures imposed by the (heavily U.S.-influenced) IMF exacerbated the economic distress and frustration of the Sierra Leonean population.

While the RUF's atrocities were unparalleled, Sierra Leone falls into a larger global pattern. The developing world is famous for its crony capitalism. What is less well known is that, almost invariably, crony capitalism arises because of the same interaction of democracy, global markets, and a market-dominant minority.

The Chinese-Friendly Dictatorships of General Suharto and Ferdinand Marcos

Take, for example, General Suharto's Chinese-friendly autocracy in Indonesia. Suharto seized power militarily in 1965, bringing to an end the "Guided Democracy" of his predecessor Sukarno, whose economic policies—including the nationalization and "indigenization" of major industries—had produced economic stagnation and widespread bankruptcies. Although in disgrace today, Suharto was for years the darling of the World Bank, the IMF, and Western investors. From early on, Suharto—a barely educated career soldier—placed his trust in foreign and foreign-trained economists, mainly from Harvard or the University of California at Berkeley. Starting in the seventies and accelerating through the eighties and nineties, Suharto embraced economic liberalization and other pro-market policies to encourage foreign investment and rapid economic growth. (Mobil Oil's massive liquefied natural gas plant in Aceh, for example, was built in the seventies.) Almost by definition, this meant that Suharto needed the help of his country's Chinese business community, who were the only ones in the country with the capital and entrepreneurial skills needed to jump-start the economy.

Suharto and the Indonesian Chinese had a nice thing going while it lasted. Just 3 percent of the population, the Chinese—like the Lebanese in Sierra Leone—were a classic vulnerable minority, the recurrent targets of popular anti-Chinese violence. In good autocratic fashion, Suharto protected the Chinese politically. He suppressed anti-Chinese labor movements, like the one in North Sumatra in 1994 that turned into a bloody riot against Chinese Indonesians. He extinguished all forms of anti-Chinese dissent and press, even jailing a prominent Jakarta journalist who published an anti-Chinese article. And he quashed, usually through armed force, political opposition of all types, including Islamic militants, Communists, and anti-Chinese political organizations. At the same time, Suharto granted the entrepreneurial Chinese the "freedom to make money," affirmatively directing lucrative business opportunities to a select few of them.[8]

In exchange, the Indonesian Chinese, with their business expertise and international connections, returned these favors, both by serving as "miracle workers" for the country's economic growth and by multiplying exponentially the personal fortune of the Suharto family. In the late 1990s the Suharto family was worth $16 billion according to Forbes, and twice that much according to an estimate attributed to the CIA. Despite their massive business holdings, Suharto and his children had poor entrepreneurial skills, and their lavish lifestyles were heavily dependent on Chinese billionaire cronies. Through much of the eighties and nineties, no one outside of his family—not even high-ranking cabinet ministers—was closer to Suharto than these cronies, who spent hours every week, golfing with the president, planning their joint investments. Most of these investments were channeled through so-called yayasans: supposedly charitable organizations that, because of their "non-profit" nature, were conveniently exempted from both taxes and auditing.[9]

Throughout his autocratic rule, Suharto called on his Chinese cronies to finance his pet projects, public as well as personal. Thus, at the president's request, Indonesian Chinese businessmen reportedly covered over $400 million in foreign exchange losses of the Bank Duta, which was indirectly owned by Suharto. As another favor to Suharto, they bailed out Indonesia's petrochemical industry after it collapsed. Suharto's Chinese cronies also financed a glowing biography of the president, bankrolled the Taman Mini theme park monorail on behalf of Suharto's wife, and accepted Suharto's children as "business partners."[10]

Using capital initially accumulated through Chinese cronies, Suharto's family grew increasingly rapacious through the 1990s. While the vast majority of Indonesians remained in chronic poverty, and with 14 million at one point unemployed, Suharto's children swept up business interests in television, radio, newspapers, airlines, banks, power plants, satellite communications, and toll roads. They brazenly set up monopolies while liberalizing the economy in ways that devastated the nation's poorest. Their shady web of businesses extended to dozens of countries, including Uzbekistan, Sudan, and Guinea-Bissau. Many of the Suharto family's projects—like the one conceived by Tommy Suharto, the general's wealthiest, flashiest son, to manufacture an Indonesia national car called Timor—were vanity-driven, colossal economic failures.[11]

As in Sierra Leone, this state of affairs led to tremendous, long-suppressed hostility among Indonesia's impoverished, largely Muslim *pribumi* majority. Suharto was aware of this hostility. Toward the end of his rule he began to distance himself from the Chinese, publicly castigating them for their "greed" and warning them of the dangers of ethnic unrest. At the same time, Suharto, in something of an about-face, began wooing influential Muslim intellectuals and religious leaders in an attempt to bolster popular support for himself. But he was too late. The intense fusion of anti-Suharto and anti-Chinese hatred exploded in the Indonesian riots of 1998, in which ordinary middle-class Indonesians participated in the mass looting and destruction of Chinese property. "It was like Christmas," one woman said, after hearing her neighbors trade stories about the various appliances they had carried out from burning Chinese stores.[12] Less festive were the hundreds of charred corpses lying in the rubble that had been commercial Jakarta.

Along with the Suharto regime, the most notorious case of crony capitalism in recent history is that of Ferdinand and Imelda Marcos in the Philippines. "He was head of government; she was head of state. It was a conjugal dictatorship," Raymond Bonner once put it.[13] In this instance, however, the backlash against democracy was even starker.

In the initial years following independence in 1946, the Philippines had relatively robust democratic elections, at least by developing-world standards. (Because of the country's extreme income disparities, vote-buying has always been common in the Philippines.) The Philippines also had relatively liberal free market policies. As a result, by the 1950s the market dominance of the Chinese was glaring: Every nook and cranny of the retail industry was owned and controlled by ethnic Chinese, many of whom had just arrived from mainland China.

Predictably, democracy in the face of pervasive Filipino poverty and disproportionate Chinese prosperity led to powerful anti-market, anti-Chinese movements, of precisely the kind described in chapter 5. In 1953, Ramon Magsaysay swept to landslide victory in the country's first presidential elections, championing "Filipinization" and promising to "wrest" the country's retail sector from Chinese hands. During this period, anti-Chinese sentiment was a constant theme of Filipino politics, and the entire Chinese-dominated food-grain industry was nationalized in the name of the "true" Filipino people. Moreover, exclusionary laws made it difficult and extremely costly for ethnic Chinese to acquire Filipino citizenship. As a result, because of their "foreigner" status, most Chinese were prohibited from participating in the professions and subjected to onerous economic restrictions.[14]

Ferdinand Marcos radically changed all this. Reliable sources report that Marcos was the illegitimate son of a Chinese lawyer, who mysteriously funded his education and political career. Among other puzzles, this would explain why Marcos throughout his life insisted that he was the direct descendant of the famous Chinese pirate Li Ma-hong.[15] In any event, Marcos during his presidency shifted the Philippines from majority-supported, anti-Chinese policies to pro-Chinese but autocratic policies.

Democratically elected in 1965, Marcos placed the entire Philippines under martial law in 1972 on the pretext of protecting the Philippines from the threat of a Communist takeover—a threat now widely acknowledged to have been a Marcos fabrication. A series of terrorist attacks, including the bombing of department stores, private companies, waterworks, even government buildings, all turned out to have been masterminded by Marcos himself, part of an elaborate plan to justify his imposition of one-man rule.[16] After declaring martial law, Marcos liberalized the economy and kicked into high-gear autocratic crony capitalism.

Using funds from the World Bank, IMF, and U.S. government, Marcos suppressed all political opposition, shutting down the *Manila Chronicle* and other major newspapers, jailing rival politicians like

Eugenio Lopez and Benigno "Ninoy" Aquino, and terminating the Philippines Congress altogether. At the same time, Marcos granted a tiny handful of cronies—some Filipino, some Chinese—massive co-conut, sugar, and tobacco monopolies, attacking in the process the wealth and power of the country's agrarian elite who had for genera-tions dominated Philippine politics. Those who suffered most from Marcos's crony capitalism were the 95 percent impoverished ethnic Filipino majority. The dozen or so people who became the most ob-scenely wealthy—Ferdinand and Imelda themselves, Marcos's resilient defense minister Juan Ponce Enrile, Marcos's fraternity brother Roberto Benedicto, Danding Cojuangco, and Imelda's brothers and sisters—"weren't entrepreneurs," writes Bonner. "They were money leeches."[17] The exception is surely Cojuangco, descendant of a nineteenth-century Chinese immigrant and a ruthlessly shrewd businessman, who is still one of the Philippines' richest men.

As for the country's predominantly ethnic Chinese business commu-nity, this group flourished under the Marcos dictatorship. One of Marcos's first acts as autocrat was to enact a new constitution in 1973 facilitating access to Philippine citizenship for all Filipino Chinese who wanted it. This change in the law opened up a host of economic oppor-tunities for the Chinese, many of whom shot to second- and third-tier tycoon status. There was of course a price: The Marcoses had to be paid off, constantly and handsomely. Imelda Marcos made herself a "silent partner" in every major corporation, almost all of which were owned by Filipino Chinese. At first she demanded a 10 percent equity interest in all businesses. Later she made it 25 percent. In addition, the Com-missions of Customs would pay an annual visit to businessmen, typically Chinese, collecting $500,000 "birthday presents" for Imelda. If someone declined, his visa would suddenly be invalidated.[18]

Still, once the Chinese realized that the Marcoses wished only to re-distribute wealth to themselves and not to the poor, the Chinese re-joiced and stock prices began steadily to climb. Despite the Marcos's gouging, the market was basically intact, and the market-dominant Chi-nese were freer than they ever had been—a 10 percent levy is far better than outright confiscation—to make their fortunes.

Indeed, many Filipino Chinese who knew Marcos remain surpris-

ingly loyal to him. He was an intelligent, in many ways simple, even as-
cetic man, they say, who ate a plain bowl of Chinese porridge every
morning. Marcos was corrupted and ultimately destroyed, they insist,
by Imelda, who by all accounts was stupid, ruthless, insatiably greedy,
and driven by a terrible inferiority complex. (Among a long list of
Imelda's failures, she once dated the now-martyred Ninoy Aquino, but
he dumped her for the shorter, far wealthier Cory.) "I cannot stand this
woman," Henry Kissinger once said of Imelda, despite her desperate attempts to court him.

Stupid or not, through her parasitic relationship with the entrepreneurial Chinese, not to mention extortion, bribery, and direct raiding of
the public treasury, Imelda was declared "one of the ten richest women
in the world" by *Cosmopolitan* magazine in 1975, her photograph appear-
ing along with those of Queen Elizabeth of England and Christina
Onassis Andreadis. On a one-day shopping spree in New York City,
Imelda spent $2 million on jewelry. According to Bonner, "A plati-
num and emerald bracelet with diamonds from Bulgari alone cost
$1,150,000. She also paid $330,000 for a necklace with a ruby, emer-
alds, and diamonds; $300,000 for a ring with heart-shaped emeralds,
and diamonds; $78,000 for eighteen-carat gold ear clips with diamonds;
$300,000 for a pendant with canary diamonds, rubies, and emeralds on
a gold chain."[19]

Imelda did not only have a large shoe-and-jewelry collection. She
was also a minor art collector. Although her taste was not widely respected, she spent some $40 million on works (largely fakes, as it would
turn out) from around the world. In addition, she had a small collection
of private aircraft: She liked to travel with an entourage of four jets,
sometimes one just for her luggage. She also collected real estate. In
September 1981, Imelda bought the Crown Building on Fifth Avenue in
New York for $51 million. Five months later she bought the Herald
Center for $60 million.[20]

During this period the Filipino Chinese as a group grew wealthier
too, although they remained at Imelda and Ferdinand's mercy right up
to the very end. On the eve of the "People Power" revolution in 1986
that finally toppled his dictatorship, and shortly before he fled the
Philippines, Marcos demanded that a Chinese businessman fork over, in

cash, 60 percent of the company's equity. Not long before, then–vice president George Bush visited the Philippines and told Marcos: "We love your commitment to democratic principles."[21]

Crony Capitalism in Kenya

Backlashes against democracy, friendly to a market-dominant minority, can also be found in East Africa. Many Kenyans, for example, would argue that their country is being milked by such an alliance today. Kenya's tiny Indian minority has always been keenly aware of its political vulnerability. In the years leading up to independence, a number of influential Indians overtly sided with the colonial authorities, opposing black majority rule. Once black African leadership became a certainty, however, Kenyan Indians changed strategies. In the country's first democratic elections in 1963, Indian business interests were the largest domestic campaign contributors to Jomo Kenyatta, who became the country's first president.

In 1967, then–vice president (now president) Daniel Arap Moi warned Africans at a political rally to "beware of bad Asians." He advised African businessmen to protect themselves from their "unscrupulous" Asian counterparts, who either had to reform or "otherwise they can pack up their bags and go." But once president, Moi found that he too needed Indian capital and entrepreneurialism—especially if he were to go after Kikuyu big business in the interests of his own Kalenjin constituency. Starting around 1978, in a complete (but predictable) about-turn, Moi entered into a symbiotic alliance with a handful of wealthy Indian businessmen. Moi protected the Indian minority politically, granting them relative economic freedom while affirmatively directing lucrative opportunities to a select few of them. In exchange, his Indian "business partners" generated vast amounts of wealth, compensating Moi and his cronies royally and allowing Moi to pursue his pro-Kalenjin agenda.[22]

Today, Moi and his cohorts jointly own extensive businesses with major Kenyan Indian families. At the same time, Kenya has retreated a long way from democracy, with Moi, like so many other African leaders, suppressing the media and political opposition, engaging in outright theft, and perpetuating himself as the country's indefinite one-man ruler. Unfortunately for Kenya's tiny Indian community—the majority of whom are middle- and upper-middle-class entrepreneurs who have received no favors from Moi other than economic freedom—the willingness of a handful of Indian tycoons to act as front men for Moi has generated tremendous, barely suppressed anti-Indian hostility. This hostility periodically explodes in the form of vicious ethnic riots, such as the one in 1982 in which mass anti-Indian looting and violence swept through not just Nairobi but other major urban centers. Today, because of Moi's flagrant cronyism, anti-Indian hatred is as or more virulent than it was in 1982.

Beyond Crony Capitalism:
Political Rule by Market-Dominant Minorities

Crony capitalism typically involves a corrupt arrangement between an indigenous autocrat and a market-dominant minority. But there are more extreme versions of the antidemocratic backlash. In some cases, a market-dominant minority itself seizes power.

A classic case is apartheid South Africa, where for generations a small white minority, backed by a police state, ruled the country and enriched itself on the backs of a disenfranchised, exploited black majority. Similar dynamics obtained in Namibia and Rhodesia (now Zimbabwe). Other examples are Rwanda and Burundi under Tutsi military rule. In all these cases an ethnic minority used military force and often truculent state repression to ensure its own economic and political dominance over subordinate majorities.

A variation on this theme existed throughout Latin America during the colonial period, and a muted version of it arguably still exists in parts of the region today. In Latin America, as in the countries of southern Africa, colonizing Europeans and their descendants seized the best land, often either killing the indigenous majorities around them or turning them into servile laborers. The oppression of the Amerindians was justified by, indeed seemed perfectly natural in light of, a deep belief in white superiority, particularly fashionable in Europe in the nineteenth century. Notwithstanding frequent revolutionary upheavals, enormous ethnic intermixing, and the rise of a pro-mestizo ideology, economic and political power in the region have remained largely concentrated in the hands of a small, "white," and to a certain extent hereditary elite.

In Bolivia, for example—where in the 1950s the revolutionary president Victor Paz Estenssoro extended universal suffrage and free education to Amerindians and conducted genuine, significant land reform—political power was never truly transferred to the country's impoverished, largely illiterate indigenous majority. (Estenssoro himself was from a wealthy landowning family and had a privileged education studying law and economics.)[23] The same is true of Ecuador, Guatemala, and Peru, where indigenous peoples represent a majority or near-majority of the population. Democracy in Latin America has historically been more formal than actual; elections notwithstanding, party control and political power have nearly always remained in the hands of the European-blooded, educated, cosmopolitan elite.

Moreover, money has a way of reasserting itself, especially in chronically poor countries. With the exception of Cuba, none of the Latin American or Caribbean countries ever became socialist economies. Within a few decades after the early wave of nationalizations, all the countries of Latin America swung back to free market, pro-foreign-investment regimes. From Mexico to Venezuela, from Bolivia to Brazil, elite leaders—sometimes from the military, sometimes from the landowning class—aggressively reprivatized land, industry, mines, oil, and railroads, generating economic growth while reinforcing the power of the market-dominant "white" minority.

In Mexico after the Second World War, for example, President Miguel Alemán declared that "Private enterprise should have complete freedom. . . . [T]he state should guarantee the rights of businessmen to open centers of production and to multiply the country's industries." Shocking ordinary Mexicans, Alemán reprivatized the oil and mining industries that Cardenas had so dramatically nationalized. In Guatemala, after seizing power in 1954, a new pro-capitalism military government reconfiscated the land previously given to the country's indigenous majority and reinstated the *latifundia* system. By 1964, Guatemala's white-owned plantations, representing just 2 percent of total farms, occupied 72 percent of the country's land. By contrast, the vast majority of the largely Mayan Indian peasantry owned either no land or too little land to survive. Today most barely eke out a living on less than two dollars a day, and roughly 60 percent do not know how to read and write. In all the Latin American countries—even in nominally democratic countries where Amerindians constitute a majority of the population—indigenous people have always been treated as politically and socially subordinate.[24]

All this, however, may be changing. Globalization is transforming and in many ways destabilizing the societies of Latin America. Western pro-democracy and human rights organizations, often partially funded by the U.S. government, are working on behalf of, and helping to mobilize, a growing number of indigenous communities throughout Latin America. Their projects vary, but typically include the promotion of indigenous rights, the empowerment of indigenous communities, and litigation alleging racial and ethnic discrimination. Many of these initiatives are extremely valuable, and long overdue. At the same time, by raising ethnic consciousness, they may inadvertently and indirectly increase ethnic conflict.

"Ethnicity" and "indigenousness" are often used by political leaders in ways not predicted by idealistic Western democracy and human rights proponents. For example, both the Amerindian movement led by Mallku in Bolivia and the Conaie movement led by Fernando Villavicencio in Ecuador are far more vitriolic, anti-market, and antiwhite than Western NGOs promoting indigenous consciousness would like. Mallku is demanding renationalization of Bolivia's natural gas reserves and vows to fight to his death both "U.S. gringo imperialism" and "minority rule by Whites and mestizos"; ten people died in the violent protests he spearheaded in 2000. In Chile, which has only a tiny Amerindian population, frustrated Mapuche Indians in southern Chile have been invading white-owned farms in a style similar to that of Zimbabwe's war veterans. Meanwhile, Venezuela's pro-*pardo,* anti-American Hugo Chavez, who "played the ethnic card" to win the presidency in free and fair elections, was never very popular in the United States, not even in left-leaning circles.

In Brazil, where Western NGOs have been particularly active, for the first time in the country's history and to the growing concern of the largely white establishment, an ethnicized all-black political party has been formed that openly champions Afro-Brazilian empowerment. Also for the first time in Brazilian history—as critics in Brazil and around the world lament—Brazil is enacting a series of "affirmative action" programs for blacks (although who is "black" enough to qualify is not obvious to anyone). Just in the last decade, dozens of emphatically black organizations and magazines have emerged, and T-shirts with slogans like "100% Negro" are suddenly a common sight in Rio de Janeiro and São Paulo.[25]

There is much about the recent ethnic reawakening in Latin America that is praiseworthy. Latin America's indigenous movements are often compared to the civil rights struggle of African-Americans in the United States during the 1960s. "[P]eople of Indian blood are fighting," writes the *Washington Post*'s Anthony Faiola, "and in many cases, winning, an unprecedented crusade for a louder political voice while celebrating and recapturing their cultural identities as never before." After centuries in which "whiteness" and Western tastes were idolized, observes Faiola, today "everything from Aztec gods to the earth symbols of Patagonian Indians have emerged as politically charged fashion statements in the T-shirts and tattoos worn by youths of the region." At the same time, there has been a boom in the publication of poetry, folklore, and textbooks in Quechua, Aymara, and other Indian languages as part of state-funded bilingual education programs. "What you're seeing is a major indigenous awakening that is having a massive impact on politics, law, and culture," says Diego Iturralde, an anthropologist based in Quito. "It is overthrowing governments, changing constitutions and generally altering the norms of society in Latin America."[26]

But there are of course dangers, too—of ethnic scapegoating and accelerating group hatred. What the future will bring for Latin America's mixed-blooded countries is impossible to know. If history is any guide, the region's wealthy, educated, globally-connected market-dominant "whites" will maintain their traditional stranglehold on both politics and the economy. In Ecuador, for example, one year after a popular Indian uprising toppled the pro-market government of President Jamil Mahuad, a new white-dominated pro-market regime is once again in place. The country's infuriated Amerindian leaders say they "were betrayed" and warn that the country faces "social explosion."[27]

In much of Latin America, as in many countries throughout the non-Western world, the two major components of globalization—markets and democracy—are on a collision course. Democratization, to the extent that it actually begins to resemble genuine majority rule, poses a serious threat to the status quo. This is particularly true in countries where most of the people are—or can be taught by media-savvy demagogues to think they are—"indigenous" or black, and where the rich can easily be depicted as colonizing "white" "outsiders." Mallku's slogans in Bolivia are frighteningly similar to those of Robert Mugabe in Zimbabwe: "We indigenous peoples are like foreigners in our own ancestral lands"; "We are governed by whites who have stolen our power and land"; "While we are ruled by this minority of whites and mestizos the crisis will continue"; "The whites should leave the country"; and, "Our blood has been spilled and must be atoned for."[28] Mallku's fellow Aymara Evo Morales, who also champions nationalization on the ground that the "indigenous people" are the "absolute owners" of the land, shocked observers by placing second in Bolivia's 2002 presidential election, behind the white mining magnate and former president Gonzalo Sanchez de Lozada.

CHAPTER 7

Backlash against
Market-Dominant Minorities

Expulsions and Genocide

I n Omarska, Keraterm, and other Serbian death camps in 1990 and 1991, torture was recreational; the victims were typically executed anyway. In one case a guard cut off one prisoner's ear and forced another prisoner to eat it. In another case a man's testicles were tied to the back of a motorcycle, which then sped off, leaving the man to die of massive blood loss.[1]

In Rwanda in the 1990s, a Tutsi woman, who had already seen seven members of her immediate family shot or hacked to death, begged a kindly Hutu couple to hide her twenty-month-old son from roaming death squads. The couple took the boy in, then killed him.[2]

Under what conditions do human beings do such things?

Ethnically targeted confiscations and autocratic crony capitalism are hardly optimal outcomes. But things can get unimaginably worse. In a frightening number of cases, democratization in the face of a market-dominant minority has led to government-encouraged attempts to "cleanse" the country of the minority altogether. Strategies for doing so include forced emigration, expulsions, and in the worst cases pogroms, extermination, and genocide. Typically, such policies are triggered by aggravating circumstances, for example an economic crisis, a border war, or the fortuitous rise of a particularly effective, hate-filled demagogue. Almost always, such policies are passionately supported by an aroused and angry "indigenous" majority, motivated by tremendous feelings of grievance and inferiority.

Induced Emigration and Expulsions

In some cases a majority backlash against a market-dominant minority takes the relatively mild form of oppressive language requirements, discriminatory education laws, and discriminatory citizenship and economic policies, all intended to "encourage" the resented minority to "voluntarily" leave the country. For example, in the non-Russian republics of the former Soviet Union, Russians were for years an economically and politically dominant "colonizer" minority, typically dominating key industrial and technical positions and occupying the best housing. Perestroika and political liberalization exposed the brutalities—including purges, deportations, and mass deaths—of the Soviet era, provoking widespread anti-Russian outrage among the indigenous majorities. In nearly all of the non-Russian republics, independence and democratization spawned a host of discriminatory laws, job-firings, and even violence. As a result, between 1989 and 1996 more than two million Russians, especially from Central Asia and Transcaucasia, abandoned their homes in favor of the chaos of post-Soviet Russia.

Meanwhile in Russia, Ukraine, and Belarus, anti-Jewish violence and political hatemongering in recent years have contributed to a large emigration of Jews to Israel (about 67,000 in 1999) and to Western countries (about 30,000 in 1999). Similarly, in Indonesia, popularly supported anti-Chinese economic policies pursued by the Habibie government in 1998, together with widespread anti-Chinese violence, prompted approximately 110,000 Sino-Indonesian families (including most of the wealthiest) to leave the country, taking tens of billions of dollars in capital with them. While many of the Sino-Indonesian families have returned, the capital has not.[3]

In Ethiopia, where members of the Eritrean minority have long dominated business, especially in key sectors such as transportation, construction, and electronics, the government took a more direct approach. Between 1998 and 1999 the Ethiopian government deported en masse 52,000 Eritrean-Ethiopians—almost the entire Eritrean community—as part of a larger war between Ethiopia and Eritrea. In classic ethnonationalist fashion, the expelled Eritreans—most of whom thought of themselves as Ethiopians—were first stripped of their citizenship. They were also deprived of education and separated from their families, with their businesses, pensions, and bank accounts subject to expropriation. Many of the deported Eritreans say they were forced to sign powers of attorney handing over their property to "full Ethiopians." The Eritreans blame their expulsion on Ethiopian "jealousy, revenge, and greed"; some have called the actions "economic cleansing."

The Ethiopian government played a major role in fomenting ethnic division and hatred within the country. Starting in 1992 the government issued to all residents identity cards providing an "ethnic" designation—for example, "Eritrean." Although Eritreans have lived in Ethiopia as long as either country has existed within defined boundaries, the Ethiopian government subsequently declared all Eritreans to be "non-Ethiopian," then "non-citizens," and ultimately "aggressors." Such scape-goating tactics have proved sadly effective in exacerbating ethnic hatred, a boon for the Ethiopian government, which looks forward to revenues from the expropriated properties and hails the awakening of a "true" Ethiopian people united "against an enemy in their midst."[4]

The Rwandan Genocide

The tragic case of Rwanda illustrates the most extreme form of majority-supported, democracy-assisted efforts to exterminate an economically dominant ethnic minority. Historically, Rwanda's roughly 85 percent Hutus were cultivators, whereas the roughly 14 percent Tutsis were herdsmen. "This was the original inequality: cattle are a more valuable asset than produce," writes Philip Gourevitch. After 1860, when Mwame Kigeri Rwabugiri, a Tutsi, ascended the Rwandan throne, the stratification between Hutus and Tutsis intensified. Rwanda essentially became a feudal kingdom in which Tutsis were overlords and Hutus their vassals. Still, the line distinguishing Hutu and Tutsi was much more porous than it would become later: The two groups spoke a common language, intermarriage occurred, and successful Hutus could "become Tutsi."

In classic divide-and-conquer fashion, the Belgian colonizers injected a sharper and much more divisive sense of ethnicity into Rwandan society—a sense of ethnicity that also happened to corroborate the

Belgians' own "scientific" beliefs about racial superiority. To facilitate their own goals of colonial subjugation, the Belgians perpetuated the myth that the Tutsi—usually stereotyped as lanky, light-skinned, and thin-lipped—were genetically superior to, and thus born to rule over, the supposedly stockier, darker, thick-lipped Hutus. According to Gourevitch,

> In addition to military and administrative chiefs, and a veritable army of churchmen, the Belgians dispatched scientists to Rwanda. The scientists brought scales and measuring tapes and calipers, and they went about weighing Rwandans, measuring Rwandan cranial capacities, and conducting comparative analyses of the relative protuberances of Rwandan noses. Sure enough, the scientists found what they had believed all along. Tutsis had "nobler," more "naturally" aristocratic dimensions than the "coarse" and "bestial" Hutus. On the "nasal index," for instance, the median Tutsi nose was found to be about two and a half millimeters longer and nearly five millimeters narrower than the median Hutu nose.[5]

In 1933–34 the Belgians conducted a "census," then issued "ethnic" identity cards. These identity cards made it almost impossible for Hutus to become Tutsis. They also allowed the Belgians to rule Rwanda indirectly through a system in which Tutsi chiefs controlled the Hutu majority, extracting their labor on behalf of the Europeans.

The Belgians openly favored the "more intelligent, more active" and more "refined" Tutsis, giving them superior education and assigning them all the best administrative and political positions. The Hutu majority was reduced to a humiliated pool of forced labor, required to toil en masse under their Tutsi taskmasters. Over the years, what French scholar Gerald Prunier has called "an aggressively resentful inferiority complex" deepened and festered among the Hutus.[6] By the time independence rolled around, the Tutsi were a starkly privileged, "arrogant," economically dominant ethnic minority. And the Hutu political activists who were calling for "majority rule" and "democratic revolution" were seeking not equality—but revenge.

In March 1957, nine influential Hutu intellectuals published a tract known as the *Hutu Manifesto*, calling for "democracy." Employing typical ethnonationalist rhetoric, the manifesto argued that Tutsis were "foreign invaders" and that "Rwanda was by rights a nation of the Hutu majority." As usual, more moderate political voices were drowned out by the more compelling voices of ethnic demagoguery. Extremists all over the country rallied large crowds with calls to unite in their "Hutuness." Meanwhile, the Belgians, seemingly oblivious to the escalating ethnic rhetoric, and now playing the role of ex-colonizer assisting the transition to independence, scheduled elections. But before the elections were even held, warfare began.

Rwanda's "social revolution," which eventually drove out the Belgians, began in November 1959. After a Hutu politician was attacked by Tutsis, violence spread throughout the country. In a popular uprising known as "the wind of destruction," Hutus, usually organized in groups of ten and led by a man blowing a whistle, conducted a campaign of pillage, arson, and murder against Tutsis. In the midst of all this, even as Hutus were torching Tutsi homes, elections were held in 1960. Not surprisingly, given Rwanda's demographics, Hutus won 90 percent of the top political posts. By then over twenty thousand Tutsis had been displaced from their homes and many thousands more killed or exiled. Hutu leaders organizing the violence were always the first to snatch Tutsi property.[7]

Rwanda was granted full independence in 1962. Inaugurated as the country's first president was Grégoire Kayibanda, one of the original authors of the *Hutu Manifesto*, who gave a speech proclaiming, "Democracy has vanquished feudalism." But this was democracy of a pathological variety. President Kayibanda, notes Gourevitch, was at best a dull leader: "Stirring up the Hutu masses to kill Tutsis was the only way he seemed able to keep the spirit of the revolution alive." In late December 1963, highly organized Hutu massacres left almost fourteen thousand Tutsis dead in the southern province of Gikongoro alone. Most of the victims were well-educated Tutsi men, although women and children were killed as well, often clubbed or speared to death, their corpses thrown into a river after their clothes were taken.[8]

In 1973 a Hutu major general by the name of Juvénal Habyarimana seized power in a coup. Calling for a moratorium on anti-Tutsi violence, and even including some Tutsis in his rubber-stamp parliament, Habyarimana ruled Rwanda as a corrupt totalitarian state for two decades, engorging himself while the majority of Rwandans lived in extreme, frustrated poverty.

In the early 1990s the wave of democratization then sweeping the world hit Rwanda. Responding to pressure from the United States and Western Europe, and particularly from France, President Habyarimana made a show of abandoning totalitarianism in favor of "pluralism" and multiparty democracy. But the new "pluralistic" politics quickly showed a dangerously ethnic face. Among the non–sham opposition parties, only one had a significant Tutsi membership. Worse, Hutu extremists, inflaming old Hutu fears and resentments, quickly captured the democratic process, turning Rwanda politics for the Hutus into a matter of survival and self-defense. Hutus had to unite and fight against their common "domestic enemy," otherwise the Tutsis would take over the country again and destroy them first. This popular movement became known enthusiastically as Hutu Power.[9]

In October 1990 a Tutsi-led rebel army calling itself the Rwandese Patriotic Army (RPF) invaded Rwanda from neighboring Uganda. According to Gourevitch, most Rwandan Tutsis had no idea that the RPF even existed. But to mobilize support for himself, Habyarimana declared all Tutsis in Rwanda to be RPF "accomplices," and Hutus who did not accept this view were branded "Tutsi-loving traitors." Hutu extremists and Hutu youth militias "promoted genocide as a carnival romp. Hutu Power youth leaders, jetting around on motorbikes and sporting pop hairstyles, dark glasses, and flamboyantly colored pajama suits and robes, preached ethnic solidarity and civil defense to increasingly packed rallies." Other Hutus "drew up lists of Tutsis, and went on retreats to practice burning houses, tossing grenades, and hacking dummies up with machetes."

Meanwhile, "freedom of the press," ironically encouraged by Amnesty International, led to the enormous influence of a newspaper called *Kangura*—"Wake It Up"—which billed itself as "the voice that seeks to awake and guide the majority people." The *Kangura,* launched in 1990, was edited by Hassan Ngeze, a diabolically effective Hutu supremacist with a knack for appealing to the ordinary Hutu. On one occasion another newspaper ran a cartoon depicting Ngeze on a couch, being psychoanalyzed by "the democratic press." The cartoon showed the following exchange:

> Ngeze: I'm sick Doctor!!
> Doctor: Your sickness?!
> Ngeze: The Tutsis . . . Tutsis . . . Tutsis!!!!!

Ngeze was apparently delighted; he ran the cartoon in his own *Kangura*. In his most famous article, "The Hutu Ten Commandments," published in December 1990, Ngeze called on Hutu women to "guard against the Tutsi-loving impulses of Hutu men"; declared all Tutsis "dishonest"; and urged Hutus to have "unity and solidarity" against "their common Tutsi enemy." The Hutu Ten Commandments were widely circulated and phenomenally popular. The eighth and most frequently quoted commandment said, "Hutus must stop having mercy on the Tutsis."[10]

In 1993, President Habyarimana signed a peace accord with the RPF. Hutu Power leaders cried treason, branded Habyarimana an "accomplice," and called for the extermination of the entire Tutsi population: for being sympathizers of the RPF—and just for being Tutsi "cockroaches." Ngeze added his voice. In *Kangura,* he warned the United Nations Assistance Mission to stay out of the way and urged Rwandans: "[L]et's kill each other. . . . Let whatever is smouldering erupt. . . . At such a time a lot of blood will be spilled."

In the spring and early summer of 1994, Hutu Power began broadcasting nationwide calls for the slaughter of Rwanda's Tutsis. In Gourevitch's words, "Hutus young and old rose to the task." In just one hundred days, ordinary Hutus killed approximately eight hundred thousand Tutsis, mostly with machetes:

> Neighbors hacked neighbors to death in their homes, and colleagues hacked colleagues to death in their workplaces. Doctors killed their patients, and schoolteachers killed their pupils. Within days, the Tutsi populations of many villages were all but eliminated, and in Kigali prisoners were released in work gangs

to collect the corpses that lined the roadsides. Throughout Rwanda, mass rape and looting accompanied the slaughter. . . . Radio announcers reminded listeners not to take pity on women and children. As an added incentive to the killers, Tutsis' belongings were parceled out in advance—the radio, the couch, the goat, the opportunity to rape a young girl. A councilwoman in one Kigali neighborhood was reported to have offered fifty Rwandan francs apiece (about thirty cents at the time) for severed Tutsi heads, a practice known as "selling cabbages."[11]

Many Westerners, including close friends of mine who are human rights advocates, insist that the horrors of Rwanda had nothing to do with democracy. Democracy, they say, does not include ethnic venom and mass killings. But to think this way is simply to define away the problem. Before 1957, when the movement for Hutu "majority rule" began, there had never been any recorded episode of systematic violence between Hutus and Tutsis.[12] Sudden political liberalization in the 1990s unleashed long-suppressed ethnic resentments, directly spawning Hutu Power as a potent political force. Undoubtedly, Belgian racism and favoritism and decades of corrupt dictatorship laid the groundwork for the genocide that followed. But the fact remains that a majority of the Rwandan people supported, indeed personally conducted, the unspeakable atrocities committed in 1994. These atrocities were in a terrible sense the expression of "majority will" in the context of mass poverty, colonial humiliation, demagogic manipulation, and a deeply resented, disproportionately wealthy "outsider" minority.

Genocide in the Former Yugoslavia

A more complicated example is the former Yugoslavia, where among many other dynamics, the Croats and Slovenes have always been, and continue to be, disproportionately prosperous vis-à-vis the more populous Serbs. The former Yugoslavia was composed of six states, which can be divided into two groups: the more economically developed northern states (Croatia and Slovenia) and the markedly poorer, less developed southern states (Bosnia, Macedonia, Montenegro, and Serbia). The Serbs were the largest ethnic group in the former Yugoslavia, numbering approximately 9.3 million and comprising more than a third of the population. By contrast, there were roughly 4.6 million Croats in the former Yugoslavia.

The northern peoples of Croatia and Slovenia traditionally enjoyed a much higher standard of living than those of the south. In 1918, the year Yugoslavia was first formed, Croatia and Slovenia accounted for roughly 75 percent of Yugoslavia's industry. Foreign investment and markets continued to favor the north, and by 1930 its share of industry had reached 80 percent.[13] The reasons for the north's market dominance are at least in part geographical and "cultural." The northern states border Italy and Austria. Moreover, Croats and Slovenes have their cultural roots in Western Europe: They are almost all Catholic, were part of the Austro-Hungarian Empire, and have traditionally used the Roman alphabet. As a result, Croats and Slovenians have long had important business and trade ties with the Western European nations, including Germany, which has been a major foreign investment partner.

The south, by contrast, was part of the Ottoman Empire; Serbia borders Romania and Bulgaria on the east. The Dinaric Alps cover most of Bosnia, Montenegro, and western Serbia, which made communications between regions historically very difficult. Most Serbs belong to the Eastern Orthodox Church and favor the Cyrillic script. Serbia suffered economically under Turkish rule. Infrastructure and industry were neglected, and the majority of Serbs continued to engage in low-technology agriculture, although oppressive rural taxes drove many farmers to the cities and neighboring states.[14]

For these and other reasons, the wealth disparity between north and south has always been striking and a fertile source of ethnic resentment in the Balkans. In 1963 the per capita income in the south was less than half that in the north. By 1997 this disparity had increased so that the south's per capita income was only 25 percent of that in the north. In 1997 the average GDP per capita in the north was $6,737, while the south's was only $1,403. As of 2001 the World Bank placed Slovenia in the high-income and Croatia in the upper-middle-income bracket, while the states in the south all fell into the lower-middle-income bracket.

Education, communication, and health levels are also notably higher in the north than in the south; the infant mortality rate in the north, for example, is approximately half what it is in the south. Little has changed since the late 1970s, when one sociologist observed:

> [T]he disparities in development and in lifestyle between the Slovenia and Croatia that I knew and [Bosnia-Herzegovina, Montenegro, and Serbia], were also striking—and troubling. Often what I saw in [the south] reminded me of what I remembered of Yugoslavia of the 1950s and at times even of what I had seen while travelling to and in India. Dirt roads, ragged children, open sewers or peasants who would get off the bus in the middle of nowhere to take a path which led across mountains to a hamlet on the other side—all these were a stark contrast to life in the "north." There, by 1978, Volkswagens had replaced tiny Fiats and major cities could boast occasional traffic congestion, shopping trips to Italy had become *de rigueur* for the growing middle class, and the yearning, and to some extent the accessibility, for the "exotic" could be seen in such things as the proliferation of new and modified dessert recipes substituting bananas, kiwis and pineapples for apples, cherries and strawberries.[15]

Once again, as with all ethnic conflict, it would be absurd to reduce the historical enmity between Croats and Serbs to economics. Among other details, Croats, with Nazi support, killed thousands of Serbs (along with Jews and Gypsies) in concentration camps in World War II. Ethnic hatred has thus long been present in the former Yugoslavia, but from 1945 to 1980 it was held in check by the charisma and iron hand of Josip Broz Tito, himself part Croat, part Slovene. Tito brilliantly played the republics off one another. To diminish Serbian power, Tito reconfigured the former Yugoslavia, creating the provinces of Kosovo and Vojvodina and drawing other boundaries that left millions of Serbs living outside the (then) state of Serbia. At the same time he filled Croatia's police and bureaucracy with Serbs, redistributed wealth from the wealthier north to the poorer south, and made ethnic nationalism a crime.[16]

As hindsight knowledge has allowed many commentators to observe, Tito's Yugoslavia was a bomb waiting to explode. And the bomb was detonated by—democratization. In Croatia the first free post–World War II elections in 1990 produced a landslide victory for demagogue Franjo Tudjman's nationalist Croatian Democratic Union party—a party basically defined by its hatred of both the ethnic Serbs living in Croatia and their cousins in Serbia. One of Tudjman's first official acts was to demote the Serbs (roughly 12 percent of the population) by giving them inferior status in the Croatian constitution. The Croatian majority loved it. "Everything for Croatia! All for Croatia!" yelled ordinary civilians.[17]

Meanwhile, 1990 democratic elections in Serbia swept Slobodan Milosevic to power on a similar wave of ethnonationalist euphoria. Now that Milosevic has been tried as an international war criminal, it is easy to forget how much the Serbian people once adored him. He was for millions, especially the great masses of frustrated, uneducated rural poor, "the saint of Serb nationalism," the long overdue champion of a Greater Serbia. Even as his chief hatemonger Vojislav Seselj was roaring to hysterical crowds, "We will kill Croats with rusty spoons because it will hurt more!" the Serb Orthodox Church blessed Milosevic's Serbian nationalism as a "new holy crusade."[18]

In 1991, Croatia and Slovenia declared independence. Led by Milosevic, the Serbs responded militarily, seizing a third of Croatia and murdering thousands. In 1992, Bosnia declared independence as well. Soon the entire region was engulfed in civil war, mass expulsions, and genocidal violence. In all, thousands of ordinary citizens, mostly men, were killed, often after being tortured in ways painful even to describe. Meanwhile, in female concentration camps, tens of thousands of women were raped, some of them more than a hundred times. One of the explicit goals was to impregnate the victims, many as young as twelve, with the "Serbian seed." Thus, victims who survived the rapes were usually released only after they were in an advanced state of pregnancy, when abortion was no longer feasible. "This baby is not a part of me, it is like a stone in my body," one pregnant, multiple-rape victim said afterward from a Sarajevo hospital. "As soon as I deliver this child the doctors had better take it away. I will kill it if I see it."[19]

There is plenty of guilt to go around, but by all accounts the more numerous Serbs, who had historically dominated the Yugoslavian military and police forces, were at the forefront of the ethnic cleansing and brutal violence. "Ejecting" or "eliminating" Croats, Slovenes, and other "foreigners" threatening Serbia's rightful power in Yugoslavia was the guiding, and sadly mass-supported, ethnonationalist principle. In a now famous speech delivered in March 1991—which contains a telling allusion to Croat and Slovene market dominance—Milosevic declared to thunderous applause: "If we must fight, then my God we will fight. And I hope they will not be so crazy as to fight against us. Because *if we don't know how to work well or to do business*, at least we know how to fight well!"[20]

The situation in the former Yugoslavia is enormously complicated, and I am certainly not offering an "explanation" for the tremendous ethnic hatred or atrocities that unfolded there in the 1990s. Indeed, this is probably a good place to reiterate what I am not arguing in this book. I am distinctly not arguing that market-dominant minorities are the source of all ethnic conflict or that market-dominant minorities are the only targets of ethnic persecution. On the contrary, in the former Yugoslavia for example, Serbs were also ethnically cleansed from the Krajina region of Croatia, while huge numbers of Albanians were exterminated en masse; neither group was a market-dominant minority.

Rather, the point is that in virtually every region of the world, against completely different historical backgrounds, the simultaneous pursuit of markets and democracy in the face of a resented market-dominant minority repeatedly produces the same destructive, often deadly dynamic. Sudden, unmediated democratization in Yugoslavia—as in Rwanda—released long suppressed ethnic hatreds and facilitated the rise of megalomaniac ethnic demagogues as well as ferocious ethnonationalist movements rooted in tremendous feelings of anger, envy, and humiliation. As in so many economically distressed countries (post-Communist Yugoslavia was mired in foreign debt) with a market-dominant minority, simultaneous economic and political liberalization directly pitted a poorer but much more populous and militarily powerful group claiming to be the "rightful owners" of the country against a hated, wealthier, "outsider" minority. In the former Yugo-slavia, the result of market liberalization and democratic elections was not prosperity and political freedom, but rather economic devasta-tion, hatemongering, populist manipulation, and civilian-conducted mass murder.

CHAPTER 8

Mixing Blood

Assimilation, Globalization, and the Case of Thailand

T he destructive ethnic dynamics described in the previous three chapters, while strikingly recurrent across different regions and countries, are not intended to be universal laws of nature. To begin with, there are some developing countries that do not have market-dominant minorities; I will discuss these countries briefly below. In addition, as people often say to me, even in countries with a market-dominant minority, surely there must be exceptions to the rule. Thailand is often pointed to as such an exception—a poor country with a market-dominant minority where the pursuit of free market democracy arguably has not generated ethnic resentment or any of the kinds of backlashes I've described. I will examine the ethnic "success story" of Thailand more closely below.

Developing Countries
without Market-Dominant Minorities

Not all developing countries have market-dominant minorities. China is an important case in point. Although the market reforms of the last decade have dramatically benefited China's coastal provinces (for example, Shanghai, Guangzhou, and Fujian) over inland provinces, and urban areas over rural areas, China does not have any economically powerful ethnic minorities. On the contrary, the Han Chinese in China, comprising 95 percent of the population, have represented an economically and politically dominant majority vis-à-vis ethnic minorities like the Tibetans, Uighurs, and Miao for three millennia.[1] Needless to say,

China has plenty of other problems: endemic corruption, immense wealth inequalities, and so on. It just happens not to have the problem of a market-dominant minority.

With China's astounding growth rates over the last decades, many have suggested that China will soon join the ranks of the "Asian Tigers"—Japan, South Korea, Hong Kong, Taiwan, and Singapore—none of which is considered "developing" anymore. Along these lines it is striking to note that none of the Asian Tigers has ever had a market-dominant minority. In all the Asian Tigers, the ethnic majority—the Japanese in Japan, the Koreans in South Korea, and the Chinese in Hong Kong, Taiwan, and Singapore—is both economically and politically dominant.

Indeed, in Japan and Korea, ethnic minorities are not merely economically disadvantaged but practically nonexistent. (It was only in 1997 that the Japanese formally acknowledged the existence of an indigenous ethnic minority, the Ainu.) In Hong Kong the English and Chinese are both relatively prosperous, but the latter, at 99 percent of the population, are today by far the economically dominant group. In Taiwan, Han Chinese, including both the Taiwanese Chinese and the mainland Chinese (descendants of the group of Chinese that arrived in Taiwan with Chiang Kai-shek in 1949), constitute roughly 99 percent of the population, with non-Han aborigines composing the other 1 percent. Even if the Taiwanese (roughly 85 percent of the population) and the mainlanders (14 percent) were viewed as distinct ethnic groups, the mainlander "minority" is not market-dominant. In Singapore, the Chinese constitute roughly 77 percent of the population and are an economically, politically, and culturally dominant majority vis-à-vis the country's Indian and Malay minorities. Among other factors, the lack of a market-dominant minority in all these Tigers probably helps explain their economic success relative to the far poorer and less stable neighboring Southeast Asian countries of Burma, Indonesia, Malaysia, and the Philippines.[2]

Nor are market-dominant minorities present today in most Eastern European countries; the terrible exception of the former Yugoslavia has already been discussed. While virtually all countries in Africa are marked by severe ethnic divisions, a few (for example, Botswana or

Sudan) do not appear to have market-dominant minorities. The countries of the Middle East will be discussed in Part Three.

Thailand: An Exceptional Case?

A few years ago a graduate student named Kanchana came to my office to see if I would be willing to supervise a paper she wanted to write on legal protections for cultural artifacts taken from Thailand, her native country. After an interesting discussion about possible approaches to her paper, I asked Kanchana a question that, in retrospect, would probably be grounds for a lawsuit under today's standards of political correctness—I asked whether she was an ethnic Chinese.

Kanchana's reply: "But the Thai *are* Chinese." She then instantly retreated: "Well—part Chinese. I have Chinese blood. Everyone in Thailand does. Well . . . *almost* everyone does."

Thailand is a fascinating case. On the one hand, it shares with the other Southeast Asian countries the phenomenon of a wildly disproportionately wealthy, market-dominant Chinese minority. The Chinese in Thailand today, although just 10 percent of the population, control virtually all of the country's largest banks and conglomerates. All of Thailand's billionaires are ethnic Chinese. On the other hand, as Kanchana's comments suggest, unlike elsewhere in Southeast Asia, the Chinese have assimilated quite successfully into Thailand, and there is relatively little anti-Chinese animus. In Thailand today, many Thai Chinese speak only Thai and consider themselves as Thai as their indigenous counterparts. Intermarriage rates between the Chinese and the indigenous majority (many of whom, at least in Bangkok, have some Chinese ancestry already) are much higher than elsewhere in Southeast Asia. Perhaps most strikingly, the country's top political leaders, including a recent prime minister, are often of Chinese descent, although they usually have Thai-sounding surnames and speak little or no Chinese.

Although interethnic socializing and intermarriage may seem perfectly normal to Westerners, it bears emphasizing how markedly Thailand differs in this regard from her Southeast Asian neighbors. In Indonesia and Malaysia, for example, rates of intermarriage between the Chinese and the indigenous majority are close to zero. The Chinese in

these countries remain a conspicuously insular minority, living, working, and socializing entirely separately from the indigenous majorities.

Many have speculated about the reasons for the starkly different
rates of intermarriage and assimilation. According to one professor of
law from Singapore, the main reason is the "pork factor." "Indonesians
and Malaysians are mostly Muslims," he explains, "and they don't eat
pork. The Chinese love pork; they eat it all the time. And for Chinese,
eating is a huge part of their lives. Thus, social interactions are impossible." This professor was being facetious, but he is clearly right that religion has played an important role: Thailand is not Muslim but largely
Buddhist, a cultural affinity that has made assimilation much easier for
the Thai Chinese, many of whom adhere to a syncretic combination of
Buddhism, Taoism, and Confucianism.

In any event, despite the persisting, glaring market dominance of the
Thai Chinese, there appears to be little anti-Chinese sentiment in
Thailand today. To be sure, some ambivalence toward the Thai Chinese
remains. Kanchana, for example, made some slightly contradictory remarks in our conversation. "All the gold shops are owned by rich
Chinese—I mean, pure Chinese," she said at one point. And: "When the
economy gets bad, then Thais resent the Chinese more." Still, the fact
remains that ethnic relations today between the Chinese and indigenous
Thais in Thailand are remarkably civilized.

Thus Thailand, which began democratizing in 1992, is arguably a
counterexample to the sobering predictions of the previous chapters. In
Thailand today, ethnic hatred and demagoguery do not seem to be problems despite recent market and democratic reforms in the presence of a
market-dominant ethnic minority.

Unfortunately, things are not quite so simple. The telltale question
with respect to Thailand is: How did the country come to be the way it
is? In significant part, the answer is decades of coerced assimilation and
cultural eradication by the Thai government, aimed at eliminating the
Chinese as a distinct ethnic group. In other words, the Thai government
in earlier decades pursued its own version of a backlash against a
market-dominant minority. If ethnic relations in Thailand do seem hope-
ful, the Thai path to assimilating its Chinese minority is unlikely to provide a useful policy model today.

"The Jews of the East"

The Chinese were not always so welcome in Thailand. After 1842 in Thailand (then known as Siam), large numbers of immigrants arrived from China. These principally male immigrants typically married Thai women and prospered. Indeed, the Chinese in this early wave of immigration were more or less completely absorbed into the Thai population.

Discord between the two peoples began after 1910, with the rise of nationalism in both China and Thailand. In 1909 the Chinese government passed a nationality law proclaiming that all persons with Chinese fathers were Chinese, no matter where they were born. This included most Thai Chinese, who suddenly found themselves with an identity crisis. There was another critical factor: After about 1910, Chinese women began accompanying their husbands and sons in significant numbers to Thailand, raising a barrier to intermarriage and assimilation. In any event, by the early twentieth century it was the strong opinion of the nationalist Thai king Vajiravudh, also known as Rama VI, that the Chinese were a "problem" for Thailand, because they remained stubbornly "ethnic Chinese," insultingly refusing to take on Thai national identity.

Thus, in his famous tract *The Jews of the East,* King Vajiravudh compared his country's Chinese minority to the European Jews. His main arguments, summarized by historian Victor Purcell, are as follows:

> In Siam . . . there exists a situation analogous to the Jewish question in countries of the West. This is "The Yellow Peril." The danger arises solely from the Chinese from whom the Siamese are even more different than Europeans are from the Jews. The first similarity between the Chinese and the Jews is in the matter of "racial loyalty." No matter where they live, what nationality they assume, Chinese remain essentially Chinese. But theirs is race loyalty, not love of country. . . .
>
> It is argued that Chinese intermarry with the people of the country: so do the Jews. But when a Chinese man marries a Thai woman, the woman becomes a Chinese and adopts Chinese customs in every detail. Their children become Chinese also. But if a

Thai man marries a Chinese woman she continues to be Chinese.
The man finds himself adopting Chinese ways and conforming to
the Chinese pattern of life. As for the children, even though they
are Thai in name they are psychologically Chinese. . . .

The second characteristic of the Jews is found developed in
the Chinese also. That is, the Chinese, like the Jews, are an ancient race, whose high civilization was developed at a time when
our ancestors had not emerged from savagery. They divide the
world into two classes—the Chinese and the barbarians. . . .
They are likely to think that we exist only to be robbed or
cheated. . . .

Chinese are willing to undergo any sort of privation for the
sake of money. Anyone who has watched Chinese coolies eat cannot help but feel a sense of revulsion, since it seems that the food
they eat would hardly attract the curs which roam the streets.
And if one speaks of the places where they lie, it is amazing that
so many persons can squeeze themselves into a space so small
that no other race on earth could manage to breathe in it. This
being the case, it is not surprising that the Chinese can manage to
corner all the available work for themselves.[3]

King Vajiravudh's pamphlet was enormously influential. Before its
publication, fear and dislike of the Chinese was principally limited to
elite Thais. After the king's pamphlet was disseminated, large numbers
of ordinary Thais were filled with suspicion and hostility toward the
Chinese in their midst. This popular anti-Chinese resentment intensified
as Chinese market dominance increasingly asserted itself at every level
of society. By the 1930s the Thai Chinese minority dominated finance,
commerce, and virtually every industry in the country, minor and major. Minor industries included food vending, salt, tobacco, pork, and the
traditional Chinese stronghold—birds' nest concessions. (The nest of
the swiflet, made of the bird's own saliva, is considered a delicacy
among the Chinese.) Major industries included shipping, petroleum,
rice milling, tin, rubber, and teak. In addition, the Chinese were major
landowners in central Siam.

By contrast, 80 percent of the indigenous Thai majority were abjectly poor rice growers. In a pattern all too familiar in Southeast Asia, the Thais came to blame their extreme poverty on the Chinese, especially Chinese moneylenders. One Thai, upon hearing in 1939 that the government had passed anti-Chinese legislation, responded: "[T]he poor peasants are liberated from the bonds of the blood-sucking 'shylocks.' "[4] Unlike the other Southeast Asian countries, however, Thailand pursued a unique strategy. It decided to "solve" its "Chinese problem" by eliminating the "Chineseness" of the Chinese minority—that is, by "turning Chinese into Thais." Starting in the 1930s the Thai government began a systematic and ruthless campaign of forced assimilation.

Prior to the 1930s, most Thai Chinese spoke Chinese, attended Chinese schools, studied Chinese history, and maintained Chinese customs. In the 1930s the Thai government declared that Chinese schools were "alien" in character. Their very purpose was "to preserve the foreign culture of a minority population, to perpetuate the Chinese language and Chinese nationalism." Accordingly, the government passed a decree requiring that in a 28-hour school week, 21 hours were to be devoted to studies in the Thai language. Mathematics, science, geography, and history were all to be taught in the Thai language. In addition, teachers in Chinese schools were required to pass difficult examinations in the Thai language.

As intended, the effect was a severe restriction of the Chinese language. As time went on, the government began closing Chinese schools altogether; twenty-five private Chinese schools were closed in July 1939, followed by seven more a month later. In addition, Chinese books were banned and Chinese newspapers shut down. Chinese social organizations were prohibited, and regulations were passed requiring "Thai dress and deportment." Chinese culture generally was suppressed in a calculated effort to destroy ethnic Chinese consciousness and identity. At the same time, more subtle pressures for assimilation played a role as well. As late as the 1960s and 1970s, any Chinese with ambitions to succeed had to pursue a Thai education, adopt a Thai surname, speak the Thai language, and, ideally, marry into a Thai family.[5]

Interwoven with these attacks on Chinese language and culture were a draconian series of anti-Chinese economic policies. Particularly in the 1930s and again in the 1950s, anti-Chinese commercial restrictions

were enacted, discriminatory taxes levied, and Chinese industries nationalized. Chinese families were harassed for showing loyalty to China;
several wealthy Thai Chinese were jailed for remitting money to the
mainland.[6] During this period, fearful of confiscation, expulsion, and
imprisonment, the Thai Chinese—like the billionaire Chiaravanont family, originally Chia—began shedding their Chinese surnames and Chinese traditions. As my student Kanchana put it, "You can tell who the
Chinese are because they're the ones with the longest last names. That's
because they felt they had to 'out-Thai' the Thai and because the Chinese
weren't allowed to take on Thai surnames that already existed."

This, then, is the darker aspect of what many have described as the
"seamless" or "blissful" integration of the ethnic Chinese minority into
Thai society. To be sure, the fact that the Thai government's assimilation
campaign worked as well as it did may reflect other factors, such as the
close cultural affinity between the Thais and the Chinese. Indeed, it is
often suggested that the Thais and the Chinese share the same "ethnic
roots." Most Thais are believed to descend from people who lived in
southwestern China until they were forced into what is now Thailand by
the Mongols.[7] It is impossible to know for sure, but a government campaign to assimilate the Chinese into Indonesia or to encourage more
ethnic intermarriage in Malaysia or the Philippines might not have
worked at all.

The fact remains that the Thai government consciously pursued, in
the name of the indigenous Thai people, policies to "eliminate" the
Chinese as a distinct ethnic minority. Although Thailand's policies were
certainly preferable to the genocide pursued by Milosevic or the Hutu
Power regime, it is obviously open to question whether an assimilation
achieved through decades of confiscation, coercive social policies, and
cultural obliteration is an end that justifies its means.

A recent final twist is worth noting. With the rise of China as an economic power in the last several years—not to mention the explosion of
market opportunities on the mainland—an increasing number of Thai
Chinese are reclaiming their Chinese identity. After decades of suppressing their Chinese heritage, many Thai Chinese are sending their children

to newly established Chinese language schools, visiting China in record numbers, investing in China, and reassuming Chinese surnames. Whether this renewed sense of ethnic Chinese pride and identity among Thai Chinese will have a destabilizing effect remains to be seen. Thus far, anti-Chinese resentment among indigenous Thais remains muted, although there are also indications that the acceptance of Thai Chinese by indigenous Thais is by no means complete. Today there are still restrictions on the use of the Chinese language. The Thai government recently forced a local cable television network to cancel its Chinese-language shows, citing long-standing regulations limiting broadcasts to Thai or English with Thai subtitles.[8]

More fundamentally, it is important to remember the limits of intermarriage and assimilation as an antidote to ethnic hatred. In Latin America and the Caribbean, extensive ethnic intermixing over many centuries has blurred ethnic lines, almost certainly helping to dampen ethnic conflict. But "ethnicity" is a highly artificial and manipulable concept, and "us against them" dynamics have repeatedly been generated even in countries where a market-dominant minority is highly assimilated or intermarrying in significant numbers with other groups. Assimilation did not protect Spanish Jews from repeated bloody attacks in the fifteenth century or German Jews in the Weimar Republic.

More recently, in the former Yugoslavia, intermarriage between Serbs and Croats was common, particularly in cosmopolitan cities like Sarajevo or Mostar. In pregenocide Rwanda, rates of intermarriage between Hutus and Tutsis were also substantial. But in neither country was assimilation or "mixing blood" sufficient to overcome the deadly fantasy of ethnicity as a source of power, a source of hate, and an excuse for mass slaughter.

PART THREE

ETHNONATIONALISM
AND THE WEST

The global spread of free market democracy has thus been a principal, aggravating cause of ethnic instability and violence throughout the non-Western world. In country after country outside the West—from Mandalay to Moscow, from Jakarta to Nairobi—laissez-faire markets have magnified the often astounding wealth and economic prominence of an "outsider" minority, generating great reservoirs of ethnic envy and resentment among the impoverished "indigenous" majority. In absolute terms the majority may actually be marginally better off as a result of markets—this was true, for example, of Indonesia and most of the Southeast Asian countries in the 1980s and 1990s—but these small improvements are overwhelmed by the majority's continuing poverty and the hated minority's extraordinary economic success, invariably including their control of the "crown jewels" of the economy.

Democracy, sadly, does not quell this resentment. On the contrary, democratization, by increasing the political voice and power of the "indigenous" majority, has fostered the emergence of demagogues—like Zimbabwe's Mugabe, Serbia's Milosevic, Russia's Zyuganov, Bolivia's Great Condor, and Rwanda's Hutu Power leaders—who opportunistically whip up mass hatred against the resented minority, demanding that the country's wealth be returned to the "true owners of the nation." As a result, in its raw, for-export form, the pursuit of free market democracy outside the West has repeatedly led not to widespread peace and prosperity, but to ethnic confiscation, authoritarian backlash, and mass killing.

What does all this have to do with the West? Is the non-Western world perhaps just hopeless—too divided, backward, and violent to sustain free market democracy? Perhaps the United States and the other Western nations should simply wash their hands of underdeveloped societies and their intractable, horrendous problems. In the end, what do market-dominant minorities and ethnonationalism have to do with us?

Actually, they have everything to do with us. Or so this final part of the book will argue.

The next four chapters will show that the explosive confrontation between a market-dominant minority and an aroused ethnonationalist majority is by no means limited to the non-Western world. On the contrary, this confrontation lurks beneath some of the most violent, abominable episodes of Western history. Moreover, even today this explosive dynamic is not confined to individual developing countries. It is being played out at regional and global levels in ways that directly affect the Western nations, particularly the United States.

CHAPTER 9

The Underside of
Western Free Market Democracy

From Jim Crow to the Holocaust

D o market-dominant minorities exist in the United States or Canada or Western Europe? The answer is: not today, at least not at the national level.

Take the United States. While some ethnic minorities have outperformed others, the United States economy is absolutely not controlled by any ethnic minority. On the contrary, if any group can be said to dominate our economy, it is the "white" majority. Generally speaking, Caucasians dominate every major economic sector: finance, technology, real estate, professions, corporate ownership and leadership, and so on. The ten richest Americans in 2001—Microsoft's Bill Gates, Paul Allen, and Steve Ballmer; Oracle's Lawrence Ellison; Warren Buffett; and five members of the Wal-Mart-founding Walton family[1]—are all white. (Incidentally, if Jewish-Americans are viewed as an ethnic minority in the United States, they do not remotely dominate the U.S. economy; unlike in Russia, for example, only one or at most two of the ten wealthiest Americans are Jewish.)

Of course, there is a good deal of artificiality in referring to "whites" as an ethnic group in the United States. Italian-Americans, for example, are counted as "whites" for census purposes, while Hispanic-Americans are treated as a separate ethnic group. Nonetheless, the core ethnic problem in the United States, as experienced by ordinary Americans, is one that pits an economically and politically dominant "white" majority against economically and politically weaker ethnic minorities.

The same is true in all the industrialized Western nations. In the

West we grapple daily with the problem of economically underprivi-leged ethnic minorities—blacks and Hispanics in the United States, African immigrants in France, aborigines in Australia, Maori in New Zealand, and so on. In stark contrast, the non-Western world today tends to be characterized by just the opposite dynamic: the presence, in country after country, of a tiny but economically powerful market-dominant ethnic minority.

The problems of ethnic conflict in the Western world today are therefore strikingly different from those outside the West, with very dif-ferent implications for free market democracy. In the developing world, markets tend to enrich ethnic minorities, while democracy tends to em-power poor, "indigenous" majorities, creating a highly combustible dy-namic. By contrast, in the contemporary Western nations both markets and democracy tend to reinforce the economic dominance of a per-ceived ethnic majority.

The Inherent Tension between Markets and Democracy

A closer look, however, reveals that the West is not free from the core dynamic—the confrontation between market wealth held by a few and democratic power held by the many—described in this book. For one thing, market-dominant ethnic minorities have existed, albeit rarely, in the Western nations in the past. As will be discussed below, the "solutions" the Western nations pursued to deal with market-dominant minorities were as ugly as any found in the developing world.

But even in the absence of a market-dominant minority, there is al-ways, in any democratic, capitalist society a potential conflict between market-generated wealth disparities and majoritarian politics. Even when the wealthy are not ethnically distinct, they are still a minority. Even when the poor do not view the rich as a different, "outsider" group, they may still feel resentment and envy toward those who em-ploy them, exploit them, and have immensely more wealth.

Societies *with* a market-dominant minority face a specially formida-ble problem: class conflict and ethnic conflict overlap in a particularly explosive way. The rich are not just rich, but members of a hated, out-sider ethnic group. In societies with *no* market-dominant minority, the division between the few who are rich and the many who are poorer is unlikely to be ethnicized—but it remains, at least potentially, a source of conflict. Wherever democracy and capitalism are joined together, mass political movements directed against the rich become a possibility, fueled by resentments and demagogic manipulation similar to (but usually less murderous than) that which arises in the presence of market-dominant minorities.

Indeed, for centuries it was thought that the danger of class conflict made universal suffrage irreconcilable with a market economy. Although largely forgotten today, leading Western statesmen, political philosophers, and economists long recognized a profound tension between market capitalism and democracy. Markets, it was thought, would produce enormous concentrations of wealth in the hands of a few, while democracy, by empowering the poor majority, would inevitably lead to convulsive acts of expropriation and confiscation. In Adam Smith's words in 1776, "For one very rich man, there must be at least five hundred poor. . . . The affluence of the rich excites the indignation of the poor, who are often both driven by want, and prompted by envy, to invade his possessions."

Similarly, James Madison warned against the "danger" to the rights of property posed by "an equality & universality of suffrage, vesting compleat power over property in hands without a share in it." David Ricardo was willing to extend suffrage only "to that part of [the people] which cannot be supposed to have any interest in overturning the rights of property." British statesman Thomas Babington Macaulay went further, portraying universal suffrage as "incompatible with property" and "consequently incompatible with civilization" itself:

> Imagine a well-meaning laborious mechanic fondly attached to his wife and children. Bad times come. He sees his wife whom he loves grow thinner and paler every day. His little ones cry for bread. . . . Then come the professional agitators, the tempters, and tell him that there is enough and more than enough for everybody, and that he has too little only because landed gentlemen, fundholders, bankers, manufacturers, railway proprietors, shopkeepers, have too much? Is it strange that the poor man

should be deluded, and should eagerly sign such a petition as this? The inequality with which wealth is distributed forces itself on everybody's notice. . . . The reasons which irrefragably prove this inequality to be necessary to the well-being of all classes are not equally obvious. . . .

[I]s it possible to doubt what the result [of universal suffrage] must be? . . . What could follow but one vast spoliation? One vast spoliation![2]

As it turned out, of course, these early doubters of free market democracy were proved wrong. Defining the terms broadly, markets and democracy have coexisted quite healthily in the United States for two hundred years, and the other leading developed countries have been both capitalist and democratic for at least a half century. That democratic politics proved compatible with capitalism in the West—that, in Claus Offe's words, the electoral "power of numbers" did not overwhelm the "power of property"—is one of the great surprises of modern history.[3]

Why didn't democracy result in confiscations and one "vast spoliation"? Why doesn't it do so today? Redistribution is one reason: All the Western nations today have enormous tax-and-transfer programs, dulling the harshest edges of class conflict. But redistribution is only part of the answer. As the West started down the road of free market democracy, a number of different institutions and cultural factors worked together to defuse the fissionable conflict between market-generated wealth and majoritarian politics. It is important to take a look at the most important of these institutions and cultural factors, to see whether they might be transplantable to countries outside the West today.

Two cautions should, however, be borne in mind. First, measures that help negotiate class conflict in societies with no market-dominant minority will not necessarily have the same success in societies where class conflict is magnified by the furies of ethnic hatred. Second, not all the devices used in the West to keep "the power of numbers" from overwhelming the "power of property" would make good exports to the non-Western world. Some of them are unique to circumstances of the early modern Western nations and could not be reproduced today. Some of them are invidious and *should* not be reproduced today.

Disenfranchisement of the Poor

In the early stages of capitalism in all the Western nations—and precisely because the wealthy were afraid that their property might be confiscated and redistributed—the poor were expressly disenfranchised. Until relatively recently, all of the Western democracies had massive exclusions from the suffrage. To take the case of the United States, after the Federal Convention of 1787 the poor were disenfranchised in virtually every state through formal property qualifications. Although such qualifications were largely eliminated by 1860, they were typically replaced by provisions denying suffrage to the very poor: for example, through taxpaying requirements and "pauper" exclusions. Moreover, as will be discussed below, blacks in the American South, and to a lesser extent throughout the United States, were effectively disenfranchised well into the twentieth century. Meanwhile, in at least fourteen states, recipients of poor relief were deprived of the franchise as late as 1934.[4]

Throughout Europe, the details differ but the basic story is the same: The poor and the propertyless were for decades, sometimes centuries, explicitly denied the right to vote. In England, a statute from 1430 provided that only those adult males with "a freehold estate the annual income from which was forty shillings" could elect members of the House of Commons. Forty shillings was the amount that in 1430 supposedly would "furnish all the necessaries of life, and render the freeholder, if he pleased, an independent man." In France, property and tax payment qualifications severely limited the franchise, even during the revolutionary period. In nineteenth-century Belgium, class domination by French speakers was perpetuated by laws limiting the vote to the propertied classes. Universal male suffrage came only in 1919.[5] The list goes on. Not only the United States, but all the Western nations had longstanding exclusions from suffrage. However repugnant, these political exclusions were arguably important to the success of the Western nations in establishing stable free market democracies.

Americans, however, have forgotten our own history. For the last twenty years the United States has been vigorously promoting instantaneous democratization—essentially overnight elections with universal suffrage—throughout the non-Western world. In doing so we are asking developing and post-Communist countries to embrace a process of democratization that no Western nation ever went through.

Capitalism Softened: The Rise of the Welfare State

As noted, in all the Western nations, and more recently Japan, the extreme wealth inequalities produced in a capitalist economy are alleviated by strong networks of redistributive institutions. The history, form, and mix of these institutions vary considerably. Generally speaking, social safety net programs have been broader, and governmental transfers larger, in Scandinavia and Western Europe than in the United States. In England, for example, the British government continues to provide broad national insurance benefits for unemployment, sickness, and disability, nationalized health care, and universally free public education, although there is constant talk of "radical" welfare reform. Germany's welfare system is supplemented by expansive pro-labor legislation. Under Japan's distinctive firm-as-extended-family employment system, Japanese firms promise (or used to promise) their employees lifetime job security. Sweden and the other Nordic countries all have extensive "cradle to grave" social legislation, including worker management rights, government-paid maternity and child support, and rent control. Not surprisingly, income tax rates in the Scandinavian countries are among the highest in the world.

Despite these variations, the bottom line is again the same. Starting in the late nineteenth century, the explosion of market activity throughout the West was accompanied by the emergence of redistributive institutions of unprecedented magnitude, softening the harshest effects of capitalism. In every developed country these institutions include not only relief to the extremely poor but also progressive taxation, social security, minimum wage laws, worker safety regulation, antitrust laws, and numerous other features of Western society that we take for granted.[6] These redistributive institutions have almost certainly helped dampen the conflict between market wealth disparities and democratic politics in the industrialized West.

By contrast, the version of capitalism being promoted outside the West today is essentially laissez-faire and rarely includes any significant redistributive mechanisms. In other words, the United States is aggressively exporting a model of capitalism that the Western nations themselves abandoned a century ago. More broadly, it is critical to recognize that the formula of free market democracy currently being pressed on non-Western nations—the simultaneous pursuit of laissez-faire capitalism and universal suffrage—is one that no Western nation ever adopted at any point in history.

Is this wise? Almost by definition, in the developing world today the poor are far more numerous, poverty is far more extreme, and inequality far more glaring than in the Western countries, either today or at analogous historical periods. The ongoing population explosion outside the West only makes things worse. If current World Bank projections are correct, the population in countries now classified as developing is expected to increase from roughly four billion today to roughly eight billion by the year 2050.[7] Meanwhile, the poor countries of the world lack the West's well-established rule of law traditions. As a result, political transitions in the developing world tend to be marked not by continuity and compromise, but rather by abrupt upheavals, military intervention, violence, and bloodshed.

In other words, today's universal policy prescription for "underdevelopment," shaped and promulgated to a large extent by the United States, essentially amounts to this. Take the rawest form of capitalism, slap it together with the rawest form of democracy, and export the two as a package deal to the poorest, most frustrated, most unstable, and most desperate countries of the world. Add market-dominant minorities to the picture, and the instability inherent in this bareknuckle version of free market democracy is compounded a thousandfold by the manipulable forces of ethnic hatred.

The Idiosyncracy of the American Dream

Disenfranchisement of the poor and the welfare state only partially explain why capitalism and democracy have proved so compatible in the West. In all the Western nations, many among the less-well-off majority do not *want* to confiscate from the rich or equalize incomes. The reasons for this, which might be described as cultural or ideological, are enormously complicated and obviously depend on the particular country in question. As an illustration, I will focus here primarily on the United States.

Poor and lower-middle-class Americans are often capitalism's biggest fans. Although there is an important racial underside to this story—to which I will return below—the fact is that a surprising percentage of America's less well off love billionaires and spurn welfare mothers. They vote Republican and fight higher taxes. The last thing they want is government interference and redistribution.

Why? Part of the answer is the American Dream. Significant numbers of Americans believe that anyone, high or low, can move up the economic ladder as long as they are talented, hardworking, entrepreneurial, and not too unlucky. A driven Vietnamese-immigrant student once explained to me, "I may be poor now, but the reason I vote Republican is because I don't plan to be poor for very much longer." And recently from *Forbes:*

> America has created a system in which anyone with talent and energy has access to the financial resources needed for success. . . .
>
> Today banks, venture capitalists, underwriters and stock brokers here don't much care who your grandfather was or whether you went to a prep school or dropped out of college. All they care about is: Can we make some bucks by backing this guy (or gal)?
>
> This is not true in Japan. It is not true in Brazil. It is not even true in France or Germany. . . . In Germany, Bill Gates might well have had to go to work for Siemens. In Japan, Gates most certainly would have ended up as salaryman for Hitachi. . . .[8]

The belief in the possibility of upward mobility has characterized America since its inception. No doubt it reflects in part our history of westward expansion and our distinctive immigrant foundations. More fundamentally, it is sustained by an impressive number of actual rags-to-riches stories. American literature, for example, is filled with such stories: from Horatio Alger's *Ragged Dick* to F. Scott Fitzgerald's *The Great Gatsby* to the recent biographies of Lee Iacocca, Arnold Schwarzenegger, and Oprah Winfrey, not to mention Bill Clinton and Bill Gates.

Ideally, the American Dream gives everyone a psychological stake in the continuing success of the market economy. At its extreme, the American Dream teaches the worse-off that their plight is the result not of an unfair or invidious economic system, but rather of their own deficiencies. In both these ways, the American Dream helps make acceptable the extreme wealth disparities inevitably produced in a capitalist economy.

It is important to recognize that the belief that anyone has a shot at fame and fortune is in some ways idiosyncratic to the United States. It has no real analogue even in the high-income countries of Western Europe, let alone the chronically poor, malnourished societies of the developing world.

Outside the West, in countries with widespread poverty and a market-dominant minority, the dream of upward mobility is largely a nonstarter. It is extremely difficult to believe in the possibility of market-generated upward mobility if you and everyone around you is mired in intractable poverty *and* the only wealthy people in the country appear to be members of a different ethnic group. (In the United States, African-Americans are probably the group who least credit the idea that in America anyone with talent and industry can "make it.") The truth is that among the impoverished indigenous majorities of the developing world, exceedingly few believe that free markets will enable them to go "from rags to riches." For this reason, anti-market backlashes are much more common outside the West than in the United States or Europe.

Racism in America: Fracturing the Poor Majority

Finally, in the United States, racism has arguably helped neutralize the conflict between markets and democracy, essentially by fracturing the poor majority. As a historical matter, it is well-established that racism hindered the formation of political alliances between poor and working-class whites on one hand, and poor and working-class minorities on the other hand. After the Second World War, for example, the

CIO's mass unionization campaign in the Southern states known as "Operation Dixie" failed dismally, unable to overcome "the insuperable task of forming unified workplace movements between white workers, who attended Klan meetings after work, and black workers."[9] And starting in the sixties, as the Democratic Party became increasingly associated with civil rights, lower-class whites in the South jumped to the Republican Party in droves.[10]

Even today, many poor and lower-middle-class whites feel more solidarity with Bill Gates or George W. Bush than with African-Americans or Hispanic-Americans of comparable economic status. Indeed, as many have observed, large numbers of working-class whites in the United States oppose welfare and increased government spending on social services, often voting against what might be expected to be their economic self-interest. It is widely suspected that racism (together with a thriving ideology of upward mobility) plays a role in this pattern.

———

To summarize, there is always an inherent instability in free market democracy. None of the Western democracies today faces this instability in its most explosive form: when the wealthy minority is also a hated, ethnic "outsider" group. Even so, every one of the Western democracies has alleviated the potential conflict between the rich few and the poor many through a host of devices, past and present, such as extensive social safety nets and redistribution, gradual expansion of the suffrage, upward mobility, and even racism. It is important to recognize, as we export free market democracy to the non-Western world, that many of these stabilizing devices do not exist in the developing world, that some of them are unsavory, and that others are, practically speaking, unreproducible.

The next section will cast a further shadow. As already mentioned, market-dominant minorities have existed in the West in the past. On the relatively rare occasions when a Western nation had to confront the problem of rapid democratization in the face of widespread poverty and a deeply resented, perceived market-dominant minority, the consequences were as terrible as any the world has seen. I will focus on just two examples here, one from the United States, the other from Western Europe.

The American South

In the United States after the Civil War, newly emancipated blacks represented a majority of the population in a number of Southern states including Alabama, Florida, Georgia, Louisiana, Mississippi, and South Carolina. In all these states—not unlike postapartheid South Africa—whites were a starkly market-dominant minority, terrified to the point of hysteria at the prospect of black majority rule. Thus, the first year after the Emancipation Declaration, "a great fear of black insurrection and revenge seized many minds," writes C. Vann Woodward in *The Strange Career of Jim Crow*. "[T]he black race," warned Southern politicians, if mobilized, "will be in a large majority, and then we will have black governors, black legislatures, black juries, black everything. . . . We will be completely exterminated, and the land will be left in the possession of the blacks, and then it will go back into a wilderness and become another Africa or St. Domingo."[11]

Southern whites responded to the threat of black majority rule by effectively disenfranchising blacks. They did so, moreover, in the name of capitalism and white supremacy. (Else, in the words of Alabama's James S. Clark, "our lovely State, with its few Caucasian inhabitants, would be converted into a kind of American Congo.")[12] To be sure, these Southerners faced the problem of the newly enacted Fifteenth Amendment, supposedly prohibiting discrimination against blacks in the suffrage. Led, however, by Mississippi, where impoverished blacks constituted 70 percent of the population in 1870, all the Southern states found elaborate ways to prevent blacks from exercising their right to vote. There were even, as late as the mid-twentieth century, delegations from the American South to South Africa to learn "tips" on how to disenfranchise and subjugate an ethnic majority.

The basic technique for establishing white minority rule in the American South was to set up barriers to voting such as property or literacy qualifications, and then to create exemptions that only white males could satisfy. Between 1895 and 1910, variations of this scheme were incorporated into the state constitutions of South Carolina, Louisiana, North Carolina, Alabama, Virginia, Georgia, and Oklahoma. Although these restrictions were highly effective in reducing the black vote, many Southern states adopted poll taxes as further obstacles.

Violence, intimidation, and racially motivated redistricting took care of most remaining blacks. As late as the 1960s it was physically dangerous for blacks as well as whites to demonstrate on behalf of black voter registration or to try to organize blacks to register and vote; some were killed for doing so.[13]

The Fifteenth Amendment of the U.S. Constitution notwithstanding, disenfranchisement of black majorities during the Jim Crow period was highly successful. In Louisiana, for example, the number of registered African-American voters fell from 130,334 in 1896 to only 1,342 in 1904. In 1896, African-Americans represented a majority in twenty-six districts; by 1900 in none. At the same time, "separate but equal" laws were proliferating. During the First World War, Maurice Evans, an Englishman who lived in South Africa, visited the American South. He found the situation there "strikingly similar" to the one he had left behind at home: "The separation of the races in all social matters is as distinct in South Africa as in the Southern States. There are separate railway cars . . . and no black man enters hotel, theatre, public library or art gallery." In addition, there were "the same separate schools, the same disenfranchisement, and the same political and economic subordination of the black man." Wealthy Southern whites were aware of the parallel as well. "There are more Negroes in Mississippi," wrote Alfred Stone, a plantation owner from the Yazoo Delta of Mississippi, "than in Cape Colony, or Natal, even with the great territory of Zululand annexed to the latter; more than in the Transvaal, and not far from as many as in both of the Boer colonies combined."[14]

After the Second World War, with the rise of the civil rights movement in the United States, the paths of the American South and South Africa dramatically diverged. Nevertheless, the bottom line remains. After the Civil War, whites in a number of Southern states suddenly found themselves in the position of a starkly market-dominant minority, fearful of "black domination," revenge, confiscation, and radical redistribution at the hands of a newly empowered black majority. Facing what it saw as the unresolvable conflict between a black-dominated democracy and the maintenance of their own wealth and status, Southern whites opted aggressively for the latter, doing everything in their power to undercut the former.

By contrast to the developing world today, Americans generally have not had to deal with the problem of sudden democratization in the face of pervasive poverty and a deeply resented, market-dominant minority. But several post–Civil War Southern states did face this precise problem, and Americans hardly rose with dignity to the challenge. As in apartheid South Africa or Rhodesia, market-dominant whites in the American South responded to the prospect of black majority rule by mass disenfranchisement.

Thus, along with the developing-world illustrations I gave in chapter 6, the American South during the Jim Crow era is a classic example of a backlash against democracy, in which a market-dominant minority, fearful of confiscation and redistribution, seizes political power. Unfortunately, the historical record of the West is darker still.

Weimar Germany and the Nazi Holocaust

Weimar Germany is a rare example of a Western nation that pursued—with catastrophic ethnonationalist consequences—free market democracy under conditions strikingly analogous to those characteristic of many developing countries today. Caution is required here. The Holocaust is in some ways so singularly evil that no straightforward comparison can be made between Nazi Germany and any other country, at any other time. To avoid misunderstanding, I offer three preliminary clarifications.

First, the Jews in Weimar Germany were not an economically dominant minority in the sense that, say, the Chinese are economically dominant in most Southeast Asian countries. Claims that "Jews ran the German economy" were patently false. Second, I am distinctly not suggesting that the roots of anti-Semitism in Weimar Germany, or anywhere else for that matter, were economic in nature. Anti-Semitism in Germany, as elsewhere in the world, existed long before Jews were particularly successful economically. (Economic grievances certainly had nothing to do with the numerous pogroms directed at poor shtetls in Russia and Eastern Europe.) Third, Weimar Germany obviously differed in profound respects from most of today's developing countries. For example, Germany was a former imperial power, with colonies and pro-

tectorates all over Africa and a formidable naval fleet and army. Weimar
Germans, including women, were far more educated than the average
inhabitant of the developing world today. Commentators have described
Weimar Germany as "a cradle of modernity." Moreover, Weimar
Germany had a powerful industrial base, an impressive network of rail-
ways and infrastructure, and a highly sophisticated banking system.[15]

Nevertheless, conditions in post–World War I Germany were more
analogous to those in the developing world today than one might think.
Most crucially, Weimar Germany was characterized by widespread economic deprivation and suffering, in large part because of inflation that
reached catastrophic proportions in 1923. (By most accounts the principal cause of the inflation was not reparations to the Allies, but rather the
excessive national debt that Imperial Germany had incurred in financing
the war.) With the plunging mark, writes historian Gordon Craig, "the
simplest of objects were . . . invested with monstrous value—the humble kohlrabi shamefacedly wearing a price-tag of 50 millions, the penny
postage stamp costing as much as a Dahlem villa in 1890. . . ." While a
few—principally industrialists and speculators—profited from the inflation, millions of working and middle-class Germans were left suddenly
impoverished. Those on fixed incomes or pensions were hit hardest. At
one point, in late 1923, only 29 percent of the total German labor force
was fully employed. Contributing to the mass frustration was a chronic
national housing shortage, estimated at 1.5 million dwellings in
1919–20. As in the developing world, malnutrition and disease in the
Weimar Republic were pervasive, particularly among children and the
old. Deaths from hunger were common.[16]

Against this background, Jews in the Weimar Republic were widely
perceived as an "outsider" ethnic minority wielding outrageously disproportionate economic power vis-à-vis the "indigenous" majority. The reality of the Jews' economic situation in the Weimar Republic was as
follows. Relative to their tiny numbers—Jews formed just under 1 percent of the total population of Germany—they were disproportionately
represented in certain professions and occupations. Between 1918 and
1933, nearly three-quarters of German Jews earned their livelihood
from trade, commerce, banking, and the professions, particularly law
and medicine. By contrast, only about one-quarter of the non-Jewish
population of Germany was similarly employed.

Thus in 1933, Jews made up around 10 percent of Germany's doctors and more than 16 percent of its lawyers and notaries public. Commerce and finance, however, were the major pursuits of most German Jews. In 1930, Jews owned 40 percent of Germany's wholesale textile firms and nearly 60 percent of the country's wholesale and retail clothing businesses. In 1932, Jews owned roughly 80 percent of all department store business. Weimar Jews were also prominent in banking. Nearly half of the country's private banks were owned by Jewish banking families like the Bleichroders, Mendelssohns, and Schlesingers. On the other hand, Jews controlled almost none of Germany's more numerous and increasingly important credit banks; nor were the modern large banks that financed the German industrialization principally controlled by Jews. Although a significant number of German Jews were extremely well off, the great majority of them belonged to the middle classes, and many Weimar Jews were poor.[17]

The economic picture of the Weimar Jews was thus a mixed one. Jews plainly did not control the Weimar economy. To the contrary, the wealthiest Germans in the Weimar Republic by and large were non-Jews: members of the nobility or landowning aristocracy as well as powerful industrialists such as Robert Bosch, Carl Friedrich von Siemens, and Hugo Stinnes.[18] On the other hand, almost no Jews were peasants, farmers, or members of the urban proletariat, and the average income of Jews was 3.2 times that of the general Weimar population.[19]

It is crucial to reiterate that the "Jewish problem" in Germany was far more than an economic problem. As many have pointed out, anti-Semitic economic hostility "is necessarily predicated upon the anti-semites' marking of the Jews as being different, identifying them not by the many other (more relevant) features of these people's identities, but as Jews, and then using this label as the *defining* feature of these people . . ."[20] The imagery and rhetoric used against German Jews was contradictory and confused. Thus, writes Gordon Craig, "the arrogant Jew" included "the flea-market and marts-of-trade and stock-market Jew, the Press and literature Jew, the parliamentary Jew, the theatre and music Jew, the culture and humanity Jew . . ." Although "materialist," Jews did not work but only "exploited." Jews were both greedy "capitalists" and the "secret force behind Communism."[21]

Nevertheless, regardless of the falsity of the charges of Jewish economic dominance, there was undeniably an economic dimension to the mobilization of German anti-Semitism. The stereotype of the Jew as rich and rapacious had long existed in Germany (as in many other European countries). Four hundred years before Hitler capitalized on this theme, Martin Luther wrote: "[T]hey hold us Christians captive in our country. They let us work in the sweat of our noses, to earn money and property for them, while they . . . mock us and spit on us, because we work and permit them to be lazy squires who own us and our realm." Similar rhetoric accompanied the vicious wave of anti-Semitism following the financial crash of 1873. Fifty years later, Jews in Weimar were widely accused, by Germans high and low, of being "uniformly prosperous," "ruling Germany financially, economically," and causing the nation's economic privations.[22] In other words, the Jews were said to be a grossly economically dominant outsider minority even though their actual level of economic success did not warrant this perception. As in many developing countries today, these charges of economic dominance provided a convenient spur to, and rationalization of, ethnic mobilization.

Weimar Germany shared another feature in common with most of today's developing countries: Germany after the First World War embarked on a period of intense marketization and democratization. Whereas normal market transactions had ground virtually to a halt during the war, Germany after 1918 saw a massive influx of foreign investment, new international trade opportunities, a burst in industrialization, and the accumulation of huge fortunes by big business and financiers. Like today's "emerging economies," the Weimar government undertook freewheeling economic liberalization, for example by eliminating import-export quotas; offering tax breaks to businesses and holders of capital; and, after 1923, repealing significant labor-law protections including, perhaps most strikingly, the eight-hour workday.

At the same time, Weimar Germany pursued intense democratization. In 1918 and 1919, over a period of barely ten months, Emperor Wilhelm II abdicated, the German people elected a National Assembly, and the National Assembly promulgated a new constitution providing for universal suffrage, direct popular election of the Reich president, and the never-before-tried practice of popular referenda. The new constitution also guaranteed a lengthy list of fundamental human rights *(Grundrechte)*.[23]

In other words, to a surprising extent Weimar Germany shared both the basic background conditions prevalent in many developing countries today and the standard policy package being pursued by these countries. In conditions of widespread economic distress and a (perceived) economically dominant minority, Weimar Germany pursued intensive market liberalization and rapid democratization. Indeed, in important respects, conditions in Weimar Germany were more propitious for the success of these policies than they are in the developing world today. For example, Weimar Germany had a much higher general level of education; an impressive array of "social safety nets"; and a much stronger legal system, whose judges were notoriously independent (and anti-Semitic).

The fate, however, of Weimar free market democracy is well known. In 1932 and 1933, the National Socialist German Workers' Party, as the Nazi Party was formally named, gained control of the German government through electoral means. Although historians over the last fifty years have repeatedly described the Nazi movement as self-contradictory and ideologically inconsistent—"a confused mixture of nationalistic, anti-Semitic, and pseudo-socialist demands"[24]—the Nazi movement led by Adolf Hitler was in fact unwaveringly and quintessentially ethnonationalist, and in this diseased sense, perfectly coherent. Point Four of the twenty-five-point party program (coauthored by Hitler and promulgated in 1920) declared: "Only members of the nation may be citizens of the State. Only those of German blood, whatever their creed, may be members of the nation. Accordingly no Jew may be a member of the nation."[25]

Like the ethnonationalist movements of the developing world, National Socialism was never truly socialist. The Nazis never undertook to abolish the institution of private property nor to eradicate all economic classes. On the contrary, Hitler repeatedly made overtures to big business, and the Nazi movement was supported by many wealthy Germans, including industrial magnates and aristocrats. Indeed, Nazism was more anti-Communist than it was anticapitalist—in either case with the same anti-Semitic thrust. Precisely because its principal commitment was to ethnonationalism, there was little need for an economic policy. (Once heard at a Nazi gathering: "We don't want higher bread prices! We don't want lower bread prices! We don't want unchanged bread prices! We want National Socialist bread prices!") Far more than any of its rivals, the Nazi Party was successful in bridging social cleavages and transcending class divisions—from industrial tycoons to farmers, but above all the middle class—in its call for a once-again-powerful Germany for "true Germans" and the destruction of Germany's "enemies" at home and abroad.[26]

Once Hitler was in power, "the destruction of the Jewish race in Europe" became a guiding principle of official state policy. Hitler began with a series of laws depriving Jews, through stringent "racial" qualifications, of their positions in the state bureaucracy, the judiciary, universities, and the professions. In 1938, for example, Hermann Goering required Jewish physicians and lawyers to liquidate their practices, then issued the more general Decree on Eliminating the Jews from German Economic Life. Soon afterward he dictated the wholesale expropriation of Jewish property and businesses. Goering insisted that expropriated Jewish property belonged to the state. In reality, private German enterprises were the main beneficiaries. At the same time, Jews were stripped of their citizenship and political rights. Hitler's "final solution" was the extermination between 1941 and 1945 of an estimated 6 million people, most of them Jews.[27]

Once again, I am making no claims here about the immediate or ultimate causes of the Holocaust. The point is simply that Weimar Germany stands as a somber warning against having excessive confidence in free market democracy as the universal solution to the problems of underdevelopment in societies with a (real or perceived) market-dominant minority. Weimar Germany marketized and democratized with a steadiness that would make most of today's international policymakers proud. Yet in Germany after World War I, the pursuit of free market democracy fueled an ethnonationalist conflagration of precisely the kind that today threatens much of the non-Western world.

Market-Dominant Minorities in U.S. Inner Cities

Are market-dominant minorities a thing of the past in the West? For the moment, the answer is yes. At the national level, none of the contemporary Western nations has an ethnic minority that comes close to controlling the economy. In the United States, self-identified "whites" make up roughly 72 percent of the population and wield roughly proportionate economic power. On the other hand, the story becomes more complex if we look both within certain pockets of the United States today and at nationwide demographic projections for the future.

In the inner cities of all the major metropolitan areas across the United States, ethnic Koreans represent an increasingly glaring market-dominant minority vis-à-vis the relatively economically depressed African-American majorities around them. In New York City, Koreans, less than .1 percent of the city's population, own 85 percent of produce stands, 70 percent of grocery stores, 80 percent of nail salons, and 60 percent of dry cleaners. In portions of downtown Los Angeles, Koreans own 40 percent of the real estate but constitute only 10 percent of the residents. Korean-American businesses in Los Angeles County number roughly 25,000, with gross sales of $4.5 billion. Nationwide, Korean entrepreneurs have in the last decade come to control 80 percent of the $2.5 billion African-American beauty business, which—"like preaching and burying people"—historically was always a "black" business and a source of pride, income, and jobs for African-Americans. "They've come in and taken away a market that's not rightfully theirs," is the common, angry view among inner-city blacks.[28]

Because Asians are relative newcomers, African-Americans view themselves as the "indigenous" and "true" inhabitants of the inner cities, who are now being ripped off, condescended to, and economically displaced by exploitative "outsiders." In 1990, a nine-month racial boycott against two Korean produce stores in Flatbush, Brooklyn, eventually drove both stores out of business. Led by the Reverend Al Sharpton, the boycotts fueled Asian-black tensions across the city. Two years later, during the Los Angeles riots that followed the jury acquittal of police officers charged with beating Rodney King, African-Americans burned or looted an estimated two hundred Korean grocery shops, smashing win-

dows and attacking Korean shopowners with knives, guns, and crow-
bars. In the end, fifty-five people died (many of them African-American), another two thousand were injured, and property losses totaled
roughly $1 billion.

Relations between Korean-Americans and African-Americans seem
to have improved since the Los Angeles riots, as leaders from both
groups have made conciliatory efforts. Nevertheless, periodic bursts of
anti-Korean baiting and violence still occur. At a December 31, 1994,
rally, Norman "Grand Dad" Reide, vice president of Al Sharpton's
National Action Network, accused Koreans of "reaping a financial harvest at the expense of black people" and recommended that "we boycott
the bloodsucking Koreans." More recently, in November 2000, African-
Americans firebombed a Korean-owned grocery store in northeast
Washington, D.C. The spray-painted message on the charred walls:
"Burn them down, Shut them down, Black Power!"[29]

Ethnic Koreans, along with other Asian subgroups such as Chinese
or Vietnamese, are not the only market-dominant minorities in America's inner cities. In certain communities—Brooklyn's Crown Heights,
for example—Orthodox Jews are a highly visible "outsider" entrepreneurial minority, deeply resented by the much more numerous, and far
poorer, African-American majorities around them. In 1991, after ethnic
violence broke out when a Hasidic Jewish driver in Crown Heights
struck and killed a black child, anger on both sides ran especially high.
"You're not going to run New York City any longer," Nancy Mere, an
African-American Housing Authority assistant, shouted at Orthodox
Jewish leaders at a news conference at city hall. "It was okay when our
mothers were cleaning your floors and taking care of your babies—that
was okay. But we're not going to have it anymore." Mere then added,
expressing a typical sentiment, "We hear about the Holocaust, the
Holocaust, the Holocaust. Well, the black man has lived through a holocaust in this city and it's terrible, and we're not taking it anymore."

Meanwhile, black community leaders have done their share in fomenting resentment against entrepreneurial minorities. At a series of
fiery rallies in 1995, and shortly after calling for anti-Korean boycotts,
Reide called for mass boycotts targeting Jewish-owned businesses.
"Nobody loves money any more than the Jewish people," he yelled in a

speech that was broadcast live on radio station WWRL. In response to charges that national black leaders like Al Sharpton and Louis Farrakhan were anti-Semitic, Reide threatened, to thunderous applause, that unless the accusations stopped, "we will marshal six million black men and women and boycott every Jewish-owned business throughout the United States." He then named specific targets: "There are 91 Waldbaum's stores; we will boycott them. There are 618 nationwide Toys 'R' Us stores; we will boycott them. There are 145 New York City Key Food shopping markets; we will boycott them. We will boycott Macy's."[30]

The "Browning of America"

According to the latest census data, in the state of California the number of whites is less than the combined number of Hispanic-, Asian-, and African-Americans. In the United States as a whole, the Census Bureau projects that whites will be a minority by 2060.[31] At that point, if these projections hold true, the United States may well have a market-dominant minority at the national level, starting in the latter half of this century.

Nevertheless, anxiety about "the browning of America" must be kept in perspective. There are powerful reasons to think that majority-based ethnonationalist movements targeting a white market-dominant minority are unlikely to develop in the United States. To begin with, given how large a percentage of America's population will still be white, it is extremely implausible that an antiwhite political movement could be democratically successful in the United States. Moreover, unlike most developing countries, there is a strong, ethnically crosscutting national identity in the United States, which would make it far more difficult for politicians to portray American whites as "outsiders" stealing the wealth from America's "true" Hispanic, black, or Asian "owners." (If Native Americans were still a majority in the United States, it might be a very different story.) In addition, rates of ethnic intermarriage and cultural assimilation are relatively high in the United States. While intermarriage is no guarantee against ethnic conflict, it is hard to imagine that American society will ever again look like a South Africa or Indonesia, where ethnic intermarriage rates are virtually nil.

Finally, as in all the Western nations, America's less well off are rich by comparison to their developing-world counterparts. In the United States, even blue-collar workers have cars, television sets, and some savings. At work they are entitled to health benefits, paid vacations, and disability compensation. Outside the West, great majorities own no property and live in hopeless, open-sewer poverty. As a result, they are much more embracing of anti-market rhetoric and confiscatory policies. In the United States, most people have CD players and a garden, think of themselves as middle-class, and, at least outside our inner cities, believe at some level in the American Dream. For all these reasons, the possibility that there might someday arise within the United States, or for that matter in any of the Western nations, an antiwhite, anti-market ethnonationalist backlash is extraordinarily slim.

Indeed, precisely because American society is so wealthy overall, America has come to occupy the role of a starkly market-dominant minority vis-à-vis the rest of world. We are now the object of intense resentment, even hatred, spurred by globalization. But this is the subject of chapter 11.

CHAPTER 10

The Middle Eastern Cauldron

Israeli Jews as
a Regional Market-Dominant Minority

The events of September 11, 2001, brought home to Americans the reality of Islamic terrorism and the importance of the Middle East conflict to American interests. The roots of that conflict have been attributed to many sources: religious fundamentalism, "ancient" Arab-Israeli animosities, the dispossession of Palestinian land, the nature of Islam, repressive regimes in the Arab states, American support for those regimes based on our need for oil, and so on.

These explanations are all partially true. But they leave out a crucial dimension of the story: the galvanizing effect of globalization on ethnic conflict. In the Middle East as elsewhere, globalization has wildly disproportionately benefited an "outsider" market-dominant minority—in this case, the Israeli Jews—fueling ethnic resentment and hatred among a massive, demagogue-incited population that considers itself the "indigenous" "true owners of the land." In the Middle East, however, this conflict occurs not at the national, but at the regional level.

Previously throughout this book I have focused on dynamics internal to nations: specifically, the danger, within individual countries, of sudden democratization in the presence of widespread poverty and a resented market-dominant minority. By contrast, the Arab-Israeli conflict spans a number of different countries, and the market-dominant minority is for the most part located in a separate sovereign jurisdiction. Moreover, the Middle East, with only a few exceptions (of which Israel is one), has so far been seemingly immune to democratization—and the United States notoriously lax in promoting it, particularly among our oil-rich Gulf allies.

The Arab-Israeli conflict is about as loaded and complex as any the world has seen, involving religion, land, geopolitics, colonization and decolonization issues, competing claims to self-determination, and much more. To suggest that the Arab-Israeli struggle is principally about economic disparities would be both absurd and offensive. In addition, it is difficult to disentangle Arab animosity toward Israeli Jews from a broader anti-Semitism or from antisecular, anti-Western hostility more generally. Nevertheless, among many other dynamics, the Arab-Israeli conflict—pitting the region's 221 million, largely poor Arabs against Israel's starkly more prosperous 5.2 million Jews'—is a classic example of an intensely popular, majority-supported ethnonationalist movement directed against a hated, market-dominant minority. But let's back up a bit and look first at some of the individual countries in the region.

The Absence of Market-Dominant Minorities in the Arab Countries of the Middle East

With a few possible exceptions, market-dominant minorities do not exist within particular countries in the Middle East. The ruling elites in the Arab states may be distinguishable in important respects from the poor masses they govern—for example, in their extreme wealth, their Western dress and orientation, or their relative religious moderation—but they are not perceived as ethnically distinct outsiders. Nor does Israel appear to have a market-dominant minority, although the Ashkenazim/Sephardim divide will be discussed in the following section.

Putting aside Israel for the moment, the Middle East can be roughly divided into three subregions: North Africa, the Gulf States, and the "Levant" or "*Mashriq*" countries. The North African countries include Algeria, Egypt, Libya, Morocco, and Tunisia. The Gulf States include Saudi Arabia, Kuwait, Bahrain, Qatar, the United Arab Emirates, Oman, and Yemen. The Levant, a colonial term (*al-Mashriq* is the Arabic equivalent), usually refers to the countries of the eastern Mediterranean including Lebanon, Syria, Jordan, and Iraq. In addition, Iran and Turkey, while not always considered part of the Middle East because their populations are not predominately Arab, are often included in the description of the Middle East region as they share the same religious traditions and an interwoven political history.

There are no market-dominant minorities today in North Africa. The major ethnic divisions in North Africa are between Arab and Berber. Self-identified Berbers make up roughly one-quarter of the population in Algeria, where political and economic friction has frequently resulted in mass demonstrations and deadly riots. Estimates of the Berber population in Morocco typically range from 30 percent to 45 percent. Berbers represent much smaller minorities in Libya and Tunisia. It is worth noting that most Berbers are also Muslim and that there has been considerable intermarriage since the rise of Islam and concurrent Arab influx some thirteen hundred years ago. In any event, Berbers are certainly not market-dominant, and if anything, disproportionately poor.

In Egypt, historically, the Christian Copt minority was disproportionately economically successful. Their market dominance, however, was largely broken up by President Gamal Abdel Nasser, whose sweeping (and economically disastrous) land reforms and nationalizations in the 1950s disproportionately targeted wealthy Copts. Today, while there remain some very successful Coptic business families, Egypt's economic elite, including many military insiders, is heavily Muslim and not perceived as ethnically distinct from the rest of the population.[2]

Similarly, there are few, if any, market-dominant minorities in the Gulf States. The main religious divide in the Gulf is between Sunni Muslims and Shia Muslims. The vast majority of the population in the Gulf States are Sunni Muslims, although each country has its own distinctive dynamic. In Bahrain, for example, the population is 70 percent Shia Muslim and only 30 percent Sunni. Because the ruling family and those with significant economic power in Bahrain are Sunni, the Shia majority often complains of their second-class status, and the kingdom has been rocked by a number of disturbances and riots over the years. Most Middle East experts agree that the Shia majority would vote out their Sunni overlords were there to be any real democratic opening.

More generally, most of the ruling families in the Gulf States are repressive and appear to be increasingly unpopular in their own countries, where they are widely viewed as morally bankrupt, toadying to the United States and living off the fat of a corrupt capitalism. Although the citizens of the Gulf countries enjoy a significantly higher standard of living than their brethren in the *Mashriq,* the consensus is that democratization in these countries would probably lead to the ouster of the current regimes. Nevertheless, with a few possible exceptions (such as Bahrain), the fact remains that the ruling families in the Gulf are not ethnically distinct from the majority of their populations.[3]

In the Levant there are significant group divisions, mostly along religious lines. Christians make up a substantial portion of the population in Lebanon (30–35 percent), Syria (10 percent), and Jordan (6 percent). Other religious divisions exist between various Muslim sects—most notably Druze in Lebanon and Alowite in Syria. In Syria, the Alowite have controlled the presidency through the military dictatorship of Hafez al-Asad and now his son, Bashir al-Asad. As with Bahrain, it is a near certainty that democratization in Syria would severely undercut the Alowite sect's current political and economic dominance.

Lebanon is perhaps the most religiously diverse country in the region, with its plethora of Muslim and Christian sects. After World War I, for reasons including the establishment by the French of a confessional power-sharing system in which the country's Christian Maronites controlled the presidency, Lebanese Christians emerged as something of a market-dominant minority, deeply resented by the country's majority Muslim population. Largely over this issue, bitter civil war erupted in 1976, causing many wealthy Lebanese to flee the country. The extraordinary market-dominance of the Lebanese minorities in Latin America and West Africa has already been noted; many of these successful expatriate Lebanese have been Christians.

Today, Lebanon is generally viewed as being on the cautious upswing, although military dominance and political interference by Syria remain serious problems. With the 1991 Taif Accord, a new power-sharing system was put in place, in theory giving the country's Muslim majority political representation more proportionate to their numbers. At the same time, many wealthy Lebanese Christians are returning to the country. Whether the problem of a market-dominant minority reasserts itself in Lebanon's struggling democracy remains to be seen.[4]

In sum, with only a few possible exceptions, none of the Arab countries has a market-dominant minority. Few, if any, are democratizing.

Rather, throughout the Arab Middle East, economic and political power tends to be concentrated in the hands of a corrupt, repressive, often hereditary ruling elite that deflects popular criticism by fomenting hatred against other, "outsider" targets.

Israel: Ashkenazim as a Market-Dominant Minority?

Israel presents a surprisingly complicated case. This is true even if we bracket off the country's Arab population for the moment and focus only on Israeli Jews. If the division between Ashkenazi Jews and Sephardic Jews is viewed as an ethnic division—I return to this question later—then the former are arguably a market-dominant minority.

In the Middle Ages, explains Bernard Lewis, the terms Ashkenaz and Sepharad (actually two ancient place names from the Hebrew Bible) were used to refer to Germany and Spain, respectively. Over time, Ashkenazim came to refer to Jews of European or Russian origin, most of whom in the past spoke Yiddish, a German dialect. By contrast, the term Sephardim came to denote Jews who came from the Arab-speaking Muslim lands, even though only a small portion of these Jews actually originated in Spain. Ashkenazim founded modern Israel, but by far the largest immigration to the country after independence was from Muslim countries. At least until recently, Sephardim made up roughly 55 percent of the Jewish population in Israel.[5]

Generally speaking, Sephardic Jews are said to be darker and to "look Arab" whereas Ashkenazi Jews "look European." Historically, Sephardic Jews from the Muslim countries were linguistically Arab and today often still speak Hebrew with an Arabic accent. Other cultural differences, more pronounced thirty years ago but still evident, include demographic patterns (orthodox Sephardim have higher birth rates), family organization (Sephardim are more patriarchal), religious observance, and so on. Provocatively, Bernard Lewis describes the Ashkenazim/Sephardim division in terms of a contest between "Jews of Christendom" and "Jews of Islam," "both groups bringing with them certain attitudes, habits, and cultural traditions from their countries and societies of origin. They have now come together in an intense symbiosis."[6]

In addition to cultural differences, there remains a substantial and persistent socioeconomic gap between Israel's Ashkenazi and Sephardic Jews. Ashkenazim have dominated the elite institutions and professions of Israel since the state was founded. By contrast, most Sephardim came from much poorer, barely industrialized countries and typically arrived in Israel with little education, capital, or modern skills. Thus, writing for a prominent Israeli newspaper in 1949, Arye Gelblum lamented of his Sephardic compatriots: "[These immigrants are] only slightly better than the general level of the Arabs, Negroes, and Berbers in the same regions. . . . These Jews also lack roots in Judaism, as they are totally subordinated to the play of savage and primitive instincts. . . . [They display] chronic laziness and hatred for work." Similarly, David Ben-Gurion saw Sephardic immigrants as lacking even "the most elementary knowledge" and "without a trace of Jewish or human education."[7]

To be sure, the category "Sephardim" is highly artificial. There is an important distinction, for example, between the Sephardi Tahor (literally "pure" Sephardi) and the more recent Sephardic arrivals from the Arab countries, known as Edot Mizrach. (In fact, during Israel's founding years, the Sephardi Tahor were a kind of Jerusalem aristocracy, who looked down on the Ashkenazi newcomers from Europe.) Further complicating the picture, many Israelis think of themselves more narrowly as, say, Yemenite Jews or Moroccan Jews rather than Sephardim, and some Sephardic communities have outperformed others. Nevertheless, on the whole, Ashkenazi Jews have many of the attributes of a market-dominant minority.

Ashkenazi Jews continue to be disproportionately represented among professionals, managers, academics, and big business, while Sephardic Jews predominate in low-skilled occupations and in poor "development" towns in outlying areas where there is high unemployment. The number of Ashkenazi Jews with university degrees is almost three times higher than that of Sephardic Jews.[8] In recent years, Israel, originally more socialist in orientation, has aggressively liberalized certain sectors of its economy. Consistent with the proposition that Ashkenazi Jews are a market-dominant minority in Israel, there is a widespread sense among the Sephardim that market reforms are "leaving them behind" while reinforcing the dominance of the Ashkenazim.

Nevertheless, it may be inaccurate today to describe Ashkenazi Jews as an *ethnic* minority within Israel. As I have repeatedly stressed, ethnic identity turns not on "biology" but on subjective perceptions, which are in turn the product of prevailing ideologies in part constructed by elites and politicians. In Israel, the powerful official ideology is that Jews—whatever their social origins—are one people, and thus one "ethnicity." When I ask Israelis whether the difference between Ashkenazi and Sephardic Jews might be seen as an ethnic difference, roughly half of them answer, "Of course it's an ethnic difference," while the other half respond with an annoyed "Of course not, that's ridiculous."

Israel is a Jewish state—this is just the problem for the country's Palestinians. As a matter of official policy, every Jew has an automatic right of admission to Israel, the famous Jewish "right of return." Judaism is the official, established state religion. Every Jewish immigrant, whether from Russia or Iraq, is subjected to strong ideological pressures to learn Hebrew as quickly as possible, to "assimilate" into mainstream Israeli society, and to make a total commitment to the Israeli state. Precisely to integrate Sephardic Jews into Israeli society, the government has instituted various "affirmative action" policies, and rates of intermarriage between Ashkenazim and Sephardim are on the increase, suggesting a trend toward the gradual merging of the two groups. By contrast, marriages between Jews and Arabs in Israel carry a strong stigma on both sides and almost never occur.

Israeli Jews as a Market-Dominant Minority in the Arab-Dominated Middle East

Internal divisions within the Middle Eastern countries, whether viewed as "ethnic" or not, pale by comparison to the defining conflict in the region: the Arab-Israeli conflict. As mentioned above, the Arab-Israeli conflict is in many ways unique and obviously is not reducible to economics. The fact remains, however, that Israeli Jews are as a group far more economically advanced and successful than the vastly more numerous, generally impoverished Arabs surrounding them. Despite the infusion of trillions of oil dollars into the Gulf States, Israel has nevertheless outperformed all of her neighbors in the Middle East under any number of economic indicators. Indeed, most Israelis and Arabs would probably agree that Jews are a market-dominant minority in the Middle East, while bitterly disputing the reasons why this is so.

But first, the undisputed facts—and there are not many of these when it comes to the Middle East. There are roughly 5.2 million Jews in the Middle East, almost all of them living in Israel. By contrast, there are over 221 million Arabs in the region. In terms of per capita wealth, Israel is starkly more prosperous than all of the neighboring Arab countries. According to the World Bank, in 2000 Israel's per capita income was roughly $16,700, compared to $7,230 in Saudi Arabia, $1,710 in Jordan, $940 in Syria, and $370 in Yemen. Per capita income is of course not the only measure of development. In 2000, Israel's infant mortality rate was roughly 5.5 per 1,000 live births, compared to approximately 43 per 1,000 live births in the rest of the Middle East. Also in 2000, 4 percent of Israel's population over the age of fifteen was illiterate, compared to 44 percent in Iraq, 45 percent in Egypt, and 54 percent in Yemen. In addition, Israel has a sophisticated welfare state, a powerful military said to have nuclear-weapon capacity, impressive infrastructure rivaling the Western nations, and a high-technology sector competitive with Silicon Valley.[9]

In stark contrast, large portions of the Arab Middle East are characterized by poverty, squalor, and mass frustration despite the region's enormous oil wealth. In Saudi Arabia, writes Seymour Hersh, "Saudi princes—there are thousands of them—have kept tabloid newspapers filled with accounts of their drinking binges and partying with prostitutes, while taking billions of dollars from the state budget." Meanwhile, the male unemployment rate is estimated at 30 percent (women are prohibited from working in all but a few occupations), and 25 percent of the total population is illiterate. Jordan too, writes Stephen Glain, considered a "bright spot" in the Middle East, "has the same problems as the rest of the Arab world: hordes of disenfranchised, unemployed, hopeless young men susceptible to poaching by extremist groups." In the still poorer Arab countries of North Africa, conditions remain primitive in many regions, comparable to Indonesia or Bangladesh, with no potable water, electricity, or sanitation among vast portions of the population.[10]

Egypt is an especially tragic case in light of its optimistic, modernizing trajectory in the fifties and sixties. In *A Portrait of Egypt,* journalist Mary Anne Weaver describes two trips she took to Cairo, one in 1977, the other in 1993. In 1977, Weaver recalls living "on the tony island of Zamalek" with its gracious if slightly shabby Edwardian mansions:

> [W]e sat on well-appointed terraces overhanging the Nile, and looked across the water at the slum of Imbaba; we speculated on *its* lifestyle. Its population density was 105,000 people per 2.2 square miles; an average of 3.7 people lived in every room. On our side of the Nile, the level of literacy was the highest in the world; in Imbaba, the average income was thirty dollars a month. Here, four languages were normally spoken at dinner parties, served by candlelight; rooms were filled with books. There, hidden away in the alleys, far from our understanding or view, sheep, goats, and children drank from open sewers, and after dark, some neighborhoods yielded to packs of wild dogs. I remember one evening in particular as I watched with friends the flickering lights of a funeral procession passing through Imbaba. The next morning, we read in the newspaper that two children had been eaten alive by rats.

Fifteen years later Weaver found that, despite immense amounts of Western aid, the disparity between rich and poor in Cairo had, if anything, intensified:

> I was struck, more than ever before, by the contrast between the poverty that seemed to be everywhere and a world of astonishing wealth. At a downtown car dealership, I listened as two men, wearing sparkling rings, argued and gesticulated, flailing their arms, over the price—$400,000—of a new Mercedes, which had just arrived. Then I watched bands of ten-year-olds lumber by in mule-drawn carts. Their faces were pretty but filthy, and they were dressed in rags; they lived among smoking piles in south Cairo's City of Garbage, and they survived by collecting rubbish along the streets.
>
> But one of my most vivid impressions on this visit was of de-

cay: of crumbling buildings seen through a patina of dust; of torn-up sidewalks and sewage in the street; of a city that was angry and was living on the edge as its population continued to grow. . . . And the more the city crumbled and the more its population swelled, the more eager it appeared to be to embrace revival of Islam."

In a region of prodigious inequality and mass poverty, Israel is like a tiny industrialized Western enclave. Indeed, a constant charge hurled by Arabs is that Israel is "an extension of the West." Compared to the rest of the region, a starkly disproportionate percentage of Israel's population is highly educated, highly skilled, and highly "Westernized." Unlike the Arab states, Israel is not considered a "developing" country; in 1996 the IMF reclassified Israel as an "advanced economy." Moreover, despite the fact that Israel has no oil, while the Gulf States sit on the largest reserves in the world, marketization and economic liberalization in the region has reinforced Israel's disproportionate prosperity as well as its industrial and technological superiority. In January 2001, Limor Nakar reported in the *Chicago Sun-Times:*

Bear Stearns has just established its first Israel office and HSBC will open its first branch in Israel early this year. They join Lehman Brothers, U.S. Bancorp Piper Jaffray and other investment companies.

These investors are responding to economic changes in Israel that began when the government instituted a reform program based on three pillars: the privatization of state-owned companies, the de-regulation of major industries and the liberalization of markets. With these policies in place, Israel's economy took off.

. . . Israel, a start-up nation, now is filled with start-up companies and second only to the United States in the number of new companies it pioneers. As a result, more venture capital dollars are invested in Israel than in anywhere outside of the Silicon Valley. . . . In the last two years, Israel also has seen the largest deals ever with U.S. firms."

In all these respects, despite the ravaging economic effects of prolonged warfare, Israeli Jews can be viewed, at the regional level, as a market-dominant minority within the overwhelmingly Arab-populated Middle East.

Reasons for Israeli Economic Dominance

If you ask Israeli Jews the reasons for their market dominance in the region, they tend to respond consistently. They invariably cite the unique origins of modern Israel, in which, beginning around 1882, thousands of well-educated European Jews came together in their common commitment to a Jewish state. They emphasize Israel's impressive tradition of the rule of law (Arabs would angrily disagree), including its well-respected independent judiciary and relatively low levels of corruption. They point out that Israel is the only democracy in the Middle East (again Arabs would disagree), an attribute that, but for constant warfare and terrorism, is attractive to foreign investors and global markets. Many Israeli Jews acknowledge, and some worry about, the tremendous amount of financial assistance that Israel has received from external sources. Between 1950 and 1985, U.S. government grants to Israel totaled approximately $21 billion, a level of aid far exceeding that provided to most other countries. (The two largest recipients of United States aid today are Israel and Egypt, which receive $3 billion and $2 billion, respectively, per year.) Over the same period, financial contributions from world Jewry totaled roughly $9.4 billion. Meanwhile, between 1950 and 1965, West Germany paid the government of Israel $780 million in Holocaust reparations. In addition, between 1950 and 1985 it paid Israeli citizens $7 billion in personal reparations.[13]

But most important, Israelis seem to agree, is the country's "human capital": its unusually skilled and educated population and their deep commitment to the survival and success of a Jewish homeland. Most developing countries suffer from "brain drain"; this is certainly true of many Arab nations. By stark contrast, Israel has always been a magnet for talented Jews who move to Israel out of ideology rather than out of hopes for a better life. (Tellingly, aliyah, the Hebrew term for the act of moving to Israel, literally means "going up," while yored, literally "one who goes down," refers to someone who moves from Israel to any other place in the world.) Most recently, over a million Russian Jews—a quarter of them engineers—have emigrated to Israel since 1990. In part because of this latest influx of engineering skill, Israel has become one of the world leaders in high technology.

If you ask Arabs in the Middle East the reasons for the disproportionate success of Israel as compared to the Arab nations, their responses also tend to be consistent, but, predictably, could not differ more from the Jewish perspective. Typically, their first reaction (not directly responsive to the question) is to emphasize the mistreatment of Palestinians within Israel and the Occupied Territories. Although Palestinians residing in the pre-1967 areas of Israel do have Israeli citizenship and the right to vote—there are a few Palestinian members of the Knesset—Palestinians in the Occupied Territories have few political rights and are treated as a conquered people. More generally, Arabs in Israel are treated as second-class citizens in numerous respects, including frequent infringement of their land rights. At least until the most recent deterioration in Palestinian-Jewish relations, many Israeli Jews disagreed with their government's policies toward the Palestinians.[14]

As for Israel's economic success vis-à-vis the other countries in the region, Arabs usually attribute it to a combination of U.S. aid and Israel's "racist" "neo-colonialism," although one often hears half-admiring, half-contemptuous grumblings about Jewish wealth, greed, and moneymaking tendencies. Generally speaking, Arabs see the Israeli Jews not as members of a persecuted minority but as a ruthless, expansionist colonizing force supported by the capitalist countries, especially the United States. Indeed, because the Zionist movement that founded modern Israel was largely European in origin and ideological inspiration, Arabs commonly describe Israel as representing, as a historical matter, "the last wave of European overseas colonization." A favorite historical parallel among Arabs is between Israeli Jews and the twelfth- and thirteenth-century Christian Crusades. The Crusaders, of course, were eventually expelled from Palestine after two centuries of precarious rule.[15]

Arab Ethnonationalism and
"Driving the Israelis into the Sea"

To describe the Middle East as a site of majority-based ethnonationalism targeting a market-dominant minority might at first seem surprising. The Middle East, after all, is not a nation but a region. Moreover, it is a region that, on the whole, has assiduously resisted democratic politics and majority rule. Nevertheless, closer examination reveals striking parallels between the defining conflict in the Middle East and the central dynamic in, say, a contemporary Indonesia or Zimbabwe.

As already established, Israeli Jews are perceived, by themselves and Arabs alike, as a disproportionately wealthy, market-dominant minority in the Middle East. In addition, Arabs perceive themselves as an exploited "indigenous" majority—the original inhabitants and "true owners" of the Middle East—who are suffering at the hands of an abusive, "outsider" colonizer minority. (On this point, of course, the Jews disagree: For them, as for the Palestinians, the Israeli-Arab conflict is in part a fight for their ancestral homeland.) Tellingly, but not necessarily accurately, in a famous Egyptian best-seller, *The Jews, History and Faith,* Dr. Kamil Safan, widely respected in Egypt as an "expert on Hebrew and Judaism," writes that in ancient times pharaohs turned on the Jews because "they tried to take control of the economy of Egypt" and "collaborated with the colonialists—the Hyksos—against the people of the country."[16] Like whites in South Africa or Chinese in Indonesia, Israeli Jews are feared as much as they are hated. Every Arab in the Middle East is conscious that Israel has the backing of the most powerful nation in the world and that between 1948 and 1973 Israel won four wars, humiliating Arab forces that outnumbered them twenty to one.

Further, although the Arab countries generally are not democratizing, the ruling elites in these countries routinely engage in populist demagoguery, deliberately fomenting anti-Israeli sentiment, both to deflect criticism from themselves and to keep their frustrated populations united against a common enemy. At the same time, nonruling demagogues, including many highly influential Islamic clerics, also engage in anti-Israel baiting, whether out of sincere zealotry or for more instrumental reasons. Meanwhile, in Arab newspapers Jews are routinely re-

ferred to as "terrorists" and perpetrators of "genocide": "Cartoons depicting Israelis and other Jews with Nazi-style uniforms and swastikas
have now become standard," writes Lewis. "These complement the
Nazi-era hooked noses and blood-dripping jagged teeth."[17] The increasingly influential Al-Jazeera, unusual in the Arab world for its journalistic
independence, is simultaneously anti-Israel and "pan-Arabist," observes
Fouad Ajami. "These are reporters with a mission."[18]

As a result, although there has been minimal democratization in the
Arab Middle East, an intense, majority-based Arab ethnonationalism,
along with tremendous hostility against Israeli Jews, nevertheless exists
throughout the region. Although it is certainly not clear that fundamentalism is supported by a majority of Arabs—sentiment on the "Arab
Street" varies considerably from country to country—there is no question that if popular elections were held throughout the Arab world,
Israel would be a common whipping boy among vote-seeking politicians.

Today very few Arab states even formally recognize Israel's "right to
exist." Worse, many Arabs in the Middle East seem committed to the
policy, officially renounced by the Palestinian Liberation Organization in
1993, of destroying Israel and "driving Israelis into the sea." As David
Remnick recently wrote: "Forget Hamas and Islamic Jihad and their culture of martyrdom and absolute victory. Last year, Faisal Husseini, a decided moderate among Yasar Arafat's leadership ranks, gave an interview
not long before he died in which he compared [the Oslo Accords of
1993] to a Trojan horse, an intermediate, tactical step leading to the
elimination of Israel. He said, 'If you are asking me as a Pan-Arab nationalist what are the Palestinian borders according to the higher strategy, I will immediately reply: From the river to the sea' "—that is, with
no Israel on the map. Meanwhile in Iran, former president Hashemi
Rafsanjani, speaking in a Tehran stadium shortly after the attacks on the
Pentagon and World Trade Center, "called for Israel's nuclear destruction. A single nuclear bomb would be sufficient to destroy Israel, he
said, whereas any Israeli counterstrike could do only limited damage."[19]

Thus, despite its ancient roots and unique status as the crucible of
religious strife, the conflict in the Middle East is also a striking manifes-
tation of an intense majority-supported movement aimed at eliminating

a despised market-dominant minority. In part, the ferocity of anti-Israeli feeling in the Middle East is sui generis. But it is also in part driven by factors familiar throughout the developing world. The ethnic hatred felt by many Middle Eastern Arabs, compounded by extreme poverty and a profound sense of powerlessness and inferiority, is analogous to the deep resentment experienced by the black majority in Zimbabwe, by Indonesia's *pribumi* majority, or by Serbs in the former Yugoslavia.

What Markets and Democracy Would Bring in the Middle East

After September 11, 2001, many prominent voices immediately called for free markets and democratization as the solution for terrorism and ethnic conflict in the Middle East. In a sense, this is no surprise: Poverty and corrupt, repressive regimes have clearly helped turn the Middle East into the cauldron of hatred that it currently is. Thus for Thomas Friedman, the solution to Middle Eastern terrorism and strife is "multi-ethnic, pluralistic, free-market democracy."[20]

Unfortunately, "multi-ethnic, pluralistic, free-market democracy" is not a policy. It is an ideal, and the problem is getting to that ideal. Even if U.S. foreign policy were unconstrained by dependence on Arab oil or other problems peculiar to the region, the basic policy prescription that America promotes elsewhere in the non-Western world—laissez-faire markets and rapid democratization—would be a very high-risk strategy in the Middle East.

It is critical to distinguish between the short-term realities and the optimistic longer term prospects of market liberalization in the Arab states. In the longer term, if the Arab economies could be genuinely opened and their societies transformed from what *Newsweek*'s Fareed Zakaria calls their present "feudal" conditions, there is good reason to think that markets could produce enormous benefits in the Middle East. Three distinctive features of the Middle Eastern states could make market reforms especially propitious. First, unlike most developing countries, the Arab states have an unusually large number of skilled and educated individuals, often with advanced degrees, who are currently unemployed. Second, the populations of the Arab states include groups famous the world over for their "entrepreneurialism." As Zakaria notes, "The Palestinians, tragically, have long been the region's best merchants and would probably respond fastest to new economic opportunities if they could put the intifada behind them."[21] Finally, again unlike most developing countries, the Arab states generally do not face the "problem" of an internal market-dominant minority, and for this reason markets are less likely to be ethnically destabilizing at the national level. Thus, with certain optimistic assumptions, markets can be a key to long-term Middle Eastern reform, both economically and politically.

In the short run, however, laissez-faire global markets in the Middle East will not transform the entrenched realities of Arab society or have a civilizing effect on ethnic relations. On the contrary, for at least a generation, the effects of marketization in the Middle East would at best produce only marginal benefits for the great mass of Arab poor. However correct in theory, free trade agreements and privatization—in the absence of major structural reforms, which are highly unlikely to occur—cannot in the short term alter the pervasive illiteracy, corruption, and Third World conditions prevailing throughout the Arab states.

Meanwhile, even if the turn to fundamentalism in the Middle East is a product of closed or repressive political regimes, it sadly does not follow that political liberalization in the region today would lead to moderation—or, for that matter, pro-market regimes. On the contrary, rapid democratization in the Arab states would likely be a recipe for extremist politics, dominated by ethnonationalist (if not fundamentalist) parties unified in their hatred of Israel and the West. As Zakaria candidly observes: "America's allies in the Middle East are autocratic, corrupt and heavy-handed. But they are still more liberal, tolerant and pluralistic than what would likely replace them [with democratic elections]. If elections had been held last month in Saudi Arabia with King Fahd and Osama bin Laden on the ballot, I would not bet too heavily on His Royal Highness's fortunes." A similar dynamic exists throughout the Arab states. In Kuwait, the democratically elected Parliament is packed with Israel-despising Islamic fundamentalists. In Jordan and Morocco, the kings are much more moderate and Western-oriented than the populations over which they rule. Finally, in the Palestinian Authority, the suicide-and-murder-bent Hamas is more popular than the arguably more moderate Palestine Liberation Organization.[22]

Many of us tend to think of the Arab-Israeli conflict as being so ancient in its roots that it is impervious to the forces of modernity. In truth, the problem is worse. Given the current realities, the principal forces of modernization—markets and majoritarian politics—are fuel to the fires of ethnic conflict in the Middle East. While free market democracy may well be the optimal end point in the Middle East, the simultaneous pursuit today of laissez-faire markets and immediate majority rule would almost certainly produce even more government-sponsored bloodshed and ethnic warfare.

CHAPTER 11

Why They Hate Us

America as a Global Market-Dominant Minority

I found myself in the middle of an argument the other evening, one of many I've been in since September 11, 2001. An outspoken Chinese friend of mine, Mei Lan—born and raised in China but about to become an American citizen, having just married a native New Yorker—asserted at a Manhattan dinner party that 99 percent of all Chinese in China were happy about the attack on America. This prompted an outcry among the American guests. *"Ninety-nine?"* someone asked incredulously. "What pollster produced *that* statistic?" To which Mei Lan replied, "Let's not get hung up on numbers. Face it, deal with it—Americans are hated."

"People like you spreading misinformation, Mei Lan, are exactly the problem," another guest heatedly interjected. He had visited China the previous summer. The Chinese were nice people, he explained, who didn't always agree with American policies but who certainly didn't hate us and in fact wanted to learn from us. Another guest, an international lawyer, agreed, and described all the sympathetic e-mails he had received from Hong Kong and Shanghai after September 11.

Mei Lan then brought up the topic of American hypocrisy about human rights, and the conversation further deteriorated after that.

In the aftermath of September 11, many Americans have experienced some version of this conversation, debating the extent of anti-Americanism throughout the world. A common problem is the tendency to generalize from an n of 2 or 3. "I got e-mails from my friends in Mexico and Chile. Anti-Americanism in Latin America is wildly exagger-

ated." Or: "My Palestinian friend e-mailed me expressing horror about
the World Trade Center. The U.S. media presents a totally distorted picture of anti-Americanism over there."

Of course not all of the Middle East hates us. Nor does 99 percent
of China hate us. The non-Western world is far from monolithic in its
attitudes toward America; generalizations on this subject are especially
perilous. Nevertheless, it is sadly untrue that Americans are loved and
admired around the world. The existence of some anti-American resentment and objections to U.S. foreign policy was apparent to anyone who
traveled outside the United States in recent years. But the depth and
passion of anti-American hatred that was revealed on September 11 was
a profound, nationwide shock.

"Once there was a time when the most evil people on earth were
ashamed to write their crime across the heavens," writes Neal Ascherson. This was not so of September 11, 2001. "Manhattan that morning
was a diagram, a blue bar-chart with columns which were tall or not so
tall. A silver cursor passed across the screen and clicked silently on the
tallest column, which turned red and black and presently vanished. *This
is how we delete you.* The cursor returned and clicked on the second column. Presently a thing like a solid grey-white cauliflower rose until it
was a mountain covering all south Manhattan. *This is how we bury you.* It
was the most open atrocity of all time, a simple demonstration written
on the sky which everyone in the world was invited to watch. *This is how
much we hate you.*"[1]

Why do they hate us? Amidst grief, anger, patriotism, defiance, and
retaliation, stunned Americans have repeatedly returned to this question. This chapter will offer one, certainly not the only, answer.

America today has become the world's market-dominant minority.
Like the Chinese in the Philippines or the Lebanese in West Africa,
Americans have attained heights of wealth and economic power wildly
disproportionate to our tiny numbers. Just 4 percent of the world's
population, America dominates every aspect—financial, cultural, technological—of the global free markets we have come to symbolize. From
the Islamic world to China, from our NATO allies to the southern
hemisphere, America is seen (not incorrectly) as the engine and principal beneficiary of global marketization. For this—for our extraordinary

market dominance, our seeming global invincibility—we have earned the envy, fear, and resentment of much of the rest of the world. Of course, not everyone who envies and resents us wants to destroy us. But there are those who do.

Anti-Americanism around the world is, among other things, an expression at the global level of popular, demagogue-fueled mass resentment against a market-dominant minority. The expression of this resentment varies enormously in intensity, ranging from benign grumbling by French bureaucrats about bad films and bad food to strategic alliances between Russia and China to terrorism. Like the ethnic cleansing of Tutsi in Rwanda, the suicidal mass murder of three thousand innocents on American soil was the ultimate expression of group hatred. The attack on America was an act of revenge directly analogous to the bloody confiscations of white land in Zimbabwe, or the anti-Chinese riots and looting in Indonesia—fueled by the same feelings of envy, grievance, inferiority, powerlessness, and humiliation.

As with Jewish market dominance in the Middle East or Kikuyu economic success in Kenya, the reasons for America's global market dominance are the subject of bitter dispute. On one view, American economic success is the result of our superior institutions, entrepreneurial spirit, and generations of hard work. On another view, our wealth and power are the spoils of plunder, exploitation, and exclusion. Even within the United States, tempers flare over which view is correct. The reality is that both carry more than a grain of truth.

On the other hand, there is astonishing global consensus on one point: that America has become the world's unrivaled market-dominant minority.

Market-Dominant America

Whether you ask an Egyptian imam, a Wall Street banker, or France's foreign minister, there is striking agreement that the United States, as a country, dominates, drives, perpetuates, and disproportionately prospers from the spread of global capitalism around the world. The facts support this perception.

To begin with, it is barely exaggerating to say that the United States

232 / ETHNONATIONALISM AND THE WEST

is responsible for the worldwide spread of free markets. No one has established this more evocatively than Thomas Friedman in *The Lexus and the Olive Tree*. Today's universal prescription of Privatization + Deregulation + Economic Liberalization "was made in America and Great Britain," writes Friedman. The Electronic Herd—Friedman's term for today's millions of anonymous traders and investors "moving money around the world with the click of a mouse"—"is led by American Wall Street bulls."

At the same time, "[t]he most powerful agent pressuring other countries to open their markets for free trade and free investment is Uncle Sam, and America's global armed forces keep these markets and sea lanes open for globalization . . ." As a historical matter, it was America, determined after the Second World War to promote capitalism and contain Communism, that drove the creation of the World Bank, International Monetary Fund, GATT, and most recently the World Trade Organization as well as a host of other free-market-oriented international institutions. In other words, writes Friedman, "even within the Cold War system America was hard at work building out a global economy for its own economic and strategic reasons."[2]

Today, America sits on top of the global economy. As with the market-dominant Chinese in Southeast Asia, global marketization has intensified America's breathtakingly disproportionate wealth and economic power. "Not so long ago," writes Mort Zuckerman, editor-in-chief of *U.S. News & World Report,* "our preoccupation was with how America could prosper in a new era of global competition against a relentless Japan, a uniting Europe, and the Pacific Rim low-wage economies." But in fact America emerged "triumphant in the new world economy."[3] According to U.S. government statistics for 2000, despite concerns about economic slowdown and recession, the United States, with a GDP of $9 trillion, is "the largest and most technologically powerful economy in the world" as well as "the leading industrial power in the world." Our exports in 2000 totaled $776 billion; this figure does not include the roughly $2 trillion worth of goods produced, assembled, and sold overseas by foreign affiliates of American companies.[4]

Needless to say, these blanket statistics hide enormous inequalities within the United States. In 1999, Bill Gates "owned as much as 40 percent of the American population put together," writes Thomas Frank. Along with Gates, hundreds of thousands of American entrepreneurs, corporate managers, and just ordinary investors have become multimillionaires, even multibillionaires, practically overnight. Between 1979 and 1997, and adjusting for inflation, reports economist Paul Krugman, the income of families in the middle of the U.S. income distribution rose 9 percent, while the income of families in the top 1 percent rose 140 percent. Meanwhile, an estimated 60 million Americans have had to accept stagnant or even declining earnings in the 1990s and, according to the U.S. Census Bureau, 34.5 million Americans (12.7 percent of the population) were officially poor in 1998. Drug addiction and violence continue to be looming problems in our inner cities. "Only the sadly impoverished and chaotic Russian Federation," notes Edward Luttwak, "has as great a proportion of its citizens in prison as the affluent and well-governed United States . . ."[5]

None of these internal blots lessens America's market dominance at the global level. The American dollar is the world's dominant currency; even *jihadis* hold their assets in dollars. English is the world's dominant language; globalization is making this increasingly so. American multinationals are the most powerful and visible in the world. It was fashionable for a while to describe multinationals as "citizens of the world," beholden to no nation. But for most of the world today there is no question that Nike, Gap, Reebok, Starbucks, Ben & Jerry's, Wal-Mart, Coca-Cola, Disney, Levi Strauss, and Toys "Я" Us are American. It is precisely the American-ness of these brands that makes them irresistible to so many—and despicable to so many others.

American fast food is globally dominant. Enough has been written elsewhere about McDonald's, but it's also worth noting that Pizza Hut operates in 86 countries around the world, Kentucky Fried Chicken in 82, and Burger King in 58, including Kuwait, Oman, Qatar, and Saudi Arabia. American stock exchanges are globally dominant; this is true despite the explosion of new stock exchanges from Shanghai to the Ivory Coast. American media are market dominant: "Where once the BBC let nation speak unto nation," a British columnist recently lamented, "now we are one world under CNN."[6] Perhaps most important, American firms are utterly dominant in the new information technology. Indeed, for the rest of the world, American economic success is exemplified by the "New Titans" of information technology: the legendary Microsoft and Intel as well as Apple, Novell, Cisco, Oracle, Sun Microsystems, America Online, and so on.

Global markets may well hold the key to long-term greater prosperity for the poor and not-so-poor countries of the world. But like Latin America's European-blooded elites or Southeast Asia's hypercapitalized Chinese, America has a massive head start over the rest of the world. Thomas Friedman suggested a few years ago that America is "the country that benefits most from today's global integration." Friedman was recently corroborated by a 2002 *New York Times* report indicating that the United States, rather than the developing world, has been the overwhelming beneficiary of globalization. "Perhaps aside from China the only country that appears to have benefited unambiguously from the trend toward open markets worldwide is the United States, where a huge inflow of capital has helped allow Americans to spend more than they save, and to import more than they export." The report goes on to quote financier and philanthropist George Soros: "The trend of globalization is that surplus capital is moving from the periphery countries to the center, which is the United States."[7]

Global Backlash

Like the market dominance of any minority in the world, American market dominance provokes intense resentment. Indeed, the rest of the world, if anything, exaggerates America's disproportionate wealth and power. Just as Russian hate-sites insist that "Yids control the entire economy," and just as indigenous Burmans often say that "the Chinese control all Mandalay," many in the world today see America as "controlling the global economy," either through its multinationals or its "puppets," the World Bank and International Monetary Fund.

Like resentment against market-dominant minorities in individual countries, anti-Americanism around the world is not a monolithic phenomenon. In some countries, anti-Americanism is particularly fierce among the elite, who in turn foment anti-American sentiment among the lower classes. Some have suggested that this is true of France. In other countries, anti-Americanism originates among the lower classes, who—even as they covet Nike sweatshirts and Madonna CDs—see and resent America as the powerful extension and protector of their own corrupt elites. This is true of many developing countries in Asia, Africa, and Latin America.

As with resentment against other market-dominant minorities, anti-Americanism is often a perverse blend of admiration, awe, and envy on one hand and seething hatred, disgust, and contempt on the other. Thus, for millions, perhaps billions, around the world, America is "arrogant," "hegemonic," and "vapidly materialistic"—but also where they would go if only they could. In Beijing, for example, many of the same screaming students who bombarded the U.S. embassy with stones after the U.S. bombing of China's embassy in Belgrade returned a few weeks later to line up for U.S. visas. One of them, interviewed by *U.S. News & World Report,* explained that he wanted to attend graduate school in America and that "If I could have good opportunities in the U.S., I wouldn't mind U.S. hegemony too much." Similarly, in another interview with *U.S. News,* Oscar Arias Sanchez, Costa Rica's former president who won a Nobel Peace Prize for brokering peace in Central America, charged that America "want[s] to tell the world what to do. You are like the Romans of the new millennium." Yet Arias vacations in the United States and has a son at Harvard and a daughter who graduated from Boston College.[8]

Another example of the world's love-hate relationship with the United States was seen when a quarter million Brazilians packed into a Rio de Janeiro concert hall to ogle U.S. teen pop idol Britney Spears. Delirious with adoration, the crowd nevertheless hissed and booed when she waved an American flag.[9] And many, of course, have pointed out that an ironic number of the cheering Palestinians, captured on television celebrating the destruction of the World Trade Center, were wearing American T-shirts, sneakers, and baseball caps.

Along with many other market-dominant minorities around the world, Americans are often accused of being "greedy," "selfish," and ungenerous, especially given our spectacular wealth. European governments frequently point out that America's foreign aid budget is a much smaller percentage of GNP than that of other OECD countries.[10] Further, what foreign aid we provide is often given on the condition that it be spent on U.S. products or consultants. (Japan is just as guilty of this as we are.) Moreover, the U.S. government is quite willing to make exceptions to our embrace of free trade for our own benefit; our farming subsidies enrage even our Australian allies. American rebuttals to these charges are, by now, also familiar. What government in the world *isn't* self-interested? What country has done more for the rest of the world than America? Who bailed out Europe in the Second World War?

It is important to stress, however, that in some respects the analogy between market-dominant minorities at the national level and America as a market-dominant minority at the global level is imperfect. For one thing, at least from an internal United States perspective, Americans are not a single "ethnicity." On the contrary, from our own point of view America is the quintessential multiethnic country, a self-proclaimed mosaic or melting pot. In addition, the "rest of the world" is not a single self-perceived "indigenous majority," in the same way that, say, blacks feel that they are "indigenous" in South Africa as opposed to whites.

On the other hand, ethnicity in any context is always a highly subjective and artificial phenomenon. This is true even in South Africa, where, at first glance, ethnic lines seem to be particularly stark. In fact, South African "whites" include diverse peoples of British, Dutch, and German Jewish origins. South Africa's whites are viewed as (and view themselves as) a single "ethnicity" only against the background of the country's predominantly "black" majority, which itself is made up of numerous different African tribes, speaking mutually incomprehensible tongues. Nevertheless, the fact remains that, as a matter of general perception, the major social fault line in South Africa today is between blacks and whites and, moreover, that whites are widely viewed as a market-dominant "outsider" minority, wielding egregiously disproportionate economic power vis-à-vis the country's indigenous majority. America occupies much the same role at the global level.

We are viewed by the rest of the world as one "people"—and for that matter, a "white" people. As one U.S. Department of Justice official put it, "with all acknowledgment to Colin Powell and Norman Mineta, the world surely thinks of our 'face' as white." More fundamentally, all over the world, American products, companies, and investors are viewed as "outsider" threats to the legitimate "indigenous" society.

America's geographic separation is no bar to this perception of Americans as a global market-dominant minority. On the contrary, most market-dominant minorities—among them the Chinese in Southeast Asia, Lebanese in West Africa, Indians in East Africa, and whites in South Africa—are all the more resented precisely because of their "insular" self-segregation. Indeed, America's increasingly restrictive immigration policies are another source of hostility for the rest of the world.

But America is unusual, compared to other market-dominant minorities, in numerous additional ways. As well as being an economic superpower, America is the world's preeminent military, political, and cultural power. As a result, global anti-Americanism reflects not only our market dominance, but also our military unilateralism, our foreign policy, and our cultural "hegemony"—all of which have provoked intense resentment in many quarters. Yet even in these respects, America's position is surprisingly comparable to that of many market-dominant minorities.

The "entrepreneurial" market-dominant minorities of Southeast Asia and Africa tend to be politically weak. Often just 1 to 2 percent of the population, they have little or no military strength or influence on governmental policy (other than through cronyism, which in any case benefits only a very few). But this is not true, for example, of the light-skinned elites in Latin America, the Tutsi minority in pregenocide Rwanda, or the white minority in apartheid South Africa and Rhodesia. All these minorities are or were both economically and politically dominant, typically controlling every sector of governmental policy and the military as well. In all such cases, as with America today, there is much more than economics behind the often-violent animosity felt by the frustrated majority. At the same time, the humiliation or oppression felt by the majority because of the minority's political dominance is inextricably woven together with, and immeasurably magnified by, the minority's wealth and economic power.

Similarly, while America's global cultural dominance today is historically unique—and certainly not reducible to mere economics—the world's reaction against American "cultural imperialism" is again strikingly parallel to standard reactions against market-dominant minorities. A characteristic feature of societies with economically powerful "outsider" minorities is the reported feeling, on the part of the "indigenous" majority, that they are in danger of being "swallowed up," their culture taken over or eradicated by the minority.[11] Thus in Rwanda, genocide was justified in the name of Hutu "self-protection" and Hutu "self-defense." A constant theme among Russian hatemongers today is that Jews "are waging a destructive campaign against our fatherland and its morality, language, culture and beliefs." A pervasive sentiment in Burma, bitterly expressed by a Mandalayan businessman, is that "we are becoming a Chinese colony." The tiny market-dominant Chinese minority, it is said, "are smothering us"; "they have turned us into second-class citizens in our own towns." "Burmese identity is being destroyed." Such sentiments are highly analogous to those expressed today by groups all over the world fearful of the invasion of American products and entertainment.

Finally, and most important, the United States differs from other market-dominant minorities in that the non-American majority is not organized in a single national territory. With the exception of the previous chapter on the Middle East, this book has focused on dynamics internal to nations: specifically, the danger, within individual countries, of rapid democratization in the face of pervasive poverty and a resented "outsider" market-dominant minority. In the case of America as a global market-dominant minority, however, there is no counterpart to democracy at the global level. Notwithstanding various efforts at global integration and the rise of numerous international political organizations, the truth is that there is no democratically elected "world government."

The closest thing there is to a world democratic government is the United Nations General Assembly, where each member state gets a vote and where, as a result, the Third World commands a substantial majority of the votes. (Of course, the national representatives to the General Assembly are usually not democratically elected.) And indeed, one finds in the General Assembly precisely the anti-U.S. and anti-market reactions that America's market-dominance would be expected to produce. These reactions range from Resolution No. 3281 in 1974, which purported to expand the authority of member states to "regulate," "supervise," and "expropriate" multinational corporations within their jurisdiction (the vote was 120 to 6, with the dissenters being five Western

European countries and the United States), to the May 2001 ouster of the United States from the United Nations Commission on Human Rights (while Sudan and Sierra Leone, for example, remain members).[12]

But the anti-Americanism expressed in the United Nations is largely symbolic and rhetorical. The real outlets are elsewhere. Against America's global market-dominance, there is not one but a host of nationalist, majority-supported backlashes, spread throughout the world, varying widely in quality and intensity, ranging from the friendly to the homicidal.

Friendly Anti-Americanism

Anti-Americanism extends to every corner of the world. This includes even the Western countries most similar to us: the United Kingdom, Canada, Australia, and New Zealand. In all these countries, the September 11 attack on America brought an instantaneous show of sympathy and support for the United States, both from the governments and from individual citizens. (Terrorism, after all, presents a common threat; bin Laden demonized not only the United States but all Western countries, and plots by terrorists thought to be associated with bin Laden have been uncovered in England, Canada, and New Zealand.) At the same time, in each country, heated debates erupted over the causes of the attack and the extent to which American attitudes or policies had contributed. There were also widespread concerns that the United States, with its military might and characteristic self-absorption, might respond with excessive force, acting unilaterally without taking into account the interests of its allies.

In the United Kingdom, America's staunchest ally in the war in Afghanistan, anti-American feeling has increased since September 11, according to a recent article in the *Guardian*. Citing a survey taken by a leading advertising agency, the *Guardian* reported that "British consumers have become more distrustful of overtly American brands" and that "more than two-thirds of British consumers are concerned the world is becoming too Americanised." As a result, there is a growing trend away from American brands to what advertising strategists call "glocal" brands—brands that savvy multinationals successfully portray as "locally relevant." Somewhat surprisingly, one of the leaders in "glocal" marketing was said to be McDonald's, which "has adapted itself so successfully to foreign markets that consumers outside the US often believe it is a domestic company." (In England, McDonald's employs "[o]vertly British advertising" and sells "British favourites, such as curry, alongside Big Macs.") By contrast, companies like Gap and Starbucks suffer because they market themselves as distinctly American.[13]

Generally speaking, however, resentment against the United States in all these English-speaking countries is, as one Canadian put it, "good-natured anti-Americanism," unlikely to become a major election issue or to be translated into anti-American policies. This is not to say that anti-Americanism in these countries is not serious, or even, in some quarters, ferocious. There are a startling number of Australian websites filled with assertions that the United States "deserved" the attacks of September 11. Mary Beard, a university lecturer in classics at the University of Cambridge, enraged many American readers when she described in the *London Review of Books* the "feeling that however tactfully you dress it up, the United States had it coming. That is, of course, what many people openly or privately think. World bullies, even if their heart is in the right place, will in the end pay the price."[14] But these views are probably unusual in their harshness. For the most part, historical connections, cultural affinities, and high standards of living go a long way in blunting anti-Americanism in our fellow English-speaking Western nations.

The European Response

It is probably safe to say that anti-American feeling is more intense in continental Europe than in, say, Canada or England. In part, this is because American culture—including not just our cowboy capitalism but language, food, and political traditions—clashes more directly, or at least more obviously, with European culture. To be sure, our Canadian neighbors hate being mistaken for Americans and, along with Australians and New Zealanders, constantly stress how different in "national character" their countries are from the United States (for example, "humble" and "quietly patriotic" as opposed to "arrogant," "preachy," and "hilariously oblivious to the rest of the world"). Nevertheless, more Europeans seem to perceive America's position of world power as a fundamental threat to their national identity.

Nowhere is this more plain than in France, where the interplay between Americanization and anti-Americanism has produced something of a national existential crisis. In the 1960s, French authors were already churning out books like René Etiemble's *Parlez-vous franglais?* (1964) and Jean Jacques Servan-Schreiber's *Le Défi américain* (1967). The former called for a campaign to save French culture from "the American 'air-conditioned nightmare.' " The latter started the publication *L'Express* to offer a French-language alternative to America's *Time* and *Newsweek.*[15]

Today, with the United States now the world's sole economic, political, and military superpower, the "American problem" has assumed unprecedented proportions, constantly in the news. Many have suggested that French anti-Americanism is principally a preoccupation of French elites, who, in culture, diplomacy, and politics, writes international historian David Ellwood, look "ever more beleaguered, overtaken and outpaced by the appeal of American dress-styles to their children, of fast-food to their youth, and of Hollywood to their cinema audiences." "The government, and the elites, realize that culture, writ large, is a battle that they're losing," observes Alain Franchon, an editorial writer for *Le Monde.* "They're very jealous of America's power to seduce. When faced with that you have to fight, even if you risk looking ridiculous."[16]

The French political class is certainly fighting. In a phrase-coining moment, Foreign Minister Hubert Vedrine recently declared that France "cannot accept a politically unipolar world, nor a culturally uniform world, nor the unilateralism of a single hyperpower." (The term has stuck; now all of Europe calls the United States "the hyperpower.") Vedrine echoed former president Mitterand's famous statement in October 1993 that no single country "should be allowed to control the images of the whole world. What is at stake is the cultural identity of our nations, the right of each people to its own culture." A few months earlier, Mitterand's minister of culture, Jack Lang, had attacked *Jurassic Park* as a threat to French national identity. More recently, Lang has argued that if France's cultural heritage is not "to dwindle into insignificance, economics and culture should learn to live together in France."

Calling for a new Ministry of External Cultural Relations, Lang wants "more energy, more openness, more international operations by French television channels and a whole-hearted build-up of a European identity 'of imagination, youth, and spirit.' " Else, "the Old World could remain frozen in the shadow of American culture. . . ." Meanwhile, *Le Monde* routinely criticizes an America "whose commercial hegemony menaces agriculture and whose cultural hegemony insidiously ruins culinary customs, the sacred gleams of French identity."[17]

In a recent, particularly acerbic essay called *"Toujours l'antiaméricanisme:* The religion of the French elite," David Pryce-Jones states that ordinary French people on the street don't have time for the "neo-Napoleonic" "inferiority complexes" of the French elite. "An American almost anywhere in France is virtually certain to receive a friendly greeting, and to hear praise for the latest Spielberg movie, and perhaps even for Euro-Disneyland, that genuine cultural freak."[18]

But as with any ethnonationalist movement targeting a market-dominant minority, it is difficult to know the extent to which French anti-Americanism is an elite-generated phenomenon as opposed to a reflection of bottom-up popular sentiment. Certainly not all French agree with José Bové, who became something of a national hero in 1999 when he vandalized a McDonald's and made Roquefort a global issue. After all, some 790 McDonald's are flourishing in France, having proliferated at a rate of around eighty per year starting in the mid-1990s. On the other hand, reports Philip Gordon of the Brookings Institution, "67 percent of the French worry that globalization threatens French identity; 52 percent reject the American economic model; and 80 percent do not want to emulate the American lifestyle." Best-sellers in France these days include *The World Is Not Merchandise, The Economic Horror,* and *Who Is Killing France?*[19]

While typically more muted, similar anti-Americanism exists in all our Western European allies—though, needless to say, each country has its own historical relationship to and distinctive set of grievances against the United States. In Germany, for example, there is an intellectual strand of anti-Americanism dating back to the poet Heinrich Heine's scorn in the 1800s for Germans who emigrated to the Americas to get rich. More recently, Germany was furious when the United States effectively vetoed Berlin's nominee to run the International Monetary Fund.

A general cultural fault line between America and Europe, however, bears directly on American market-dominance. François Bujon de l'Estang, French ambassador to the United States, put it this way: "What we may see emerging now is a new ideological rift. On one side is the American model of free-market capitalism, which was emulated by Margaret Thatcher's United Kingdom. On the other is a milder, European model that includes a stronger social safety net with attributes such as a national health care system and government-funded retirement and unemployment plans. Most Europeans, as well as the Canadians, are very attached to that model." Philip Gordon suggests that there is a feeling in Europe, and especially in France, "that globalization is playing to America's strengths by reinforcing the dominance of our economic model and business practices. . . ."[20]

Many of the European nations—among them France, Germany, and Spain—were of course once great world powers, both militarily and culturally. For these countries, being eclipsed today by America's upstart, hotdogging rise to global dominance is additionally grating. The same might be said of Great Britain. As Jonathan Freedland recently wrote in London's *Spectator* only half-facetiously, "After all, it was the Yanks who dared pushed Britain off its top perch in the first half of the last century," and then had "the impertinence to force us to give up our empire by stopping our adventure in the Suez." On the other hand, Britain has an advantage over Europe because of its linguistic, cultural, and historical links to the United States, which arguably give Britain a better shot at influencing Washington—"playing Athens to America's Rome," as Prime Minister Harold Macmillan once put it.[21]

In any event, far more so than in Great Britain, European anti-Americanism has translated into concrete economic and political policies that, while not exactly inimical to U.S. interests, are clearly directed at offsetting America's global power. Most crucially, the interest in a stronger, more united Europe—indeed, the European Union itself—is based in large part on the hope of making Europe competitive with, if not superior to, America as a global economic and political power. "[T]alk of European integration has increasingly gone hand in hand with anti-American rhetoric," James Kitfield noted recently. "The whole debate in Europe is now dominated by charges of U.S. 'hegemony' and 'unilateralism,' " adds an editor with *Suddeutsche Zeitung*. "Germans are rallying to the common cause of 'Euronationalism,' fueled in part by anti-American sentiment."The deputy director of a Berlin think tank agreed: "[W]e are beginning to catch the 'French disease,' which holds that you can only build greater European unity around anti-American rhetoric."[22]

Similarly, the euro is in part a desire to counter the global dominance of the American dollar, although only the French government has openly admitted this. European plans for a new "Euro-army"—formally, the European Rapid Reaction Force—have alarmed analysts on both sides of the Atlantic. In December 2000, then–defense secretary William Cohen warned France that a Euro-army "could, if mismanaged, render NATO a relic." More recently, a British official criticized the Rapid Reaction Force as indicative of the "virulent strain of anti-Americanism in Europe," which reflected the rivalrous "political ambitions" of "some in Europe" and was "in danger of infecting the whole transatlantic relationship."[23]

Nevertheless, the European nations—even France, which has been the most obstreperous—remain allies that the United States can generally count on in moments of great import. All the European nations ultimately supported the United States' war in Afghanistan. Again, it helps that these countries enjoy high standards of living and the distractions of affluence. In any case, while anti-Americanism in Europe has triggered both reactive nationalism and rising "Euronationalism," these movements, by and large, have not reflected totalizing mass hatred or confiscatory backlashes—and certainly not the desire to kill. Unfortunately, the same cannot be said of great parts of the non-Western world.

Anti-Americanism in the Developing World

If America's global dominance produces resentment even among our Western allies—who have plenty of wealth and influence of their own—anti-American hostility is a thousandfold more intense in the non-Western world. Moreover, anti-Americanism outside the West has increased over the last few decades, coinciding with the United States' emergence as the world's sole superpower.

Why? As proponents of free markets correctly point out, global capitalism has, in certain important respects, done wonders for the world, including many developing countries. Global per capita income has tripled in the last thirty-five years. Technology has transformed even small villages. Life expectancy and adult literacy rates have, on the whole, increased significantly in the developing world. Global infant mortality rates are lower than ever.

Unfortunately, these macro statistics are not what real people in the real world experience. To begin with, many "advances"—for example, the spread of the Internet and television, and even improvements in education—are two-edged swords, often producing growing discontent along with growing awareness. Globalization generates not only new opportunities and hopes, but also new social desires, stresses, insecurities, and frustrations. At the same time, the benefits of global markets have been distributed extremely unequally, both across and within countries. The spread of global markets in recent decades has unambiguously widened the gap between developed and underdeveloped countries. Today, the richest 1 percent of the world's population own as much as the poorest 57 percent. Half the world's population live on less than two dollars a day; more than a billion people live on less than one dollar a day. Meanwhile, the top 20 percent of those living in high-income countries account for 86 percent of all of the world's private consumption expenditures.[24]

In a newly released report, the World Bank, one of the most ardent institutional promoters of markets, notes that over two decades ending in the late 1990s some two billion people, particularly in sub-Saharan Africa, the Middle East, and the former Soviet Union, have not benefited from globalization. To the contrary, the economies in these regions have generally contracted while poverty has risen. On a more positive note, the report notes that twenty-four developing countries increased their integration into the world economy. These countries, home to some three billion people, enjoyed an average 5 percent growth rate in per capita income. The report goes on to note, however, that even within these countries that have succeeded in breaking into global markets, integration has not, typically, led to greater income equality.[25]

This was not what globalization promised.

Just a decade ago, in the early 1990s, hundreds of millions of the world's poorest, from Johannesburg to Rio de Janeiro, believed that it was only a matter of time before market liberalization, democratic reforms, and globalization would hike their standard of living closer to that enjoyed by Americans. American policymakers and pro-market developing-country politicians were equally irresponsible in cultivating these dangerously inflated expectations. Today, as London's *Financial Times* recently put it, "Americans are richer while people in most transition economies and emerging markets still struggle, their frustration heightened by cheap, almost universal access to images and information about how much better Americans live." While anti-Americanism used to be driven by what America did, "now it is also motivated by what America is."[26]

And what is America? In the eyes of the vast majority of the developing world, America is the antithesis of what they are. America is rich, healthy, glamorous, confident, and exploitative—at least if Hollywood, our multinationals, our supermodels, and our leaders are any indication. America is also "almighty," able to "control the world," whether through our military power or through the IMF-implemented austerity measures we have heartlessly forced on developing populations. They, on the other hand, are hungry, poor, exploited, and powerless, often even over the destiny of their own families. Obviously their condition is not all America's fault. But like the wildly disproportionately wealthy Chinese in Indonesia, Indians in East Africa, or Jewish "oligarchs" in Russia, America is an obvious scapegoat, practically calling out to be hated.

And Americans are indeed hated in the developing world. Of course, "the poor" in developing countries are not homogeneous, and surely— hopefully—the prominent Hanoi professor who said he believed "fully 80 percent of the world's population" "privately praise[d] the September 11 attacks" was exaggerating.[27] Nevertheless, the fact remains that after the two towers of the World Trade Center collapsed—horrifically killing three thousand men, women, and children—many outside the United States rejoiced.

In Indonesia and Malaysia, gleeful, hate-filled youths went from one luxury hotel to another, looking for Americans. In Brazil, Osama bin Laden masks rolled off assembly lines, not fast enough to satisfy exploding consumer demand. "I don't give a shit," wrote a Chinese man in an inflammatory anti-American e-mail that circulated in Australia and Europe. "America deserves this, because of all the suffering it has caused humankind," said a Vietnamese university student, interviewed on September 13, 2001. "The United States is king of the jungle," said another. "When the king is attacked, the other animals are happy." And: "I feel sorry for the terrorists who were very brave because they risked their lives."[28]

Many hundreds of millions of others in the developing world take a more moderate view, condemning the killing of innocent people but at the same time firmly declaring that "America had it coming," "This is what they get," and "What do Americans expect?" Indeed, this seems clearly to be the dominant, majority-held view in the developing world: condemnation of the attack but sympathy for the attackers and the causes motivating them.

Moreover, across Africa, Asia, and Latin America, the theme of American market dominance repeatedly emerges, with more frequency, bitterness, and clarity than the charges against American foreign policy with which they are sometimes interwoven. Thus, Daijhi, a popular Nepalese commentator, condemned the attack on America as follows:

> Those men who carried out the plane bombings . . . chose specific targets. The World Trade Centre was the High Temple of capitalism. It housed thousands of highly paid financial workers who were seen as soldiers fighting an economic war that forces 80% of mankind to live in poverty. The bombers did not see them as innocent civilians. They felt these workers were directly responsible for the suffering of millions. . . . We should never rejoice in the death and suffering of other people even if they are our enemies. But America should not ignore the widespread hatred that is felt against it. No empire can successfully oppress other nations and cultures indefinitely. Unless the wealth of the whole is fairly shared among all its members there will always be rebellion and terrorism.[29]

And from Michel Fortin of *Africana Plus*:

> The World Trade Centre was a symbol of the scandalous thirst for profit on the part of the Western countries, which practice a one-way commercial traffic. It was attacked by terrorists who wished

to humiliate the Financial Monster, the leader of the modern world. Whatever the background, this attack deserved of course the strongest condemnation. . . . Yet we have to recognize that this deplorable act of aggression may have been, at least in part, an act of revenge on the part of desperate and humiliated people, crushed by the weight of the economic oppression practiced by the peoples of the West.

It is therefore the interference of the West in the economies of the Third World which has produced the underdevelopment which it was supposed to be curing. . . . Development agencies are becoming increasingly aware that multinational companies are siphoning off the wealth of poor countries.[30]

These excerpts are representative of literally thousands of similar statements from inhabitants of the developing world. Much less representative is the following defense of America from the November 2001 Internet-issue of *Brazzil* magazine after a slew of post–September 11 anti-American diatribes:

The reaction of Brazilians to the attack on the United States by Muslim terrorists portrays the dubious nature of [the] human mind. [The] United States is the country that the government and people of Brazil try to imitate as much as they possibly can, not to mention the ever-present long lines of Brazilians waiting to obtain their travel visas at American Embassies and Consulates all over the country.

If the people of the United States and their government are such bad people that deserve to be slaughtered as on September 11, 2001, I wonder why anybody would want to visit the country. I don't see the same long lines of Brazilians in Iraqi, Iranian, Libyan, and Saudi Arabian embassies waiting for visas to travel to those countries.

My theory regarding the reactions of Brazilians and, in fact, of people in many other third world countries is that those reactions are a mixture of envy and frustration. These are countries that have failed to move forward in economic development. Even though Americans are always the first to arrive with help at a scene of disaster anywhere in the world, that is not what people think about when they think of the United States. They just want to live the way Americans live without realizing that Americans worked hard to get to where they are, and still work hard, and do things the right way to stay there. The dubious nature of [the] human mind makes these people feel good when the so-called mighty is brought down because they somehow irrationally believe that that would make everyone equal.[31]

In sum, the vicious, passionate, often self-contradictory anti-Americanism experienced by so many among the world's poor is strikingly analogous to the resentment directed against market-dominant minorities around the world. The difference is that in this case America is a *global* market-dominant minority. Like resentment against the Chinese in Southeast Asia, anti-Americanism is not always active. But it is an ever-present vein of hatred, waiting to be mined, whether by a charismatic demagogue or a triggering event.

Still, it is important to keep in mind that justifying or even praising the September 11 attack after the fact is not the same thing as participating in it. Most people, however frustrated or angry, do not kill others, however "arrogant" or resented. Indeed, until relatively recently, anti-Americanism in the developing world typically found expression not in killing Americans—although there were certainly isolated cases of anti-American violence abroad—but rather through confiscations of American businesses or property in the name of the "rightful owners of the nation." Like the expropriation of white-owned land in Zimbabwe or of Eritrean businesses in Ethiopia described in chapter 5, these confiscations are examples of a backlash against markets, targeting an "outsider" market-dominant minority.

Anti-market Backlash against Western Investors

For a hundred years throughout the developing world, the market dominance of Western foreign investors has provoked the same anti-market backlashes that have been directed at domestic market-dominant minorities. Indeed, from the viewpoint of the "indigenous" majorities, marketization and privatization campaigns in Africa, Southeast Asia, and Latin America have been virtually synonymous with "handing over to foreigners" ownership and control of the country's most valuable industries and resources, including oil, gas, timber, communications, utilities, transportation, and gold, silver, and copper mines. As American investors and corporations have become increasingly preeminent in global markets, Americans have come to bear the brunt of the reaction.

Confiscations of foreign-held property are an integral part of the history of most developing countries, often wrapped up with their most celebrated revolutionary movements. In the late 1930s, for example, Mexico's President Lázaro Cárdenas famously nationalized the country's railways, seizing control from wealthy American and British bondholders. More dramatically, decrying the "innumerable outrages [and] abuses" by foreign oil companies that pursued "private, selfish, and often illegal interests" while relegating Mexicans to "misery, drabness, and insalubrity," Cárdenas nationalized the entire oil industry. This nationalization was immensely popular at every level of society, from bishops to bartenders to university students. Hundreds of thousands of ordinary Mexicans marched through Mexico City carrying mock coffins inscribed with "Standard Oil" and the names of other fallen American behemoths.[32] As is always true of expropriations targeting a market-dominant minority, Cárdenas's nationalizations proved economically disastrous. Nevertheless, in Mexico to this day, Cárdenas stands for the promise of a "Mexico for the Mexicans."

In Argentina, laissez-faire economic policies in the late nineteenth and early twentieth centuries led to the humiliating domination of Argentina's economy by American companies like Swift, Armour, Wilson, Goodyear, and ITT. By 1935 roughly 50 percent of the country's industrial capital was owned or controlled by American or other Western investors. Anti-American sentiment intensified, culminating in a powerful nationalist reaction under the charismatic populist leader Juan Perón. Masterfully inciting hatred against foreign capitalists and the landed estancieros, Perón nationalized Argentina's foreign-owned railroads, gasworks, and utilities in the name of the "true Argentinians."[33]

Similar majority-supported, anti-market confiscations targeting

Western foreign investors, often along with internal market-dominant minorities, have occurred throughout the developing world. In Chile in the early 1970s, democratically elected president Salvador Allende nationalized hundreds of private businesses, including the American Anaconda and Kennecott copper companies, in the name of "Chile for the Chileans." In Uruguay, Don José Batlle y Ordóñez swept to electoral victory on an antiforeigner, nationalist platform; once in office Batlle nationalized the foreign-dominated railway, electricity, and insurance industries. In Burma, the country's revered first prime minister U Nu nationalized major British teak, cement, sugar, and transportation companies along with Burmese Indian and Burmese Chinese businesses in the name of "Burmanization." In Indonesia, Sukarno's sweeping nationalizations in the late fifties and sixties targeted not just Indonesian Chinese but also enormous Dutch enterprises. In Uganda in the 1960s, President Milton Obote partially nationalized major European companies, including Shell-BP. Around the same time in Tanzania, President Julius Nyerere nationalized all major foreign firms, including the entirety of the British- and Indian-dominated banking, insurance, and import-export sectors.[34]

The list goes on. A startling percentage of the world's developing countries have at some point confiscated the assets or businesses of market-dominant foreign investors. Invariably, these nationalizations were majority-supported—usually with wild popular enthusiasm.

With the fall of the Soviet Union in 1989, many imagined that the pressures for nationalization in the developing world would evaporate. But as discussed earlier, this prediction was based on the erroneous assumption that nationalization in the developing world was motivated principally by socialist or Communist ideals. In reality, with a few exceptions (China, Cuba, Vietnam), nationalization in developing countries was never so much an expression of socialism as it was of intense nationalism and ethnonationalism, directed at both Western and internal market-dominant minorities.

The events of 1989, while perhaps discrediting socialism, did nothing to diminish nationalist and ethnonationalist pressures. Indeed, as chapter 5 discussed, ethnonationalist confiscations targeting market-dominant minorities have occurred frequently since 1989, for example, in Ethiopia, Indonesia, and most recently Zimbabwe. At the same time, nationalist resentment against Western "economic aggression" and IMF free market "austerity" measures has intensified. In recent years, with the rising dominance of the United States and the growing visibility of American multinationals, such nationalist resentment increasingly vents itself in concentrated anti-American hatred.

But unlike in the 1930s or even 1970s, anti-American backlash these days rarely takes the form of confiscation or nationalization of American holdings. This is not because nationalism or anti-Americanism has lessened. (When President Bill Clinton visited India in 2000, furious protests broke out, and well-known poet Kaifi Azmi wrote a poem for Clinton, saying: "Your bill is counterfeit. O shark of the markets / We know you truly well. O benevolent / intruder from the distant land.")[35] Rather, anti-American nationalizations are rare because of America's tremendous global clout—economic, political, and military. Any country daring to expropriate American property today risks serious consequences, whether in the form of capital flight, crippling lawsuits, economic sanctions, or worse. The poor countries of the world, governments and citizens alike, fear America. That's partly why they hate us.

Indeed, the few episodes of near-confiscation in recent years have typically involved unusual circumstances and some degree of American botch-up. In 1999, for example, the Wall Street firm Kohlberg Kravis Roberts (KKR) managed the hostile takeover of Russia's Lomonosov Porcelain Factory by American shareholders. But KKR underestimated the importance of the factory as a symbol of Russian cultural identity. Established by Peter the Great's daughter in 1744, the Lomonosov Factory produced tea sets, gilded figurines, and even porcelain paintings for generations of tsars. After the Communists took over in 1917, the factory's product line "became more politically correct: plates bearing Lenin's visage and chess sets with manacled proletarians as pawns." Apparently, Jane Fonda once ordered Lomonosov china, painted environmental green with the rust-colored slogan "Earth to the Workers."[36]

For many Russians the idea of foreigners, especially Americans, owning the factory was anathema, or, as one factory spokeswoman put it, akin to "selling part of the Hermitage art collection." Nor did it help matters that KKR had employed an unpopular local intermediary to carry out the actual transaction. In any event, self-interested managers of the factory sued for renationalization, on grounds that it had been illegally privatized—singling it out of ten thousand other similar privatizations. In the end, however, after initial losses in lower St. Petersburg courts, the American investors ultimately prevailed.[37]

Enron, much in the news these days, fared considerably worse in India. As late as 1991, India's power sector was a state-owned economic nightmare. Almost half of the electricity produced in the country was given away free, and roughly another quarter was stolen. Meanwhile, India's economy was plodding along at almost zero growth. Pushed by the World Bank, India's new pro-market government came up with a familiar solution: jump-start the power sector through privatization and foreign investment.

In 1993, in what seemed like a match made in heaven, Enron entered into a contract with the state government of Maharashtra to build the $2.8 billion Dabhol power plant, representing by far India's largest foreign investment. But like Coca-Cola and IBM, who were "persuaded" by Indira Gandhi in the 1970s to close down their operations in India, Enron ran into intense anti-American, antimultinational sentiment. Shortly after the deal was signed, Hindu nationalist parties rode to power in elections in Maharashtra. The new leaders condemned the terms of the contract as theft and "neo-colonialism," favorable only to Enron and its corrupt local cronies while forcing the already impoverished local Maharashtrians to pay higher, survival-threatening prices.

"Why do we need foreigners when we have so many Indian industrialists?" demanded the new leaders as they "reviewed the legitimacy" of the contract. "Kill the Dabhol project!" "America out!" and "Enron into the sea!" became popular slogans. In what many Westerners view as a form of confiscation, Enron eventually had to renegotiate the terms of the contract.[38] (Critics of Enron say its willingness to renegotiate merely confirms how outrageous their original profit margin must have been; Enron's defenders argue that Enron, having already sunk $300 million in construction costs, was basically held up and extorted.)

Enron's troubles in India were far from over. Even after the new contract was signed in 1995, with reduced electricity rates for the Maharashtrians, Enron stood as a hated symbol of American exploitation. Anti-Enron demonstrations, vandalism, and threats to storm the power plant persisted through spring of 2001. Enron ended up paying for local police to provide additional security, then got entangled in further scandal when New York–based Human Rights Watch issued a 166-page report charging the police with beating and illegally detaining anti-Enron protesters. At one point, the report said, "the pregnant wife of a village activist was dragged naked from her home and beaten in the street."[39]

But the Lomonosov Porcelain and Enron cases are exceptional. The truth is that while American multinationals are more resented than ever, and often the subject of sporadic local protest or retaliation, they are also more confident and powerful in the developing world than ever, backed by the strongest nation in the world. In India, for example, despite the Enron fiasco and seething popular antimultinational hostility, recent economic liberalizations have brought American giants like Coca-Cola and IBM charging back in. Because of the United States' "hyperpower" status, developing-country governments—at least for now—no longer view expropriation of American assets as a viable option. As one developing-country commentator put it, "Developing countries are entirely dependent on, and controlled by, the international financial system. In short, we are at the mercy of the United States."

Thus, even as anti-American hostility in developing countries mounts, one outlet for its expression—expropriation of American holdings—has essentially been closed off. On one level this is a cause for celebration: Perhaps what Westerners call "the rule of law"—meaning basically the sanctity of contract and protection of private property—is finally taking hold in the developing world. The problem, however, is that the pervasive, underlying hatred of the market-dominant minority remains. And there are outlets for group hatred infinitely more terrible than economic confiscations.

Destroying America

Market-dominant minorities are often the victims of homicidal fury. The Chinese in Southeast Asia, Tutsi in Rwanda, Jews in Germany, Ibo in Nigeria, and Croats in the former Yugoslavia were all, at some point, murdered en masse by enraged members of a frustrated, relatively impoverished majority who saw themselves as the humiliated "true" owners of the nation.

The September 11, 2001, killings had much in common with other mass killings of market-dominant minorities. First, they revealed an all-consuming group hatred that may have shocked Americans but is distinctly parallel to the hatred felt, for example, by the Hutu when they murdered Tutsis, who had dominated them economically and politically for four hundred years. In the eyes of the killers on September 11, as in every case when market-dominant minorities are massacred, the victims were no longer individuals but faceless embodiments of corrupt wealth, arrogance, and abusive power.

Second, this intense group hatred was fomented by a calculating, charismatic demagogue. In this respect, Osama bin Laden has his counterparts in Adolf Hitler and Slobodan Milosevic. In all these cases the leaders found great wells of anger, disgust, and spiritual misery waiting to be exploited.

Third, like other mass killings aimed at "cleansing" the nation of a hated "outsider" market-dominant minority, one of the main objectives of Islamic terrorism has been to eliminate the presence of America from the Middle East. A stunning feature of this terrorism is its global reach. Nevertheless, one of bin Laden's primary missions has been to "purge" the "lands of Islam" of Western and particularly American infidels. "For more than seven years," bin Laden declared in 1993, "the United States has been occupying the lands of Islam in the holiest of its territories, Arabia, plundering its riches, overwhelming its rulers, humiliating its people, threatening its neighbors, and using its peninsula as a spearhead to fight neighboring Islamic peoples."[40]

Similarly, after the 1996 twin bombings of U.S. embassies in Kenya and Tanzania—in which over 250 people died and more than 5,500 were injured—bin Laden's associate Abdul-Bari Atwan published an article called "American Harvest of Blood," defending the suicide attacks as "the logical results of the unjust and demeaning policies which the United States has been pursuing in the Arab region and in the Islamic world." A litany of grievances followed, summarized by Yossef Bodansky in his recent biography of bin Laden, with the main criticism aimed at the United States' policy of sponsoring corrupt dictators in the Arab world, hypocritically "prevent[ing] the democratic tide from spreading to the region . . ." According to Atwan, "America's insistence on imposing its own puppets on the Muslim world in order to expedite exploitation of oil and other riches—and not U.S.-Israeli relations—was at the core of the Islamist eruption."[41]

After the September 11 attacks, bin Laden himself issued a strongly worded warning to Americans in a recorded statement broadcast on Al-Jazeera television. Describing the American victims generically as "killers, who have abused the blood, honour, and sanctuaries of Muslims," bin Laden swore "by God, who has elevated the skies without pillars," that "neither America nor the people who live in it will dream of security before we live it in Palestine, and not before all the infidel armies leave the land of Muhammad."[42]

Fourth, like all acts of violence against market-dominant minorities, the September 11 attacks were an act of revenge by the weak against the powerful, motivated by tremendous feelings of humiliation and inferiority. "Weakness" is a complicated matter, with a large subjective component. Poverty breeds feelings of weakness. But so does being from a poor country. As many have pointed out, the pilots who flew their planes into the World Trade Center were well educated, with middle-class backgrounds. But they were also from countries that in their own eyes had been raped and humiliated by the West. Slobodan Milosevic was not poverty-stricken, but his statement "[I]f we don't know how to work well or to do business, at least we know how to fight well!"[43] reveals much about the psychology of a majority that perceives itself as dominated and degraded.

"Power" can also be subjective and complicated—but in the United States' case, it is not. As a country, America is not merely disproportionately wealthy, but economically, politically, culturally, technologically, and militarily dominant over the rest of the world.

"America is the most powerful nation on Earth," wrote Nepalese columnist Daijhi, shortly after September 11. "Its economic force controls every field of commerce. Its military strength can destroy any other nation. It is effectively both the global government and the global policeman. But a small group of dedicated people armed only with fruit knives and a passionate cause was able to bring death, destruction and humiliation upon it. The spectacular attack on New York and Washington was the most important international event since the collapse of Communist Russia."[44] Although Daijhi condemned the attack on America, the hint of pride in his tone is unmistakable. "So America is not so invincible after all," hundreds of other developing-country commentators observed.

Many on the Arab street gloated more expressly. "Bulls-eye!" cheered taxi drivers in Egypt as they watched over and over footage of the hijacked planes slamming into the twin towers of the World Trade Center. *"Mabrouk! Mabrouk!* (Congratulations!)," shouted jubilant crowds huddled around televisions in shop windows.[45] While most Muslims are not fundamentalists, the September 11 killings nevertheless prompted many of them to celebrate and give special thanks to Allah. "[T]here can be no question," writes Martin Peretz, "that today, it is in the lands of Islam where the greatest number of lives are invigorated by ecstatic hatred of the United States. We see this ecstasy, at once joyful and enraged, from Gaza to Egypt to the Gulf to South Asia."[46]

Demographics exacerbate the problem. The majority of the population in the Middle East are young. "Seventy percent of the Arab population has been born since 1970," Robert Kaplan warned presciently in his 1994 essay "The Coming Anarchy." "The most distant recollection of these youths will be the West's humiliation of colonially invented Iraq in 1991. Today seventeen out of twenty-two Arab states have a declining gross national product; in the next twenty years, at current growth rates, the population of many Arab countries will double. These states . . . will be ungovernable through conventional secular ideologies."[47]

The statement bin Laden aired shortly after the September 11 attacks, nauseating to grief-stricken Americans, hit just the right chord with millions throughout the Middle East: "I bear witness that there is no God but Allah and that Mohammed is his messenger. There is America, hit by God in one of its softest spots. Its greatest buildings were destroyed. Thank God for that. There is America, full of fear from its north to its south, from its west to its east. Thank God for that. What America is tasting now is something insignificant compared to what we have tasted for scores of years."[48]

The momentary jubilation, however, of the millions of poor and exploited people around the world who rejoiced at the mass murder of Americans reflects profound weakness. In the words of Turkish writer Orhan Pamuk, "It is neither Islam nor even poverty itself that directly engenders support for terrorists whose ferocity and ingenuity are unprecedented in human history; it is, rather, the crushing humiliation that has infected the third-world countries." Pamuk continues as follows:

> At no time in history has the gulf between rich and poor been so wide. . . . at no time in history have the lives of the rich been so forcefully brought to the attention of the poor through television and Hollywood films. . . . But far worse, at no other time have the world's rich and powerful societies been so clearly right, and "reasonable."
>
> Today an ordinary citizen of a poor, undemocratic Muslim country, or a civil servant in a third-world country or in a former socialist republic struggling to make ends meet, is aware of how insubstantial is his share of the world's wealth; he knows that he lives under conditions that are much harsher and more devastating than those of a "Westerner" and that he is condemned to a much shorter life. At the same time, however, he senses in a corner of his mind that his poverty is to some considerable degree the fault of his own folly and inadequacy, or those of his father and grandfather. The Western world is scarcely aware of this overwhelming feeling of humiliation that is experienced by most of the world's population . . .[49]

Like other group hatred movements directed against market-dominant minorities, Islamic fundamentalism offers an alternative to humiliation. It offers a scapegoat, a mission, an identity, and a chance—however deluded—for the powerless to regain power.

CHAPTER 12

The Future
of Free Market Democracy

T he bottom line is this. Democracy can be inimical to the interests of market-dominant minorities. There were good reasons why the Indians in Kenya and whites in South Africa, Zimbabwe, and America's Southern states resisted democratization for generations. Market-dominant minorities do not really want democracy, at least not in the sense of having their fate determined by genuine majority rule.

Some readers will surely protest. Many market-dominant minorities—the Chinese in Malaysia, for example, or Jews in Russia, and Americans everywhere—often seem to be among the most vocal advocates of democracy. But "democracy" is a notoriously contested term, meaning different things to different people.

When entrepreneurial but politically vulnerable minorities like the Chinese in Southeast Asia, Indians in East Africa, or Jews in Russia call for democracy, they principally have in mind constitutionally guaranteed human rights and property protections for minorities. In other words, in calling for democracy, these "outsider" groups are precisely seeking protection against "tyranny of the majority."

Similarly, when the European-blooded elites in Bolivia, Ecuador, or Venezuela discuss democratization, they invariably mention the "rule of law" in the same sentence. What these elites decidedly don't want from democracy is to have property rights and economic policies suddenly determined by their countries' poorly educated, impoverished Indian-blooded majorities. (Witness the horror of the Venezuelan elite when populist leader Hugo Chavez swept to power and the subsequent efforts to remove him.) On the contrary, by democratization, Latin America's

elites usually mean a very gradual process of majority inclusion, beginning first with educational reform, perhaps local elections, and some
political participation of the masses—but always tempered by, and subordinated to, an overriding concern for the stability of property rights,
foreign investment, and the status quo.

In the Middle East, Israeli Jews are justly proud of the strength of
Israel's democratic institutions, which are almost unique in the Middle
East. But even Israel does not extend suffrage to the roughly 3 million
Palestinians living in the West Bank and Gaza Strip. Among other reasons, enfranchising the Palestinians of the Occupied Territories would
significantly dilute Israel's "Jewish character" and could even lead to
Jews eventually becoming a minority in Israel. Nor is it clear that democratization of the Arab states would be in Israel's best interests. In
Egypt, for example, rapid democratization might very well bring to
power a regime much more hostile to Israel than Hosni Mubarak's autocratic military rule.

Finally, when Americans call for world democratization, we don't
mean world democracy. For Americans, global democratization means
democracy for and within individual countries. That is, we envision a
world in which brutal and unjust dictatorships are replaced by freely
and fairly elected leaders, accountable to their citizens. We imagine ourselves, moreover, at the helm of such a world. As President Clinton predicted in his second inaugural address: "The world's greatest democracy
will lead a whole world of democracies."[1] By contrast, the last thing
most Americans want is a true world democracy, in which our economic and political fate is determined by a majority of the world's
countries or citizens. The idea, for example, of the U.N. General
Assembly controlling U.S. foreign investments would probably not be
appealing to most Americans. Like other market-dominant minorities,
we don't trust the relatively poor, frustrated, resentful majorities surrounding us necessarily to act in our best interests.

Democracy or Markets?

Deservedly or not, market-dominant minorities—with their disproportionate capital, skills, business networks, and control over the mod-

ern economy—drive global capitalism. Any backlash against market-dominant minorities, whether the Chinese in Indonesia, Ibo in Nigeria, or America at the global level, is thus also a backlash against markets.

In other words, in societies with a market-dominant minority, democracy can pose a grave threat not only to the minority, but to markets themselves. Rather than reinforcing the market's liberalizing, wealth-producing effects, the sudden political empowerment of a poor, frustrated "indigenous" majority often leads to powerful ethnonationalist, anti-market pressures. And these pressures, as Rwanda, Indonesia, and the former Yugoslavia vividly show, are more likely to lead to confiscation and ethnic killing than to the widespread peace and prosperity that proponents of free market democracy envision. There is always an inherent tension between market capitalism and democracy. But in societies with a market-dominant minority, this tension is inflamed by the dark energies of ethnic hatred. As a result, throughout the non-Western world today, markets and democracy—at least in the raw forms in which they are currently being implemented—are not typically mutually reinforcing. On the contrary, their combined pursuit in the face of a hated market-dominant minority is a recipe for ethnic conflagration.

So where does this leave us? What are the implications of market-dominant minorities for national and international policymaking?

Influential writer Robert D. Kaplan recently offered this general answer: hold off on democracy until free markets produce enough economic and social development to make democracy sustainable. In *The Coming Anarchy*, Kaplan argues that a middle class and civil institutions—both of which he implicitly assumes would be generated by market capitalism—are preconditions for democracy. Contrasting Lee Kuan Yew's prosperous authoritarian Singapore with the murderous, "bloodletting" democratic states of Colombia, Rwanda, and South Africa, Kaplan fiercely condemns America's post–Cold War mission to export democracy abroad, to "places where it can't succeed."[2]

This position—markets first, democracy later, if at all—has a long and impressive pedigree. In 1959, noted sociologist Seymour Martin Lipset wrote that "the more well-to-do a nation, the greater the chances that it will sustain democracy." And in his 1968 *Political Order in Changing Societies* political scientist Samuel P. Huntington made what continues to be the most powerful and subtle case against rapid democratization in modernizing societies.[3] Not surprisingly, this view also finds support among many leaders of non-Western nations, who argue that democracy is a Western value that should not indiscriminately be imposed on other cultures.

In 1992, for example, Saudi Arabia's King Fahd publicly stated that the "democratic system prevailing in the world does not suit us in the region . . . Islam is our social and political law. It is a complete constitution of social and economic laws and a system of government and justice."[4] Similarly, Malaysia's prime minister Dr. Mahathir Mohamad has frequently attacked the "moral degeneration" of Western democracy and the superiority of "Asian values."[5]

Singapore's Lee Kuan Yew recently explained in an interview in *Foreign Affairs* that "Asian societies are unlike Western ones. The fundamental difference between Western concepts of society and government and East Asian concepts"—referring to China, Japan, Korea, and Vietnam, as distinct from Southeast Asia—"is that Eastern societies believe that the individual exists in the context of the family. He is not pristine and separate." On democracy, Lee Kuan Yew responded, "What are we all seeking? A form of government that will be comfortable, because it meets our needs, is not oppressive, and maximizes our opportunities. And whether you have one-man, one-vote or some-men, one vote or other men, two votes, those are forms which should be worked out. I'm not intellectually convinced that one-man, one-vote is best."[6]

Singapore, with its astounding rise to prosperity, modernity, and civil stability, has proved an alluring exemplar for those who question the wisdom of democratizing developing societies. According to Kaplan, the American urge to democratize others is arrogant, provincial, and irresponsible. "To think that democracy as we know it will triumph—or is even here to stay—is itself a form of determinism, driven by our own ethnocentricism," argues Kaplan.[7]

Although Kaplan's view is refreshingly unromantic, I ultimately differ from him. To begin with, as one writer has quipped, "If authoritarianism were the key to prosperity, then Africa would be the richest continent in the world." There is no way to ensure that any given dictator will be beneficent, farsighted, and pro-market. Ask (as some do) for an Augusto Pinochet or an Alberto Fujimori, and you may get an Idi Amin or a Papa Doc Duvalier. As many political economists have observed, there is no clear correlation between authoritarianism and economic growth.[8] While democracy is certainly no panacea for corruption, many of history's most predatory regimes, from the Marcos dictatorship in the Philippines to Burma's repugnant SLORC, have been autocratic.

More fundamentally, Kaplan overlooks the global problem of market-dominant minorities. Kaplan stresses the ethnic biases of elections, but neglects the ethnic biases of capitalism. At the same time he is overly optimistic about the ability of markets alone to lift the great indigenous masses out of poverty. The awkward reality is that markets in developing societies favor not only some people over others, but some ethnic groups over others. Worse, they often benefit a hated ethnic minority, leaving the vast majority of the nation in frustrated poverty. Overlooking this reality, Kaplan blames too much of the world's violence and anarchy on democracy.

Consider, for example, the brutal takeover of Sierra Leone by diamond-hungry, limb-chopping rebels; the confiscations of white land in Zimbabwe; or the 1998 anti-Chinese riots in Indonesia that triggered $40 billion of capital flight and helped economically destabilize all of Southeast Asia. In all these cases and many more, markets set up the disasters by reinforcing the stark economic dominance of an "outsider" minority and by fomenting intense resentment among the poor, frustrated "indigenous" majority. Once such intense resentment among the majority exists, Kaplan is absolutely right that suddenly holding free and fair elections could well produce catastrophic results. What he fails to see is that unrestrained markets—superimposed on postcolonial societies with massive initial ethnic imbalances in financial and human capital—have helped create intolerable and volatile conditions in these societies, the very conditions that unrestrained democracy detonates.

The remainder of this chapter will be based on three assumptions. First, the best economic hope for developing and post-socialist countries lies in some form of market-generated growth. Second, the best political hope for these countries lies in some form of democracy, with constitutional constraints, tailored to local realities. And third, avoiding ethnic oppression and bloodshed must be a constant priority. But if these goals are to be achieved—if global free market democracy is to be peaceably sustainable—then the problem of market-dominant minorities, however unsettling, must be confronted head-on. The answer is not to swing from one wishful panacea to another, for example by scapegoating democracy and glorifying markets, or vice versa.

Rather, the next several sections will address the following specific topics: (1) the possibility of "leveling the playing field" between market-dominant minorities and the impoverished "indigenous" majorities around them; (2) ways of giving the poor, frustrated majorities of the world a greater stake in global markets; (3) ways of promoting liberal rather than illiberal democracies; and (4) approaches that market-dominant minorities themselves might take to forestall majority-based, often murderous ethnonationalist backlashes. If we stop peddling cure-alls—both to ourselves and others—and instead candidly address the biases and dangers inherent in both markets and democracy, there is in many cases room for optimism.

Leveling the Playing Field:
Addressing the Causes of Market Dominance

The first, most obvious step is to isolate, where possible, and to address, where appropriate, the causes of the market dominance of certain groups. In South Africa, for example, expanding educational opportunities for the black majority—relegated for more than seventy years to inferior Bantu schooling—is properly a national priority and should be vigorously supported by the international community to the extent that it has an interest in promoting the stability of a democratic South Africa. Throughout Latin America as well, the market dominance of the European-blooded elite reflects at least in part centuries of subjugation, exclusion, and corrupt, oligarchic rule. Educational reform and equalization of opportunities for the region's poor indigenous-blooded majorities are imperative if global markets are to benefit more than just a handful of cosmopolitan elites.

Similarly, to the extent that political favoritism has contributed to the astounding wealth of certain market-dominant minorities, eliminating such favoritism would plainly be a step in the right direction. The monopolies awarded by indigenous leaders, always in exchange for kick-backs, to outsider market-dominant minorities not only are inefficient, but fuel invidious group stereotypes and aggravate ethnic resentment.

On the other hand, we have to be realistic. The truth is that the un-derlying causes of market dominance are poorly understood, difficult to reduce to tangible factors, and in any event highly intractable. Research, for example, suggests that additional educational spending, if not ac-companied by major socioeconomic reforms, produces depressingly few benefits.[9] (Educating girls, however, might have a significant indirect payoff: Research results are strong that young women with more educa-tion have smaller families, and population pressures exacerbate all the problems of poor countries, including those related to market-dominant minorities.) Likewise, while political favoritism is a frequent, exacerbat-ing problem in societies with a market-dominant minority, such fa-voritism tends to be more the consequence than the cause of market dominance. Most market-dominant minorities, whether the Bamiléké in Cameroon or Indians in Fiji, are disproportionately economically suc-cessful at every level of society, including small traders, retailers, and shopkeepers with no political connections whatsoever. Further, many market-dominant minorities have been successful notwithstanding long histories of official discrimination against them. This is certainly true of the Chinese in Southeast Asia, Lebanese in West Africa, and Jews almost everywhere.

Sociologists and anthropologists have been trying for years to under-stand the economic success of some groups over others. Ever since Max Weber argued that Protestantism was more conducive to capital accu-mulation than Catholicism, religion has often been cited as a critical de-terminant of group economic success. More recently, many have stressed cultural factors—for example, group differences in work habits, savings propensities, or attitudes toward education, commerce, and wealth—to explain differentials in group economic performance.[10]

To the extent that religion and other cultural factors play a signifi-cant role in producing the market dominance of certain groups, the ap-propriate policy implications are by no means clear. Even if there were a demonstrable relationship between certain religions and economic success, an effort to instill "entrepreneurialism" through, say, group conversions to Protestantism (or Judaism or Confucianism, depending on the theory) would seem unpromising. Attempts to inculcate a "work ethic" may seem more attractive, but have not proved any more effective. Indigenous elites in developing countries have frequently encouraged their fellow citizens to emulate market-dominant minorities and to become more "diligent" and "motivated." Malaysia's prime minister Mahathir, for example, has often urged his Malay constituents to model themselves on their more "hardworking" and commercially "astute" Chinese counterparts.[11] Not surprisingly, such governmental "cultural revolutions"—attempting to change culture from the top down—have been notoriously unsuccessful.

Apart from the issue of feasibility, there is also a moral question. "Culture" cannot simply be treated as an inconvenient impediment to free markets. Even if it were possible to transform every developing-world villager into a consumer entrepreneur, it is hardly obvious that this ought to be the goal of development policy.

But the fundamental point is this. To "level the playing field" in developing societies—to try to bring impoverished, often illiterate majorities up to the level where they can compete successfully with the hypercapitalized market-dominant minorities in their midst—will be a painfully slow process, taking generations if it is possible at all. As a result, over-reliance on this strategy is unwise. Leaving in place for years or even decades the existing ethnic economic imbalances, long-term efforts to "level the playing field" assume a horizon of social stability that many non-Western countries do not have. Indeed, in the short term, investment in education and other forms of human capital can contribute to ethnonationalist movements. As many have pointed out, the relationship between education and ethnonationalism is by no means straightforward; Osama bin Laden's Al Qaeda pilots were very well educated.

Policies to expand education and promote equal opportunity, while comforting and uncontroversial, do not directly address the pressing, potentially explosive problems of ethnic resentment and ethnonationalist hatred that threaten so many developing and post-socialist societies today. To address these problems it will be essential to try to devise measures and create institutions restraining the worst excesses of markets and democracy—excesses that in the presence of a market-dominant minority often lead to confiscations, authoritarian backlash, and mass slaughter.

Stakeholding: Spreading the Benefits of Markets

The essential problem is that in societies with a market-dominant minority, laissez-faire capitalism leaves significant numbers of the relatively impoverished majority feeling that they have no stake in globalization or a market economy. There are at least four basic strategies for redressing this problem. Each has drawbacks; some are more controversial than others; and some might be inappropriate or infeasible in particular contexts. But all should be seriously considered.

The first and most familiar strategy for wealth-spreading is redistribution through tax-and-transfer programs. As discussed in chapter 9, not a single Western nation today has anything close to a laissez-faire economic system. Yet laissez-faire markets are precisely what the United States, along with powerful international institutions like the IMF, have been promoting for decades throughout the non-Western world.

In the West, strong redistributive measures such as progressive taxation, social security, and unemployment insurance, as well as antitrust and financial regulation, temper the harshest effects of capitalism. In the non-Western world, it is equally imperative to try to spread the benefits of markets. There is no good reason why, in some of the poorest countries in the world, the tax rate for the very wealthy is effectively zero. At a minimum, when exporting Western market institutions, the advanced countries should also be working toward the creation of the social safety net programs and tax-and-transfer institutions familiar throughout the Western nations.

Unfortunately, the realistic redistributive potential of tax-and-transfer policies in the developing world is limited, at least in the near future. To put it bluntly, there is not enough to tax, and nearly no one who can be trusted to transfer.[12] While Westerners take sophisticated tax systems for granted (and complain about them all the time), establishing the institutions and practices necessary to effectuate tax-and-transfer programs is immensely difficult in countries where the state is weak, money scarce, and corruption pervasive.

A second strategy for spreading market wealth was recently proposed by Hernando de Soto in *The Mystery of Capital:* give the poor in the developing world formal, legally defendable property rights. Specifically, de Soto advocates integrating extralegal businesses into the formal property system and giving squatters legal title rather than evicting them. Based on de Soto's proposals, countries like Peru (de Soto's home country) and the Philippines have implemented bold new titling programs, attempting to debunk the prevailing view in the developing world that capitalism is a "private club," only benefiting the West and the already-rich. [13]

A passionate and brilliant champion of both capitalism and the poor in the Third World, de Soto has managed to capture the imaginations of influential figures like Margaret Thatcher and Milton Friedman, along with millions who are currently excluded from globalization's benefits. Insofar, however, as de Soto believes that mere "titling," combined with a market economy, can eliminate poverty quickly and on a large scale, his proposals are probably idealistic. Some of the new "titled" communities established on de Soto's model are located in remote areas and still lack sewage and basic infrastructure. More broadly, de Soto's book does not account for the fact that the existing property rules do not seem to have impeded wealth accumulation by certain ethnic groups—market-dominant minorities—many of whom began with no property at all. As a result, while de Soto's proposals are eminently worth pursuing, I fear that a mere change in formal property rules may not substantially alter the realities of entrenched poverty and the current extreme ethnic maldistributions of wealth. Nevertheless, by drawing international attention to the urgency of trying to expand popular participation in the market system, and by offering a concrete way of doing so, de Soto has performed a tremendously important service and represents a courageous step in the right direction.

A third strategy for spreading the benefits of free markets involves finding ways to give the poor majorities of the world an ownership stake in their country's corporations and capital markets. In the United States, a solid majority of Americans, even members of the middle and lower-middle classes, own shares in major U.S. companies, often through pension funds, and thus feel that they have a stake in the U.S. market economy. This is not the case in the non-Western world, where corporations are often privately owned by single families belonging to a market-dominant minority group and where extremely few members of the general population have any stake in the corporate sector.

If this state of affairs could be changed—if large numbers of the "indigenous" population had an ownership stake in their society's capital markets—the benefits might be considerable, economically and politically. As Columbia Law School professor John Coffee has put it, "Encouraging equity markets to develop and encouraging dispersed ownership may . . . imply not only efficiency gains but also a more open society, one less dominated by banks" and "crony capitalism" and "more attractive to entrepreneurship."[14]

Fourth, a more controversial strategy for addressing the problem of market-dominant minorities consists of government interventions into the market, consciously designed to "correct" ethnic wealth imbalances. Such ethnic-based interventions on behalf of an economically disadvantaged group are known as affirmative action programs in the West. Particularly in the United States, these programs have been the subject of increasingly bitter criticism in recent years.

Whatever the merits of these criticisms in the West, it is important not to confuse apples with oranges. In the West, affirmative action policies are intended to benefit disadvantaged ethnic *minorities*—African-Americans in the United States, aborigines in Australia, or Maori in New Zealand, for example. By contrast, affirmative action policies in countries with a market-dominant minority are intended to benefit disadvantaged *majorities*—for example, blacks in South Africa, Quechua and Aymara Indians in Bolivia, or the 80 percent indigenous *pribumi* majority in Indonesia. This is a rather major difference.

For one thing, even putting aside questions of justice, a situation in which the great majority of citizens in a country live in extreme poverty, while a tiny ethnic minority controls most of the nation's wealth, is extremely unstable, particularly when combined with sudden democratization. For another thing, affirmative action programs in these countries, if voted in by a majority of the population as is the case in South Africa, represent a democratic outcome—and therefore an outcome that it would be awkward for, say, the IMF or the United States to overturn in the name of markets. In any event, Western policymakers, especially American policymakers, have to be careful not to project their own negative feelings about affirmative action or identity politics onto societies where the conditions and demographics are totally different.

Indeed, many Americans are unaware that other countries, including a number of Western countries, have pursued ethnically based affirmative action programs—some with notable success. Canada, for example, has had considerable success addressing the problem of a market-dominant minority at the provincial level. In Quebec, aggressive affirmative action policies in the 1960s helped raise the economic status of the severely economically disadvantaged 80 percent French Canadian majority vis-à-vis the market-dominant English-speaking minority, who historically controlled Quebec's banks, insurance companies, trade, and manufacturing—indeed, the virtual entirety of the modern economy.[15]

But conditions in Quebec forty years ago were considerably more propitious than those prevailing in the non-Western world today. (Quebec was part of a prosperous, industrialized country and the recipient of generous federal funding from the Canadian government.)[16] A much more relevant example for today's developing countries is Malaysia's affirmative action program for its indigenous Malay majority. Following the 1969 race riots in Kuala Lumpur, which were similar in many respects to those that recently erupted in Indonesia, the Malaysian government adopted the "New Economic Policy" (NEP), aggressively seeking to achieve "national unity . . . expressed as the improvement of economic balances between the races." At that time indigenous Malays, or *bumiputra,* represented roughly 62 percent of the population but owned a minuscule 1.5 percent of the country's capital assets.[17] Along with foreign investors, Malaysia's entrepreneurial Chinese minority controlled all of the country's most lucrative, large-scale commercial enterprises, both agricultural and nonagricultural.[18]

To redress these extreme ethnic wealth imbalances, the Malaysian government adopted sweeping ethnic quotas on corporate equity ownership, university admissions, government licensing, and commercial employment. It also initiated large-scale purchases of corporate assets on behalf of the Malay majority. After 1976, under what was effectively compulsory corporate restructuring, many Malaysian Chinese companies were required to set aside 30 percent of their equity for Malay interests—typically with no choice about the identity of their new Malay "business partners." More recently, privatized entities, and companies seeking to list on the Kuala Lumpur Stock Exchange, were required to have a *bumiputra* shareholding of at least 30 percent.[19]

In many respects the results of the NEP have been impressive. While the NEP has not lifted the great majority of Malays (particularly in the rural areas) out of poverty, it has helped to create a substantial Malay middle class. Between 1970 and 1992 the percentage of Malays occupying the country's most lucrative professional positions went from 6 percent to 32 percent. The proportion of *bumiputra* doctors rose from 4 percent to 28 percent; dentists from 3 percent to 24 percent; architects from 4 percent to 24 percent; and engineers from 7 percent to 35 percent. In the corporate sector the *bumiputra* ownership share of corporate stock at par values jumped from 1.5 percent in 1969 to 15.6 percent in 1982 to 20.6 percent in 1995. There is no possibility that free markets could have produced such results.[20]

By creating a small but visible Malay economic elite and by bringing Malay participation into important economic sectors—for example, the construction, rubber, tin, shipping, and communications sectors (all formerly dominated by foreign investors or Chinese and Indian Malaysians)—the NEP has helped promote a sense among the *bumiputra* that a market economy can benefit indigenous Malays, and not merely foreign investors and entrepreneurial "outsiders." According to Prime Minister Mahathir, who frankly concedes that the NEP has tended to favor elite, well-connected Malays, the NEP serves an important symbolic function:

> [I]f these few Malays are not enriched the poor Malays will not gain either. It is the Chinese who will continue to live in huge houses and regard the Malays as only fit to drive their cars. With the existence of the few rich Malays at least the poor can say their fate is not entirely to serve rich non-Malays. From the point of view of racial ego, and this ego is still strong, the unseemly existence of Malay tycoons is essential.[21]

Today, in addition to a number of Malay tycoons, some of Malaysia's best doctors and attorneys are Malay—a fact acknowledged even among the Chinese, who just thirty years ago made no secret of their contempt for Malays.[22]

Neighboring Indonesia provides a useful counterpoint. The massive capital flight and ethnic violence suffered after 1998 by Indonesia contrasts sharply with the situation in Malaysia, where the Asian financial crisis produced no anti-Chinese backlash or rioting, no ethnic confiscations, and very little capital flight. While the comparison between Malaysia and Indonesia has its limits,* there is a strong consensus that Malaysia's systematic market interventions over the last thirty years have helped improve the country's ethnic relations.[23]

At the same time, the accomplishments of the NEP should not be overstated. It is unclear how well the NEP would have fared in the absence of the extraordinarily dynamic growth rates of the 1970s and 1980s. More critically, the NEP has failed to achieve some of its most ambitious objectives. Despite inflated official claims, for example, the NEP has not succeeded in "eradicating poverty," one of its major goals.[24] Further, even after decades of sustained governmental intervention, the Chinese minority remains starkly economically dominant vis-à-vis the *bumiputra* majority. To repeat: Market dominance is surprisingly intractable, and resistant to government-sponsored "corrective" ethnic policies. Worse yet, there is always the danger that government affirmative action policies will exacerbate rather than ameliorate ethnic conflict, by entrenching ethnic divisions.[25]

For all these reasons, it would be irresponsible to champion affirmative action as the one-size-fits-all solution for developing countries that have a market-dominant minority. This is not to say that the NEP or Quebec's ethnic preference programs cannot be helpful models. But in the deeply divided societies of the non-Western world, government leaders are themselves ethnic partisans; indeed, they are often the chief instigators of ethnonationalist sentiment. Sadly, there is a slippery slope between narrowly tailored, ethnic preference programs of limited duration on one hand, and vicious, confiscatory, often murderous "group-

---

*Malaysia and Indonesia differ in important respects: Malaysia has a much smaller absolute population than Indonesia; the Chinese community in Malaysia comprises a much larger percentage of the total population (roughly 30 percent) than that in Indonesia (roughly 3 percent); and Malaysia also has a large Indian community.

payback-time" programs on the other. In their own minds, Zimbabwe's Robert Mugabe, Serbia's Slobodan Milosevic, and Rwanda's Hutu Power leaders were all conducting a form of "affirmative action" on behalf of a long-exploited and humiliated majority.

Democracy: Against Hypocrisy and Beyond Majority Rule

When I recently visited Bolivia, I noticed enthusiastic political slogans ("MNR!") spray-painted on the roofs and walls of tiny dirt-floor houses, even in isolated desert villages. When I mentioned these to my Quechuan guide Osvaldo, he dismissed them with a wave of his hand. "The people in those houses can't even read," he laughed bitterly. "But if they let the government paint those slogans, they get a sack of potatoes, or maybe some sugar."

Democracy in the developing world is often more nominal than real. In many countries the great majority of the impoverished electorate do not have a substantial political voice, whether because of lack of access to information or because the wealthy control the political process through lobbying or corruption.[26] This is true even of "success stories" such as the Philippines, where, despite impressive strides toward democracy in the last twenty years, it remains the case that a few landowning, dynastic families along with powerful Chinese business interests continue to dominate the political process.

In other words, Western triumphalism about democracy in the developing world rests in part on a certain hypocrisy. If universal suffrage were a reality rather than a sham, one might wonder whether most of today's marketizers, foreign investors, and international organizations would be supporting it. Indeed, even today, there are many within the international community who, at the first sign of a possible trade-off between markets and democracy, make clear that their first commitment is to the former. As a beaming U.S. economist said to me just after Venezuela's democratically elected president Hugo Chavez was deposed in a military coup (and before he was reinstated), "Democracy is not necessarily the most efficient form of government."

It is better to be an open advocate of the priority of markets than to be a self-congratulatory advocate of sham democracy. The difficulty, however, with a genuine commitment to democracy is that, for all the reasons discussed in this book, majority rule in many countries outside the West could indeed produce anti-market, ethnically violent outcomes.

So what is to be done?

The answer is that democracy has to mean more than majority rule. Just as the United States should not promote unrestrained laissez-faire capitalism (a form of markets that the West itself has repudiated) throughout the non-Western world, so too the United States should not promote unrestrained, overnight majority rule (a form of democracy the West has repudiated). In the West the primary restraints on the excesses of majority rule take the form of constitutional safeguards: minority protections and guarantees against arbitrary government confiscations. But as with the Western-style welfare state, Western-style constitutional safeguards may not be realistic or adequate outside the West.

Constitutional protection of minorities and private property require, for example, an independent (and not ethnically biased) judiciary as well as mechanisms through which the judiciary's judgments can be reliably enforced. But these institutions are notoriously weak in non-Western countries. In Zimbabwe, President Robert Mugabe proceeded with his popular seizures of white land in open defiance of a judicial determination that they were unconstitutional. And in Venezuela, populist President Hugo Chavez, while at the height of his popularity, oversaw the overnight enactment of a radical new constitution to support his anti-market, anti-elite agenda.

In short, while constitutional safeguards and human rights protections should of course be encouraged in developing and transitional countries, they cannot be relied on as an answer to the problem of market-dominant minorities. On the contrary, outside the West constitutional checks on majority will are often swept away by the very ethnonationalist risings they are intended to forestall.

Instead of looking for means to check or halt an already aroused hateful majority, the emphasis has to be on prevention. This means first and foremost that the process of democratization must be rethought. Throughout the non-Western world, if democracy and markets are to be peaceably sustainable, democratization cannot be reduced to shipping out ballot boxes for national elections—a process almost calculated to maximize ethnic politics in deeply divided societies. Ballot boxes brought Hitler to power in Germany, Mugabe to power in Zimbabwe, Milosevic to power in Serbia—and could well bring the likes of Osama bin Laden to power in Saudi Arabia.

Americans often forget that there are many different models of democracy, even within the Western nations. Democracy can vary along a large number of axes: for example, U.S.-style presidentialism versus U.K.-style parliamentarism; first-past-the-post electoral systems versus proportional representation; bottom-up democratization (starting with local village elections) versus top-down democratization (starting with national, presidential elections). These different versions of democracy can have significantly different effects on ethnic politics.

Finally, it has to be remembered that the democratization process occurring in the non-Western countries is nothing like the democratization process that unfolded in the West. In particular, as discussed in chapter 9, the rapidity of democratization in developing and transitional countries today contrasts sharply with the gradual extension of the suffrage in Europe and the United States. Universal suffrage emerged in the West incrementally, over many generations. By comparison, in the nations of the non-Western world, universal suffrage is being implemented on a massive scale, almost overnight. Limitations on the suffrage are not an acceptable option today. But there are other ways to slow down and stabilize the process of democratization.

China, although it does not have a market-dominant minority, is an interesting case in point. Conventional wisdom in the West has it that since 1980, China has been rapidly marketizing without democratizing. Politics professor Minxin Pei, however, questions this conventional wisdom in a recent *Foreign Affairs* article called, "Is China Democratizing?" According to Pei, China has pursued significant political liberalization over the last two decades. But these changes have gone largely unnoticed in the United States, because "American politicians and news media measure the progress of political reform in other countries against a single yardstick—the holding of free and open elections" at the national level.[27]

China's political reforms, however, have had far-reaching effects. Throughout China there are now semi-open local village elections, which, despite their limitations, offer a nontrivial measure of political participation and, more critically, legitimate competitive elections as an important part of the political process. Nationally, while the Chinese Communist Party (CCP) retains its dictatorial position, significant measures have made even the national government somewhat more responsive to popular grievances and attitudes. For example, new mandatory retirement rules for government and CCP officials, while attracting little attention abroad, transformed a ruling elite dominated by aging, anti-market revolutionaries into one composed mostly of middle-aged, well-educated technocrats who have much more progressive economic and political outlooks.

At the same time, the National People's Congress (NPC) is no longer just a rubber stamp, but increasingly a potential challenger to the CCP's power. Recent polls indicate that citizens view the NPC, along with a more independent legal community and local people's congresses, as channels for popular grievances and political participation. In addition, writes Pei, the Chinese government has shifted "from mass to selective repression," targeting a relatively small number of highly visible dissidents while granting the great majority of citizens far more economic and personal freedoms than they have enjoyed in generations.[28]

But despite these and other political reforms, China today remains fundamentally autocratic at the national level. Indeed, advocates of the "markets first, democracy later" approach often cite China as a case in their favor. China, after all, stunningly quadrupled its per capita income in just eighteen years, by contrast to, say, democratic Russia, which in Robert Kaplan's words, "remains violent, unstable, and miserably poor despite its 99 percent literacy rate." "My point," writes Kaplan, "hard as it may be for Americans to accept, is that Russia may be failing in part because it is a democracy and China may be succeeding in part because it is not." Kaplan may be right. At the same time, I wonder whether the real lesson China holds for other non-Western countries is not that authoritarianism may best promote markets, but rather that democratization comes in many guises. It is still too early to tell.

The Middle East: The Long Road Toward Democracy?

As I suggested in chapter 10, if some version of free market democracy is the long-term goal in the Middle East, holding overnight elections is probably not the best way to achieve it. On the contrary, immediate majority elections in many of the Arab states would likely bring to power intensely anti-market, anti-Israel, anti-American, anti-globalization regimes. Moreover, counterintuitively, democratic elections in many Middle Eastern countries could well sweep in antidemocratic regimes. As Fareed Zakaria puts it, many "Islamic fundamentalist parties are sham democrats. They would happily come to power through an election but then set up their own dictatorship. It would be one man, one vote, one time."[29]

What are the alternatives? In the long term, prominent Egyptian intellectual Saad Eddin Ibrahim believes that, despite their extremism, "Islamic militants are tamable through accommodative politics of inclusion. Running for office, or once in it, they recognize the complexities of the real world and the need for gradualism and toleration."[30] Meanwhile, a number of thoughtful Middle Eastern scholars, such as Abdolkarim Soroush of Iran, have called for the gradual establishment of democracy within an Islamic framework. There are few, if any, examples of successful "theocratic democracies"—which, unlike American democracy, do not call for a sharp separation of church and state—but this avenue may offer some long-term hope for at least certain countries in the Middle East.[31]

In the meantime, the United States must, even if just for our own security interests, make much more concrete efforts to stop the breeding of fanaticism and terrorism among Middle Eastern populations. The goal should not be holding elections as soon as possible, but neither should it be uncritically propping up the current authoritarian regimes. Instead, as Zakaria says, the U.S. government should continually press the Arab states on an array of other issues:

[t]he Saudi monarchy must order a comprehensive overview of its funding (both private and public) of extremist Islam, which is now the kingdom's second largest export to the rest of the world. It must rein in its religious and educational leaders and

force them to stop flirting with fanaticism. In Egypt, we must ask President Mubarak to insist that the state-owned press drop its anti-American and anti-Semitic rants, end the glorification of suicide bombers and begin opening itself up to other voices in the country. In Qatar we might ask the emir, who launched Al-Jazeera, to make sure that responsible, moderate Muslims appear as regularly on his network as extremist bin Laden sympathizers. None of this will produce democracy, but it will slow down the spread of illiberal voices and viewpoints.[32]

Market-Dominant Minorities: Taking the Lead against Ethnonationalism

The previous sections on markets and democracy did not offer any quick fixes to the problem of market-dominant minorities and ethnonationalist backlash. There is a reason for this: Even assuming that free market democracy is the optimal end point for most non-Western countries, in the short run markets and democracy are themselves part of the problem. So long as markets continue to reinforce the stark economic dominance of a resented ethnic minority, as they have throughout the non-Western world, then the introduction of democratic politics, putting political power into the hands of the impoverished "indigenous" majority, will always be a source of tremendous potential instability. And we can only "adjust" and "restrain" market capitalism and democracy so much before we undermine them altogether.

Fortunately or unfortunately, then, the best hope for global free market democracy lies with market-dominant minorities themselves. This is adamantly not to blame market-dominant minorities for the ethnonationalist backlashes against them. But it is to suggest that market-dominant minorities may be in the best position to address the most pressing challenges threatening free market democracy today.

One of the ironies about market-dominant minorities is that they are so often perceived as "leeches" "draining away the nation's wealth" and "a menace to the economy" when in fact they are usually a crucial source of national economic vitality and growth. This irony makes the problem of market-dominant minorities a special case of ethnic conflict, presenting both distinctive obstacles and opportunities. The obstacles stem from the overlap of class and ethnic division: In addition to all the usual problems of ethnic hatred, market-dominant minorities face the specific problem of economic resentment, often associated with stereotypes of greed, selfishness, disloyalty, and exploitation. The opportunities stem from the reality that market-dominant minorities have the skills and resources to contribute to economic growth and development.

The challenge is to grapple with these obstacles and take advantage of the opportunities. In what follows, I begin by addressing a topic that is often treated as taboo: whether market-dominant minorities engage in objectionable practices that reinforce or exacerbate ethnic hatred. I then discuss possible affirmative measures that market-dominant minorities might take to forestall majority-based ethnonationalist backlashes against them. Ideally, and if only out of self-interest, market-dominant minorities would voluntarily take steps to foster the reality and the perception that they are vital, public-spirited contributors to the national interest rather than "arrogant" and "exploitative" "outsiders."

Objectionable Practices

It should be stressed at the outset that there are some market-dominant minorities who are victimized solely because of their ethnic difference and their disproportionate wealth. It should also be stressed that even where objectionable practices by these minorities can be identified, they in no way justify or excuse the kinds of violence and human rights abuses often inflicted on them. On the other hand, it is unfortunately often the case outside the West that some members of market-dominant minorities engage in practices—such as bribery, discriminatory lending practices, and violation of workplace regulations—that not only are illegal or otherwise objectionable in themselves, but also reinforce invidious ethnic stereotypes. Although there is no guarantee that eliminating these practices would improve ethnic relations, it seems important nonetheless, given the special dangers associated with market-dominant minorities, to identify such practices and take measures to curb them as much as possible.

Corrupt relations between members of the indigenous ruling elite and members of market-dominant minorities have a long history in the developing world and invariably fuel bitter resentment among the indigenous majority. In Indonesia, for example, the intense anti-Chinese violence that erupted in May 1998 was inseparable from the association of a few Chinese magnates with the Suharto regime's "crony capitalism." As is sadly often the case, vicious popular reaction unleashed itself not on the relatively few wealthy Chinese who were actually complicit—and who used their wealth to go into hiding abroad—but rather on ordinary, struggling, middle-class Chinese Indonesians, whose shops were burned and looted.

Similarly, in post-Communist Russia, the symbiotic relationship between President Yeltsin and a tiny handful of Jewish entrepreneurs galvanized the deep anti-Semitism latent in Russian society; honest, middle-class Russian Jews pay the highest price, often in the form of violence and desecration. In Kenya, the corrupt cronyism between President Moi and a few Indian tycoons has fueled massive resentment of Kenya's Indian community generally, who are the regular objects of ethnic brutality and looting.

But it is not only the wealthiest members of market-dominant minorities who engage in illicit practices; the problem is often more general. Throughout Southeast Asia many Chinese-controlled firms routinely violate tax laws, banking and lending laws, and laws concerning overtime regulations and worker safety. Even more disturbing in Southeast Asia is the common practice among Chinese businessmen, particularly in Indonesia, Thailand, and the Philippines, of importing tens if not hundreds of thousands of illegal workers from mainland China. As is true even in the United States, local workers fume when illegal immigrants take over jobs at lower wages.[33] Indeed, in Indonesia, where roughly 6 million working-age Indonesians (almost all *pribumi*) were unemployed in 1996, the violent protest that erupted when a Chinese conglomerate imported a thousand illegal workers from China seems understandable.[34]

Similarly, allegations that market-dominant Western investors expose local workers to hazardous and exploitative conditions are all too familiar. In 1995–96, writes Naomi Klein in *No Logo*, the Gap's freshly scrubbed facade was further exfoliated to reveal a lawless factory in El Salvador where the manager responded to a union drive by firing 150 people and vowing that "blood will flow" if organizing continued. In May 1996, U.S. labor activists discovered that chat-show host Kathie Lee Gifford's eponymous line of sportswear (sold exclusively at Wal-Mart) was being stitched by a ghastly combination of child laborers in Honduras and illegal sweatshop workers in New York.

In June 1996, *Life* magazine created more waves with photographs of Pakistani kids—looking shockingly young and paid as little as six cents an hour—hunched over soccer balls that bore the unmistakable Nike swoosh.[35]

To be sure, not all child labor is conducted under "indentured slave" conditions. Moreover, members of the "indigenous" business community also violate workplace and safety laws, and "indigenous" political elites often tolerate such violations in exchange for bribes or kickbacks. But the perception among an economically disadvantaged majority that a disproportionately wealthy "outsider" minority disregards the country's laws and exploits the indigenous population can only exacerbate ethnic resentment.

What to do about such illicit practices is less obvious. As economists put it, there is a "collective action" problem. In theory, if any single firm decides to comply with workplace and other regulations when its competitors do not, the likely effect is to put the compliant firm out of business. As a result, calling on individual businesses to take corrective measures is unlikely to have much effect. On the other hand, looking to the state is not promising either. The obvious problem is that the governmental actors who would have to implement reform are often the same ones corruptly benefiting from the violations.

One as-yet unexploited resource may be the surprisingly strong ethnic organizations, both commercial and social, that many market-dominant minorities already have in the developing world. Chinese "chambers of commerce" and "clan associations" can be found throughout Southeast Asia; Indian and Lebanese counterparts exist, respectively, in East and West Africa; similar associations exist among the Bamiléké,

Ibo, Kikuyu, and other "entrepreneurial" African groups. The success of these organizations in overcoming collective action problems in a variety of commercial contexts—through informal trust, peer pressure, and monitoring practices—has been widely observed. If leaders of the minority communities in a given developing country can be persuaded of the importance of, and overall gains to be had from, eliminating corrupt or illicit business practices, these organizations may have the right set of incentives and capabilities to play a significant role.

Apart from breaking the law, market-dominant minorities sometimes engage in behavior that indigenous majorities find objectionable for a variety of reasons, some of which are themselves objectionable. Market-dominant minorities are often criticized for acting "insularly," for indulging in "conspicuous consumption," or for "flaunting" their ethnic pride. As a Chinese-Indonesian economist presciently worried in 1997:

> I see the problem through the eyes of my *pribumi* friends: I see the shopping malls, the posh restaurants, the hotels and lavish weddings, full of young Chinese who don't seem to have any interest in national problems. These people don't know they're living on a time bomb. They don't mix with native Indonesians, so they don't know how much they're envied and resented.[36]

But what is to be done about ethnic minorities who "don't mix" with the indigenous majorities around them? This is a tricky and morally complex issue. It is hardly clear that forced assimilation and acculturation, even if it were possible, would be desirable. Nevertheless, as will be discussed in the next section, there are important constructive measures that market-dominant outsider groups might take to counter the perception (justified or not) of their insularity and indifference to the welfare of the nation.

A More Honorable Way:
Voluntary Generosity by Market-Dominant Minorities

After my aunt was murdered in 1994, my other family members in the Philippines hired personal bodyguards, erected barbed-wire fences, and bought some man-eating watchdogs. This is also how many whites in South Africa, Jewish oligarchs in Russia, and other market-dominant minorities live—in fear.

Similarly, after September 11, Americans across the country despaired that our lives might never be the same again. We spoke of our "loss of innocence" and worried that we might have to give up our free and open way of life in order to protect ourselves from those savagely and psychotically angry at us around the world. Most Americans ultimately rejected that vision of life. Otherwise, "the terrorists would win."

But what is to be done about the underlying hatred, not just against Americans at the global level, but against market-dominant minorities everywhere in the world?

One long-term strategy—in my mind more likely to be effective and certainly more dignified than erecting barbed-wire fences—is for market-dominant minorities to make significant, visible contributions to the local economies in which they are thriving. Although such efforts to date have been relatively few and by no means always successful in promoting goodwill, some valuable models can be found.

In East Africa, powerful families of Indian descent—among them the Madhvanis, Aga Khans, Mehtas, and Chandarias—have made immense contributions to their local communities, often concentrating heavily on indigenous African welfare and development. Indians, for example, were principally responsible for creating the University of Nairobi, East Africa's first nonracial institution of higher education. More recently, the Madhvanis, owners of the largest industrial, commercial, and agricultural complex in East Africa, not only provide educational, health, housing, and recreational facilities for their African employees, but also employ Africans in top management and offer a number of wealth-sharing schemes. Similarly, Kenya's powerful industrialist Manu Chandaria, who owns fourteen companies and employs five thousand workers in Kenya, has become a household name because of the millions he has poured into local education, health, and environmental conservation.[37]

In Russia, in a somewhat bizarre turn of events, Jewish billionaire

Roman Abramovich was recently elected governor of the godforsaken, poverty-stricken region of Chukotka, where temperatures commonly drop to minus thirty degrees Celsius. Abramovich bought his popularity by spending tens of millions of dollars of his own money airlifting food, parkas, boots, and medicine, buying computers and textbooks for the schools, and even flying three thousand children to sunny vacation destinations so they could swim in warm water.[38] A shrewd entrepreneur, Abramovich, who favors jeans and sneakers but models himself on American "robber barons" like Andrew Carnegie, wants to economically transform Chukotka and become "the first New Russian philanthropist." So far, he is succeeding. "I love him," said one local citizen, expressing a common sentiment. "Since he came in the new year, we have been receiving salaries on time. There have been no problems. All hope is on him."[39] While many wonder about his motives, the fact remains that Abramovich, over a period of just a few years (and while two of his fellow oligarchs were being exiled), turned himself into a revered figure, seen by the local people as genuinely committed to helping their community.

Meanwhile, a growing number of Western multinationals have begun to view corporate philanthropy as part of a long-term profit-maximization strategy in developing countries. It is Coca-Cola's official position, for example, that "In the nearly 200 countries where we do business, the Coca-Cola system gives back to the community." In Mexico City, American multinationals played a crucial role in funding the building of El Papalote, one of the world's outstanding children's museums. Roughly five thousand poor and lower-middle-class children from all parts of the country visit the museum each day and, rightly or wrongly, associate the prominently displayed names of Hewlett-Packard and Procter & Gamble with the beneficial dispersion of science and education. Since its Pakistan soccer ball scandal, Nike has enacted a code of conduct and spent millions of dollars in philanthropy, specifically aimed at improving long-term opportunities for children and women in developing countries.[40]

Ideally, voluntary contributions by market-dominant minorities would be highly visible and directed at large numbers of ordinary members of the disadvantaged majority. To be sure, any material redistribution effected by these contributions would itself be desirable, but as a practical matter the more important consideration may well lie in their symbolic implications. A principal focus of nationalist and ethnonationalist anti-market reactions in the non-Western world has been the humiliating domination by "outsiders" of a nation's economic symbols: oil wells in Latin America, gold mines in South Africa, forests in Burma and Indonesia, Lomonosov porcelain in Russia, or other sectors that have come symbolically to be associated with national identity. Perhaps market-dominant minorities can turn symbolism around in their favor.

A good question for market-dominant business communities to ask is whether there are, in a given developing country, important national sectors or symbols to which they could make visible, valuable contributions. Thus, such communities might learn from the recent example of a number of wealthy businesspeople in the United States, who, in several highly publicized gestures, have donated tens of millions of dollars toward scholarship funds for inner-city children. Along similar lines it might be an important demonstration of national solidarity for market-dominant "outsider" groups, which are often urban-centered, to fund rural development projects. In societies where child mortality is a constant source of sorrow, the contribution of new hospital facilities, water treatment plants, or even just antibiotics would certainly be appreciated. Major conspicuous contributions to infrastructure providing tangible benefits to ordinary citizens are another possibility.

Given the extraordinary needs and deficits of developing societies, the opportunities for building interethnic goodwill are plentiful, and there is considerable room for creativity. For example, many have observed the tremendous unifying power of sports all over the world, across both class and ethnic lines. In the United States, nothing has improved race relations more over the last two decades than the idolization of such figures as Michael Jordan, Sammy Sosa, and Tiger Woods. In France the national soccer team is now invariably "a rainbow of colors from France's imperial history." Thus, out of the twenty-two glorified members of the team that won the world trophy in 1998, eight were black or brown-skinned, including a Ghanaian adopted by a French priest.[41] In Indonesia, where anti-Chinese sentiment is about as fierce and entrenched as it can get, ordinary *pribumi* citizens openly adore Susi

Susanti and Alan Kusuma, ethnic Chinese badminton stars (now husband and wife) who won gold medals for Indonesia at the Barcelona Olympics—the first golds ever taken by Indonesian athletes.[42]

Odd or trivial as it may seem, contributions by "outsider" groups to a national sport or team—perhaps by funding the acquisition of a star soccer player or by donating athletic facilities—may be a way of deploying the power of national symbols constructively. (Indeed, the feeling of passionate, almost irrational identification with a favorite sports team bears a certain resemblance to nationalism and ethnonationalism.) I am certainly not suggesting here that a few strategic charitable contributions will cure ethnic conflict. Anti-Indian sentiment remains intense in East Africa despite the philanthropic efforts described above, and in a shocking and disappointing recent incident, Susi Susanti's car was vandalized in Indonesia as part of an ethnic hate crime.[43] There are no easy fixes for group hatred.

But there have been moments from which hope can be drawn. In a now-famous gesture in 1995, with all of newly democratic South Africa watching, Nelson Mandela embraced the country's largely white rugby team by donning its green and gold jersey and attending its world championship game. Mandela's gesture, coupled with the ensuing victory, produced a moment of rare ethnic reconciliation that has helped sustain South Africa's fragile democracy to this day.[44]

And what about the United States? What should the world's market-dominant minority do about the growing anti-Americanism around the globe? Pulitzer Prize–winning author Jared Diamond recently offered one answer, much along the lines of what I have proposed for other market-dominant minorities. In an essay entitled, "Why We Must Feed the Hands That Could Bite Us," Diamond urges Americans to combat the forces of poverty and hopelessness on which international terrorism feeds through three basic strategies: providing health care, supporting family planning, and addressing chronic environmental problems such as deforestation that infuriate local populations. Diamond recognizes that these measures will not eliminate the immediate threat of terrorism. But as he points out, the "few active terrorists [who carried out the September 11 attacks] depended on many more people, including desperate populations who have tolerated, harbored and even taken part in terrorist activities. When people can't solve their own problems, they strike out irrationally, seeking foreign scapegoats, or collapsing in civil war over limited resources. By bettering conditions overseas, we can reduce chronic future threats to ourselves."[45]

Other influential figures have taken a similar position. Not long after September 11, 2001, World Bank president James D. Wolfensohn joined the United Nations secretary general, Kofi Annan, and British chancellor of the exchequer Gordon Brown, in calling for a $50 billion increase in foreign aid to poor countries, calling it "an insurance policy against future terrorism." Similarly, former U.S. treasury secretary Robert Rubin has called for an international campaign to raise public support for increased aid budgets, particularly in the United States.[46]

Not surprisingly, the "more foreign aid" view has its acerbic critics, both from the left and the right. Gregory Clark, for example, a commentator for the *Japan Times,* mocks the liberal notion that addressing poverty will solve the problem of terrorism. "If people in the Third World want to use force against their governments or the West, that is because of perceived injustice. Large outpourings of aid will just add to the long history of aid waste and corruption." In Clark's view, terrorist attacks will continue as long as the United States continues its overseas "meddling" and its hypocritical support of oppressive regimes.[47]

Similarly, but for vastly different reasons, Daniel Pipes argues that U.S. foreign aid is not the right response to the September 11 attacks. In an essay called "God and Mammon: Does Poverty Cause Militant Islam?," Pipes answers his own question with a vociferous no. "Indeed," writes Pipes, "if one turns away from the commentators on militant Islam and instead listens to the Islamists themselves, it quickly becomes apparent that they rarely talk about prosperity. As Ayatollah Khomeini memorably put it, 'We did not create a revolution to lower the price of melon.' " In Pipes' view, militant Islam is ultimately about a struggle for power. Thus, "economic assets for Islamists represent not the good life but added strength to do battle against the West."[48]

Clark, Pipes, and many others are obviously right that anti-Americanism, including the particularly virulent Islamicist strain, stems from much more than just economic deprivation. Moreover, it is fantasy to think that U.S. monetary assistance might be able to do anything more than make a small dent in eliminating world poverty, at least in the near future. In my opinion, however, the wisdom of recent calls for American beneficence lies in their potentially far-reaching symbolism. Rightly or wrongly, for millions around the world, the World Trade Center symbolized greed, exploitation, indifference, and cultural humiliation. (John Cassidy recently observed that, relative to the size of our economy, the United States has the smallest aid budget of any advanced country: around 0.1 percent of GDP.)[49] Like other market-dominant minorities around the world, perhaps America should try to turn symbolism around in our favor. There is no long-term promise in retreating into belligerent isolationism, or glorifying American parochialism—a recent number-one country song celebrates not knowing "the difference between Iraq and Iran." It is difficult to see, in any event, how a little generosity and humility could possibly hurt.

Afterword

In March 2003, three months after the U.S. publication of *World on Fire*, the United States went to war with Iraq, commencing our preemptive strike with the awesome bombing of Baghdad. We went to war without United Nations authorization and without the support of traditional NATO allies such as France, Germany, and Canada. Of the major European powers, Great Britain alone, led by Tony Blair, fought beside us.

The U.S. government's principal justification for war was national security—specifically, Saddam Hussein's sponsorship of terrorism and the "grave danger to global peace and security" posed by Iraq's "massive stockpile" of biological and chemical weapons and its efforts to produce nuclear weapons. At the same time, an equally powerful sub-theme— formally laid out in "The National Security Strategy of the United States of America" issued by the White House in September 2002—was the U.S. government's commitment, including through military means, to replacing brutal, repressive dictators like Saddam Hussein with free market and democratic institutions. According to the Strategy, "We will actively work to bring the hope of democracy, development, free markets, and free trade to every corner of the world." And in his March 31, 2003 Letter to the Speaker of the House of Representatives, President George W. Bush explained that "disarming and liberating Iraq" was merely "a first step" toward "the development of a free-market democracy in Iraq."

The U.S.–British victory in Iraq was swift and decisive. Despite

Saddam Hussein's bizzare claims that "The enemy . . . is in trouble now" and "Victory will soon be ours," his reviled Ba'athist regime fell in just over forty days, prompting dancing and cheering—not to mention looting—throughout Iraqi streets. Since that initial jubilation, however, one thing has become painfully clear: The United States dramatically underestimated the difficulty of turning Iraq into a liberal, Western-style free market democracy.

Before the war, optimists (including Secretary of Defense Donald Rumsfeld) pointed to American successes in reconstructing post-Second-World-War Germany and Japan, both of which transitioned smoothly to free market democracy. But neither post-war Germany nor Japan is an apt comparison for Iraq, for one simple reason: Neither country was riven by ethnic, religious or tribal schisms remotely comparable to those in Iraq. On the contrary, by 1945 Germany had exterminated most of its non-Aryans and Japan had for centuries been strikingly ethnically and religiously homogeneous. Unfortunately, a far better parallel for post-Saddam Iraq is post-Tito Yugoslavia.

Like the former Yugoslavia, Iraq's ethnic and religious dynamics are extremely complicated. They involve cross-cutting conflicts across Kurds, Shias, Christians, and Sunnis; many horrendous massacres; wholesale confiscations; and deep feelings of hatred and need for revenge. In particular, Iraq's Shias represent a 60 percent long-oppressed majority in Iraq. It is impossible to know what kind of candidate—fundamentalist or moderate, conciliatory or vengeful—they would vote for in free elections. It is clear that the collapse of Saddam Hussein's brutal (but secular) Ba'athist police state, while long overdue, has also fueled religious demagoguery among vying Islamic clerics and unleashed powerful fundamentalist movements throughout the country. Needless to say, these extremist movements are intensely anti-American, anti-foreign-investment, and illiberal. They have especially grievous implications for girls and women.

Perhaps because of beliefs in the "melting pot" and the U.S.'s own relatively successful—though halting and incomplete—history of ethnic assimilation, Americans don't always understand the significance of ethnicity, both in the U.S. and especially in other countries. Interestingly, British imperial governments were fastidiously conscious of ethnic divisions. Of course, their ethnic policies are a dangerous model. When it was the British Empire's turn to deal with nation-building and ethnicity, the British engaged in divide-and-conquer policies, not only protecting but favoring ethnic minorites, and simultaneously aggravating ethnic resentments. As a result, when the British decamped, the time-bombs often exploded, from Africa to India to Southeast Asia. By contrast, at least before the war, the U.S. government's ethnic policy for Iraq was essentially to have no ethnic policy. Instead, U.S. officials seemed strangely confident that Iraq's ethnic, religious, and tribal divisions would dissipate in the face of democracy and market-generated wealth. In President George W. Bush's words, "freedom and democracy will always and everywhere have greater appeal than the slogans of hatred."

But in countries as deeply divided as Iraq, everything—even freedom and wealth—has ethnic and sectarian ramifications. Who will comprise the police? Who has experience in engineering and oil or the skills to run a stock exchange? Given Saddam Hussein's sadistically unfair and repressive regime, some groups—namely, the Sunni minority, particularly the Ba'athists—will almost certainly have a head start in terms of education, capital, and economic and managerial experience. Consequently, as is true in so many other non-Western countries, laissez-faire markets and overnight democracy in Iraq could well favor different ethnic or religious groups in the short run, creating enormous instability.

At the same time, because the United States is the world's most powerful and most resented market-dominant minority, every move we make with respect to Iraq is being closely—and perhaps even unfairly—scrutinized. Despite Saddam Hussein's barbarous gulags, gross human rights violations, and repeated refusals to comply with U.N. requirements, international public opinion was overwhelmingly against the United States going to war with Iraq, even in countries such as Canada and the United Kingdom, not to mention China, Russia, France, and the Arab states. It is important to see that this opposition to U.S. policies was closely bound up with deep feelings of resentment and fear of *American* power and cynicism about *American* motives.

Unfortunately, the latest developments in Iraq seem only to be fueling these suspicions. U.S. troops have not yet found weapons of mass destruction. Moreover, it has become clear that at best the U.S.

government was operating on an oversimplistic view of what a post-Saddam Iraq would look like.

Instead of a gratitude-filled Iraqi people cooperating with the United States in a rapid transition to multi-ethnic free market democracy (which ideally would produce a domino effect across the Middle East), Iraq today teeters on the brink of lawlessness. In June 2003 in Najaf, L. Paul Bremer III, the head of the American military occupation in Iraq, unilaterally cancelled local elections, even though the Iraqis were eager and ready to vote. Mr. Bremer based his decision on the ground that conditions in Najaf were not yet appropriate for elections. A senior official in his office elaborated: "The most organized political groups in many areas are rejectionists, extremists and remnants of the Ba'athists . . . They have an advantage over the other groups." Not surprisingly, the barring of elections in Najaf—and the U.S.'s decision more generally to postpone Iraqi self-government—has produced tremendous anger throughout Iraq. Attacks on coalition forces continue, and demonstrating crowds yelling "No Americans, No Saddam" and "Yes to Freedom and Islam" are increasingly common.

Deep ethnic and religious devisions remain in Iraq, but ironically one theme unifying the Iraqi people at the moment is their intensifying opposition to American and British occupation. Meanwhile, in the words of one observer, the vast majority of Arabs in the Middle East are "perched at the edge of their seat waiting for the U.S. to fail. . . . Many Arabs feel that any work in Iraq now—be it humanitarian relief work, governance, or helping the economy—is feeding into the occupation of one of the strongest Arab nations."

Many Americans today are bewildered—outraged—at the depth and pervasiveness of anti-Americanism in the world. "Why do so many people want to come here if we're so terrible?" frustrated Americans demand. "What would France be doing if *it* were the world's super-power?" "Why do they hate *us*?" These are reasonable points. But the fact of the matter is that because the United States is the world's sole superpower, we are going to be held to a higher standard than everyone else—market-dominant minorities always are. (The Chinese in Southeast Asia and the Indians in East Africa have been those regions' principal economic engines, generating enormous growth over the generations. Yet if you ask ordinary Indonesians or Kenyans on the street, they will insist that these minorities are "leeches" "sucking out the wealth of the nation" and the reason for their country's poverty.) For this reason, it is in the United States' own interest to avoid taking actions that suggest hypocrisy, look glaringly exploitative, or display lack of concern for the rest of the world, including of course the people of Iraq.

It is easy to criticize the United States, just as it is easy to hide behind facile calls for "free market democracy." With the international community watching, I prefer to view this moment as a critical opportunity for the United States to surprise a skeptical world. One thing, however, is clear: The United States cannot simply call for elections and universal suffrage and at the same time support an economic system that is seen as benefiting only a tiny, privileged minority—whether an ethnic or religious minority or U.S. and British companies. To do so would be a recipe for disaster. Already, according to the director of one NGO in Iraq, "Anti-Americanism is growing here. There is a strong perception that U.S. companies plan to rape the country of its resources. This is particularly dangerous as there is currently no sense of control or ownership on the part of the Iraqi people." Once basic services and order are restored, the single most important thing for the United States to do is to change this perception: To give the Iraqi people a sense of control and ownership over their own resources and destinies. Perhaps most important of all, it is vital that the United States remain true to our word and take visible, symbolic measures to ensure that the new Iraqi government—unlike Saddam Hussein's regime—includes the Iraqi people in the benefits of Iraq's oil wealth.

———

A final clarification. This book is not about blame, but about unintended consequences. My own view, for example, is that the results of democratization in Indonesia have been disastrous. But if forced to place the blame somewhere, I would point to thirty years of plundering autocracy and crony capitalism by Suharto. Similarly, in Iraq, overnight elections might well bring undesirable results. But that is not *democracy's* fault. On the contrary, if anything, the blame rests with the cruelly repressive regime of Saddam Hussein. Nevertheless, this doesn't take away from the reality that given the conditions that actually exist now in many post-colonial countries—conditions created by history, colonialism, divide-and-conquer policies, corruption, autocracy—the combination of laissez-faire capitalism and unrestrained majority rule may well have catastrophic consequences.

July 1, 2003
New Haven, CT

Notes

Introduction

1. My discussion of the kidnapping industry in the Philippines is based principally on a series of interviews I conducted in Manila during May 2001. Because law enforcement officials in the Philippines are generally thought to have close ties to kidnapping gangs, many families of kidnapped Chinese victims simply pay the demanded ransom rather than report the crime to authorities. As a result, there is little rigorous documentation of the phenomenon. For journalistic accounts, see Caroline S. Hau, "Too Much, Too Little," *Philippine Daily Inquirer,* June 15, 2001, p. 9; Abigail L. Ho, "Chinese traders won't flee, won't invest either," *Philippine Daily Inquirer,* August 6, 2001, p. 1; and Reginald Chua, "Country Held Hostage," *Straits Times,* February 28, 1993, p. 7.

2. Estimates of Chinese economic control in the Philippines vary somewhat, but usually hover between 50% and 65%. For an up-to-date, if slightly gossipy, report on the wealth and holdings of Chinese Filipino tycoons, see Wilson Lee Flores, "The Top Billionaires in the Philippines," *Philippine Star,* May 16, 2001. See also "A Survey of Asian Business," *The Economist,* April 7, 2001; Cecil Morella, "Ethnic Chinese Stay Ready, Hope to Ride out Crime Wave," *Agence France-Presse,* April 30, 1996; and Rigoberto Tiglao, "Gung-ho in Manila," *Far Eastern Economic Review,* February 15, 1990, pp. 68–72.

3. The statistics I cite relating to poverty, health, and sanitation in the Philippines are from: "Annual Poverty Indicators Survey," released September 15, 2000, by the Income and Employment Statistics Division, National Statistics Office, Republic of Philippines; The World Bank, *World Development Report 2000/2001* (New York: Oxford University Press, 2001); The World Bank, *Entering the Twenty-First Century: World Development Report 1999/2000* (New York: Oxford University Press, 2000); United Nations

Children's Fund, *UNICEF Statistical Data: The Philippines* (from UNICEF website, updated December 26, 2000); and Mamerto Canlas, Mariano Miranda, Jr., and James Putzel, *Land, Poverty and Politics in the Philippines* (London: Catholic Institute for International Relations, 1988), pp. 52–53.

4. Roy Gutman, "Death Camp Horrors," *Newsday*, October 18, 1992, p. 3, and Laura Pitter, "Beaten and scarred for life in the Serbian 'rape camps,' " *South China Morning Post*, December 27, 1992, p. 8.

5. Bill Berkeley, *The Graves Are Not Yet Full* (New York: Basic Books, 2001), p. 2.

6. See Margot Cohen, "Turning Point: Indonesia's Chinese Face a Hard Choice," *Far Eastern Economic Review*, July 30, 1998, p. 12.

7. Lee Hockstader, "Massive Attack Targets Another Palestinian City," *Washington Post*, April 4, 2002, p. A1.

8. Indira A. R. Lakshmanan, "Pakistan Backs Us, Despite Warning by Afghanistan," *Boston Globe*, September 16, 2001, p. A5.

9. I borrow this phrase from Orhan Pamuk, "The Anger of the Damned," *The New York Review of Books*, November 15, 2001.

10. This story is reported in Jacques deLisle, "Lex Americana?: United States Legal Assistance, American Legal Models, and Legal Change in the Post-Communist World and Beyond," *University of Pennsylvania Journal of International Economic Law* 20 (1999):179–308 (citing William Kovacic).

11. This description is taken from Matt Biven's hilarious and eye-opening article, "Aboard the Gravy Train: In Kazakhstan, The Farce That Is U.S. Aid," *Harper's*, August 1, 1997, p. 69. The balloon episode was never actually produced, on the grounds that it would be too expensive.

12. Thomas L. Friedman, *The Lexus and the Olive Tree* (New York: Anchor Books, 2000), pp. ix, xvi, 12.

13. John Lewis Gaddis, "Democracy and Foreign Policy" (transcript of Devane Lecture, delivered at Yale University on April 17, 2001, available at http://www.yale.edu/yale300/democracy, p. 8.

14. Thomas L. Friedman, "Today's News Quiz," *New York Times*, November 20, 2001, p. A19.

15. See Mihai Constantin and Sabina Fati, "Vadim Tudor: Demagogue in Waiting?" CNN.com, December 9, 2000, and Andrei Filipache and Alexandru Nastase, "PRM's Tudor Attends Antonescu Ceremony, Threatens to 'Hang' Hungarians," World News Connection (NTIS, U.S. Dept. of Commerce), June 2, 2001.

16. Ann M. Simmons, "On Zimbabwe Farms, Push Now Comes to Shove," *Los Angeles Times*, July 1, 2000, p. A1 (quoting Agrippa Gava, executive director of the Zimbabwean National Liberation War Veterans Association).

17. "Leader Urges Zimbabwe Blacks to Menace the White Residents," *New York Times,* December 15, 2000, p. A8.

18. Adam Roberts makes these points in "The Great Manipulator," *Times Literary Supplement,* March 8, 2002, p. 78. See also Donna Harman, "Land Reform: An African Issue," *Christian Science Monitor,* March 13, 2002.

19. Thomas Frank, *One Market under God: Extreme Capitalism, Market Populism, and the End of Economic Democracy* (New York: Doubleday, 2000), p. xv.

20. See The World Bank, *Globalization, Growth and Poverty: Building an Inclusive World Economy* (New York: The World Bank and Oxford University Press, 2002), chapter 1.

21. See "Interviewing Chomsky; Preparatory to Porto Alegre," http://www.zmag.org/chomskypa.htm. Lori Wallach's quotes are from "Brazil: World Social Forum for Global Equity, Says Activist," *Agence France-Presse,* February 2, 2002, and "Lori Wallach and Others on the WTO's Dubious 'Doha Round,'" lists.essential.org/pipermail/tw-list/2001-November/000101.html.

22. For various conceptions of "democracy," see Joseph A. Schumpeter, *Capitalism, Socialism, and Democracy* (3d ed.) (New York: Harper & Brothers Publishers, 1950), p. 269; Robert A. Dahl, *Democracy and Its Critics* (New Haven: Yale University Press, 1989), pp. 121–22, 220–22; Jon Elster and Rune Slagstad, eds., *Constitutionalism and Democracy* (Cambridge: Cambridge University Press, 1988), p. 1; and Philippe C. Schmitter and Terry Lynn Karl, "What Democracy Is . . . and Is Not," in Geoffrey Pridham, ed., *Transitions to Democracy: Comparative Perspectives From Southern Europe, Latin America and Eastern Europe* (Aldershot, England: Dartmouth Publishing, 1995), pp. 3–16.

23. Donald L. Horowitz, *Ethnic Groups in Conflict* (Berkeley, Los Angeles, and London: University of California Press, 1985), pp. 51–92. "The ethnic tie is simultaneously suffused with overtones of familial duty and laden with depths of familial emotion," writes Horowitz. For various perspectives on the larger question of "what is ethnicity?," see Harold R. Isaacs, *Idols of the Tribe* (Cambridge, MA and London: Harvard University Press, 1989), pp. 38–45; Anthony Smith, *The Ethnic Origins of Nations* (Oxford: Blackwell Publishers, 1986), pp. 11–13, 32; John Breuilly, *Nationalism and the State* (2d ed.) (Manchester, UK: Manchester University Press, 1993), pp. 19–24; and John Hutchinson and Anthony Smith, eds., *Ethnicity* (Oxford and New York: Oxford University Press, 1996).

24. See Philip Gourevitch's magnificent book, *We wish to inform you that tomorrow we will be killed with our families* (New York: Picador USA, 1998), especially chapter 4.

1. As reported in Thomas Frank, *One Market under God: Extreme Capitalism, Market Populism, and the End of Economic Democracy* (New York: Doubleday, 2000), p. 12.
2. Mitchell Landsberg, "Race, Resentment Fuel Attacks on Indians in Fiji," *Los Angeles Times,* June 22, 2000, p. A3.
3. Frank, *One Market under God,* p. 12.
4. See Anna Gelpern and Malcolm Harrison, "Ideology, Practice, and Performance in Privatization," *Harvard International Law Journal* 33 (1992): 240–54; Sander Thoenes, "Trust of People Key to Reform," *Financial Times,* July 11, 1996, p. 3; and Jack Epstein, "Brazil's Economy Lagging Behind," *San Francisco Chronicle,* February 28, 1994, p. A8.

Chapter 1

1. Donald L. Horowitz, *The Deadly Ethnic Riot* (Berkeley, Los Angeles, and London: University of California Press, 2001), pp. 96, 185, 211–12. The contemporary observer was the Britishman Maurice Collins. His account can be found in Maurice Collins, *Trials in Burma* (London: Faber and Faber Limited, 1945), pp. 140–45.
2. My discussion of Burma relies heavily on David I. Steinberg, *Burma: The State of Myanmar* (Washington, DC: Georgetown University Press, 2001), and Mya Maung, *The Burma Road to Capitalism: Economic Growth Versus Democracy* (Westport, CT: Praeger, 1998), especially pp. 156–207. An authoritative discussion of Chinese (along with Indian and British) economic dominance in colonial Burma can be found in Frank H. Golay, Ralph Anspach, M. Ruth Pfanner & Eliezer B. Ayal, *Underdevelopment and Economic Nationalism in Southeast Asia* (Ithaca and London: Cornell University Press, 1969), chapter 4.
3. In describing the recent Chinese economic takeover of Mandalay and Rangoon, I draw freely on the eyewitness accounts of Anthony Davis, "Burma Casts Wary Eye on China," *Jane's Intelligence Review,* June 1, 1999; Anthony Davis, "China's Shadow," *Asiaweek,* May 28, 1999, p. 30; Abby Tan, "Mandalay Preparing to Shake Off Frontier Image," *Asia Today,* July 1996; Steve Raymer, "British Era Fades, China Gains in Myanmar," *Los Angeles Times,* April 3, 1994, p. A20; Philip Shenon, "Burmese Cry Intrusion," *New York Times,* March 29, 1994, p. A4; Nirmal Ghosh, "Making Money in Mandalay," *Business Times (Singapore),* July 20, 1993; and "Road to Lashio is Paved with Good Fortune for Chinese Businessmen," *Guardian (London),* July 16, 1994, p. 16.

4. "Myanmar and China: But Will the Flag Follow Trade?" *The Economist,* October 8, 1994, p. 35.

5. Christopher S. Wren, "Road to Riches Starts in the Golden Triangle," *New York Times,* May 11, 1998, p. A8.

6. Ibid., p. A8. See also Tony Emerson, "Burma's Men of Gold," *Newsweek,* April 20, 1998, p. 24. The early exploits of Lo Hsing-han, Olive Yang, and other opium warlords are described in Bertil Lintner, *Burma in Revolt: Opium and Insurgency Since 1948* (Boulder, CO: Westview Press, 1994), and Martin Smith, *Burma: Insurgency and the Politics of Ethnicity* (London and New Jersey: Zed Books Ltd., 1991).

7. On Burma's legal and illegal teak activities, see John Pomfret, "China's Lumbering Economy Ravages Border Forests, *Washington Post,* March 26, 2001, p. A19. See also James Fahn, "Little the world can do to help Burma's forests," *Nation,* December 17, 1998; Raymer, "British Era Fades," p. A20; and Rainforest Relief's website, "Campaign to End Purchase of Teak from Burma," November 4, 1998, http://forests.org/archive/asia/teakwee2.htm. On "May Flower" Kyaw Win, see the special report on "Burmese Tycoons" published in the *Irrawaddy* newsmagazine in July 2000, available at http://www.irrawaddy.org/database/2000/vol8.7/report.htm.

8. Raymer, "British Era Fades," p. A20.

9. See Maung, *The Burma Road to Capitalism,* pp. 168–71, 204.

10. Ibid., pp. 170, 204, and Emerson, "Burma's Men of Gold," p. 24.

11. See Steinberg, *Burma: The State of Myanmar,* pp. xx, 139–40, 206, and U.S. Embassy, Rangoon, *Country Commercial Guide: Burma (Myanmar)* (U.S. & Foreign Commercial Service and the U.S. Department of State, 2000), chapter 2.

12. See U.S. Embassy, Rangoon, *Country Commercial Guide: Burma (Myanmar),* chapter 2. See also Steinberg, *Burma: The State of Myanmar,* pp. 136, 206–10.

13. See Maung, *The Burma Road to Capitalism,* pp. 156–57, and Shenon, "Burmese Cry Intrusion," p. A4.

14. The descriptions in this paragraph are from Davis, "China's Shadow," p. 30; Raymer, "British Era Fades," p. A20; and "Myanmar and China: But Will the Flag Follow Trade?" p. 35. On anti-Chinese hatred stemming specifically from Chinese connections with SLORC, see Steinberg, *Burma: The State of Myanmar,* pp. 165, 227–28, and Blaine Harden, "Grim Regime: A Special Report: For Burmese, Repression, AIDS and Denial," *New York Times,* November 14, 2000, p. A1.

15. Maung, *The Burma Road to Capitalism,* p. 166.

16. Shenon, "Burmese Cry Intrusion," p. A4.

17. One of the best comprehensive histories of the Chinese in Southeast Asia remains Victor Purcell, *The Chinese in Southeast Asia* (2d ed.) (London: Oxford University Press for the Royal Institute of International Affairs, 1965). Grand Eunuch Cheng Ho's seven voyages to Southeast Asia are described on pp. 16–18.

18. See Clifford Geertz, *Peddlers and Princes: Social Development and Economic Change in Two Indonesian Towns* (Chicago and London: University of Chicago Press, 1963), pp. 24–27.

19. Lynn Pan, *Sons of the Yellow Emperor* (Boston, Toronto, and London: Little, Brown and Company, 1990), pp. 31–33.

20. Ibid., pp. 32–33 (citation omitted).

21. This discussion of Chinese economic dominance in Vietnam is reproduced in large part from pp. 92–105 of my own article, Amy L. Chua, "Markets, Democracy, and Ethnicity: Toward a New Paradigm for Law and Development," *Yale Law Journal* 108 (1998): 1–105, which in turn draws heavily on Golay et al., *Underdevelopment and Economic Nationalism in Southeast Asia,* chapter 7; Stanley Karnow, *Vietnam: A History* (New York: Penguin Books, 1984); and Tran Khanh, *The Ethnic Chinese and Economic Development in Vietnam* (Singapore: Institute of Southeast Asian Studies, 1993).

22. Khanh, *The Ethnic Chinese and Economic Development in Vietnam,* pp. 18–19, and Purcell, *The Chinese in Southeast Asia,* pp. 183–84.

23. The statistics regarding Chinese dominance in Vietnam during the colonial era are from Golay et al., *Underdevelopment and Economic Nationalism in Southeast Asia,* pp. 395–96, and Khanh, *The Ethnic Chinese and Economic Development in Vietnam,* pp. 20–21, 41, 47, 57. The anti-Chinese epithets are from Purcell, *The Chinese in Southeast Asia,* p. 190. The intensification of Chinese dominance during the Vietnam War is discussed in Khanh, *The Ethnic Chinese and Economic Development in Vietnam,* p. 80. On the branding of the Chinese as bourgeois capitalists, see Henry Kamm, "Vietnam Describes Economic Setbacks," *New York Times,* November 19, 1980, p. A9, and James N. Wallace, "A Ray of Hope," *U.S. News & World Report,* August 6, 1979, p. 50.

24. See "Chinese Vietnamese Work Hard for Big Success," *Saigon Times Daily,* February 1, 2001; Leo Dana, "Mastering Management: Culture is of the Essence in Asia," *Financial Times,* November 27, 2000; Steve Kirby, "Saigon's Chinatown Bounces Back from Dark Years after 1975," *Agence France-Presse,* April 28, 2000; and Gail Eisenstodt, "Caged Tiger," *Forbes,* March 25, 1996, p. 64.

25. My discussion of the Chinese in Thailand (and Southeast Asia more generally) draws on Gary G. Hamilton and Tony Waters, "Ethnicity and Capitalist Development: The Changing Role of the Chinese in Thailand," and Linda Y. C. Lim and L. A. Peter Gosling, "Strengths and Weaknesses of Minority Status for Southeast Asian Chinese at a Time of Economic Growth and Liberalization," both of which appear in Daniel Chirot and Anthony Reid, eds., *Essential Outsiders: Chinese and Jews in the Modern Transformation of Southeast Asia and Central Europe* (Seattle and London: University of Washington Press, 1997), the former at pp. 258–84, the latter at pp. 285–317. The study of Thailand's largest business groups was conducted by Suehiro Akira. See his book *Capital Accumulation in Thailand, 1855–1985* (Japan: Centre for East Asian Cultural Studies, 1989).

26. See Sumit Ganguly, "Ethnic Politics and Political Quiescence in Malaysia and Singapore," pp. 233–72, in Michael Brown and Sumit Ganguly, eds., *Government Policies and Ethnic Relations in Asia and the Pacific* (Cambridge: MIT Press, 1997); Lim and Gosling, "Strengths and Weaknesses of Minority Status for Southeast Asian Chinese at a Time of Economic Growth and Liberalization," pp. 285–317; and "Empires without Umpires," in Asian Business Survey, *The Economist*, April 7, 2001, pp. 4–5.

27. On Robert Kuok's economic empire, see "Empires without Umpires," pp. 4–5, and http://www.forbes.com/2002/02/28/billionaires.html.

28. On the concentration of land in the Philippines—the most inequitable in Asia—see Mark Mitchell, "This Land is Your Land," *Far Eastern Economic Review*, March 29, 2001, p. 27. On the increase in the economic prominence of the Filipino Chinese during the 1980s and 1990s, see Lim and Gosling, "Strengths and Weaknesses of Minority Status for Southeast Asian Chinese at a Time of Economic Growth and Liberalization," pp. 285–317; Rigoberto Tiglao, "Gung-ho in Manila," *Far Eastern Economic Review*, February 15, 1990, pp. 68–72; and Wilson Lee Flores, "The Top Billionaires in the Philippines," *Philippine Star*, May 16, 2001, pp. BL1–3.

29. On the growing economic role of the Chinese in Cambodia and Laos, see Dan Eaton, "China, Vietnam, play out old rivalry in Cambodian visits," *Agence France-Presse*, November 12, 2000, and Dana, "Mastering Management," p. 12.

30. The World Bank, *Globalization, Growth and Poverty: Building an Inclusive World Economy* (New York: The World Bank and Oxford University Press, 2002), chapter 1.

31. Clifford Geertz's description of Mojokerto's bean curd industry can be found on pp. 66–70 of *Peddlers and Princes*.

32. On Indonesia's struggling tofu industry today, see Dan Murphy, "The IMF

and the Economics of Jakarta Tofu," *Christian Science Monitor,* May 10, 2001, p. 8; "Indonesia's Soybean Imports Still High," *Jakarta Post,* July 23, 2001, p. 10; and "Tempeh Makers Left Without a Bean," *Jakarta Post,* August 21, 1998.

33. The story of the phenomenal rise of the CP Group is based primarily on the group's website as well as on Hamilton and Waters, "Ethnicity and Capitalist Development: The Changing Role of the Chinese in Thailand," pp. 275–77, and Carl Goldstein, "Full Speed Ahead," *Far Eastern Economic Review,* October 21, 1993, pp. 66–68.

34. Max Weber, *The Protestant Ethic and the Spirit of Capitalism,* Talcott Parsons, trans. (London and New York: Routledge, 1992) (1930).

35. For additional reading from a variety of perspectives, see Francis Fukuyama, *Trust: The Social Virtues and the Creation of Prosperity* (New York: Free Press, 1995); Lawrence Harrison, *Who Prospers? How Cultural Values Shape Economic and Political Success* (New York: Basic Books, 1992); Joel Kotkin, *Tribes: How Race, Religion, and Identity Determine Success in the New Global Economy* (New York: Random House, 1993), pp. 165–200; and Thomas Sowell, *Migrations and Cultures: A World View* (New York: Basic Books, 1996).

36. My discussion of the Chinese in Indonesia during the Suharto period draws heavily on Michael R. J. Vatikiotis, *Indonesian Politics under Suharto* (3d ed.) (London and New York: Routledge, 1993), and R. William Liddle, "Coercion, Co-optation, and the Management of Ethnic Relations in Indonesia," pp. 273–319, in Michael Brown and Sumit Ganguly, eds., *Government Policies and Ethnic Relations in Asia and the Pacific* (Cambridge: MIT Press, 1997).

37. The statistics regarding Chinese economic dominance are from Leo Suryadinata, "Indonesian Politics toward the Chinese Minority under the New Order," *Asian Survey* 16 (1976): 770–87, and "A Taxing Dilemma," *Asiaweek,* October 20, 1993, pp. 57–58. See also Michael Shari and Jonathan Moore, "The Plight of the Ethnic Chinese," *Business Week,* August 3, 1998, p. 48.

38. Michael Shari, "A Tycoon under Siege," *Business Week,* September 28, 1998, p. 26. See also William Ascher, *Why Governments Waste Natural Resources* (Baltimore: Johns Hopkins University Press, 1999), pp. 74–77.

39. Vatikiotis, *Indonesian Politics under Suharto,* p. 14.

40. On the recent forest fires in Indonesia, see Alan Khee-Jin Tan, "Forest Fires of Indonesia: State Responsibility and International Liability," *International and Comparative Law Quarterly* 48 (1999): 826–55. See also Edward A. Gargan, "Lust for Teak Takes Grim Toll," *Newsday (New York),* June 25, 2001, p. A7.

41. Friedman, *The Lexus and the Olive Tree,* p. 13.

42. Ravi Velloor, "Fix Chinese Issue, Indonesia Told," *Straits Times,* October 10, 1998, p. 2. On the 1998 riots, see also Gregg Jones, "Fear Overwhelming Indonesia's Chinese," *Dallas Morning News,* October 4, 1998, p. 1A, and Shari, "A Tycoon under Siege," p. 26.

43. Margot Cohen, "Indonesia: Turning Point," *Far Eastern Economic Review,* July 30, 1998, p. 12.

44. The comparative economic statistics for Indonesia and Singapore are from The World Bank, *World Development Report 2000/2001* (New York: Oxford University Press, 2001).

45. On Bengali economic dominance and anti-Bengali violence in Assam, India, see Donald L. Horowitz, *Ethnic Groups in Conflict* (Berkeley, Los Angeles, and London: University of California Press, 1985), pp. 112–13; Sanjoy Hazarika, "India's Assam Cauldron Bubbles Dangerously Again," *New York Times,* December 2, 1982, p. A2; and Ashutosh Varshney, "After the Assam Killings," *Christian Science Monitor,* March 22, 1983, p. 27.

46. Sowell, *Migrations and Cultures,* p. 28. See also Horowitz, *Ethnic Groups in Conflict,* pp. 155–56, 245–46, 616–17.

47. On the "Pentagon gang," see "Kidnap gang brings new terror to southern Philippines," *China Daily,* August 23, 2001, available at http://www.chinadaily.net/news/2001–08–23/28651.html. On Burmese bear bile, see "Life on China's Edge," *The Economist,* September 14, 1996, p. 41.

Chapter 2

1. As loosely translated and reported in "Talks with Farm Leader Break Down," *Press Association,* October 2, 2000.

2. Peter McFarren, "Bolivia Farmer Talks Break Down," *Associated Press,* October 1, 2000.

3. Paul Keller, "Natural-born Rebel with a Cause to Stir," *Financial Times,* February 2, 2002, p. 2, and Clifford Krauss, "Bolivia Makes Key Concessions to Indians," *New York Times,* October 7, 2000, p. A8.

4. "Talks with Farm Leader Break Down."

5. For general discussions of Bolivia in English, see Maria L. Lagos, *Autonomy and Power: The Dynamics of Class and Culture in Rural Bolivia* (Philadelphia: University of Pennsylvania Press, 1994); Waltraud Queiser Morales, *Bolivia: Land of Struggle* (Boulder and Oxford: Westview Press, 1992); and Robert Barton, *A Short History of the Republic of Bolivia* (La Paz and Cochabamba, Bolivia: Los Amigos del Libro, 1968).

6. Manning Nash, "The Impact of Mid-Nineteenth Century Economic Change upon the Indians of Middle America," pp. 170–83, in Magnus Mörner, ed.,

Race and Class in Latin America (New York and London: Columbia University Press, 1970).

7. Tristán Marof, "La Tragedia del Altiplano," *Editorial Claridad* (Buenos Aires, 1934). On the process of *"encholamiento,"* see Salvador Romero Pittari, "Las Claudinas," *Editorial Karaspas* (La Paz, 1988).

8. "Bolivia: Congress Passes Controversial Land-Reform Law," IAC (SM) Newsletter Database (TM), Latin American Database, October 18, 1996.

9. See Seymour Martin Lipset, "Values and Entrepreneurship in the Americas," pp. 77–140, in *Revolution and Counterrevolution: Change and Persistence in Social Structures* (rev. ed.) (New Brunswick and Oxford: Transaction Books, 1988), especially pp. 84–87; Frederick B. Pike, *Chile and the United States, 1880–1962* (Notre Dame: University of Notre Dame Press, 1963), pp. 280–87; and Jaime Vicens Vives, "The Decline of Spain in the Seventeenth Century," pp. 121–95, in Carlo M. Cipolla, ed., *The Economic Decline of Empires* (London: Methuen, 1970). The term "gentleman's complex" is usually attributed to the Brazilian sociologist Gilberto Freyre.

10. "Patience Runs Out in Bolivia," *The Economist,* April 21, 2001; Clifford Krauss, "Bolivia Falls Short," *New York Times,* July 12, 1998, p. 3.

11. William Finnegan, "Leasing the Rain," *The New Yorker,* April 8, 2002, pp. 43–53; Krauss, "Bolivia Falls Short," p. 3; and "Don't Run My Stop Signs," *Newsweek,* May 4, 1998, p. 64 (interview with Bolivia's former vice president Jorge Quiroga Ramirez). See also http://www.converge.org.nz/iac/articles/news990801a.htm.

12. Magnus Mörner, *Race Mixture in the History of Latin America* (Boston: Little, Brown and Company, 1967), pp. 22, 24.

13. This list was compiled by Magnus Mörner in Ibid., p. 58. My discussion of pigmentocracy draws heavily on Mörner, especially Ibid., pp. 1–2, 21–27, and pp. 53–68.

14. Ibid., p. 13.

15. See Ibid., pp. 43, 60, 99, 140–41; Magnus Mörner, *The Andean Past* (New York: Columbia University Press, 1985), p. 181; and David Bushnell and Neill Macaulay, *The Emergence of Latin America in the Nineteenth Century* (New York and Oxford: Oxford University Press, 1988), p. 5.

16. See "The right not to be Hispanic," *The Economist,* March 7, 1998, p. 88, and Enrique Krauze, "The new nativism," *World Press Review,* June 1998, p. 47. See also James F. Smith, "Mexico's Forgotten Find Cause for New Hope," *Los Angeles Times,* February 23, 2001, p. A1; Ginger Thompson, "Mexican Rebel Chief Says the Fight is Now for Peace," *New York Times,* January 30, 2001, p. A3; and Kevin Sullivan, "Chiapas Indians Pin Hopes on Fox," *Washington Post,* December 5, 2000, p. A34.

17. See Joel Millman, "Mexico's Clubby Corporate World Gets Jolt from U.S. over Insider Trading," *Wall Street Journal,* May 14, 2001, p. A16.

18. Anthony DePalma, "Going Private: A Special Report," *New York Times,* October 27, 1993, p. A1.

19. See Jonathan Kandell, "Yo Quiero Todo Bell," *Wired Magazine,* January 2001, available at http://www.wired.com/wired/archive/9.01/slim_pr.html.

20. My discussion of Carlos Slim draws heavily on Ibid.; Andrea Mandell Campbell, "Carlos Slim, El Hombre Mas Rico de America Latina," *Financial Times,* July 16, 2000; and David Luhnow, "It's Going to be Fine," *Wall Street Journal Europe,* February 8, 2001, p. 24. On Telmex's postprivatization improvements, see Elliot Blair Smith, "Mexico Struggles with Networks," *USA Today,* June 26, 2001, p. 14E.

21. Jared Diamond, *Guns, Germs, and Steel: The Fates of Human Societies* (New York and London: W. W. Norton & Company, 1999), pp. 68, 70–73. There is a voluminous interdisciplinary literature on the Spanish Conquest and subjugation of Latin America's indigenous populations. In addition to Jared Diamond, my discussion draws principally on John Hemming, *The Conquest of the Incas* (New York: Harcourt Brace Jovanovich, 1970); Mörner, *The Andean Past,* pp. 30–48; Mörner, *Race Mixture in the History of Latin America,* pp. 23–25; and Nash, "The Impact of Mid-Nineteenth Century Economic Change upon the Indians of Middle America," pp. 170–83.

22. As reported in Mörner, *The Andean Past,* p. 34.

23. Ibid., pp. 35–37. For discussions of the *encomienda* system, see Marvin Harris, *Patterns of Race in the Americas* (New York: Walker and Company, 1964), pp. 18–24, and Mörner, *The Andean Past,* p. 38.

24. See Nash, "The Impact of Mid-Nineteenth Century Economic Change upon the Indians of Middle America," pp. 173–74. See also Harris, *Patterns of Race in the Americas,* p. 22.

25. See Lipset, "Values and Entrepreneurship in the Americas," p. 85.

26. See Jeff Silverstein, "Mexico on the Brink of a New Revolution," *San Francisco Chronicle,* November 27, 1991, p. A8; Sally Bowen, "Peru set to sweep away 27-year-old 'land reform' laws," *Financial Times,* July 18, 1995, p. 29; and Linda Diebel, "Women harvest the grapes of NAFTA," *Toronto Star,* May 27, 1995, p. A18.

27. See Nancy Scheper-Hughes, *Death without Weeping: The Violence of Everyday Life in Brazil* (Berkeley and Los Angeles: University of California Press, 1992), which includes on pp. 152–57 a discussion of the disturbing studies of the Zona da Mata cane workers conducted by Nelson Chaves and his disciples. Chaves's quote can be found at Ibid., p. 153. See also the vivid ac-

counts in Linda Diebel, "Bittersweet sugar plantations dominate northeastern Brazil," *Toronto Star,* December 6, 1998, p. B1, and John Vidal, "The Long March Home," *Guardian (London),* April 26, 1997, p. T14.

28. Lipset, "Values and Entrepreneurship in the Americas," pp. 107–9. See also Magnus Mörner (with Harold Sims), *Adventurers and Proletarians: The Story of Migrants in Latin America* (UNESCO, Paris: University of Pittsburgh Press, 1985); Raymond Vernon, *The Dilemma of Mexico's Development* (Cambridge: Harvard University Press, 1965), chapter 6; and W. Paul Strassman, "The Industrialist," pp. 161–85, in John J. Johnson, ed., *Continuity and Change in Latin America* (Stanford: Stanford University Press, 1964).

29. Judith Laikin Elkin, *The Jews of Latin America* (rev. ed.) (New York and London: Holmes & Meier, 1998), pp. 131, 136.

30. See Ibid., pp. 80, 145–46. See also Henrique Rattner, "Economic and Social Mobility of Jews in Brazil," pp. 187–200, in Judith Laikin Elkin and Gilbert W. Merkx, eds., *The Jewish Presence in Latin America* (Boston: Allen & Unwin, 1987). For discussions of the prominent role played by Jews in Panama's commercial sectors, see Jon Mitchell, "The Panama Free Zone: Paradise for would-be millionaires," April 28, 1998, available at http://www.foreignwire.com/cf2.html, and Michele Labrut, "Picking Up the Pieces in Panama," *Jerusalem Report,* November 15, 1990, p. 35.

31. On Argentina's Jewish community see Haim Avni, *Argentina and the Jews,* Gila Brand, trans. (Tuscaloosa: University of Alabama Press, 1991). On the Elsztain family, see Clifford Krauss, "This Year in Argentina, Two Brothers Build an Empire," *New York Times,* April 14, 1998, p. D1.

32. See Rex A. Hudson, "Country Study & Country Guide for Uruguay," June 4, 1992, available at http://www.1upinfo.com/country-guide-study/uruguay/uruguay11.html.

33. On the late-nineteenth- and early-twentieth-century waves of mass immigration from Europe to Argentina, Chile, and Uruguay, see Mörner, *Race Mixture in the History of Latin America,* especially pp. 133–34, and Mörner and Sims, *Adventurers and Proletarians,* chapters 3 and 4.

34. Pike, *Chile and the United States, 1880–1962,* pp. 289–93.

35. See Anthony W. Marx, "Contested Citizenship: The Dynamics of Racial Identity and Social Movements," pp. 177–82, in Charles Tilly, ed., *International Review of Social History: Citizenship, Identity, and Social History* (Supplement 3) (Cambridge: Cambridge University Press, 1995), and Charles H. Wood and Jose A. M. Carvalho, *The Demography of Inequality in Brazil* (Cambridge: Cambridge University Press, 1988), chapter 6. See also David L. Marcus, "Melting Pot Coming to a Boil," *Dallas Morning News,* January 16, 1994, p. 1A.

36. See Eugene Robinson, *Coal to Cream: A Black Man's Journey Beyond Color To an Affirmation of Race* (New York: Free Press, 1999). Robinson's encounter with Vilma is described on pp. 10–14. See also pp. 11, 32. On the racial inequity Robinson encounters, see especially chapters 7 and 8. Scholarly treatments of race and racism in Brazil include France Winddance Twine, *Racism in a Racial Democracy: The Maintenance of White Supremacy in Brazil* (New Brunswick: Rutgers University Press, 1998), and Wood and Carvalho, *The Demography of Inequality in Brazil,* chapter 6.
37. See Harris, *Patterns of Race in the Americas,* pp. 61–63; Twine, *Racism in a Racial Democracy;* Marx, "Contested Citizenship," pp. 179–80; and Marcus, "Melting Pot Coming to a Boil," p. 1A.
38. Robinson, *Coal to Cream,* pp. 145, 181.
39. Anthony Faiola, "Peruvian Candidate Reflects New Indian Pride," *Washington Post,* March 31, 2000, p. A1.
40. Finnegan, "Leasing the Rain," p. 50.
41. See John Otis, "Popular Uprising," *Houston Chronicle,* September 28, 2000, p. A16; Larry Rohter, "Bitter Indians Let Ecuador Know Fight Isn't Over," *New York Times,* January 27, 2000, p. A3; and Nicole Veash, "Ecuador on the Verge of Anarchy as Indians Revolt," *Independent (London),* January 14, 2000, p. 16.
42. Veash, "Ecuador on the Verge of Anarchy as Indians Revolt," p. 16.
43. My discussion of hip-hop in Brazil draws heavily on Jennifer Roth-Gordon, "Hip-Hop Brasileiro: Brazilian Youth and Alternative Black Consciousness Movements" (presented at the American Anthropology Association meeting held on November 18, 1999). See also Stephen Buckley, "Brazil's Racial Awakening, *Washington Post,* June 12, 2000, p. A12.

Chapter 3

1. See Chrystia Freeland, *Sale of the Century: Russia's Wild Ride from Communism to Capitalism* (New York: Crown Business, 2000), which is based on Freeland's personal interviews of the oligarchs. I draw extensively on Freeland's book throughout the chapter. Other books covering the oligarchs include Paul Klebnikov, *Godfather of the Kremlin: Boris Berezovsky and the Looting of Russia* (New York, San Diego, and London: Harcourt, Inc., 2000), and Matthew Brzezinski, *Casino Moscow* (New York: Free Press, 2001).
2. See John Lloyd, "The Autumn of the Oligarchs," *New York Times Magazine,* October 8, 2000, pp. 88–94.
3. Freeland, *Sale of the Century,* p. 128.
4. Ibid., p. 175; Klebnikov, *Godfather of the Kremlin,* p. 212.
5. For two rather different descriptions of the loans-for-shares deal, see

Freeland, *Sale of the Century,* chapter 8, and Klebnikov, *Godfather of the Kremlin,* chapter 8.

6. As reported in Rachel Blustain, "Too Many Jews in the Kremlin?" *Forward,* April 4, 1997, p. 14.

7. See National Conference on Soviet Jewry, Anti-Defamation League, "The Reemergence of Political Anti-Semitism in Russia: A Call for Action" (presented to Secretary of State Madeline Albright on January 21, 1999), pp. 6–7, available at http://www.adl.org/international/russian_political_antisemitism.html, and The World Bank, *World Development Report 2000/2001* (New York: Oxford University Press, 2001). Determining the size of the Jewish population in Russia is complicated by a number of factors. The main problem is definitional: Different Jewish groups (e.g., Orthodox Jews as opposed to Reform Jews) apply different standards in determining who "counts" as Jewish. In Russia, many individuals with a single Jewish grandparent, or even just a "Jewish-sounding" surname, self-identify, and are perceived by others, as Jewish. At the same time, because of the long legacy of anti-Semitism in the country, many Russian Jews are not open about their heritage.

8. On the Jews during the Middle Ages, see Solomon Grayzel, *A History of the Jews* (New York and Ontario: Jewish Publication Society of America, 1968), pp. 276–367, especially pp. 362, 365. See also Michael Grant, *The Jews in the Roman World* (London: Weidenfeld and Nicolson, 1973).

9. On the "commanding economic position" of the Jews in interwar Romania, see Barbara Jelavich, *History of the Balkans: Twentieth Century* (Cambridge: Cambridge University Press, 1983), p. 160; in interwar Poland and Lithuania, see Ezra Mendelsohn, *The Jews of East Central Europe Between the World Wars* (Bloomington: Indiana University Press), pp. 23, 26, 226; and in interwar Hungary, see Peter Pulzer, *The Rise of Political Anti-Semitism in Germany and Austria* (rev. ed.) (London: Peter Halban Publishers, 1988), pp. 10–11, 13. An accessible summary of the economic history of the Jews in Europe can be found in Thomas Sowell, *Migrations and Cultures: A World View* (New York: Basic Books, 1996), pp. 238–82.

10. My discussion of Jews in tsarist Russia draws heavily on Zvi Gitelman, *A Century of Ambivalence: The Jews of Russia and the Soviet Union, 1881 to the Present* (2d expanded ed.) (Bloomington: Indiana University Press, 2000), especially chapter 1, and John Doyle Klier, *Imperial Russia's Jewish Question, 1855–1881* (Cambridge: Cambridge University Press, 1995), especially pp. 13–50, 285–331.

11. Gitelman, *A Century of Ambivalence,* p. 11.

12. Ibid., pp. 50, 52; Klier, *Imperial Russia's Jewish Question, 1855–1881,* pp. 290–91, 311–13.

13. Gitelman, *A Century of Ambivalence*, pp. 14, 49–52; Sowell, *Migrations and Culture*, p. 64.

14. See Gitelman, *A Century of Ambivalence*, chapters 2, 5, and 6, especially pp. 151–54; Sowell, *Migrations and Culture*, pp. 271–72; and Paul Johnson, *A History of the Jews* (New York: Harper & Row, 1987), pp. 450–55, 568–72.

15. Freeland, *Sale of the Century*, p. 171.

16. See Annalise Anderson, "The Red Mafia: A Legacy of Communism," in Edward P. Lazear, ed., *Economic Transition in Eastern Europe and Russia: Realities of Reform* (Stanford: Hoover Institution Press, 1995).

17. Freeland, *Sale of the Century*, pp. 114–15.

18. Ibid., pp. 116–19.

19. Ibid., p. 118. See also Robert Cottrell, "Foreigners are reluctant but locals are confident," *Financial Times*, July 2, 2001, p. 5.

20. Lloyd, "The Autumn of the Oligarchs," p. 90.

21. Freeland, *Sale of the Century*, pp. 146–56, 194, 239–41.

22. Ibid., p. 148.

23. Ibid., pp. 121–26, 182–86.

24. Khodorkovsky's wealth and holdings are documented in Bernard S. Black, Reinier Kraakman, and Anna Tarassova, "Russian Privatization and Corporate Governance: What Went Wrong?" *Stanford Law Review* 52 (2000): 1731–1803, pp. 1748, 1768; Oksana Yablokova, "Forbes List's Rich Russians Get Richer," *Moscow Times*, March 4, 2002, p. 1; and Sabrina Tavernise, "Fortune in Hand, Russian Tries to Polish Image," *New York Times*, August 18, 2001, p. C3.

25. Freeland, *Sale of the Century*, p. 121.

26. See Black, Kraakman, and Tarassova, "Russian Privatization and Corporate Governance," pp. 1754–55, and Tavernise, "Fortune in Hand, Russian Tries to Polish Image," p. C3.

27. Freeland, *Sale of the Century*, p. 135.

28. Klebnikov, *Godfather of the Kremlin*, pp. 89–90.

29. For a vivid and detailed description of the Avva scheme, see Ibid., pp. 140–43.

30. Freeland, *Sale of the Century*, pp. 137–41. See also Daniel W. Michaels, "Capitalism in the New Russia," *Journal of Historical Review* 16 (1997): 21–27, p. 24.

31. Freeland, *Sale of the Century*, pp. 141–45.

32. See Peter Baker, "An Unlikely Savior on the Tundra," *Washington Post*, March 2, 2001, p. A1; John Lloyd, "A miracle worker," *Financial Times*, January 6, 2001, p. 1; and Sabrina Tavernise, "An Aluminum Behemoth is Born in Russia," *New York Times*, April 6, 2001, p. W1.

33. Freeland, *Sale of the Century,* pp. 127–33.

34. Ibid., pp. 128, 172–89.

35. Lloyd, "The Autumn of the Oligarchs," p. 88.

36. "Putin says 1996 Chechnya pullout was 'major error,'" *BBC Summary of World Broadcasts,* March 20, 2000.

37. "Putin versus the oligarchs?" *The Economist,* June 17, 2000.

38. Robert Siegel, Jacki Lyden, Lawrence Sheets, "Boris Berezovsky to release documentary in London," *All Things Considered,* National Public Radio, February 21, 2002.

39. Ibid. (interviewing Moscow journalists Masha Lipman and Stanislav Kucher).

40. Brzezinski, *Casino Moscow,* pp. 180–81.

41. On Friedman, see Cottrell, "Foreigners are reluctant but locals are confident," p. 5. On Khodorkovsky's new attitude, see Maura Reynolds, "An 'Oligarch's' U-Turn toward Probity," *Los Angeles Times,* December 26, 2001, p. A26.

42. As reported in Barry Schweid, "Jewish group says Putin's 'instincts' help fuel bias," *Seattle Times,* March 16, 2001.

43. On Abramovich's recent replacement by Geraschenko, see Andrei Grigoriev, "Twelve and a Half," *What the Papers Say,* January 22, 2002, pp. 17–21. On the recent rise of political anti-Semitism, see National Conference on Soviet Jewry, "The Reemergence of Political Anti-Semitism in Russia," pp. 1–4.

44. Judith Matloff, "Russians seek scapegoats in hard times," *Christian Science Monitor,* August 13, 1999, p. 9.

45. Michael R. Gordon, "Russian Jews Turning Edgy as the Country's Chaos Creates an Ugly Mood," *New York Times,* March 9, 1999, p. A12.

46. National Conference on Soviet Jewry, "The Reemergence of Political Anti-Semitism in Russia," p. 4.

47. Ibid., p. 5.

48. Ibid., p. 6; Matloff, "Russians seek scapegoats in hard times," p. 9.

49. Nabi Abdullaev, "New Political Party Campaigns against Jews," *Moscow Times,* February 28, 2002.

Chapter 4

1. Ryszard Kapuściński, *Another Day of Life* (San Diego, New York, and London: Harcourt Brace Jovanovich, 1987), pp. 10, 23–24, 66–67. For additional reading on Angola, see Gerald J. Bender, *Angola under the Portuguese* (Berkeley and Los Angeles: University of California Press, 1978). See also Reference Center, "Virtual Historical Tour of Angola," http://209.183.193.172/

referenc/history/virtualtour.html and "Angola—A History," http://www.
africanet.com/africanet/country/angola/history.htm.

2. The World Bank, World Bank Country Brief on Angola, July 2001, available
    at http://www.worldbank.org/afr/ao2.htm.

3. David J. Lynch, "A Wary Nation Looks to a Time of Transition," *USA Today*,
    December 15, 1997, p. 17A. The quote from Namibia's President Nujoma
    is from "Namibia: President raps commercial farmers for firing workers
    'arbitrarily,' " *BBC Worldwide Monitoring*, March 29, 2001.

4. On the historical economic dominance of South Africa's English speakers
    vis-à-vis the more numerous Afrikaners, see Milton J. Esman, "Ethnic
    Politics and Economic Power," *Comparative Politics* 19 (1987): 395–418.
    General histories of South Africa include Michael Attwell, *South Africa:
    Background to the Crisis* (London: Sidgwick & Jackson, 1986), and T. R. H.
    Davenport, *South Africa: A Modern History* (4th ed.) (London: Macmillan,
    1991).

5. The statistics I cite on the persisting economic dominance of South Africa's
    white minority, and the continuing mass poverty of the black majority, are
    from recent reports by South Africa's Black Economic Empowerment
    Commission (2000 and 2001), available at http//www.bmfonline.co.za/
    bee_rep.htm. See also Maurice Hommel, "Escaping Poisonous Embrace of
    Racism," *Toronto Star*, August 24, 2001, p. A21; "Skin Deep," *The Economist*,
    July 21, 2001; Hardev Kaur, "Affirmative Action Plan Calls for
    Advancement of Blacks," *New Straits Times (Malaysia)*, May 24, 2001, p. 10;
    Hardev Kaur, "Blacks Continue to Live in Poverty," *New Straits Times
    (Malaysia)*, May 23, 2001, p. 10; and Christopher Ogden, "The Post-
    Miracle Phase," *Time International*, September 16, 1996, p. 46.

6. On colonial Namibia, see Jan-Bart Gewald, *Herero Heroes: A Socio-Political
    History of the Herero of Namibia, 1890–1923* (Athens: Ohio University Press,
    2001). On the persisting extreme economic inequality between the white
    minority and the black majority, see the 2001 Country Review on Namibia
    written by CountryWatch.com and the World Bank Africa Live Database.
    See also The World Bank Group, "Namibia," September 2000, available at
    http://www.worldbank.org/afr/na2.htm, and "Namibia," *The Economist*,
    November 7, 1992, p. 49.

7. See Nicholas Stein, "The De Beers Story: A New Cut on an Old
    Monopoly," *Fortune*, February 19, 2001, p. 186.

8. See Ibid., p. 186; Rob Edwards, "Mining Giant Goes to Court," *Scotsman*,
    April 20, 1997, p. 8; and Daniel J. Wakin, "Surf's Up in Swakopmund,"
    Ottawa Citizen, December 4, 1999, p. K6. The 2000 sanitation statistic is

based on *The World Bank, World Development Report 2000/2001* (New York: Oxford University Press, 2001).

9. For further reading on Zimbabwe (formerly Rhodesia), see David Blair, *Degrees in Violence* (London and New York: Continuum, 2002), and Robert Blake, *A History of Rhodesia* (London: Eyre Methuen, 1977).

10. Jeremy Hardy, "Farming Today," *Guardian (London),* April 8, 2000, p. 22.

11. See "State lists 57 more white farms for Mugabe land grab," *Deutsche Presse-Agentur,* September 15, 2000, and Simon Baynham, "Redistribution of Land Angers Many," *Jane's Intelligence Review,* February 1, 1998, p. 13.

12. My account of Cholmondeley and the decadent years of Kenya's Happy Valley is based on James Fox, *White Mischief* (New York: Random House, 1982). See also Louise Tunbridge, "Whites take up politics 'to halt Kenya's decay,' " *Daily Telegraph,* December 23, 1997, p. 19.

13. My description of the Kenyan Cowboys draws on Danna Harman, "Past echoes in infamous Kenyan club," *Christian Science Monitor,* February 15, 2001, p. 1. On the Leakeys, see Tunbridge, "Whites take up politics 'to halt Kenya's decay,' " p. 19, and "Big-game safari," *The Economist,* July 31, 1999.

14. John M. Cohen, "Ethnicity, Foreign Aid, and Economic Growth in Sub-Saharan Africa: The Case of Kenya" (Development Discussion Paper 520, Harvard Institute for International Development, November 1995). See also Paul Kennedy, *African Capitalism* (Cambridge: Cambridge University Press, 1988); Frank Holmquist and Michael Ford, "Kenya: State and Civil Society the First Year after the Election," *Africa Today* 41 (1994): 5–25; and Shin-wha Lee and Anne Pitsch, "Kikuyu, Kisii, Luhya, and Luo in Kenya," October 1999, http://www.cidcm.umd.edu/inscr/mar/kenkik.htm.

15. See Bill Berkeley, "An Encore for Chaos?" *Foreign Affairs,* February 1996.

16. For a wonderful description of the Onitsha Marketplace, and Africa generally, a must-read is Ryszard Kapuściński, *The Shadow of the Sun,* Klara Glowczewska, trans. (New York and Toronto: Alfred A. Knopf, 2001), pp. 298–305.

17. See Donald L. Horowitz, *Ethnic Groups in Conflict* (Berkeley, Los Angeles, and London: University of California Press, 1985), pp. 27–28, 154–55, 164–66, 243–49.

18. See Ibid., pp. 112, 153, 245–46.

19. Probably the best English source on the economically dynamic Bamiléké in Cameroon is Victor T. Le Vine, *The Cameroon Federal Republic* (Ithaca and London: Cornell University Press, 1971). More recent articles documenting the market dominance of the Bamiléké are James Brooke, "Informal Capitalism Grows in Cameroon," *New York Times,* November 30, 1987, p.

D8, and Richard Everett, "The Bamiléké—Merchant Tribe of Cameroon," *Record,* August 10, 1986, p. A48.

20. On Rwanda, see Philip Gourevitch, *We wish to inform you that tomorrow we will be killed with our families* (New York: Picador USA, 1998), especially chapter 4, and Gérard Prunier, *The Rwanda Crisis: History of a Genocide* (New York: Columbia University Press, 1995), especially pp. 26–45. On Burundi, see Rene Lemarchand, *Burundi: Ethnocide as Discourse and Practice* (Cambridge and Washington, DC: Cambridge University Press and Woodrow Wilson Center Press, 1994).

21. An excellent discussion of the highly successful (and recently deported) Eritrean business community in Ethiopia can be found in Noah Benjamin Novogrodsky, "Identity Politics," *Boston Review,* summer 1999. On the economically advanced Ewe in Togo and Chagga in Tanzania, see Horowitz, *Ethnic Groups in Conflict,* pp. 37, 46, 149, 152, 154, 159. On the Baganda in Uganda, see Horowitz, *Ethnic Groups in Conflict,* pp. 163–64; Mahmood Mamdani, *Politics and Class Formation in Uganda* (New York and London: Monthly Review Press, 1976), pp. 29–34, 41–44, 120–22; and Bill Berkeley, "An African Success Story?" (Uganda), *The Atlantic,* September 1994, p. 22. The Susu in Guinea are discussed in the country reports compiled by Freedomhouse (http://www.freedomhouse.org) and the University of Minnesota Human Rights Library (http://www1.umn.edu/humanrts/africa/guinea.htm).

22. Hazel M. McFerson, "Ethnicity, Individual Initiative, and Economic Growth in an African Plural Society: The Bamiléké of Cameroon," in *U.S. AID Evaluation Special Study* No. 15 (1983), and Etienne Tasse, "Cameroon Politics: It Just Takes a Spark to Ignite Ethnic Fires," *Inter Press Service,* July 11, 1995.

23. See Karl Vick, "A New View of Kenya's 'Asians,' " *Washington Post,* March 15, 2000, p. A21, and Simon Baynham, "Racial fears flare in Kenya," *Jane's Intelligence Review,* February 1, 1997, p. 11.

24. See Vick, "A New View of Kenya's 'Asians,' " p. A21, and Baynham, "Racial fears flare in Kenya," p. 11.

25. See, for example, Michael Cowan and Scott MacWilliam, *Indigenous Capital in Kenya* (Helsinki: Institute of Development Studies, University of Helsinki, 1996).

26. The "Goldenberg case" is discussed in "Kenya's Man in the Middle," *Business in Africa,* June 18, 2001. On the history and economic success of Indians in East Africa, see J. S. Mangat, *A History of the Asians in East Africa* (London: Oxford University Press, 1969), and Thomas Sowell, *Migrations and Cultures: A World View* (New York: Basic Books, 1996), chapter 7.

27. See Keith B. Richburg, "Tanzanian Reforms Opening Up Socialist, One-

Party System," *Washington Post,* March 24, 1992, p. A14, and Scott Straus, "In Zambia, Race Hatred Simmers," *Baltimore Sun,* January 26, 1996, p. A2.

28. Moyiga Nduru, "Behind the Scenes of a Democratic Election," available at http://www.oneworld.org/index_oc/news/kenya231297.html. On the 1982 riots, see Alan Cowell, "A Fearful Reminder Lingers for Asians in Kenya," *New York Times,* September 1, 1982, p. A2.

29. See James Traub, "The Worst Place on Earth," *The New York Review of Books,* June 29, 2000, pp. 61–66, and "The Darkest Corner of Africa," *The Economist,* January 9, 1999, p. 41.

30. Neil O. Leighton, "Lebanese Emigration: Its Effect on the Political Economy of Sierra Leone," in Albert Hourani and Nadim Shehadi, eds., *The Lebanese in the World: A Century of Emigration* (London: Centre for Lebanese Studies, 1992), pp. 579–601, especially pp. 582–84.

31. Ibid., pp. 584–97, and H. L. van der Laan, *The Lebanese Traders in Sierra Leone* (The Hague: Mouton & Co., 1975), chapter 9.

32. Graham Greene, *The Heart of the Matter* (New York: Penguin Books, 1948), p. 6.

33. See "The Inner Circle of the Taylor Regime," January 1, 2001, available at http://www.theperspective.org/innercircle.html.

34. The statistics on population and ethnic demographics cited throughout the chapter are from *Africa South of the Sahara* (29th ed.) (London: Europa Publications, 1999). Most of the statistics relating to poverty, illiteracy, and other measures of development are from United Nations Development Programme, *Human Development Report 2001* (New York: Oxford University Press, 2001).

Part Two Preface

1. John Lewis Gaddis, "Democracy and Foreign Policy," p. 8 (Transcript of Devane Lecture, delivered at Yale University on April 17, 2001, available at http://www.yale.edu/yale300/democracy. See also Thomas Carothers, *Aiding Democracy Abroad* (Washington, DC: Carnegie Endowment for International Peace), pp. 40–44.

Chapter 5

1. See Catherine Buckle, *African Tears: The Zimbabwe Land Invasions* (Johannesburg and London: Covos Day Books, 2001), pp. 31, 50–55, 72, 74, and Adam Roberts, "The great manipulator," *Times Literary Supplement,* March 8, 2002, p. 7.

2. See Buckle, *African Tears,* p. 32; Roberts, "The great manipulator," pp. 7–8;

and "Leader Urges Zimbabwe Blacks to Menace the White Residents," *New York Times,* December 15, 2000, p. A8.

3. Roberts, "The great manipulator," p. 7.
4. Seumas Milne, "Colonialism and the new world order," *Guardian (London),* March 7, 2002, p. 20, and Roberts, "The great manipulator," p. 7. For a history of Zimbabwe under Robert Mugabe, see Martin Meredith, *Our Votes, Our Guns* (New York: Public Affairs, 2002).
5. See Buckle, *African Tears,* p. 140, and Rupert Cornwell, "Zimbabwe Crisis: Mugabe Declares War on Country's White Farmers," *Independent (London),* April 19, 2000, p. 13.
6. Peter Beinart, "Beloved Country," *The New Republic,* April 1, 2002, p. 6, and Milne, "Colonialism and the new world order," p. 20.
7. Rosie DiManno, "In Zimbabwe, Change is Just a Word," *Toronto Star,* March 26, 2001. See also Roberts, "The great manipulator," p. 7.
8. Claire Keeton, "Thousands of S. African squatters facing government wrath," *Agence France-Presse,* July 4, 2001; and "South Africa: Pan Africanist Congress urges summit to discuss land issue," *BBC Worldwide Monitoring,* July 8, 2001.
9. Michael Dynes, "South Africa's license for black redress," *The Times (London),* February 7, 2001.
10. Frank H. Golay, Ralph Anspach, M. Ruth Pfanner & Eliezer B. Ayal, *Underdevelopment and Economic Nationalism in Southeast Asia* (Ithaca and London: Cornell University Press, 1969), pp. 137, 158, 166, 181, 191–95, 197–98.
11. See Dennis Austin, *Democracy and Violence in India and Sri Lanka* (London: Printer Publishers Limited, 1994), pp. xvii, 66–70, and Donald L. Horowitz, *Ethnic Groups in Conflict* (Berkeley, Los Angeles, and London: University of California Press, 1985), pp. 383, 683.
12. Golay et al., *Underdevelopment and Economic Nationalism in Southeast Asia,* pp. 209, 211, and Martin Smith, *Burma: Insurgency and the Politics of Ethnicity* (London and New Jersey: Zed Books, 1991), pp. 200–201.
13. Omar Noman, *Pakistan* (London and New York: Kegan Paul International, 1990), pp. 20, 41, 75–80, 93–94; Richard F. Nyrop, ed., *Pakistan: A Country Study* (5th ed.) (Washington, DC: U.S. Government Printing Office, 1984), pp. 104, 137; Stanley Wolpert, *Zulfi Bhutto of Pakistan* (New York and Oxford: Oxford University Press, 1993), pp. 124–26, 135–39; and Ian Talbot, *Pakistan: A Modern History* (London: Hurst and Company, 1998), pp. 215, 233.
14. See Robert Barton, *A Short History of the Republic of Bolivia* (La Paz and Cochabamba, Bolivia: Los Amigos del Libro, 1968), pp. 255–75; Magnus

Mörner, *The Andean Past* (New York: Columbia University Press, 1985), pp. 69, 205, 221–22; and "Victor Paz Estenssoro," *The Economist,* June 23, 2001, p. 84.

15. I have documented this in more detail in Amy L. Chua, "The Privatization-Nationalization Cycle: The Link between Markets and Ethnicity in Developing Countries," *Columbia Law Review* 95 (1995): 223–303.

16. Thomas L. Friedman, *The Lexus and the Olive Tree* (New York: Anchor Books, 2000), p. 450 (citing Larry Diamond).

17. Clifford Geertz, "Starting Over," *The New York Review of Books,* May 11, 2000, pp. 22, 24.

18. Tom McCawley Serang, "A People's Economy," *Asiaweek,* December 18, 1998, p. 62.

19. See David Jenkins, "The Business of Hatred," *Sydney Morning Herald,* October 28, 1998, p. 8; "Indonesia's Anguish," *New York Times,* October 16, 1998, p. A26; Ravi Velloor, "Fix Chinese Issue, Indonesia Told," *Straits Times,* October 10, 1998, p. 2; and Kafil Yamin, "Economy-Indonesia: Not Too Happy With Very Strong Currency," *Inter Press Service,* July 2, 1999.

20. See Warren Caragata, "One Lousy Job," *Asiaweek,* February 16, 2001, p. 27, and "Nationalizing Indonesia: Commanding Depths," *The Economist,* July 24, 1999, p. 61.

21. Caragata, "One Lousy Job," p. 27, and "Privatization should be reactivated," *Jakarta Post,* December 31, 2001.

22. Fyodor Dostoyevsky, "The Jewish Question," Kenneth Lantz, trans., *A Writer's Diary* (March 1877) (Evanston, IL: Northwestern University Press, 1997), pp. 905–6.

23. My accounts of rising political anti-Semitism in Russia are based on the following sources: National Conference on Soviet Jewry, Anti-Defamation League, "The Reemergence of Political Anti-Semitism in Russia: A Call for Action" (presented to Secretary of State Madeline Albright on January 21, 1999), pp. 1–4, available at http://www.adl.org/international/russian_political_antisemitism.html; Michael R. Gordon, "Russian Jews Turning Edgy as the Country's Chaos Creates an Ugly Mood," *New York Times,* March 9, 1999, p. A12; and Paul Goble, "Russia: Analysis From Washington—Another Outburst of Anti-Semitism," available at http://www.rferl.org/nca/features/1998/12/F.RU.981216135725.html. On anti-Semitic demagoguery in Krasnodar, see Celestine Bohlen, "Where Russians Are Hurting, Racism Takes Root," *New York Times,* November 15, 1998, p. A3.

24. See Igor Semenenko, "Top Official: Invalidate Unfair Sell-Off Deals,"

Moscow Times, March 10, 1999, and "TV analyses developing parliamentary election race in Russia," *BBC Summary of World Broadcasts,* January 19, 1999.

25. See Vladimir Todres and Eduard Gismatullin, "Russia Shuts Down Last Nationwide Private TV Channel," *Bloomberg News,* January 22, 2002; "Blank Screens," *The Economist,* January 26, 2002; and "Democracy is Step One, Mr. Putin," *Los Angeles Times,* April 19, 2001, p. B10.

26. Judith Matloff, "Russians seek scapegoats in hard times," *Christian Science Monitor,* August 13, 1999, p. 9.

27. Nabi Abdullaev, "New Political Party Campaigns against Jews," *Moscow Times,* February 28, 2002.

28. Larry Rohter, "A Combative Leader Shapes Venezuela to a Leftist Vision," *New York Times,* July 28, 2000, pp. A1, A8. For a historical synopsis of the often symbiotic relationship between Venezuela's roughly 20 percent white elite and the country's military, see Heinz R. Sonntag, "Crisis and regression: Ecuador, Paraguay, Peru, and Venezuela," in Manuel Antonio Garretón M. and Edward Newman, eds., *Democracy in Latin America* (Tokyo, New York, and Paris: United Nations University Press, 2001), chapter 6.

29. See Rohter, "A Combative Leader Shapes Venezuela to a Leftist Vision," pp. A1, A8; and "Back to the soil," *The Economist,* April 28, 2001.

30. Linda Diebel, "Seattle Fallout Drifts South," *Toronto Star,* December 26, 1999; Bart Jones, "Venezuelans Overwhelmingly Approve New Constitution," *Associated Press,* December 16, 1999; Rohter, "A Combative Leader Shapes Venezuela to a Leftist Vision," pp. A1, A8; and "Venezuelan president replaces profit with food in the 'peaceful revolution,' " *Irish Times,* October 12, 1999, p. 10.

31. Fabiola Sanchez, "Venezuela central bank director says no nationalization despite presidential threats," *Associated Press,* December 18, 2001, and "Chavez Seeks to Tax Financial Transactions," *LatinFinance,* February 1, 2002, p. 6.

32. See David Adams, "Twelve killed in Venezuelan street protests," *The Times (London),* April 12, 2002. On the disastrous economic effects of Chavez's policies, see "Consolidating Power in Venezuela," *New York Times,* August 2, 2000, p. A24.

33. See Andy Webb-Vidal, "Strengthened Caracas leader strikes a more moderate tone," *Financial Times,* April 15, 2002, p. 7, and Ginger Thompson, "Behind the Upheaval in Venezuela," *New York Times,* April 18, 2002, p. A8.

Chapter 6

1. James Traub, "The Worst Place on Earth," *The New York Review of Books,* June 29, 2000, pp. 61–66; Colin Muncie, "On a mission to hell and back," *Medical Post,* August 25, 1998, p. 19; and Alex Duval Smith, "This is a nation of husbands who have seen their wives executed and their children's hands chopped off," *The Independent,* January 23, 1999, p. 1.

2. See William Reno, *Corruption and State Politics in Sierra Leone* (Cambridge: Cambridge University Press, 1995), pp. 72–73, and H. L. van der Laan, *The Lebanese Traders in Sierra Leone* (The Hague: Mouton & Co., 1975), pp. 9, 58–62, 280–81.

3. Reno, *Corruption and State Politics in Sierra Leone,* pp. 4, 87, 110–11, 118–20.

4. David Fashole Luke, "The Politics of Economic Decline in Sierra Leone," *Journal of Modern African Studies* 27 (1989): 133–41, p. 137, and "Waxing fat on a diet of shrimps, diamonds—and good connections," *South,* December 1982, p. 60.

5. Reno, *Corruption and State Politics in Sierra Leone,* pp. 155–60, 172–74; Traub, "The Worst Place on Earth," p. 61; and "Waxing fat on a diet of shrimps, diamonds—and good connections," p. 60.

6. Traub, "The Worst Place on Earth," p. 61.

7. See Kathryn Ellis, "Diamonds Are Fundamental to Sierra Leone Conflict, U.S. Editor Says," State Department Information Programs, available at http://usinfo.state.gov/regional/af/security/a1062501.htm. On the Lebanese exodus, see "Fuel Crisis New Worry to War-Weary Sierra Leone," January 27, 1999, available at http://www.cnn.com/WORLD/africa/9901/27/sierra.leone.01.

8. Michael R. J. Vatikiotis, *Indonesian Politics under Suharto* (3d ed.) (London and New York: Routledge, 1993), pp. 14–15, 32–59, 105–6, 126–30; Leo Suryadinata, "Indonesian Politics toward the Chinese Minority under the New Order," *Asian Survey* 16 (1976): 770–87; and R. William Liddle, "Coercion, Co-optation, and the Management of Ethnic Relations in Indonesia," pp. 273–319, in Michael F. Brown and Sumit Ganguly, eds., *Government Policies and Ethnic Relations in Asia and the Pacific* (Cambridge: MIT Press, 1997), p. 318.

9. Vatikiotis, *Indonesian Politics under Suharto,* pp. 15, 51. The estimates of the Suharto family's wealth are from George J. Aditjondro, "Suharto & Sons (and Daughters, In-Laws, and Cronies)," *Washington Post,* January 25, 1998, p. C1.

10. William Ascher, *Why Governments Waste Natural Resources* (Baltimore and London: Johns Hopkins University Press, 1999), pp. 75–76.

11. Vatikiotis, *Indonesian Politics under Suharto,* p. 151, and Salil Tripathi, "Children of a Lesser God," *Far Eastern Economic Review,* June 4, 1998, p. 66.

12. Vatikiotis, *Indonesian Politics under Suharto,* pp. 156–61, 227.

13. Raymond Bonner, *Waltzing with a Dictator* (New York: Times Books, 1987), p. 162.

14. For discussions of pre-Marcos anti-market backlashes against the Chinese in the Philippines, see Frank H. Golay, Ralph Anspach, M. Ruth Pfanner & Eliezer B. Ayal, *Underdevelopment and Economic Nationalism in Southeast Asia* (Ithaca and London: Cornell University Press, 1969), chapter 2, and Edgar Wickberg, "Anti-Sinicism and Chinese Identity Options in the Philippines," pp. 152–83, in Daniel Chirot and Anthony Reid, eds., *Essential Outsiders: Chinese and Jews in the Modern Transformation of Southeast Asia and Central Europe* (Seattle and London: University of Washington Press, 1997), pp. 168–74.

15. See Sterling Seagrave, *The Marcos Dynasty* (New York: Harper & Row, 1988), pp. 22–27.

16. See Bonner, *Waltzing with a Dictator,* pp. 112–27, especially p. 125.

17. Ibid., pp. 256–63.

18. Ibid., pp. 127, 161.

19. Ibid., pp. 161–62, 247–48. On Imelda's courting of Kissinger, and its results, see Ibid., p. 155. As for Imelda's being dumped by Ninoy Aquino, see Ibid., pp. 21–22.

20. Ibid., pp. 388–89; Seagrave, *The Marcos Dynasty,* pp. 234–35.

21. See "Was Marcos Misunderstood?" *BusinessWeek Online,* October 11, 1999, available at http://www.businessweek.com/1999/99_41/b3650091.htm. For testimony regarding Marcos's demand for 60 percent of a Chinese company's equity, see Jovito R. Salonga, *Presidential Plunder: The Quest for Marcos' Ill-Gotten Wealth* (Quezon City: University of the Philippines & Regina Publishing, 2000), pp. 335–37.

22. On the antidemocracy positions taken by prominent Indian leaders before independence, see Michael Cowan and Scott MacWilliam, *Indigenous Capital in Kenya* (Helsinki: Institute of Development Studies, University of Helsinki, 1996), p. 113. For a detailed discussion of Indian contributions to President Kenyatta's political campaign, see pp. 114–15. On President Moi's evolving relationship with Kenya's Indian minority, see pp. 117–19, 129–30.

23. "Victor Paz Estenssoro," *The Economist,* June 23, 2001, p. 84.

24. See Rodolfo Stavenhagen, "Social Dimensions: Ethnicity," in Manuel Antonio Garretón M. and Edward Newman, eds., *Democracy in Latin America* (Tokyo, New York, and Paris: United Nations University Press, 2001), chapter 7, and Joseph Contreras, "Rise of the Indian," *Newsweek,*

August 13, 2001, p. 20. On President Alemán's reprivatization campaign, see Peter H. Smith, "Mexico Since 1946: Dynamics of an Authoritarian Regime," in Leslie Bethell, ed., *Mexico Since Independence* (Cambridge and New York: Cambridge University Press, 1991), pp. 321, 337, 339–40. On Guatemala, see Thomas and Marjorie Melville, *Guatemala: The Politics of Land Ownership* (New York: Free Press, 1971), pp. 81–94, 297–99, and Contreras, "Rise of the Indian."

25. On Brazil's emerging racial consciousness, see Stephen Buckley, "Brazil's Racial Awakening, *Washington Post,* June 11, 2000, p. A12; Andrew Downie, "Brazil creates race quotas to aid blacks," *Washington Times,* August 28, 2001, p. A10; "I'm black, be fairer to me," *The Economist,* October 20, 2001; and "Brazilian political movement aims to get blacks to take pride in their race," NPR, *All Things Considered,* October 24, 2001.

26. Anthony Faiola, "Peruvian Candidate Reflects New Indian Pride," *Washington Post,* March 31, 2000, p. A1.

27. Larry Rohter, "Bitter Indians Let Ecuador Know Fight Isn't Over," *New York Times,* January 27, 2000, p. A3, and "The Indians and the dollar," *The Economist,* March 4, 2000.

28. Paul Keller, "Natural-born rebel with a cause to stir," *Financial Times,* February 2, 2002, p. 2, and Clifford Krauss, "Bolivia Makes Key Concessions to Indians," *New York Times,* October 7, 2000, p. A8.

Chapter 7

1. Roy Gutman, "Death Camp Horrors," *Newsday,* October 18, 1992, p. 3.

2. Bill Berkeley, *The Graves Are Not Yet Full* (New York: Basic Books, 2001), p. 259.

3. On anti-Russian policies in the former Soviet Union, see Jeff Chinn and Robert Kaiser, *Russians as the New Minority* (Boulder, CO: Westview Press, 1996), especially pp. 1–3, 12, and Gail W. Lapidus and Victor Zaslavsky, with Philip Goldman, *From Union to Commonwealth* (Cambridge: Cambridge University Press, 1992), especially pp. 45–70. On the departure of Jews from Russia, Ukraine, and Belarus, see Tel Aviv University, "Anti-Semitism Worldwide 1999/2000: Former Soviet Union," available at http://www.tau.ac.il/Anti-Semitism/asw99-2000/fsu.htm. See also Jay Solomon, "Indonesia's Chinese Move to Increase Civil Rights after a Decades-Long Ban on Political Activities," *Wall Street Journal,* June 9, 1998, p. A14.

4. My discussion of the recently deported Eritrean business community in Ethiopia draws heavily on Noah Benjamin Novogrodsky, "Identity Politics," *Boston Review,* summer 1999, and Julia Stewart, "Ethiopian government under fire for deportation of Eritrean businessmen," *Birmingham Post,*

November 7, 1998. See also "Eritrean rights group claims Ethiopia intends to seize Eritreans' property," *Agence France-Presse,* March 1, 2000.

5. Philip Gourevitch, *We wish to inform you that tomorrow we will be killed with our families* (New York: Picador USA, 1998), pp. 47–49, 55–56.

6. Berkeley, *The Graves Are Not Yet Full*, p. 258, and Gérard Prunier, *The Rwanda Crisis: History of a Genocide* (New York: Columbia University Press, 1995), especially pp. 26–45.

7. Gourevitch, *We wish to inform you that tomorrow we will be killed with our families,* pp. 58–60.

8. Ibid., pp. 60–61, 64–65.

9. Ibid., pp. 82, 89–92.

10. Ibid., pp. 82–83, 85–88, 93.

11. Ibid., pp. 100, 115.

12. Ibid., p. 59.

13. The population figures for Serbs and Croats in the former Yugoslavia are based on the 1981 census, as reported in Bruce McFarlane, *Yugoslavia* (London and New York: Pinter Publishers, 1988), p. 2. The economic figures from 1918 and 1930 are from Branka Prpa-Jovanović, "The Making of Yugoslavia: 1830–1945," in Jasminka Udovički and James Ridgeway, eds., *Burn This House* (Durham, NC: Duke University Press, 1997), p. 54.

14. On the different cultural and religious roots of the north and south, see Hugh Poulton, *The Balkans* (London: Minority Rights Publications, 1991), pp. 7, 22–24, 34–35; Marcus Tanner, *Croatia: A Nation Forged in War* (New Haven and London: Yale University Press, 1997), pp. 29–40, 187, 192, 195–97; and Jasminka Udovički, "The Bonds and the Fault Lines," in Udovički and Ridgeway, eds., *Burn This House,* pp. 14–21.

15. Dijana Pleština, *Regional Development in Communist Yugoslavia* (Boulder, CO: Westview Press, 1992), p. xxi. The statistics on the stark economic, health, and educational disparities between north and south are from: Jack C. Fisher, *Yugoslavia* (San Francisco: Chandler Publishing, 1966), p. 72; United Nations, *InfoNation,* available at http://www.un.org/Pubs/CyberSchoolBus/infonation/e-infonation.htm; and the World Bank's "country at a glance" data, available at http://www.worldbank.org/data/countrydata/aag/yug_aag.pdf.

16. Stephen Engelberg, "Carving Out a Greater Serbia," *New York Times,* September 1, 1991, p. 19. See also Pleština, *Regional Development in Communist Yugoslavia,* pp. 13–58, 69–71.

17. See Tim Judah, *The Serbs: History, Myth and the Destruction of Yugoslavia* (New Haven and London: Yale University Press, 1997), chapters 8 and 9, especially pp. 165, 177.

18. Johanna McGeary, "Face to Face with Evil," *Time,* May 13, 1996, p. 46. See also Blaine Harden, "Serbian Leader in Firm Control Despite Protests," *Washington Post,* March 10, 1992, p. A12, and Eric Margolis, "The End for Slobodan?" *Ottawa Sun,* July 19, 1999, p. 15.

19. Richard Beeston, "Rape and Revenge," *The Times,* December 17, 1992, and Laura Pitter, "Beaten and scarred for life in the Serbian 'rape camps,' " *South China Morning Post,* December 27, 1992, p. 8.

20. Engelberg, "Carving Out a Greater Serbia," p. 19 (emphasis added).

Chapter 8

1. Along with most China scholars, I assume here that the "Han" Chinese in China may be viewed appropriately as a single ethnic group, even though the category of "Han" is highly artificial. See, for example, John King Fairbank and Merle Goldman, *China: A New History* (Cambridge: Belknap Press, 1998), p. 23.

2. On Singapore, see Joseph B. Tamney, *The Struggle Over Singapore's Soul* (Berlin and New York: Walter de Gruyter, 1996), pp. 20, 96–103, 187. On Japan, see "Japanese Parliament Passes 'Ainu' Minority Rights Bill," *Agence France-Presse,* May 8, 1997. On Taiwan, see Alan M. Wachman, *Taiwan: National Identity and Democratization* (Armonk, NY: M. E. Sharpe, 1994), pp. 15–17.

3. Victor Purcell, *The Chinese in Southeast Asia* (2d ed.) (London: Oxford University Press for the Royal Institute of International Affairs, 1965), pp. 85, 92–93, 115–23.

4. Ibid., p. 131. On Chinese economic dominance in Thailand, see pp. 127–31, 139.

5. Ibid., pp. 143–47, and David K. Wyatt, *Thailand: A Short History* (New Haven and London: Yale University Press, 1984), pp. 254–55, 292.

6. Purcell, *The Chinese in Southeast Asia,* pp. 134–40.

7. G. Bruce Knecht, "Thais that Bind," *National Review,* November 21, 1994, p. 58.

8. Michael Vatikiotis, "Sino Chic," *Far Eastern Economic Review,* January 11, 1996, pp. 22–23.

Chapter 9

1. See "The Forbes Four Hundred," September 27, 2001, available at http://www.forbes.com/2001/09/27/400.html.

2. Thomas Babington Macaulay, "The People's Charter" (May 3, 1842) in *Miscellanies* (Boston and New York: Houghton, Mifflin & Company, 1900), volume 1, pp. 263–76. The quotes from Adam Smith, James Madison, and

David Ricardo are from: Adam Smith, *An Inquiry into the Nature and Causes of the Wealth of Nations* (1776) (Chicago: University of Chicago Press, 1976), book V, chapter I, part II, p. 232; James Madison, "Note to His Speech on the Right of Suffrage" (1821), in Max Farrand, ed., *The Records of the Federal Convention of 1787* (New Haven: Yale University Press, 1966), volume 3, pp. 450, 452; and Piero Sraffa, ed., *The Works and Correspondence of David Ricardo,* volume VII (Cambridge: Cambridge University Press, 1952), pp. 369–70.

3. Claus Offe, *Modernity and the State: East, West* (Cambridge, England: Polity Press, 1996), p. 154. See also Adam Przeworski, "The Neoliberal Fallacy," in Larry Diamond and Marc F. Plattner, eds., *Capitalism, Socialism, and Democracy Revisited* (Baltimore, MD: Johns Hopkins University Press, 1993), p. 47.

4. Forest McDonald, *Novos Ordo Seclorum* (Wichita: University Press of Kansas, 1985), p. 26; Chilton Williamson, *American Suffrage: From Property to Democracy, 1760–1860* (Princeton: Princeton University Press, 1960), p. 280; and Robert J. Steinfeld, "Property and Suffrage in the Early American Republic," *Stanford Law Review* 41 (1989): 335–76, especially p. 353. This chapter is based on an earlier article of mine. See Amy L. Chua, "The Paradox of Free Market Democracy: Rethinking Development Policy," *Harvard International Law Journal* 41 (2000): 287–379, especially pp. 293–308.

5. Regarding suffrage limits in England, see McDonald, *Novos Ordo Seclorum,* pp. 25–26. On France, see Henry W. Ehrmann and Martin A. Schain, *Politics in France* (5th ed.) (New York: HarperCollins, 1992), pp. 199–200. On Belgium, see Pierre van den Berghe, *The Ethnic Phenomenon* (New York: Elsevier, 1981), p. 202.

6. Others have recently made this point. See, for example, Robert A. Dahl, *On Democracy* (New Haven and London: Yale University Press, 1998), pp. 175–76, and John Gray, *False Dawn* (New York: New Press, 1998), pp. 17–18.

7. Nancy Birdsall, "Population Growth," *Finance and Development,* September 1984, pp. 10–14.

8. Reuven Brenner, "Land of Opportunity," *Forbes,* October 12, 1998, p. 66.

9. Mark Barenberg, "Federalism and American Labor Law," in Ingolf Pernice, ed., *Harmonization of Legislation in Federal Systems* (Baden-Baden, Germany: Nomos Verlagsgesellschaft, 1996), pp. 93, 110.

10. Frances Fox Piven and Richard Cloward, *The Breaking of the American Social Compact* (New York: New Press, 1997), pp. 12, 92.

11. C. V. Woodward, *The Strange Career of Jim Crow* (New York: Oxford

University Press, 1966), p. 23, and James Oakes, *The Ruling Race* (London and New York: W. W. Norton & Company, 1998), p. 234 (quoting a Georgia commissioner speaking before the Virginia secession convention).

12. Oakes, *The Ruling Race,* p. 238 (quoting James S. Clark).

13. Woodward, *The Strange Career of Jim Crow,* pp. 83–88. There is a large litera- ture on the Jim Crow era in the United States. In addition to Woodward, works particularly relevant here include the classic W. J. Cash, *The Mind of the South* (New York: Doubleday, 1956), and John W. Cell, *The Highest Stage of White Supremacy: The Origins of Segregation in South Africa and the American South* (Cambridge: Cambridge University Press, 1982).

14. Woodward, *The Strange Career of Jim Crow,* pp. 85, 111–12.

15. See Gordon A. Craig, *Germany, 1866–1945* (New York and Oxford: Oxford University Press, 1978), pp. 80–86, 119–24, 312, 470, 478, and Hajo Holborn, *A History of Modern Germany, 1840–1945* (New York: Alfred A. Knopf, 1969), pp. 374–83.

16. These statistics about poverty and economic distress in Weimar Germany are from Craig, *Germany, 1866–1945,* pp. 435, 450–55, and Hans Mommsen, *The Rise and Fall of Weimar Democracy,* Elborg Forester and Larry Jones, trans. (Chapel Hill and London: University of North Carolina Press, 1996) (1989), pp. 117–18. On the chronic housing shortage, see Richard Bessel, *Germany after the First World War* (Oxford: Clarendon Press, 1993), pp. 167–94.

17. The figures regarding the Jewish economic position in Weimar Germany are based on: Richard Grunberger, *The 12-Year Reich: A Social History of Nazi Germany, 1933–1945* (New York: Da Capo Press, 1995) (1971), p. 456; Holborn, *A History of Modern Germany, 1840–1945,* p. 279; and Donald L. Niewyk, *The Jews in Weimar Germany* (Baton Rouge: Louisiana State University Press, 1980), pp. 13–15.

18. James Pool, *Who Financed Hitler* (New York: Pocket Books, 1997), pp. 63, 301–5.

19. Holborn, *A History of Modern Germany, 1840–1945,* pp. 278–79, and Niewyk, *The Jews in Weimar Germany,* p. 16.

20. Daniel Jonah Goldhagen, *Hitler's Willing Executioners* (New York: Alfred A. Knopf, 1996), p. 40.

21. See Craig, *Germany, 1866–1945,* p. 153; Goldhagen, *Hitler's Willing Executioners,* pp. 284–85; and Pool, *Who Financed Hitler,* pp. xxxi, 79.

22. See Goldhagen, *Hitler's Willing Executioners,* p. 113; Grunberger, *The 12-Year Reich,* p. 456; and Peter Pulzer, *The Rise of Political Anti-Semitism in Germany and Austria* (rev. ed.) (London: Peter Halban Publishers, 1988), pp. 144–45. The quote from Martin Luther is from Raul Hilberg, *The*

Destruction of the European Jews (rev. ed.) (New York: Holmes & Meier, 1985), volume 1, p. 16.

23. On the rapid marketization during the Weimar period, see Bessel, *Germany after the First World War,* pp. 143, 164–65; Craig, *Germany, 1866–1945,* pp. 451–52; and Mommsen, *The Rise and Fall of Weimar Democracy,* pp. 116–18, 121, 125, 134. As to Weimar democratization, see Craig, *Germany, 1866–1945,* pp. 397, 416.

24. Craig, *Germany, 1866–1945,* p. 550.

25. Goldhagen, *Hitler's Willing Executioners,* p. 85.

26. See Craig, *Germany, 1866–1945,* pp. 550–51; Mommsen, *The Rise and Fall of Weimar Democracy,* pp. 345–47; Pool, *Who Financed Hitler,* pp. 107–14, 152, 301–5; and Pulzer, *The Rise of Political Anti-Semitism in Germany and Austria,* pp. 281–82. The quote regarding "National Socialist bread prices" is from Craig, *Germany, 1866–1945,* p. 550.

27. Craig, *Germany, 1866–1945,* pp. 633–37, 750.

28. The statistics on Korean market dominance are from Heather MacDonald, "Their American Nightmare," *Washington Post,* May 7, 1995, p. C1, and William Booth, "Mercy for the Motherland," *Washington Post,* December 21, 1997, p. A1. On the black beauty products industry, see Philip Dine, "Blacks Resent Korean Competition," *St. Louis Post-Dispatch,* July 30, 1995, p. 1B.

29. On the Flatbush boycott, see MacDonald, "Their American Nightmare," p. C1. On the Los Angeles riots, see "Rebuilding South Central," *California Journal,* July 1, 1997. For Norman Reide's quote, see Wendell Jamieson, "Rev. Al's Friend Pushed Boycotting Other Shops," *Daily News,* December 14, 1995, p. 4. On the more recent firebombing in Washington, DC, see Petula Dvorak, "Boycotted Store is Firebombed," *Washington Post,* December 1, 2000, p. B1.

30. On the Crown Heights conflict, including the quote from Nancy Mere, see William Bunch, "Racial Rift Spills to City Hall Steps," *Newsday,* August 27, 1991, p. 29. The anti-Jewish boycotts are discussed in Jamieson, "Rev. Al's Friend Pushed Boycotting Other Shops," p. 4.

31. "Changing population in California, where whites are no longer the majority," NPR, *Talk of the Nation,* June 18, 2001.

Chapter 10

1. Population estimates for the Middle East vary considerably. My figure for the region's total Arab population is a conservative one, based on the 1990 estimate reported in Youssef M. Choueiri, *Arab Nationalism: A History* (Oxford: Blackwell Publishers, 2000), p. vii. The estimate for Israeli Jews is from the Israeli daily newspaper *Ha'aretz,* as of April 15, 2002. The esti-

mates I use for the ethnic and religious breakdowns in specific Arab countries are from the CIA World Factbook.

2. On the Berbers in North Africa, see "The Kabylie Erupts: Algeria's Berbers Are Heard From," *The Estimate,* May 4, 2001, and The Political Risk Services Group, "Berbers," in *Morocco Country Forecast: Political Framework,* November 1, 2001, p. 28. On the Copts in Egypt, see Anthony McDermott, *Egypt from Nasser to Mubarek: A Flawed Revolution* (London: Croom Helm, 1988), pp. 185–86, and "Copts in Egypt," *The Economist,* May 23, 1998, p. 42.

3. For additional reading see Michael Herb, *All in the Family: Absolutism, Revolution and Democracy in the Middle Eastern Monarchies* (Albany: State University of New York Press, 1999), and F. Gregory Gause, III, *Oil Monarchies* (New York: Council on Foreign Relations Press, 1994).

4. For different perspectives on Syria and Lebanon, see William L. Cleveland, *A History of the Modern Middle East* (Boulder, CO: Westview Press, 1994); William W. Harris, *Faces of Lebanon* (Princeton: Markus Wiener Publishers, 1997); and Kamal Salibi, *A House of Many Mansions* (Berkeley, Los Angeles, and London: University of California Press, 1988).

5. Bernard Lewis, *Semites and Anti-Semites* (New York and London: W. W. Norton & Company, 1999), pp. 64–65. See also Yitzchok Adlerstein, "Israel's Jewish Problem and the Archbishop of Canterbury," *Jewish Law Commentary,* available at http://www.jlaw.com/Commentary/archbishop.html.

6. Lewis, *Semites and Anti-Semites,* pp. 79–80, and Pierre L. van den Berghe, *The Ethnic Phenomenon* (Westport, CT and London: Praeger, 1980), pp. 233–34.

7. As reported in Ella Shohat, *Israeli Cinema* (Austin: University of Texas Press), p. 116.

8. Yinon Cohen and Yitchak Haberfeld, "Second-generation Jewish immigrants in Israel: have the ethnic gaps in schooling and earnings declined?" *Ethnic and Racial Studies* 21 (1998): 507–28, especially pp. 512–15.

9. The per capita income, literacy, and infant mortality figures are from The World Bank, *2000 World Development Indicators Database* (updated April 2002).

10. See Seymour M. Hersh, "King's Ransom," *The New Yorker,* October 22, 2001, p. 35, and Stephen Glain, "Slide Rule," *The New Republic,* November 19, 2001, p. 20. The literacy statistic for Saudi Arabia is from the CIA World Factbook, available at http://www.cia.gov/cia/publications/factbook/geos/sa.html. On unemployment, see Mark Katz, "Saudi Economic Woes Could Have Implications for Anti-Terrorism Campaign," *Eurasia Insight,* December 18, 2001, available at http://www.eurasianet.org/departments/insight/articles/eav121801.shtml.

11. Mary Anne Weaver, *A Portrait of Egypt* (New York: Farrar, Straus & Giroux, 2000), pp. 11–12, 81–83.

12. Limor Nakar, "Peace slow, but Israeli economy on fast track," *Chicago Sun-Times,* January 27, 2001, p. 16.

13. These statistics are from Michael Wolffsohn, *Israel: Polity, Society, Economy, 1882–1986,* Douglas Bokovoy, trans. (New Jersey: Humanities Press International, 1987), especially pp. 268–69.

14. See, for example, David Remnick, "In a Dark Time," *The New Yorker,* p. 51.

15. Van den Berghe, *The Ethnic Phenomenon,* p. 232.

16. As reported in Lewis, *Semites and Anti-Semites,* p. 229.

17. Ibid., p. 269.

18. This is from an interview with Fouad Ajami, professor of Middle East Studies at Johns Hopkins University, by Neal Conan on NPR's *Talk of the Nation,* broadcast November 13, 2001.

19. Remnick, "In a Dark Time," p. 51, and Abraham Rabinovich, "Hezbollah fires on Israeli border," *Washington Times,* February 7, 2002.

20. Thomas L. Friedman, "Today's News Quiz," *New York Times,* November 20, 2001, p. A19.

21. Fareed Zakaria, "How to Save the Arab World," *Newsweek,* December 24, 2001, p. 22.

22. Ibid.

Chapter 11

1. Neal Ascherson, "11 September," *London Review of Books,* October 4, 2001 (italics added).

2. Thomas L. Friedman, *The Lexus and the Olive Tree* (New York: Anchor Books, 2000), pp. xix, 13, 381–82.

3. Mortimer B. Zuckerman, "Still the American century," *U.S. News & World Report,* February 10, 1997, p. 72.

4. These figures are from the CIA's official website. See http//www.cia.gov/cia/publications/factbook/geos/us.html.

5. Thomas Frank, *One Market under God: Extreme Capitalism, Market Populism, and the End of Economic Democracy* (New York: Doubleday, 2000), p. 12; Edward Luttwak, *Turbo-Capitalism: Winners and Losers in the Global Economy* (New York: HarperCollins Publishers, 1999), pp. 1, 2, 22; and Paul Krugman, "America the Polarized," *New York Times,* January 4, 2002, p. A21. On poverty in the United States, see *Almanac of Policy Issues,* available at http://www.policyalmanac.org/social_welfare/poverty.shtml.

6. Jonathan Freedland, "The Right Turns against America," *Spectator,* April 21, 2001, pp. 22–24.

7. See Friedman, *The Lexus and the Olive Tree,* p. 437, and Joseph Kahn, "Globalization Proves Disappointing," *NewYork Times,* March 21, 2002, p. A8.

8. See Thomas Omestad, Bay Fang, Eduardo Cue, and Masha Gessen, "A world of resentment," *U.S. News &World Report,* March 5, 2001, p. 32.

9. Ibid., p. 32.

10. See James Kitfield, "A Tale of Two Allies," *National Journal,* February 10, 2001, p. 398.

11. See Donald L. Horowitz, *Ethnic Groups in Conflict* (Berkeley, Los Angeles, and London: University of California Press, 1985), pp. 175–78.

12. On the 1974 U.N. resolution, see Alan C. Swan and John F. Murphy, *Cases and Materials on the Regulation of International Business and Economic Relations* (2d ed.) (New York: Matthew Bender & Company, 1999), pp. 1057–58. On the May 2001 ouster of the United States from the U.N. Commission on Human Rights, see Dalia Acosta, "Rights: Cuba Applauds U.S. Removal from U.N. Rights Commission," *Inter Press Service,* May 4, 2001.

13. Claire Cozens, "U.S. brands suffer as anti-American feeling runs high," *Guardian (London),* December 21, 2001.

14. Mary Beard, "11 September," *London Review of Books,* October 4, 2001.

15. See David Ellwood, "French Anti-Americanism and McDonald's," *History Today,* February 1, 2001, p. 34–35.

16. As reported in Ibid., p. 34.

17. On Vedrine, see Philip H. Gordon, "The French position," *National Interest,* fall 2000. Mitterand's and Lang's statements, and the quote from *Le Monde,* are reported in Ellwood, "French Anti-Americanism and McDonald's," pp. 34–36.

18. David Pryce-Jones, *"Toujours l'antiaméricanisme:* The religion of the French elite," *National Review,* June 11, 2001, p. 45.

19. Ellwood, "French Anti-Americanism and McDonald's," pp. 34, 36; Gordon, "The French position"; and Pryce-Jones, *"Toujours l'antiaméricanisme,"* p. 45.

20. Kitfield, "A Tale of Two Allies." See also Elizabeth Pond, "Europe's 'anti-Americanism' may reflect worry over Soviet military power," *Christian Science Monitor,* July 15, 1981, p. 3.

21. As reported in Gordon, "The French position." See also Freedland, "The Right Turns against America," p. 22.

22. These quotes are from Kitfield, "A Tale of Two Allies."

23. The former defense secretary is quoted in Ibid. See also Jason Beattie, "Cook to Launch Staunch Defense of Euro Army," *The Scotsman,* April 25, 2001, p. 11.

24. See George Soros, *On Globalization* (New York: Public Affairs, 2002), p. 10 (citing the 2001 United Nations Human Development Report). See also

Robert P. Weiss, introduction to "Criminal Justice and Globalization at the New Millennium," *Social Justice* 27 (Summer 2000): 1–15, and John Cassidy, "Helping Hands," *The New Yorker,* March 18, 2002, p. 60.

25. See The World Bank, *Globalization, Growth and Poverty: Building an Inclusive World Economy* (New York: The World Bank and Oxford University Press, 2002), chapter 1.

26. "Why the world loves to hate America," *Financial Times,* December 7, 2001, p. 23 (quoting Greek writer Takis Michas).

27. Michael Mathes, "Many Vietnamese happy with attacks on U.S.," *Deutsche Presse Agentur,* September 13, 2001.

28. Ibid.

29. See www.Daijhi.com. Daijhi is a weekly columnist for Nepal's *Samacharpatra* newspaper. He is known in the West as Richard Morley.

30. Michel Fortin, "Reflections on the Occasion of an Act of Terrorism," *Africana Plus,* October 2001, available at http://pages.infinit.net/africana/terrorism.htm.

31. *Brazzil,* November 2001, available at www.brazzil.com (letter to the Editor submitted by Paul Betterman).

32. Robert Ryal Miller, *Mexico: A History* (University of Oklahoma Press, 1985), pp. 320–21; Harry K. Wright, *Foreign Enterprise in Mexico* (Chapel Hill: University of North Carolina Press, 1971), pp. 67–70; and Alan Knight, "The Rise and Fall of Cardenismo," in Leslie Bethell, ed., *Mexico Since Independence* (Cambridge and New York: Cambridge University Press, 1991), pp. 279–84.

33. David Rock, *Argentina, 1516–1982* (Berkeley and Los Angeles: University of California Press, 1985), pp. 258, 262–63, 283–86, 312, and James R. Scobie, *Argentina: A City and a Nation* (New York, London, and Toronto: Oxford University Press, 1971), pp. 143, 188, 196, 222–23, 235.

34. On nationalizations in Chile, see Philip O'Brien, ed., *Allende's Chile* (New York: Praeger Publishers, 1976), pp. 223–30; in Uruguay, see M. H. J. Finch, *A Political Economy of Uruguay Since 1870* (New York: St. Martin's Press, 1981), pp. 207–11; in Burma and Indonesia, see Frank H. Golay, Ralph Anspach, M. Ruth Pfanner & Eliezer B. Ayal, *Underdevelopment and Economic Nationalism in Southeast Asia* (Ithaca and London: Cornell University Press, 1969), pp. 188, 209–11, 215; and in Africa, William Redman Duggan and John R. Civille, *Tanzania and Nyerere* (New York: Orbis Books, 1976), pp. 192–94.

35. Vidyadhar Date, "Trade Unions, Academics Plan Protests against Clinton's Visit," *Times of India,* March 24, 2000.

36. David Lynch, "U.S. investors caught in Russian tug of war," *USA Today,* De-

cember 17, 1999, p. 1B. See also John Varoli, "Revolutions Come and Go, but a Porcelain Factory Endures," *New York Times,* December 21, 2000, p. F6.

37. Lynch, "U.S. investors caught in Russian tug of war," p. 1B, and Varoli, "Revolutions Come and Go, but a Porcelain Factory Endures," p. F6.

38. See Marcus W. Brauchli, "We Were the Guinea Pigs," *Wall Street Journal,* April 27, 1995, p. A1.

39. Donna Bryson, "U.S.-based energy company linked to human rights abuses," *Associated Press,* January 24, 1999. See also "Anti-Enron Protesters to Step Up Campaign," *Gulf Daily News,* February 10, 2001.

40. Fouad Ajami, "The Sentry's Solitude," *Foreign Affairs,* November/December 2001, p. 2.

41. Yossef Bodansky, *Bin Laden: The Man Who Declared War on America* (Roseville, CA: Prima Publishing, 2001), pp. 269–70.

42. Translation supplied by Associated Press, October 7, 2001, available at http://www.guardian.co.uk/waronterror/story/0,1361,565069,00.html.

43. Stephen Engelberg, "Carving Out a Greater Serbia," *New York Times,* September 1, 1991, p. 19.

44. See www.daijhi.com.

45. Lamia Radi, "Bulls-eye say Egyptians as they celebrate anti-US attacks," *Middle East Times,* available at http://www.metimes.com/2K1/issue2001-37/eg/bulls_eye_say.htm.

46. Martin Peretz, "Death Trap," *New Republic,* December 31, 2001 and January 7, 2002, p. 12.

47. Robert Kaplan, *The Coming Anarchy* (New York: Random House, 2000), p. 42.

48. Translation supplied by Associated Press, October 7, 2001, available at http://www.guardian.co.uk/waronterror/story/0,1361,565069,00.html.

49. Orhan Pamuk, "The Anger of the Damned," *The New York Review of Books,* November 15, 2001, p. 12.

Chapter 12

1. As reported in Thomas Carothers, *Aiding Democracy Abroad* (Washington, DC: Carnegie Endowment for International Peace, 1999), p. 5.

2. Robert D. Kaplan, *The Coming Anarchy* (New York: Random House, 2000), pp. 63–78.

3. Seymour Martin Lipset, "Some Social Requisites of Democracy: Economic Development and Political Legitimacy," *American Political Science Review* 53 (1959): 69–77, and Samuel P. Huntington, *Political Order in Changing Societies* (New Haven and London: Yale University Press, 1968).

4. Youssef M. Ibrahim, "Saudi King Rules Out Free Elections," *New York Times,* March 30, 1992, p. A6.

5. See Takashi Inoguchi and Edward Newman, "Introduction: 'Asian Values' and Democracy in Asia," available at http://www.unu.edu/unupress/asian-values.html.

6. Fareed Zakaria, "Culture is Destiny: A Conversation with Lee Kuan Yew," *Foreign Affairs,* March/April 1994, pp. 113, 119.

7. Kaplan, *The Coming Anarchy,* p. 60.

8. See the excellent essays in Larry Diamond and Mark F. Plattner, eds., *Capitalism, Socialism, and Democracy Revisited* (Baltimore and London: Johns Hopkins University Press, 1993), and especially Adam Przeworski, "The Neoliberal Fallacy," pp. 39–53. See also Larry Diamond, "Democracy and Economic Reform: Tensions, Compatibilities, and Strategies for Reconciliation," in Edward P. Lazear, ed., *Economic Transition in Eastern Europe and Russia: Realities of Reform* (Stanford: Hoover Institution Press, 1995), pp. 107–246.

9. See Robert Klitgaard, *Adjusting to Reality* (San Francisco: ICS Press, 1991), pp. 214–15, and Harry Anthony Patrinos, "Differences in Education and Earnings across Ethnic Groups in Guatemala," *Quarterly Review of Economics and Finance* 37 (1997): 809–21.

10. For further reading, see the sources listed in notes 34 and 35 to chapter 1.

11. See Klitgaard, *Adjusting to Reality,* p. 188.

12. Gunnar Myrdal, "International Inequality and Foreign Aid in Retrospect," in Gerald M. Meier and Dudley Seers, eds., *Pioneers in Development* (New York: Oxford University Press, 1984), pp. 151, 154.

13. Hernando de Soto, *The Mystery of Capital* (New York: Basic Books, 2000).

14. John C. Coffee, Jr., "The Future as History," *Northwestern University Law Review* 93 (1999): 641, 706.

15. Milton J. Esman, "Ethnic Politics and Economic Power," *Comparative Politics* 19 (1987): 395–418, especially pp. 396–401.

16. Ibid., pp. 395–96, 399.

17. See Sumit Ganguly, "Ethnic Policies and Political Quiescence in Malaysia and Singapore," in Michael Brown and Sumit Ganguly, eds., *Government Policies and Ethnic Relations in Asia and the Pacific* (Cambridge: MIT Press, 1997), pp. 233–72.

18. Ibid., p. 251.

19. See James V. Jesudason, *Ethnicity and the Economy* (Singapore and New York: Oxford University Press, 1989), pp. 72, 137, 141; Ganguly, "Ethnic Policies and Political Quiescence in Malaysia and Singapore," pp. 257–63; and Steve Glain, "Malaysia's Grand Social Experiment May

Be Next Casualty of Asian Crisis," *Wall Street Journal,* April 23, 1998, p. A15.

20. These statistics are from Ganguly, "Ethnic Policies and Political Quiescence in Malaysia and Singapore," p. 261, and K. S. Jomo, "A Specific Idiom of Chinese Capitalism in Southeast Asia," in Daniel Chirot and Anthony Reid, eds., *Essential Outsiders: Chinese and Jews in the Modern Transformation of Southeast Asia and Central Europe* (Seattle and London: University of Washington Press, 1997), pp. 237–57, especially p. 244.

21. Thomas Sowell, *Preferential Policies: An International Perspective* (New York: William Morrow & Company, 1990), p. 49.

22. See Murray Hiebert and S. Jayasankaran, "Formative Fury: Affirmative action policies enacted after riots 30 years ago still play a vital role in fostering racial harmony," *Far Eastern Economic Review,* May 20, 1999, p. 45.

23. Ibid., p. 45.

24. Sowell, *Preferential Policies,* pp. 49–50, and Jill Eyre and Denis Dwyer, "Ethnicity and Industrial Development in Penang, Malaysia," in Denis Dwyer and David Drakakis-Smith, eds., *Ethnicity and Development* (Chichester and New York: John Wiley & Sons, 1996), pp. 181–94.

25. See Sowell, *Preferential Policies,* pp. 15, 53, 57, 74–75, and Myron Weiner and Mary Fainsod Katzenstein, *India's Preferential Policies* (Chicago: University of Chicago Press, 1981), p. 147.

26. On this point, see the excellent essays in Manuel Antonio Garretón M. and Edward Newman, *Democracy in Latin America* (New York, Paris, and Tokyo: United Nations University Press, 2001). See also Mariano Tommasi and Andrés Velasco, "Where Are We in the Political Economy of Reform?" *Policy Reform* 1 (1996): 187, 220.

27. Minxin Pei, "Is China Democratizing?" *Foreign Affairs,* January/February 1998, p. 68.

28. Ibid.

29. Fareed Zakaria, "How to Save the Arab World," *Newsweek,* December 24, 2001, p. 22.

30. As reproduced in Jonathan G. Katz, "Muslims Caught in the Middle," *Sunday Oregonian,* September 30, 2001, p. B1.

31. Abdolkarim Soroush, "Tolerance and Governance: A Discourse on Religion and Democracy," in *Reason, Freedom & Democracy in Islam,* Mahmoud Sadri and Ahmad Sadri, trans. (Oxford and New York: Oxford University Press, 2000).

32. Zakaria, "How to Save the Arab World," p. 22.

33. See Linda Y. C. Lim and L. A. Peter Gosling, "Strengths and Weaknesses of Minority Status for Southeast Asian Chinese at a Time of Economic

Growth and Liberalization," in Daniel Chirot and Anthony Reid, eds., *Essential Outsiders*, pp. 285–317, especially p. 293; Michael R. J. Vatikiotis, *Indonesian Politics under Suharto* (3d ed.) (London and New York: Routledge, 1993), p. 41; and Jomo, "A Specific Idiom of Chinese Capitalism," p. 252.

34. Leah Makabenta, "Indonesia: Ethnic Chinese Economic Success Fuels Racial Tension," *Inter Press Service*, March 25, 1993.

35. Naomi Klein, *No Logo* (New York: Picador, USA, 1999), pp. 327–28.

36. As reported in Peter Waldman and Jay Solomon, "As Good Times Roll, Indonesia's Chinese Fear for Their Future," *Wall Street Journal*, June 5, 1997, p. A18.

37. See Robert G. Gregory, *The Rise and Fall of Philanthropy in East Africa* (New Brunswick, NJ: Transaction Publishers, 1992), pp. 43–65, especially pp. 55 and 205, and "Building Capacity," *Business in Africa Online*, available at http://www.businessinafrica.co.za/kenar.html.

38. See Peter Baker, "An Unlikely Savior on the Tundra," *Washington Post*, March 2, 2001, p. A1, and John Lloyd, "A miracle worker," *Financial Times*, January 6, 2001, p. 1.

39. As reported in Baker, "An Unlikely Savior on the Tundra," p. A1.

40. See Anthony DePalma, "In Mexico City, A State-of-the-Art Children's Museum," *New York Times*, November 18, 1993, p. C4, and Christine MacDonald, "Hands-On Museum Catches Kids' Fancy," *Dallas Morning News*, December 21, 1993, p. C5. See also the Coca-Cola and Nike home websites.

41. "United by rugby?" *The Economist*, October 30, 1999.

42. Christopher Clarey, "This Is No Picnic: In Southeast Asia, Respect Rides on a Shuttlecock," *New York Times*, June 25, 1996, p. B14.

43. See World Huaren Federation, "Contributions and Achievements: Susi Susanti & Alan Budi Kusuma," available at http://www.huaren.org/contributions/.

44. Ian Thomsen, "Rugby: South Africa Ascends World Stage," *New York Times*, May 26, 1995, p. B9.

45. Jared Diamond, "Why We Must Feed the Hands That Could Bite Us," *Washington Post*, January 13, 2002, p. B1.

46. Alan Friedman, "World Bank Presses U.S. to Increase Aid," *International Herald Tribune*, January 31, 2002, p. 1, and John Cassidy, "Helping Hands," *The New Yorker*, March 18, 2002, pp. 60, 66.

47. Gregory Clark, "More aid, more regrets later," *Japan Times*, January 22, 2002.

48. Daniel Pipes, "God and Mammon: Does Poverty Cause Militant Islam?" *National Interest*, Winter 2001/2002, p. 14.

49. Cassidy, "Helping Hands," p. 64. Cassidy also notes that in absolute dollar terms, the U.S. spends more on aid than any other country apart from Japan.

Index

Argentina, 15–16, 21, 58–59, 67, 67–69, 250

Assimilation, 177–85. *See also* Intermarriage

countries without market-dominant minorities, 177–79

forced, of Chinese in Thailand, 179–85

Austerity measures, 128, 150–51, 252

Australia, 239–40

Aven, Pyotr, 78, 85

Aymara, 49–52

Backlash against democracy, 10–11, 125, 147–62

Chinese-friendly dictatorships in Indonesia and the Philippines, 43–45, 151–57, 280

crony capitalism and, 30, 147–58, 164–65

crony capitalism in Kenya, 113–14, 157–58

countering, 279–82

political rule by market-dominant minorities, 158–62

in Sierra Leone, 147–51

Backlash against market-dominant minorities, 10, 11, 12, 125, 163–75, 254–58. *See also* Ethnic violence

against Americans, 254–58

expulsions and genocide as, 163

forced assimilation in Thailand, 181–84

genocide in former Yugoslavia, 170–75

genocide in Rwanda, 165–70

induced emigration and expulsions, 164–65

Backlash against markets, 10–11, 124–25, 127–45

anti-Semitism and nationalization in democratic Russia, 138–42

backlash against Western foreign investors, 249–54

ethnic confiscation in post-Suharto Indonesia, 136–38

history of nationalization in developing world, 131–35

in Venezuela, 142–45

in Zimbabwe, 127–31

Baganda, 112

Bahrain, 213

Bamiléké, 111–12, 281

Bean curd business, 38–42

Belgians, 15, 165–67

Belgium, 193

Benin, 110, 115, 119

Berezovsky, Boris, 78, 87–89, 90–91, 141

bin Laden, Osama, 255–57. *See also* World Trade Center attack

Black markets, 26, 83–84

Blacks

in Brazil, 69–72, 74–75, 160–61

in post–Civil War U.S. South, 199–201

in South Africa, 99–100, 236 (*see also* Africa)

in U.S. inner cities, 207–9

U.S. racism and, 197–98

Bolivia, 49–57, 64, 65, 134, 159–60, 162

Bosnia, 173

Botswana, 178

Brazil

affirmative action programs, 160–61

American culture and, 235

ethnic consciousness in, 69–75, 160–61

Jews in, 67

Portuguese in, 95

reaction in, to World Trade Center attack, 246–49

white dominance in, 65, 69–72

British. *See also* England

in Kenya, 103–4

in Southern Africa, 99, 101–2